Political Economy of Federalism in India

Indian Federalism is at a crossroad. On one hand, the legacy of colonialism, partition, and the vision of nation-building all contrived to create a centralized federation. On the other hand, the ongoing transition to a free market has brought the contradictions of centralized federal arrangements to the fore.

This book incorporates economic perspectives on political institutions, more comprehensively than ever attempted before and is divided into three parts

- Historical review of the Indian Federal System
- Economics of Indian Federalism
- Political Economy and Intergovernmental reforms

It further emphasizes the emergence of coalition governments at the Centre, and the increasing importance of regional parties which have brought out the contradictions in the efficient governance of the federation.

To Devaki, Sunil, and Sneha for their constant love
and support and for the time and things they missed
—M. Govinda Rao

To my parents, and to Inderjit, Bhairav, and Keshav
for their constant love and support
—Nirvikar Singh

The Political Economy of Federalism in India

M. GOVINDA RAO

AND

NIRVIKAR SINGH

OXFORD

UNIVERSITY PRESS

OXFORD
UNIVERSITY PRESS

Oxford University Press is a department of the University of Oxford.
It furthers the University's objective of excellence in research, scholarship,
and education by publishing worldwide. Oxford is a registered trademark of
Oxford University Press in the UK and in certain other countries

Published in India by
Oxford University Press
2/11 Ground Floor, Ansari Road, Daryaganj, New Delhi 110 002, India

First Edition published in 2005
Oxford India Paperbacks 2006

ISNB-13 (print edition): 978-0-19-568693-7
ISNB-10 (print edition): 0-19-568693-4

ISNB-13 (eBook): 978-0-19-908785-3
ISNB-10 (eBook): 0-19-908785-7

Printed in India by Repro Knowledgecast Limited, Thane

Contents

Preface

Indian federalism is at a crossroad. On the one hand, the 'idea of India' is still contested. The legacy of colonialism, partition, and the vision of nation building all contrived to create a centralized federation, which still exercise a strong influence. Centralized planning as the development strategy adopted soon after independence, required further concentration of economic powers. On the other, the recent transition to market-based development and the accompanying opening up of the economy have brought the contradictions of centralized federal arrangements to the fore. On the political front, the end to single-party rule at the Centre and states, the emergence of coalition governments at the Centre, and increasing importance of regional parties in the political affairs of the country have brought into focus various contentious issues in the efficient governance of the federation.

The challenges thrown up by market-based development in a globalizing environment require the various governmental units in Indian federalism to act in a manner that provides cost-effective physical and social infrastructure, creates the proper enabling environment for growth, and efficiently regulates, the market where necessary. This is a challenge for any single government, and the Central, state and even local governments in India must accomplish this with some degree of coordination. However, in practice, current institutional arrangements involve acute, often destabilizing, political and economic competition. For example, the emergence of regional parties in pivotal roles at the Centre, and the instabilities inherent in coalition politics as evident from frequent changes in political alliances and repeated elections have made achieving national interests more difficult. There are genuine concerns that some regions of the country are being permanently left behind.

The solution is not obvious. While the dominance of a single political party in the government at Central and state levels for over three decades provided stability, it did not allow mechanisms towards dispute resolution, or systems and institutions to create adequate checks and balances to adequately evolve. If anything, the dominant party itself decayed internally, as did some of the other institutions of government. Facing emerging challenges of accelerating the pace of development, particularly in regions lagging behind, requires a careful evaluation of India's federal framework, including the various institutions of political and economic governance.

Many books written on Indian federalism look purely at economic issues of assignment, overlapping, and transfers. Even here the issues of Centre–state relations have been looked at in isolation from state–local relations. From the perspective of political science, most studies deal with party politics or with legal and constitutional issues, without looking at economic aspects. This book is an attempt at a synthesized framework, combining both elements in a political economy prism, more comprehensively than has been attempted before. Since we are both economists, any tilt is towards economic issues, but we have incorporated economic perspectives on political institutions as well. Ultimately, we believe, only such a framework can provide a useful guide to implementable reform of policies and institutions.

This book has evolved over nine years. Its genesis goes back to 1995 when the authors met at a conference in New Delhi, organized by Professor Mancur Olson under the aegis of the Institutional Reform and the Informal Sector (IRIS) project. What was originally envisaged as a small monograph has, over the years, expanded into a major project which has now come to fruition. During the course of these years, there has been a number of changes in intergovernmental fiscal arrangements and the political and economic situation in India. It has indeed been a challenge to work and rework on several chapters to keep up with the changes.

On many chapters, first drafts were written independently. We then exchanged and commented extensively on each other's drafts, and rewrote them many times, taking full advantage of e-mail and word processing technologies that developed just in time for us to carry out a long-distance collaboration. Nirvikar Singh has been based at the University of California, Santa Cruz, throughout this period, but also worked on the project while a visitor at the Centre for Research in Economic Development and Policy Reform (CREDPR), Stanford University. Govinda Rao started work on the book while he was at the National Institute of Public Finance and Policy (NIPFP) in 1995, and completed it in 2004, back in the same institution after working on it in several other institutions. The major portion of the work was carried out in Australia South Asia Research Centre (ASARC), Research School of Pacific and Asian Studies, the Australian National University, and the Institute for Social and Economic Change (ISEC), Bangalore. The work was greatly facilitated by visits of Govinda Rao to University of California, and Nirvikar Singh to ASARC, NIPFP, and ISEC at various times during this period. We even managed to find time to discuss our project in the midst of conferences in Cornell, Stanford, Bangalore, and Chennai. We are particularly grateful to our host institutions, which provided all the facilities and environment for carrying out these studies.

Many chapters in the book have been presented or published in earlier versions as papers. Publication outlets have included the working papers of the economics department at the University of California, and CREDPR (now named the Stanford Center for International Development), and several conference volumes. Between us we presented papers in conferences and seminars held at Harvard University, Columbia University, the University of Michigan, Cornell University, the University of Birmingham, the Australian National University, Stanford University, the IMF, ISEC, the Madras School of Economics (Chennai), the Northeastern Universities Development Conference, the Econometric Society North American Winter Meetings, and the NIPFP, New Delhi. We are grateful to all these institutions, and to the many audiences who responded to our work on these occasions.

We have received comments on various parts of the book from several friends and colleagues in the profession, who have discussed our work informally, and sometimes collaborated on related projects. There are too many of our friends who are guilty of this but mention must be made of Richard Bird, Albert Breton, Wallace Oates, T.N. Srinivasan, Nicholas Hope, K.P. Kalirajan, Ric Shand, Anwar Shah, Robert Ebel, and Ehtisham Ahmad. Without implicating them in any manner for the errors and shortcomings in the book, we would like to acknowledge the numerous and generous comments and suggestions that we have received from them. We must also admit that it is our families that bore the brunt of the burden. It is not just prolonged absences from the family that inflicted costs; even when we were present, we were often inaccessible. We hope this book at least partially justifies the sacrifices made by them.

M. GOVINDA RAO
NIRVIKAR SINGH

PART I

THE SETTING

1

Political Economy of Federalism
Challenges of Reforming Policies and Institutions

FEDERALISM AND DECENTRALIZATION

The failure of the centralized state, both in economic and in political governance, has swung the pendulum in favour of decentralized systems in recent years across the globe. This phenomenon is not confined to constitutionally declared federations but also seen in unitary systems, spanning countries with varying ideological spectrums and levels of development (Bird and Vaillancourt, 1998). The emergence of the European Union has underlined the advantages of an enlarged common market, while keeping distinct national identities. The collapse of Soviet Union has demonstrated the unsustainability of autarchic and centralized policy regimes. Changes in development strategies in favour of the market have further underlined the need for decentralized governance. In fact, experience has demonstrated that centralized planning negates federalism. An equally important motivation for the trend towards decentralizing has been the need to have more responsive governments in societies with diverse ethnic, linguistic, social, and cultural demands. It is also argued that decentralized systems help to enhance efficiency and minimize transaction costs in the provision of services, encourage innovation by activating intergovernmental competition, and ensure greater participation of the people in the decision-making process (Breton, 1995). While some free-market economists consider decentralization to be an effective check against a leviathan government, even those who argue for active state intervention prefer a greater role for sub-national governments to minimize transaction costs and improve access to information (Bardhan, 2002).

Much of the gains attributed to fiscal federalism in the mainstream literature pertain to decentralization, not federalism per se. Fiscal federalism deals with degree of decentralization, not whether the system is unitary or federal (Oates, 1972). What distinguishes federalism from decentralization is the ownership of inextinguishable constitutional powers (Breton, 2000). The powers assigned to different levels of government in a federation cannot be extinguished, unless the Constitution is ignored, abandoned, or drastically modified.[1] Ownership of powers is necessary for sub-national governments to exercise unfettered choice in their assigned domain, and provide public services as desired by their citizens. In this respect, constitutional assignment is much like ownership of property rights, which improves the incentives for investment decisions for the optimal provision of public services, at the same time enhancing efficiency and accountability. Assignment is also the source of competition between different tiers of government and between different units within each of the tiers. While constitutional assignments can change over time, depending on changing circumstances, in the short run the assignment rights are assured.

Assignment of powers to different levels of government enables both vertical and horizontal competition. In a democratic set-up, with electorates and opposition parties comparing the supply performances of their government with benchmarks set by the standards in their competitors, sub-national governments are forced to compete.[2] This competition may have positive as well as negative implications for resource allocation. Also, however perfectly the assignment is done, overlapping of powers, both vertical and horizontal, is unavoidable. In addition to the possible negative consequences of competition overlapping of powers adds to the case for coordination. Where 'Coasian bargains' are possible, representing negotiation based on clearly assigned rights, this may be called cooperative federalism. However, cooperative federalism succeeds only in cases where there is an innate motivation to enter into such bargains for mutual gains. In other cases, a higher-level government, or the judicial branch may have to serve as monitor and referee.

Underlying the different possibilities for federal governmental structures

---

[1] Thus, one needs sufficient safeguards against the encroachment upon these rights in federal systems. A system of checks and balances partially ensures that these jurisdictions are protected.

[2] Pierre Salmon (1987), using the logic of rank order tournaments, constructs the case wherein the electorate and opposition parties benchmark the performances of the competitors. In a more recent analysis, Besley and Case (1995) make a similar analysis where jurisdictions are compared with each other and this mechanism ensures accountability.

and the roles of competition and cooperation are two alternative perspectives on the nature of governance. The classic economic approach to federalism, associated with the seminal work of Musgrave (1959), implicitly assumes benevolent government decision makers. In contrast, Buchanan (1960) emphasizes the self-interest of government decision makers, and the need to keep such motives in check. To the extent that self-interest leads to larger government, federal structures are seen to reduce the size of government through competition among sub-national governments for constituents and for capital. More recent work on the political economy of federalism tends to lean towards the latter view, with varying degrees of emphasis on different aspects of the political economy of governance. In particular, key contributions have been made by Breton (1995), with his analysis of 'competitive governments', and by Weingast (1995), with the concept of market-preserving federalism. These contributions have helped to refine the economic case for federalism, while providing insights into the implications of different federal structures for efficiency, equity, and political stability. They provide the analytical underpinnings and some of the motivation for our own work.

ANALYSIS OF FEDERALISM IN INDIA

This book is about federalism in India. It deals with the system, institutions, and outcomes arising from the interplay of political and economic forces in Indian federalism. The book makes an attempt at broadening the conceptual framework for analysing Indian federalism to include the political elements and institutions and their strategic interaction with fiscal elements. The studies have not attempted to combine the political and economic elements shaping Indian federalism in a systematic manner. Most analyses of Indian federalism have adopted the framework of the fiscal federalism literature, or have focused on describing the political events and motivations associated with India's federal institutions, and have not explicitly considered the importance of institutions and incentives. While such economic analysis of federalism—the Musgravian approach to fiscal federalism—ignores the political objectives of forming a federation like political participation and protection of individual rights and liberties, the political theories do not consider the importance of efficient public service delivery and formation of common market in the country in their analyses.

Further, the traditional literature on fiscal federalism does not even consider the requirement of constitutions to assign and enforce fiscal powers to multilevel governmental units. It simply assumes the existence and efficient functioning of the institutions. Economic objectives of a federation can be fulfilled only under an appropriate institutional setting and structure of incentives. In reality, governance structures in most developing economies are weak, and as such the existing literature on fiscal federalism is not very helpful as a guide to policy in most federations (Litvack et al., 1999).

Analysis of federalism involves serious political economy issues and this has brought to the fore the inadequacy of conventional analyses of fiscal and political federalism. Much of the mainstream literature on fiscal federalism assumes away the influence of political factors and effect of institutions on which the fiscal arrangements are placed. In contrast, much of the literature on federal finance in India is descriptive. Indeed, both the fiscal federalism and federal finance strands of the literature are important in themselves in understanding the multilevel fiscal system in a country as diverse as India. However, in order to understand the dynamics of Indian federalism, it is necessary to analyse the strategic interplay of political and economic elements. A systematic study of the political economy of Indian federalism is overdue.

In the emerging globalizing environment, it is important to ensure that both policies and institutions, of which intergovernmental institutions are of great significance, play an effective role in facilitating development. In this environment, it is important to redesign the institutions not only to meet the narrow objective of ensuring responsive and efficient provision of public services, but also to achieve a broader objective of establishing a secure, predictable political foundation for the structure of governance (Williamson, 1994). The issue of analysing the governance structure has acquired significance for an additional reason as well. The changes in the Indian polity in terms of the disappearance of single-party rule, emergence of coalition politics at the Centre on the one hand, and the increasing importance of regional parties in the determination of national economic and political decision making on the other, have underlined the need to strengthen the institutions and the governance structures in the country. The resulting decline in the time horizon of the political parties and politicians has only contributed to further weakening of the governance structure and institutions of governance.

India embarked upon market-oriented reforms since the early 1990s. Around the same time, it initiated decentralizing reforms by amending the Constitution to give statutory recognition to the third tier of the government. In spite of the attempted changes in policies and institutions, the system and institutions have remained largely unaffected. Much remains to be done to make the institutions of governance in the country more market-friendly. The vestiges of planning have continued to plague policies and institutions, and considerable reforms are still needed in this dimension. Besides, the system that evolved over the years to meet the requirements of an economy with perennial shortages needs to be reorganized. Rationing and segmentation of the market may be appropriate in a closed economy characterized by scarcity, but will impede growth in a globalized environment. The reforms have to be carried not just at the central, but also at sub-central levels. In the emerging globalizing environment, sub-national governments will have to take a lead in creating an accommodating market environment by providing physical and social infrastructure.

IMPORTANCE OF INSTITUTIONS

The normative framework implicit in the mainstream literature assumes the Benthamite view that governments are benevolent despots, and do whatever is necessary to counter market failures. The agents of the government are supposed to work towards enhancing the welfare of the people. It does not explain why politicians and bureaucrats in fact behave in the manner they actually do or why there are serious instances of elite capture of public services provided, even in formal democratic societies characterized by oligarchic power structures. Consequently, the analyses do not provide much guidance on how the institutions and incentives can be structured to achieve the economic and political goals of federalism. When, in fact, the institutions create a structure of incentives which leads to redistribution in favour of special interest groups, the very concept of decentralization and its ability to enhance efficiency in service delivery is questioned.[3]

However, there have been some recent attempts to extend the conceptual framework to include additional institutional dimensions of multi-level governments. Inman and Rubinfeld (1997), for example, extend traditional economic analysis to explicitly consider political goals in government objective functions and examine trade-offs between political and economic objectives. More importantly, the new literature in institutional economics underlines the importance of clearly defined and enforced property rights, a reliable law on contracts, and rules of third-party enforcement in reducing market uncertainties and providing incentives for investment (North, 1981). While this requires the state to be strong

---

[3] See, for example, Prud'homme (1995), Bardhan and Mookherjee (2000), and Breton (2002).

enough to protect property rights, it is also necessary to establish ... 'a secure foundation that limits the ability (of) the state to confiscate wealth by altering those rights and systems' (Weingast, 1993). Like the 'leviathan' theorists (Brennan and Buchanan, 1980; Niskanen, 1971), the proponents of 'Market Preserving Federalism' (MPF), suggest that sub-national control over their respective jurisdictions within a common market provides an effective check against the abuse of power by the Central government while intergovernmental competition over mobile sources of revenue contains individual sub-national governments. Similarly, Breton (1995, 2002) explains the design of federal institutions including the design of the constitution itself in terms of vertical and horizontal intergovernmental competition. Nevertheless, our understanding of the institutions and their associated incentive structures is not secure enough to ensure successful policy design and implementation. We are still trying to find out the preconditions necessary for beneficent intergovernmental competition to ensure economic and political efficiency.

The above background suggests that design of policies and institutions to effectively achieve economic and political goals in a federal economy requires the analysis to be done from an institutional perspective. This implies in the first instance, proper assignment of rights: first, between the private and public sector and second, between different levels of government and among different governmental units within each of the levels. The assignment of rights between public and private sector determines the scope of the government vis-à-vis the market, and assignments between the levels of government determine the role of degree of decentralization in the delivery of public services. The assignment system provides the rules of the game.

Efficiency in assignment, and in its enforcement, creating appropriate market incentives and efficiently delivering public services, depends on the nature of institutions and structure of incentives. Incentive structures for a given assignment determine efficiency in its functioning. Enforcement of the rights can be done when there are institutions to administer the rules and monitor the observance of rules by various players, and bargain, adjudicate, and penalize when necessary. The structure of incentives ensures self-enforcement of the rules and enhances efficiency in the market for both private and public goods. Institutions and incentives depend upon both political and economic factors.

The assignment of property rights affects the structure of incentives and the latter in turn is affected by the former. Normative theory suggests that assignment of rights between the public and private sectors should be based on market failure arguments. Enforcement of this calls for the creation of a structure of incentives (including institutions). At the same time, the extent to which market failure arguments are valid depends upon the nature of institutions and incentives prevailing in the economy. Similarly, normative theory suggests criteria for the assignment of tax and expenditure functions for different levels of government based on principles of comparative advantage. However, these can vary widely across countries depending upon the nature of the institutions, differences in the capacity to administer various taxes and expenditure functions, and the structure of incentives. Thus, the assignment system not only determines the nature of institutions and structure of incentives but is also determined by it. Analysis of intergovernmental fiscal relations, to be useful as a policy guide, should, therefore, consider both the aspects.

CHALLENGES FOR INDIAN FEDERALISM

Thus, Indian federalism has to face manifold challenges in the emerging environment in terms of changing policies and institutions, even as it faces severe constraints. Transforming the economy to join the comity of developed nations within a reasonable time span is the most difficult of all the challenges and this alone requires accelerating the reform process at both national and sub-national levels. Motivating the states to undertake economic reforms towards outward orientation and coordinating the reform efforts of the Centre and states needs to be done in order to accelerate growth, reduce poverty, and hasten human development. These reforms should not only ensure efficient fiscal, financial, and regulatory systems and mechanisms to provide public services by financing them through the least distortionary ways but also create a market-friendly environment. Accomplishing these in a multilevel fiscal system is by no means an easy task.

The transition from plan to market necessarily envisages a greater role for decentralized levels of government. At the same time, not all of India's states are equally equipped to access the opportunities afforded by the market. Despite the adoption of a planned developmental strategy, there are significant differences in the levels of development, market penetration, and governance capacity. There are also significant inter-state variations in the capacity to generate revenues and standards of physical and social infrastructures provided. The intergovernmental transfer mechanism has failed to offset the fiscal disabilities between the states in a satisfactory manner. The preconditions for successful intergovernmental competition—competitive equality and cost–benefit appropriability—also do not exist to create a competitive environment. Political elements have intervened in significant ways to influence the transfer system. In addition, there are various types of invisible inter-state transfers due to price, quality, and regulatory controls introduced as a part of the planning process or to aid supply management in a shortage economy and such transfers tend to be inequitable. Offsetting the disabilities of the disadvantaged states in initial conditions, and ensuring a level playing field to enable the states to access market opportunities, continue to be important challenges faced in Indian fiscal federalism.

The issue of critical importance is that all these have to be accomplished in a constrained environment. The different parties in power at the Centre and in the states make it difficult to create a coordinated policy environment at the two levels. While the assignment system and the planning process over the years have created a strong Centre, the emergence of a coalition government at the Centre has weakened its ability to carry forward strong reforms. At the same time, emergence of regional parties as ruling parties in states and their ability to leverage power at the central coalition has placed strain on both intergovernmental policies and institutions. In addition to all these, the shortening time horizon of politicians in virtually all political parties as a result of high political turnover is an important factor that has exerted serious adverse effects on the governance at all levels.

PLAN OF THE BOOK

This book deals with the political economy of Indian federalism, with economic analysis at the forefront. It tries to analyse intergovernmental policies in the context of politics and institutions. The book is divided into three parts. The first part deals with the system and its setting. Issues of Centre–state economic relations are dealt with in the second part. The third part deals with various political economy issues in intergovernmental reform.

In Chapter 2, we review economic and political theories of federalism. While the political theories broadly see federalism as a bargain among constituent units of the federation to preserve group identities while securing security and stability, economic theories emphasize the efficiency and equity impacts on resource allocation, for private as well as public goods and services. Chapter 3 briefly reviews the history of India's federal structures, and will be useful for those without any familiarity with the country, but may be redundant for those who study India. Chapter 4 begins our analysis proper with a further consideration of historical and institutional issues in the context of our theoretical perspective. We discuss asymmetries in India's federal structures, problems of commitment for the Central government, and issues of bargaining between the Centre and states, and between the Centre and various constituent groups. Chapter 5 examines India's federal institutions along various dimensions, including political parties, the judiciary, and the bureaucracy, to try to understand how these fit in with the political structures that are typically the focus of analysis of federations.

The second part of the book deals with Centre-state economic relations and efficiency and equity implications of the constitutional arrangements and their actual working. The critical issue in economic relations, as pointed out above is the assignment question. Chapter 6 deals with this issue in detail. As pointed out earlier, what distinguishes federalism from decentralization is the assignment of powers. This is akin to giving property rights to sub-national governments and is critical to provide the necessary incentives and accountability in the provision of services. The entire working of a federation hinges on clarity in assignments and means to safeguard these property rights. However, even in the most ideal assignment systems, concurrency and overlapping cannot be avoided. Equally important is the fact that the assignment system is the basis on which intergovernmental competition works. The implications of concurrency, overlapping, and competition, therefore, have been analysed in some detail in Chapters 6 and 7.

The mechanisms to resolve problems arising from concurrency and methods to activate beneficent competition lie in adopting a well-designed intergovernmental transfer system (Chapter 8). We also discuss the ideal mix of general-purpose and specific-purpose transfers and the appropriate designs of these transfers. In light of this, we try to evaluate the transfer system in India, in Chapter 9. Unlike in developed market economies where much of the inter-regional resource flows depend on either the regional policies or intergovernmental transfers, regulations and controls on prices and quantities introduced as a part of the central planning process does have important inter-regional redistributive implications. In a political economy situation in which the more developed states wield greater powers, implicit transfers may be an important way to significantly offset the progressive impact of explicit transfers. It is also important to note that many of these instruments have outlived their utility and need to be phased out in the interest of both efficiency and equity.

A very important aspect of Centre–state economic relations is the assignment of natural resources. This has been a major issue of contention in federations like Nigeria and even in a developed country such as Canada, where the assignment of oil to the provinces has been a source of major distortions. In the Indian context, the major overlap has been in the case of sharing of river waters. Assignment of inter-state river waters to the Centre, and of exploitation of river water for irrigation to the states, has created a contentious environment between upper riparian and lower riparian states. This is one case where bargains have failed, and neither the Central government nor the Supreme Court has been able to enforce the spirit of the Constitution. Besides non-optimal harnessing of water resources, the overlap in the assignment system has led to some important ecological problems as well. We discuss these issues in Chapter 10.

Part three of the book deals with political economy of intergovernmental reforms. The analysis of the system of assignments and transfers lead us to analyse the political economy elements in intergovernmental transfers in Chapter 11. We cover the issue of incentives and implications of the intergovernmental fiscal system on the states' finances in some detail. We also produce some quantitative evidence on the political elements in determining the transfer system. These are closely related to the issue of inter-state disparities and regional dimensions of economic growth in India, which we examine in Chapter 12. We also review the recent literature on convergence of incomes in Indian states. Accentuation of disparities does not bode well for Indian federalism. In Chapter 13, we analyse the recent attempts to decentralize governance below the state level and bring out some important problems in both design and implementation of the system. The analysis of political economy of Indian federalism helps us to formulate some important policy and institutional dimensions of reform, which are discussed in Chapter 14. Of course, these need to be calibrated carefully by separating the short-term and longer-term dimensions. Finally, in Chapter 15, we conclude with a discussion of Indian federalism in the context of globalization, and India's overall economic reform programme.

2

Political and Economic Theories of Federalism

THE CASE FOR FEDERALISM

This chapter reviews political and economic theories of federalism. Political theory of federalism considers the federation as an outcome of bargain by the various parties to preserve group identities while securing security and stability. The case of federalism from political perspective rests in wider freedom of choice and better representation of different constituents. This may be called the 'holding together federalism' in contrast to the 'coming together federalism' in which smaller independent entities come together to form a federation for reasons of stability and security.

The economic case for government is based on the market failure argument, associated in particular with the existence of public goods. Federal structures in this case can support more diversity in the provision of non-market goods, by permitting more effective exercise of the mechanisms of exit (moving to different jurisdictions within a federation) and of voice (through voting). The optimal decentralized structure will involve attention to efficiency in the provision of public goods and services, as well as to equity across all the members of the federation. Factors that will influence the precise trade-offs and the institutional structures chosen include the extent of economies of scale, transaction costs of multiple jurisdictions, the degree of access to and ability to respond to information, and the types and extent of externalities or spillovers across jurisdictions. Indeed, the critical issue in economics of federalism is the question of assignment of powers, which is akin to assigning property rights. This not only helps to ensure optimal provision of public services but also provides a platform for healthy intergovernmental competition. As the powers cannot be extinguished, and as there are checks and balances instituted in a federal set-up, the ownership is real.

The political economy focus of our analysis leads us to highlight two aspects of government behaviour in a federal system. First, one cannot assume that different governments in a federation will automatically cooperate, as is assumed in 'cooperative federalism'. Instead, intergovernmental (vertical) and interjurisdictional (horizontal) competition prevail, particularly in a liberal or market environment. The design of institutions to maximize efficiency in competitive federalism must take this behaviour into account. Second, governments at all levels are composed of self-interested individuals, and therefore the design of federal structures must take into account rent-seeking and influence activities, as well as electoral considerations and mechanisms that affect responsiveness to voters' preferences.

POLITICAL THEORIES OF FEDERALISM

One can approach federalism from two directions, depending on the initial conditions. The political case for a federal structure in an existing nation can be made on the basis of enhancing freedom and the representation of constituents in their government. This is a possible argument for India in the present, or for a currently democratizing Russia. On the other hand, starting with smaller independent entities, the political goals of stability and security may be better achieved through a federation. Several historical examples of this exist including the original thirteen states which constituted the United States of America, and the ongoing evolution of the European Union. As these last two contrasting examples illustrate, the degree of political union may vary considerably under the broad term 'federation'. India at independence also faced the issue of combining smaller entities, namely the princely states, and many of them chose to enter the Indian Union based on the political realities of security and survival.[1] Of course, as these examples illustrate, the political and economic rationales for federalism are intertwined: economic cooperation and free trade within a federation may promote political stability if they reduce the incentive for aggression—the rationale behind the conception of the original European Economic Community. However, we shall try to separate political from economic factors in our discussion to the extent possible.

---

[1] Bardhan (2002) following Stephan and Lintz (quoted in Bardhan) makes a distinction between 'coming together federalism' like the US and 'holding together' federalism. It is possible that the 'coming together' federalism might eventually become a 'holding together' federalism.

Freedom and Representation

The idea of enhancing freedom and constituents' representation can be viewed in instrumental terms, as affecting the provision of goods and services by governments to constituents: this is actually an economic argument that we discuss below as the 'decentralization theorem'. Therefore the 'pure' political case must be based on non-instrumental grounds (Elster, 1994), whereby enhancing the ability to participate and to affect outcomes in the political process is in itself desirable, irrespective of the benefits of the outcomes themselves. A federal structure, in which there exist one or more lower levels of government, increases people's participation in the political process, by increasing the number of issues on which they directly vote, and, in smaller constituencies, at least notionally increasing the value of their votes in determining outcomes. These ideas of political participation have at least partly motivated various attempts in India to strengthen local governments under the general concept of panchayati raj. The issue of local government in India is taken up in Chapter 13.

It may be argued that a federal structure is not necessary for achieving greater participation in government, since this can be effected via devices such as referenda on single issues. This is certainly an alternative in some circumstances. However, two conceptual points should be noted. First, if such referenda are on sub-national issues, the constituency that votes on such an issue should be appropriately restricted. Presumably, there could be a mechanism for determining which issues are voted or which do not require a governmental entity at the corresponding level. To illustrate, if there is a decision to be made about whether to build a road in a particular district, even if there is no district-level government, an appropriate number of signatures presented to the state government administrator who is appointed at the district level could trigger a referendum on the issue. One can argue that a federal structure that includes a district-level government is therefore unnecessary.

However, this is where the second point must be brought in. From a political perspective, any representative government might be considered inferior to direct democracy in terms of participation of citizens in decision making. However, it is well recognized that, beyond a point, direct democracy will be unwieldy, costly, and even self-defeating if citizens tire of constantly having to pass judgement on decisions that may affect them only slightly (Downs, 1957). Thus, representatives are delegated to make such judgements, subject to periodic review through the electoral process.[2] In some sense, then, one is saying that political purity of participation must inevitably be tempered by considerations of efficiency. Together with the fact that some issues are always sub-national, or even local in character, this brings one back to a case for two or more tiers of government, that is, federalism. In fact, such efficiency considerations imply that in practice, there are multiple tiers of government even in the case of unitary or centralized systems. What distinguishes federal structures from such cases of multiple tiers is the ownership of powers that sub-national constituents have. We shall discuss some of the theoretical aspects further in this chapter, and issues of control throughout the book.[3]

Group Identities

So far, we have made the abstract case for federalism that derives from classical liberal political theory. This approach is based on the individual as the sole relevant unit, and it has a powerful normative appeal. However, all practical attempts at devising national constitutions, or systems of government more generally, have to come to grips with the heterogeneity of populations. This heterogeneity includes the larger historic divisions of gender and race, as well as more specific diversities in language, religion, ethnicity, and culture. To some extent, every nation attempts to transcend such heterogeneity, to stress national citizenship above all else. This has been the case for the United States and emerging European nations in the nineteenth century, as well as for newly independent nations such as India in the twentieth century. In some cases, such as the United States and European countries such as France, there is no constitutional or legal basis for recognizing heterogeneity along the dimensions of religion or language, though this is now under debate in these countries, as they become more diverse in these ways. India, however, because of its size and its history, has always recognized various kinds of diversity in its constitutional

---

[2] In the example of the administrator constrained to follow the dictates of a referendum procedure, one is essentially making her/him an agent of the local constituency, as would be a locally elected official. The difference is that the administrator's agency role is very restricted, and her/his incentives are still chiefly determined by the parameters of the state-level organization. These issues of incentives will be taken up in more detail at various points of our analysis.

[3] Verney, in Arora and Verney (1995), has provided a detailed taxonomy of different forms of hierarchical government, including federalism. We may also note that, in addition to Verney's scheme, there are many terms used to describe different forms of tiered government, including decentralization, deconcentration, delegation, and devolution (e.g., Rondinelli, 1981). To some extent, we will try to avoid getting caught up in semantic issues in this work. However, we return to the issue of different types of federalism below.

and legal structures, and much of this recognition has been expressed through the political structures of federalism.[4]

We shall take up the details of the interaction between the workings of Indian federalism and factors such as language, religion, and ethnicity in Chapter 8. Here we concentrate on the theoretical basis for incorporating such factors in federal structures. The key idea to be noted is that, in allowing considerations of this nature to influence federal structures, in cases such as drawing state (or other sub-national jurisdictional) boundaries on the basis of language, or creating ethnically based local councils within states, one is acknowledging that the group (however defined) is in itself a significant political unit. Why should this be any different from purely geographic subunits in a homogeneous nation? Presumably, the difference is in the strength of within-group ties, the possible barriers for those not in the group, and the resultant competition with national identity. At the same time, it must be recognized that heterogeneity is real, and simply ignoring it in designing the federal structure will not remove it: cultural identities (broadly conceived to include the various dimensions mentioned above) are quite durable.[5] Thus, while demands for linguistically organized states were resisted by the Central government in India after independence, by 1966 all the major demands for reorganization by linguistic groups had been acceded to.

The recognition of group identities is actually a strong feature of the Indian Constitution, in features such as the provision that different laws may apply to different religious groups, or in the creation of reserved seats for erstwhile untouchables or similar groups. Thus, the incorporation of such group identities in the federal structure is one aspect of a broader approach that has characterized the designing of India's system of governance. The two non-federal examples just mentioned have also been significant flashpoints in the evolution of India's polity, and illustrate the depth of the issues raised by such factors. In this work, we will not, of course, be able to provide a comprehensive analysis of these issues. However, we will explore how concerns about group identity have

[4] It is important to remember the centrality of this issue and the pervasiveness of this approach. There has been a tendency to contrast the homogeneous Western industrialized nation with developing countries driven by religious, linguistic, or tribal conflicts. However, the examples of the United Kingdom (England vs. Scotland, Wales, and Northern Ireland) and Spain (the Basque Country and Catalonia) illustrate the universality of such concerns.

[5] One can make an efficiency argument here also, in that states with more than one language group would be administratively unwieldy, or would favour one linguistic group over another. To some extent, this problem is unavoidable, especially at the national level, but having sub-national government jurisdictions matching linguistic boundaries to the greatest extent possible would presumably minimize the problem.

influenced the evolution of India's federal institutions, including not only the constitutional and legal structures, but also the resulting pattern of fiscal transfers from higher to lower levels of government.

To return to the initial argument—that federalism may be desirable to promote greater freedom and representation of citizens—one can view the issue of group identity as supplementary, in that it provides guidelines beyond geography for the demarcation of sub-national jurisdictions in a federation justified only by the objective of promoting representation of individuals. However, the desire of a group to constitute a separate political unit may be an independent justification also. Both these factors are manifest in the most basic feature of India's federal structure: the demarcation of states. The larger states have had their boundaries redrawn where necessary, or where demanded, to reflect linguistic boundaries, but have typically not been divided up further. India's north-eastern region, however, is composed of a number of smaller states, in some cases carved out of existing states, based almost entirely on ethnic and related criteria, rather than pure concerns for representation of individual citizens.[6] In other words, group identity has served as an independent basis for determining the structure of the federation.[7] Again, we will take up the analysis of cases such as this in Chapter 8.

Security and Stability

In contrast to the non-instrumental rationale for federal political structures as a way of promoting greater freedom and representation in an existing nation, the political justification for federation, when starting from the opposite end of the spectrum (namely multiple independent entities), is purely instrumental: the promotion of security and stability. One can therefore almost cast this case entirely in economic terms, where security and stability are viewed as public goods subject to economies of scale in production, or where the competitive provision of these goods by multiple entities creates negative spillovers: increasing one entity's security via military spending reduces its neighbour's security. A federation that involves only a higher-level government providing external security avoids these spillovers and takes advantage of economies of scale. In fact,

---

[6] An alternative view is that the greater cultural (ethnic, linguistic) diversity in the region is associated with greater preference diversity, which in turn would imply smaller government units according to the decentralization theorem that we discuss later in this chapter (Arora, 1995).

[7] Even in the existing major states, group identities based on ethnicity play a role, as evidenced in the demands for autonomous regions by Gorkhas in West Bengal and by the tribal population of Jharkhand in Bihar.

without some political justification such as security, the previous political arguments discussed would make a case for separate nations rather than a federation. Finally, it should be recognized that accommodation of group identities in the federal structure in special ways, alluded to earlier, also reflects security concerns: the north-eastern states, for example, have strategic significance for India.

Riker (1975) dismisses the 'ideological' reasons in favour of federalism discussed in the previous subsection,[8] and strongly argues for understanding federalism as 'a constitutional bargain among politicians', with the motives being 'military and diplomatic defence or aggression' (pp. 113–14). Riker (1964) offered the following sole conditions for such a bargain to be struck:

1. A desire on the part of politicians who offer the bargain to expand their territorial control by peaceful means, usually either to meet an external military or diplomatic threat or to prepare for military or diplomatic aggrandizement.

2. A willingness on the part of politicians who accept the bargain to give up independence for the sake of the Union either because they desire protection from an external threat or because they desire to participate in the potential aggression of the federation (Riker, 1975, p. 114).

Birch (1966) added the desire to deter internal threats to the above conditions. The essence remains unchanged by the extension. Riker's emphasis is that the establishment of a federal government is a rational bargain among politicians. He goes on to argue, in surveying the experience

---

[8] Riker (1975, pp. 156–8) discusses three arguments: that federalism promotes democratic polity, that it promotes democracy by promoting an interest in sub-national government, and that it maintains individual freedom, and tends to dismiss them as 'absurd'. Similar reservations about decentralization in general have been recently expressed by Prud'homme (1995). These issues will recur throughout this work. However, two points may be made here. First, Riker raises serious questions concerning the positive content of statements such as, 'federalism promotes democratic polity'. A more refined and cautious statement, for which we develop arguments in the body of this chapter, is that within a democratic framework, federalism allows for greater democracy, in the sense of local control over local issues. Riker seems to think that this is not true either, that 'nonfederal governments do not necessarily interfere with local policymaking on local issues' (1975, p. 158). However, the Indian experience, and that of other centralized federations, suggests the contrary. Second, there are normative issues mixed into Riker's discussion: his point about the lack of civil rights for blacks in the southern United States, because of the application of federal principles, is a powerful and common one, but it involves a normative judgement. Typically, such values are enshrined in the constitution of a country, and the problem identified by Riker is one of the failure to apply such values. It is not clear that federal principles caused this failure. Such issues, once again, are critical in Indian federalism, and are discussed in Chapters 8 and 11.

of many different federations, that every successful federation satisfied the above two conditions, while they were absent from every failure. Therefore, Riker argues that actual federalism can only be understood from a particular positive, instrumental viewpoint: the normative aspects discussed in the previous subsection are irrelevant (see footnote 7 also).

We conclude this subsection by briefly commenting further on the relevance for Indian federalism of the issues of voluntary combination through a political bargain. We noted the fact that there was some element of combination involved in the absorption of the princely states at the time of Indian independence. However, while almost all the princes voluntarily joined the Union, recognizing the political difficulties (in terms of security and stability), or even impossibility, of staying independent, in one or two cases, at least, the Indian government used coercion to incorporate princely states. This was facilitated where the princely state was completely surrounded by the Indian Union such as the princely state of Hyderabad. One very important special case where this was not true was the princely state of Jammu and Kashmir, which acceded to the Union under very special circumstances, and for which special provisions were made in India's Constitution,[9] reflecting the idea of federation much more than in cases of other princely states joining the Union. Aside from the example of Kashmir, therefore, what resulted was not a federation, as in the case of the United States, Australia or Canada, where the original boundaries of constituent units have mostly remained unchanged, but something quite different. In fact, the Indian Constitution avoids the words 'federal' and 'federation' entirely (Verney, 1995). While issues of external security have certainly been extremely important in shaping India's polity since independence, they have been motivated much more by the Central perspective of a unitary state, or a nation with a geographical (and cultural) centre and peripheries, rather than by the idea of a voluntary federation of otherwise autonomous entities (the states). This is further substantiated by the fact that there is no provision for exit in the Constitution (though this is true of 'more federal' countries than India also), and the general power of the Centre to change state boundaries or even extinguish a state altogether.[10]

---

[9] Kashmir, therefore, provides an important example of what Arora calls asymmetric federalism. The north-eastern states have also had special provisions inserted in the Constitution to encourage their continued membership in the 'federation'. We take these cases up in detail in Chapter 8.

[10] Again Kashmir is an exception. Furthermore, of course, political realities, in the form of group identities constrain the Centre beyond the limits placed by the Constitution.

Political Structures and the Measurement of Federalism

Riker (1975) builds on his analysis of federalism as a political bargain to discuss the nature and measurement of this institution. His (1964) definition of the term is 'a political organisation in which the activities of government are divided between regional governments and a Central government in such a way that each kind of government has some activities on which it makes final decisions'. According to this definition, on one side of federations are alliances or leagues, while on the other side lie centralized or unitary governments. Within the range of federations, the degree of centralization is reflected in the narrowness or breadth of the final decision-making authority of the different levels of government. Towards one extreme is centralized federalism, at the other is peripheralized federalism. The former is distinguished from the latter by the ability of the Central government to force constituent governments to do its bidding with respect to those functions that are assigned to the Centre. In a peripheralized federal structure, constituents will obey only if they agree with the decision.[11]

Riker discusses the development of centralized federalism, beginning with the United States' constitutional convention of 1787, as a significant departure from historical precedent. He traces the direct and indirect influence of the US model on numerous other federal systems of government, from early nineteenth-century Latin America to Europe and the British colonies in the twentieth century. The spread and strengthening[12] of centralized federalism was the result of the success of this mode of government, which in turn was helped by the ability of the Centre to raise resources through taxation more effectively than in a peripheralized structure.

Within the category of centralized federalism, Riker is forced to make a further distinction, between fully and partially centralized cases. In the first, the majority of significant political decisions are made at the Centre, and the notion of state or provincial rights is meaningless, as in the old Soviet Union, or in Mexico. In partially centralized federalism, many

---

[11] A useful way to think of this for economists is that in peripheralized federalism, the Centre must respect the 'participation' or 'individual rationality' constraints of the constituent governments, while it does not have to do so in centralized federalism.

[12] Riker is careful to distinguish political from technological centralization. The former is the result of a reassignment of functions. The latter is the more effective or broader application of a function already assigned to the Centre as a result of technological improvements such as faster communication. Of course, from the economic perspective, technological change which increases economies of scale or scope may prompt a legal or a de facto political reassignment of functions towards the Centre: the two kinds of centralization are intertwined.

significant political decisions are made by constituent governments, and the notion of state or provincial rights is meaningful. According to Riker, 'this category would surely include Canada and Australia and perhaps India and even the United States' (1975, p. 133). Given this range, Riker seeks to measure federalism in terms of the degree of centralization, using observable variables.

The focus of Riker's measure is the degree of centralization of the structures of political competition, in particular, the structure of political parties. He notes that in all fully centralized federations, the political party system is also fully centralized, while in all partially centralized federations the political party system is relatively decentralized. He gives examples from the United States, Canada, and Australia to illustrate the latter correlation. On India, he observes, 'India is decreasingly centralized constitutionally and politically as the state governments and state politicians assert themselves, especially since the death of Nehru' (p. 136). This fits in with the earlier characterization of India as a case of partially centralized federalism.

The classification of party centralization, in turn, depends on two factors:

1. Whether or not the party in control of the national government is in control of constituent governments.
2. Whether or not party discipline exists on legislative and executive matters.

The second of these is difficult to measure objectively in a manner that permits comparison across different federations, but the first dimension provides one possible measure of the degree of centralization in a federation. Based on the work of Shapley and Shubik (1954), who constructed a 'power index' for coalitional decision making, Riker and Schaps (1957) devised an 'index of disharmony' to measure the degree of difference of control between the Central and the constituent governments in a federation. The details of this index follow.

Shapley and Shubik's power index is the percentage chance that a member of a governing body has to be pivotal. To be pivotal means to be the last added member of a minimal winning coalition. The power index is constructed by examining all possible winning coalitions, and calculating the fraction of those in which the individual or party is pivotal. Riker and Schaps use this to construct their index of disharmony as follows. Suppose that there is a party (or a coalition of parties) at the Centre that has a power index greater than 0.5. This party or coalition is identified as the 'governing party'. For example, if a single party has an absolute majority at the centre, its power index would be one, since it is, by itself, always the minimal winning coalition. Now for the central 'governing party', calculate its power index in each of the constituent (state or provincial governments). Average these over all constituent governments (e.g. weighted by population size). Then subtract this average 'constituent government power index' to get Riker and Schaps's index of disharmony. Clearly, the index will be between zero and one, and the larger the number, the greater the degree of decentralization according to this measure. For the United States, for example, Riker and Schaps calculated this index of disharmony biennially from 1937 to 1955, obtaining values ranging from 0.31 in the first year to 0.55 at the end of the period. Ranges calculated for Canada and Australia showed greater variation, from as low as 0.10 or 0.20 to highs of 0.85 or 0.90.

While the effectiveness of this index is somewhat limited in focusing on political parties alone, and in not considering the complexities of the parties themselves—particularly in India, where sometimes the same party at the Centre and the state level may be quite different entities in terms of personal loyalties—it clearly provides one possible, and useful quantification of the degree of centralization in a federation. However, one key feature missing from this scheme is the economic aspect, particularly the relative control of resources at the two levels. For example, if the Centre controls almost all public expenditure and revenues, a high index of disharmony, calculated according to Riker and Schaps's procedure, will be misleading in suggesting a high degree of decentralization. In this case, combining the political measure with a measure of economic centralization may be more appealing. In fact, this illustrates a central message of our analysis that political and economic (especially fiscal) factors must be combined in understanding the workings of Indian federalism. This analysis will be developed in Chapter 12.

This concludes our brief excursion into political theory and its relevance for understanding Indian federalism. While political issues such as electoral weight, coalitions of power, and relative bargaining strength will be important components of our analysis in subsequent chapters, as Riker and Schaps's use of an idea developed by economists shows, one can treat these issues within the usual analytical apparatus of economics. Therefore, we next give some detailed consideration of the possible economic rationales for federal structures of government.

ECONOMIC THEORIES OF FEDERALISM

We begin with a discussion of the economic rationale for government as the provider of certain types of goods and services that may not be well provided by the market mechanism. We then turn to an analysis of hierarchical government, decentralization and federal structures as seen from an economic perspective, focusing on incentive issues. We next discuss issues of competition among constituent governments as an essential aspect of understanding the working of federal structures, and then proceed to examine the links between competition and incentives also. We close with a discussion of issues of revenue raising, separately and in relation to the expenditure responsibilities of different levels of government.

Public Goods and Government

As we have seen, to some extent economic theories of federalism overlap with instrumental political theories. The essence of economic theories of government is the idea that the market mechanism may not be in a position to supply certain goods and services at appropriate levels. The reason for this is in the nature of the goods[13] themselves, or in the technology of production or provision of the goods. Briefly, if a good can be consumed by someone without reducing its availability to others (that is, it is 'non-rival') and if others cannot be prevented from consuming it (that is, it is 'non-exclusive'), it is termed a pure public good, and it is a candidate for provision by government. The classic examples of public goods are defence and law and order, and historically, of course, providing these has been the initial rationale for a basic governmental structure.

In reality, of course, there are two complications. The first is conceptual: few goods are pure public goods. They may be non-rival but exclusive, rival but non-exclusive, or lie somewhere along either continuum of rivalry or exclusivity. As an example of the latter, a busy road or a park that is subject to congestion is partially non-rival: one person's consumption does not preclude another's enjoyment, but does diminish it (Breton, 1965; Olson, 1986; Cornes and Sandler, 1996). The congestion example is of particular interest, because it suggests a reason for multiple provision of the good: up to a point, a bigger park may be feasible, but at some stage, two parks may be preferable,[14] and these may conceivably be provided by two separate entities—private (clubs) or public (local governments). The second complication is practical: governments rarely restrict themselves

---

[13] Here, we shall take goods to mean goods and services. This is sensible from the perspective of economic theory, which makes no distinction between the two categories in the satisfaction of wants. However, in legal documents, such as the Indian Constitution, the failure to comprehend services in the category of goods has caused some problems: see Chapter 4.

[14] Perhaps this point is more compelling with examples such as swimming pools and schools.

to providing only public goods. There are various possible reasons for this, including a desire to control private monopolies,[15] paternalism in general, or, less benignly, a desire to extract surplus from constituents.[16] We will touch on some of these issues of government objectives and incentives in our discussion of theories of federalism and Indian practice. For the moment, however, we will continue the exposition of theory by referring to governments providing public goods only.

Hierarchies of Government and Decentralization

So far, we have briefly described an economic rationale for the existence of government, without exploring its hierarchical structure. The initial reason for considering this question arises because there are some public goods that are non-rival or non-exclusive only up to a point. Geographic distance, in particular, can matter, in limiting the number who benefit from provision of a public good. Once the possibility of local or, more broadly, sub-national public goods, is admitted, one should consider the possibility of provision of these goods by governments whose constituencies match the locus of beneficiaries. In a world of perfect information and benevolent governments, however, just as the broader theoretical choice between markets and governments becomes moot (either will deliver the goods), the issue of hierarchical structure of government becomes irrelevant. A single, benevolent, perfectly informed government can provide local public goods just as well as it does national public goods, and there is no economic case for a federal or any other hierarchical structure of government.

Now consider the more realistic case where the information available to governments is not perfect. The key aspect of information is, of course, the benefits that individuals derive from the provision of a public good. Without knowing this, a benevolent government cannot perfectly achieve

---

[15] The classic argument here is that, with increasing returns to scale, which are the result of indivisibilities or high fixed costs of production, competition will not be feasible or stable: there is a 'natural monopoly'. This suggests either regulation by government as an agent of consumer citizens, or government ownership and production (nationalization). This kind of argument has underlain much of the thinking on government intervention in industry, in India and elsewhere. As a theoretical aside, it is useful to note that there is a very close connection between this rationale for government intervention, and that based on the notion of non-rival goods. Pure non-rivalry can ultimately be traced back to indivisibilities in the production technology, and the presence of fixed costs: this point is made very clearly in Olson (1986).

[16] Some of this surplus may, in fact, flow back to particular groups of constituents, so-called 'special interest groups'. This will be an important issue in discussing federal structures, and decentralization in general.

an objective of maximizing social welfare, which will be (in a formalization of the idea of benevolence) some aggregate of individual welfare levels. One possible argument is that information about constituent preferences, especially with respect to sub-national public goods, is better at levels below the national level. According to this argument, governments at sub-national levels will therefore be better able to provide quantities of public goods. Thus, the argument continues, a federal structure of governments, or more generally, decentralization, will do a better job of providing such goods than would a unitary government. To some extent, this is the usual presentation of what is sometimes called the 'decentralization theorem' (e.g., Oates, 1972).

However, the above logic is not complete, for the following reason. If governments are benevolent, there is no reason why local knowledge of preferences should not be passed on to higher levels: there is nothing that requires separate government entities at lower levels—one only needs local functionaries within a unitary, but hierarchical government. So incomplete information alone, while it motivates a hierarchical government does not by itself provide a rationale for a federal system. One possible way around this is to note that the transmission of information is costly (an example of the more general case of what are known as 'transaction costs'), and this would work in favour of decentralization. This argument would have carried more force in the days before modern means of communication, however, and it is useful to distinguish such exogenous transaction costs from the endogenous costs associated with the structure of incentives.

This brings us to the other idealized assumption, that of automatic benevolence of government decision makers. Once one relaxes this assumption, one can provide a theoretical rationale for tiers of government. The argument is as follows. Suppose that government decision makers are self-interested, as are all economic agents. Then they must be provided with incentives to act in a manner beneficial to their constituents. The electoral process provides one way of doing this: more effective provision of public goods to constituents means a higher chance of re-election, and staying in office is preferable for the government decision maker. Now, elections are based on performance with respect to multiple dimensions of public good provision, so incentives are not perfect. However, having tiers of government allows incentives that operate through the electoral process to be more refined. For example, if voters can only choose at the national level, they must base their decisions on performance with respect to national as well as sub-national and local provision of public goods. If there are several tiers of government, these decisions can be unbundled:

the choice in a national election can be based on the provision of national public goods such as external security, at the state level on the provision of state-level goods such as education, and at the local level on the provision of local goods such as street lighting and sanitation. Presumably, local politicians, judged on the basis of local performance alone, have greater incentives to do a good job of satisfying constituents than a national politician being judged on the basis of national defence as well as local sanitation (Seabright, 1996).[17]

It is worth noting that the incentive argument is to some extent independent of the information argument, since it operates even in the case of perfect information about constituent preferences. Government decision makers may know exactly what to do to satisfy constituents, but still not do it in the absence of appropriate incentives. Typically, however, reflecting the real world, the two arguments are combined in presenting the economic case for a federal structure of governments.

Competition Among Governments and Spillovers

There is also another dimension of the incentive argument, in addition to the one we have described, which focuses on the refinement of incentives provided by unbundling of performance measures through a tiered structure of government. This other dimension is based on the mobility of citizens within a country. In terms of Hirschman's well-known terminology, the first case involves 'voice', while the second deals with 'exit' as an incentive device for government decision makers. In the case of public good provision, this approach has its roots in Tiebout's (1956) famous model of competition among localities for residents. We will not go into the details of the model and assumptions here, but the intuition is that competition among localities, through the mechanism of resident's mobility ('voting with one's feet') will lead to an efficient provision of local public goods, and that would not be achieved in the absence of such competition. The implication, therefore, is that a federal structure which creates 'competitive governments' (using Breton's succinct term) will do a better job of providing public goods efficiently, in the sense of matching such provision with the preferences of citizens, than will a unitary government not subject to the rigours of competition.

---

[17] This discussion can be related back to the discussion of referenda as an alternative means of allowing political expression. If bureaucrats or administrators, as agents of higher-level politicians, are responsible for implementing or making decisions at the local/sub-national level, this introduces one more step in the chain of incentives that are required. In general, incentives will be more effective where they are more direct, and based on more accurate and specific performance measures. See Milgrom and Roberts (1990), Chapter 7.

The arguments developed so far provide a case for the allocation of decision making to different levels of government based on the locus of beneficiaries. Superficially, this is quite similar to the kind of argument made by Breton (1965) and Olson (1969) for determining the scope of jurisdictions. However, that case was made on the basis of internalizing externalities or spillovers, and a fully explicit rationale for having lower-level governments at all was not provided there.[18] We have not considered spillovers so far, but wherever they exist, they raise the possibility of centralization to internalize them, hence avoiding the inefficiency that comes about when certain costs and benefits are not accounted for in making a decision.[19] In the absence of the need for refinement of incentives, spillovers of any kind would move one in the direction of centralization, and unitary government. The incentive argument then implies a trade-off between the need to provide effective incentives and the need to internalize externalities. The optimal structure of tiers of government and of jurisdictions might then not involve all spillovers being internalized, unlike in Olson's analysis. On this point, one can also note that Coase's (1960) perspective on the resolution of externality problems would also favour more decentralization, to the extent that local governments can negotiate to overcome such inefficiencies in a mutually beneficial manner.[20]

---

[18] Olson (1986) does substantially extend his earlier analysis, and argues as follows: '[W]hen the government is far larger than many of the public goods of exogenous domain, there is the political problem of the "internality" that also leads to nonoptimality. The gains from providing a local public good of exogenous domain can greatly exceed the costs of providing it, but, with a unitary national jurisdiction, the number of losers from the national taxes that would finance the public good will be far larger than the number of gainers. Thus the provision of the local public good will fail to command a majority of the larger jurisdiction.' Olson's analysis here does not permit the kind of possibility discussed earlier, where a sub-national constituency alone might vote on a 'local' public good, even without a separate government for that constituency. Of course, optimality would require the financing of the good to be through taxes restricted to the beneficiaries, rather than the national taxes assumed by Olson. Again, it is possible to conceive of locality-or region-specific taxes without a full-fledged government for that area: such taxes would be collected by an agent of the Central government. Once again, we are left with incentives as the driver of institutional structure.

[19] For example, a wooded local park might provide some benefits to actual users, as well as positive spillovers for nearby non-users who benefit from the resultant cleaner air. Neglecting the latter benefit by a local government might adversely affect the decision to build such a park.

[20] Coase's argument is usually presented as a case of bargaining between two individuals: well-defined initial property rights will lead to efficiency when costless bargaining is possible, overcoming inefficiencies created by externalities without government intervention or centralization to internalize the externality. Once again, if there is perfect information, the issue of centralization versus decentralization becomes somewhat irrelevant, since either will

The incentive argument interacts with the Coasean perspective somewhat subtly, since if spillovers are pervasive and uniform, this is tantamount to saying that the locus of beneficiaries is not properly defined, and incentives would be improved by widening the geographic scope of the government in question. In the limit, then, one has a concordance with the Olson (1969, 1986) analysis.

The discussion of spillovers provides help to extend the idea that public goods having national scope should be provided by the national government. In a sense, the concept of spillovers is a generalization from a situation where there are very well-defined groups who are equal beneficiaries, or not at all, to one where there is a gradient of benefits, often associated with geographic distance, so that even 'outsiders' are not completely excluded from benefits. Furthermore, while we have focused on positive spillovers, it is well known that externalities can be negative (e.g. building an urban amenity might create pollution for surrounding rural areas), and the discussion of Coasean bargaining applies to such cases as well. This, too, could be incorporated in the idea of a locus of beneficiaries by allowing for negative benefits.

We next turn to another aspect of federalism, the interaction of different levels of government. This has not been an issue at all in the preceding discussion. However, an alternative to the Coasean or centralization solutions to spillovers between lower-level jurisdictions is the use of externality-correcting taxes and subsidies by the higher-level government. This remedy was proposed by Pigou (1932) and is often discussed in the context of externalities between individual agents, but it can be applied to sub-national governments as well, just as it is applied to organizations such as firms. In practice, explicit taxes on subordinate governments are rare, but restrictions on pricing of government goods, ceilings on tax rates, and so on, may all act as taxes on lower-level governments. Such restrictions are quite common in the Indian case, and will be discussed in the chapters on assignment of functions, transfers, and regulation (Chapters 4–7). Whether these policies are motivated by concerns such as externality correction will also be discussed there. 'Subsidies' to lower-level governments are much more common in federal systems, in the form of intergovernmental transfers. Again, the motivations for such transfers, both theoretical and practical, are much more complex than externality

---

lead to the optimal allocation. On the other hand, with incomplete information about benefits or preferences, it is not clear that Coase's 'theorem' holds true, since an imperfect, centralized solution may, under some circumstances, do better than bargaining from initial property rights: see Farrell (1987).

correction, and it is not easy to disentangle their causes and effects. Given the importance of Central transfers to states in the Indian federal system, understanding their mechanisms and outcomes is a major focus of this study. Chapters 6 and 7, in particular, examine these transfers.

Spillovers across jurisdictions within a federation are basically what economists refer to as externalities, as we have indicated through our usage of the terms. In fact, the way we have described them, they are 'technological' externalities, where this term equally applies to preferences, since preferences and technology are the two fundamental primitives of any economic analysis. In the analysis of a perfectly competitive market system, however, one also has the notion of 'pecuniary' externalities, for example where one individual's purchase of a good raises the price that others have to pay (Marshall, 1920). With perfect competition, complete markets, and no public goods, the fact that such pecuniary externalities exist has no negative implications for efficiency. However, when markets are incomplete, as is typically the case in the real world, pecuniary externalities do matter. More broadly, whenever there is competition that does not fit the price-mediated model of perfect competitive equilibrium, there is no presumption that the outcome will be allocatively efficient. Thus, in general, the Nash equilibrium of a non-cooperative game is not Pareto efficient.[21]

In this context, the models of Tiebout (1956) and Oates and Schwab (1988), where competition among governments—in dimensions such as the levels of public goods provided, taxes on residents, and subsidies to attract capital into a jurisdiction—leads to an optimal or efficient outcome in terms of the allocation of resources, are very special. Typically, relaxing any of the assumptions of these models leads to a violation of optimality. In extreme cases, the equilibrium outcome may be quite undesirable, in the sense not only of inefficiency, but also of inequity.[22] For example, the levels of taxation may be too low (the so-called 'race to the bottom'), or residents may flee from one location so that its infrastructure is inefficiently

[21] The technical terms used here may be loosely defined here for non-economists. A game is, very roughly, any strategic situation. A non-cooperative game is one where agreements to cooperate are not binding or cannot be enforced. A Nash equilibrium is a choice of strategies by all the players such that each game player's choice is a best response to the others' equilibrium choices, i.e. no one has an incentive to unilaterally deviate from the equilibrium. A Pareto efficient or Pareto optimal outcome is one where no one can be made better off without making someone else worse off: it represents a minimal notion of optimality. Equity concerns can be incorporated on top of Pareto optimality, but they do not conflict with it, nor does the Pareto criterion have any implications for equity.

[22] In fact, an equilibrium outcome may be inequitable even when it is Pareto efficient: see the previous footnote.

utilized or the location even becomes economically unviable as a jurisdiction. These kinds of phenomena create a role for a higher-level government, which may not only set the rules of the competition among subordinate governments, for example through legislation, but also continually monitor and influence their competition through policies such as intergovernmental transfers. The role of the national government in a federation therefore includes that of referee or monitor, though it extends beyond merely enforcing the rules of competition, to interpreting and altering them as well.[23] This role has been particularly stressed by Breton (1995). We may view it as a generalization of the idea that the higher-level government's role in a federal system includes the correction of externalities, since the non-optimality of strategic behaviour in general is closely related to the externalities imposed by each player on others in the game.

In these kinds of strategic competition, it should also be noted that there might be multiple equilibria, even for a given set of rules of the game. The policy of the superior government may then be aimed at moving the lower-level governments towards an equilibrium that is more socially desirable. A further complication arises if there is a tendency to move further away from the desirable equilibrium whenever some external shock causes an initial displacement from equilibrium (the desirable equilibrium is 'unstable').[24] In this case, a higher-level government may be better off changing the rules of competition, rather than forever trying to compensate for the instability. Note that Breton (1995) uses the term 'instability' in a somewhat loose sense, to encompass the existence of undesirable equilibria as well as the problem of instability of desirable equilibria. As long as the usage is clear, there is no problem, and we shall tend to use Breton's terminology as a convenient shorthand for both problems.

Competition and Incentives

The preceding discussion emphasized the monitoring role for a higher-level government in a federation, taking it beyond the provision of

---

[23] One can insert a conceptual remark on federalism here: a federal structure involves not only sub-national control rights, for example, through sub-national representative governments, but also limits on national government encroachment on those rights. Thus, a federation will involve *some* limits on how much the national government can alter the rules.

[24] Note that, properly speaking, the ideas of 'stable' and 'unstable' require some specification of the process of adjustment, something that is not specified in the notion of equilibrium itself. An 'unstable' equilibrium is therefore one where the process of adjustment to a shock that disturbs the equilibrium does not bring one back to the initial situation, but rather a different one (or away from any equilibrium at all): the usual physical analogy is that of a pyramid which is in a stable equilibrium resting on its base, but an unstable one balancing on its point.

national-level public goods. In some sense, of course, monitoring and refereeing by the national government of sub-national governments' competition can be viewed as the provision of a particular national public good. Recall that the argument for decentralization was based on the sharper incentives provided to government decision makers, acting as agents of constituents. This argument was made without regard to competition among governments: the competition was implicitly among those potentially willing and able to serve in government.

Here, we examine the interaction between incentives of government decision makers and the existence of competition among governments. Models such as those of Oates and Schwab, or variants of the Tiebout model typically assume that government decision makers will automatically maximize the welfare of constituents. However, if they are exploitative (or, to use a less pejorative term, rent seekers),[25] and set taxes higher than is optimal in the absence of competition to maximize their own welfare, as in the Leviathan model of government of Brennan and Buchanan (1980) or the bureaucratic revenue-maximizing model of Niskanen (1971), 'race to the bottom' type competition will counter this tendency, and is to be preferred for this reason. The argument here is, of course, very close to the argument for competition over monopoly in markets for private goods provided by firms, where competition leads to lower prices and higher welfare for consumers, though firms are only interested in maximizing their own profits. Put in another way, competition among governments creates incentives for their decision makers that are beneficial to constituents.

The Brennan–Buchanan argument implicitly assumes that other incentive mechanisms are not sufficient, or perhaps are absent. For example, electoral competition in a unitary government might not be enough to restrain 'Leviathan', and competition among governments adds another incentive device. In Brennan and Buchanan's work, therefore, electoral competition within a jurisdiction and competition among jurisdictions are separate but complementary incentive devices, with the first not being strong enough on its own. Breton (1995) has highlighted the work of Salmon (1987), which combines the two phenomena as follows. The idea is that citizens of a jurisdiction can use information about the goods

---

[25] The term comes from Krueger (1974), but the idea can be traced to Tullock (1967). It refers to the idea of economic rent, which is the excess or surplus beyond what someone would receive in their next best alternative occupation. Barriers to entry and economies of scale help to create economic rents, and self-interested government decision makers can create rents through policy choices, as well as seek a share of these rents by making them available to private sector rent seekers such as firms or interest groups. Other noteworthy contributions to the literature on rent seeking include Olson (1965, 1982) and Becker (1983).

provided elsewhere to evaluate the performance of their own government, in the manner of a contest or tournament (Lazear and Rosen,
1981).[26] Therefore, competition among governments not only affects
policies to attract or keep citizens, but it also interacts with electoral
incentives. Accordingly, '[e]ach government has an incentive to do better
than governments in other jurisdictions in terms of levels and qualities of
services, of levels of taxes or of more general economic and social indicators.' Empirically, whether this happens (and this is a question that needs
to be examined in the Indian context) depends on 'the possibility and
willingness of citizens to make assessments of comparative performance ...
and [on] the impact these assessments have on the well-being of politicians' (Salmon, 1987, p. 32). Breton (1995, p. 237) argues that the 'Salmon
incentive mechanism' is quite important in understanding the diffusion of
policies and programmes among jurisdictions in federations. To the extent
that mobility costs restrict 'voting with one's feet' in India, electoral
incentives are more important, and performance measures that also look
at relative performance can strengthen or refine electoral incentives.

An important extension of the Brennan–Buchanan approach is the
concept of Market Preserving Federalism (MPF), introduced by Weingast
(1993, 1995). In addition to stressing the importance of decentralized
governments that compete effectively with each other (and therefore have
appropriate powers assigned to them), MPF has two additional key
ingredients (Oates, 1999). First, the federation must constitute a common
market, without any internal trade barriers. Second, sub-national governments must face 'hard budget constraints', which means that they cannot
create money, access unlimited credit, or get bailouts from higher-level
governments in times of fiscal distress. The term is derived from Kornai's
(1986) identification of 'soft budget' constraints as a problem for government-owned enterprises in centrally planned economies. Thus, MPF and
Breton's concept of 'competitive governments' overlap, with different
relative emphases on government–market boundaries, the details of how
competition between sub-national governments is analysed, and the incentive structures in place between different levels of government.

Government Revenues and Federalism

Up to now, we have treated the question of financing the provision of
public goods only tangentially. Now we discuss it more explicitly, and

---

[26] In general incentive models, incentives are not perfect from the principal's point of
view because the performance of the agent (here the government) is subject to noise. Hence,
performance is not a perfect indicator of effort. Relative performance can help to reduce this
noise in evaluating effort: see Milgrom and Roberts (1990), Chapter 7.

explore the implications for federal structure of government. The key ideas of information and incentives that have been discussed throughout this section so far will recur in the following.

In the model of a benevolent and omniscient government, government decision makers know the preferences of constituents, in particular their marginal benefits from the provision of any public good, or from an increase in its level. Therefore, it is easy to assign cost shares, in the form of taxes or user charges, to individuals in a manner such that every individual's marginal cost equals her or his marginal benefit. Such an outcome is Pareto optimal.

Now consider the case where benevolence still holds, but the government does not know constituents' preferences for the public good to be provided. We discussed this case earlier, but did not explicitly consider the issue of paying for the good. One possibility is that such public goods are financed by general taxes, which are not explicitly linked to benefits. The benevolent government can choose such taxes to be as efficient as possible,[27] but it will not know how much of the public good to provide, or whether to provide it at all. The non-rivalry characteristic of public goods creates a crucial problem here. For a private good, if people understate their marginal benefits, and as a result the good is under provided, they will consume less of the good than would be best for them: the incentive to understate one's desire is not present.[28] For a non-rival good, given what everyone else says their benefits from the good are, an individual will have an incentive to misrepresent her or his benefit, if there is any link perceived between this expression of benefit and the share of the cost that is paid by the individual, because others' willingness to pay will lead to the good being provided, and then consumed by the 'free-riding' individual. This is because of non-rivalry (others' consumption does not reduce the

[27] The main idea here is as follows. In the absence of problems of monopoly or other departures from 'perfect' competition, taxes that affect individuals' marginal incentives, as do income and sales taxes, create distortions in resource allocation by driving wedges between marginal benefits and marginal costs. If a given amount of revenue has to be raised through taxes, this can be done to minimize such distortions. 'Lump-sum' taxes such as taxes on endowments (unimproved land, native ability) or head taxes avoid these marginal distortions, but may not be feasible for informational reasons, because of equity concerns (as in a pure poll tax, where a rich and a poor person would pay exactly the same tax), because they violate individual endowment constraints (the poor cannot afford to pay), or because of a variety of possible political reasons.

[28] The caveat that should be emphasized is that this is strictly true for competitive markets with a large number of buyers and sellers. In bilateral bargaining, as anyone in India will know, it can be an optimal strategy to understate one's desire for a good to get a better deal.

availability to the 'free rider', and also non-excludability (the other characteristic of a pure public good), since that person cannot be excluded from consuming the available public good.[29]

The implications of this logic are as follows. If the government wants to give constituents an incentive to reveal their true benefits from a public good, it cannot link their payments for the good to their announced benefits. Various incentive schemes can be devised, such that each individual has a positive incentive to report her or his true benefits:[30] each person's payment depends only on others' reported benefits, not on her own report. Alternatively, taxes could be assessed on the basis of fixed characteristics, such as a lump-sum tax per head (a poll tax). In this latter case, however, an individual has an incentive to overstate her benefit from the public good, since she perceives that the marginal cost of the public good to her is zero. In the terminology of Breton (1995), the Wicksellian connection (between revenues/costs and expenditures/benefits at the margin) is broken. This leaves one with the complicated incentive schemes that elicit the truth. In these schemes, overstating one's desire for the public good is also costly, as is understating it.

Of course, a government typically does not ask constituents for reports on potential benefits of a project to provide a public good, and the nature of the payment schemes to elicit truthful demand revelation does not seem to correspond to any actual mechanism, at least in this context.[31] At the same time, there are often voting schemes such as referenda to decide on whether or at what level a public good should be provided. In some cases,[32] even when voters realize that they will be taxed to finance the public good (as must be the case if they are not to over-demand the good), the voting mechanism leads to an optimal choice of the public good level. Thus, it is possible to think of such decisions on public goods—including an appropriate scheme for taxing to cover the costs of the public good—as being made by constituents through voting, in an optimal way, without the government decision maker having to know constituents' preferences, and, indeed, without the government decision maker having to be benevolent. Here, of course, government is just administration, carrying out the

[29] Non-excludability also works against charges in the nature of entry fees, as well as charges for marginal use that would approximate the usual prices for private goods. Note that 'user charges' or other prices are often used by or recommended for governments because the goods they provide are not pure public goods, they provide are not pure public goods, but have some or all of the characteristics of private goods.

[30] For example, see Groves and Ledyard (1977), or Cornes and Sandler (1996), Chapter 7.

[31] On the other hand, mechanisms with similar incentive properties do seem to be used in auctions and similar situations.

[32] For example, see Bowen (1943) and Cornes and Sandler (1996).

wishes of the electorate, without any substantive decisions being delegated to it by constituents.

The optimality result for voting holds only under special circumstances. Furthermore, if government decision makers choose the levels of public goods and of taxes to finance them, as they do in practice for economizing on transaction and decision costs, what matters is not voting directly by constituents on such matters, but voting on the performance of the government decision makers, as has been discussed in the previous subsections. There, we emphasized the provision of the 'correct' levels of public goods, but, clearly, making the costs to constituents 'correct' also matters. The Brennan–Buchanan–Niskanen viewpoint is that voters cannot effectively discipline government decision makers in this manner. One can note some of the problems here. If there is just a single public good to be decided on, voters can observe what they get and how much they pay, and a vote on the performance of the government decision maker is very much like a vote on the public good and its financing. Problems of information (the technology of provision, for example) may exist in both cases, but they should be comparable in the two elections. There is a difference in timing, in the sense that the vote on the office-bearer comes after performance, but the rational office-bearer will anticipate the election and incorporate this in making decisions on the public good (putting aside issues of 'taking the money and running'), and this is ironed out if such situations are repeated. However, an office-bearer typically makes many such decisions, and the vote on her performance is therefore a less-refined incentive scheme than separate votes on individual cases of public good provision. Again, note that the former scheme is preferred because it economizes on resources involved in making decisions. Yet, there is a cost involved because of the blunting of incentives. Once again, federal or other hierarchical structures allow some unbundling of voting; they potentially create competition among jurisdictions that can improve outcomes, and they provide benchmarks for judging performance of government decision makers. All the previously discussed analysis carries over with the recognition that individuals will look at their net benefits (benefits minus costs) in judging performance.

Does this mean that one does not need to consider issues of government revenues separately from those of expenditures on public goods? Even in a unitary system, this might not be the case. The key idea here is that spending and taxing decisions are delegated to government office-bearers to economize on decision-making costs. This is particularly pertinent for expenditure decisions, where expertise may be required. Decisions on raising revenue may also require expertise, in terms of deciding on the mix of user charges and taxes, and on the kinds of taxes and rates. One can think of options on such policies being prepared by experts, and then put to a vote, but this also may be costly in terms of time and decision-making effort. However, there still may be differences in the degree of delegation that constituents find optimal for revenue decisions vis-à-vis expenditure decisions. For example, they may allow complete freedom to their representatives in deciding the pattern of spending on public goods (subject to the performance review of periodic elections), but place limits on tax rates, or require that tax increases be approved in specific votes. Thus, even for a single government, one may wish to examine incentive issues for revenues separately from those for expenditures.

In a federal system, the relation between revenues and expenditures becomes considerably complicated. There are several reasons. First, the technologies of provision of services and of collection of revenues may be very different. For example, there may not be economies of scale in providing many public goods, which makes them candidates for sub-national provision, but revenue collection may benefit greatly from a centralized system of collection: there may be economies in having a national database, a national tax collection agency, etc. One can argue that such a national agency could also act as a collection agency for sub-national governments, where certain taxes and their rates are decided by the sub-national governments. For example, a state might decide its own income tax or sales tax rates, but piggyback on the collection by the Centre, which collects its own income tax or sales taxes (including excise duties). However, there might be incentive issues within the tax collection agency: where should collection and auditing efforts be focused, on central taxes or those of the states? The problem can be understood as one of common agency, where the different governments require the services of the same agent: this might suggest bidding mechanisms to determine the allocation of the agency's resources. In any case, in such a scenario, each state government has clearly assigned tax revenues, with control over rates. The agency problem in collection would be faced even with its own dedicated tax collection organization.

The second issue on the revenue side in federal structures is somewhat more serious, and brings one to some core issues in federalism. The consequences of allocational efficiency of different tax assignments may be quite significant, because the incentive effects are quite different. Essentially, mobility across jurisdictions within a federation is greater than mobility across nations. A tax base that is mobile may shrink dramatically in response to a tax. Therefore, it is harder for sub-national jurisdictions to raise revenue from taxes than it is for the Centre. One can think of the problem as being one of tax 'capacity': this being lower for the sub-national jurisdictions. If this factor implies that more taxes should be collected by the Centre, there will be a tendency for there to be a mismatch between revenues and expenditures for sub-national jurisdictions, to the extent that sub-national governments are relatively better able to respond to diversity of preferences, for the reasons discussed in the previous subsections.

It is still possible that this problem can be avoided to some extent by coordination of taxes among sub-national jurisdictions. For example, different states might agree to charge the same sales tax rate or income tax rate. Unlike national taxes, these would only be on state-level tax bases, but the incentive for the activities that are taxed to move to other, less-taxed locations would be removed. There are clearly enforcement problems in such agreements, since each state might wish to cheat, either directly reneging, or using non-transparent subsidies to compensate for the taxes, say to attract capital to their own jurisdictions. One response to this might be central imposition of some degree of coordination, for example, minimum or maximum tax rates. This would be an example of the monitoring-type role of the Centre in a federation, emphasized by Breton (1995). On the other hand, if the Centre removes competition entirely, the idea of federalism itself is negated, at least in the dimension of revenue decisions. In general, there is no simple answer to these issues of coordination and competition. What is clear for the Indian case is the relative absence of coordination, and the resulting 'disharmony' in sub-national taxation policies, with severe resource allocation distortions resulting. These points are developed in Chapters 4 and 5, along with the basic issue of 'assignment' of revenue sources and expenditure responsibilities to the different levels of government.

If tax coordination among the constituent governments of a federal system is difficult, the argument in favour of raising revenue centrally remains, and the question of the mismatch between revenues and expenditures, the 'vertical imbalance' present to some extent in all federal systems, must be tackled. One possibility is that taxes are assigned to the Centre, to avoid the adverse incentives and disharmony associated with sub-national taxes, but the proceeds are shared with sub-national jurisdictions. This is also a common feature in federal systems, and an important feature of the Indian case. Depending on the precise institutional arrangements, the ownership of the tax revenue in such cases is more or less shared, according to law or precedent. Again, there may be incentive problems because the Centre is collecting taxes on behalf of the states. Such a tax-sharing arrangement is different from the agency problem discussed earlier, to the extent that the states or other sub-national jurisdictions may not have any freedom to alter tax rates. To illustrate this point, consider three different income tax schemes. In the first, there is a national income tax, the rates decided by the Centre, but shared with the states. In the second, only the states impose income taxes in their own jurisdictions, and decide their own rates, but the tax is collected by a central agency. In the third, both the Centre and the states impose income taxes, each deciding their own rates, but these are all collected by the same central agency. The first of these scenarios corresponds to tax sharing in the Indian case.

In tax sharing, one earmarks certain revenue sources of the Centre for sharing with sub-national governments. However, the Central government may also make transfers from its general funds (from all revenue sources, including borrowing) to sub-national jurisdictions. These may be in the form of grants or loans, with or without conditions attached. There is presumably greater discretion in these transfers than in tax-sharing transfers decided by law or by precedent. The basic motivation for a benevolent Centre is the vertical imbalance created by the likely mismatch between revenues and expenditures for lower-level governments, since it wishes to ensure that public goods are well provided by the subordinate governments. Another possible motivation for a benevolent Centre is the correction of spillovers, as discussed in a previous subsection, to the extent that jurisdictional boundaries are not and cannot be drawn to avoid all such spillovers. If the national government responds instead to the incentives provided by its national constituency, it may make transfers for two reasons. It may only want national public goods to be provided, if that is the basis on which it is going to be judged. Or it may make transfers because it will receive political support in return, in a situation where sub-national coalitions embodied in regional governments can affect the electoral outcome at the Centre.

Two additional complications need to be noted. We have treated sub-national jurisdictions as a bloc so far. But the vertical imbalance may be quite different across sub-national jurisdictions. Hence, transfers to different sub-national jurisdictions may be different. This is compounded by equity concerns at the national level, which may exist due to the concerns of a benevolent government decision maker, or because equity is a national public good, or because the Centre in its role as monitor of sub-national competition wishes to level the playing field (Breton, 1995). This may be a rationale for larger transfers to poorer jurisdictions, not just to jurisdictions with a greater fiscal imbalance. Note that this becomes a difficult issue because of our second complication that the imbalance is itself endogenous, since the desired expenditures and revenues of the sub-national governments on local public goods depend on the transfers made. This also raises important issues of incentives, with respect to tax effort and expenditure decisions (the Wicksellian connection again), and with respect to efforts by sub-national governments to directly influence transfers (rent seeking again). It also raises issues of information, since designing transfers to avoid perverse incentives may put a strain on the information gathering and processing capacity at the Centre, something in which federal structures are meant to help. We shall conclude here by noting the general theoretical complexities, and return to these issues in Chapters 6 and 7 in the Indian context.

3

A Historical Review of Indian Federalism

INTRODUCTION

In this chapter, we provide a synoptic history of developments in the structures of Indian federalism. Our main purpose in this volume is neither historical nor institutional analysis in the traditional sense, but to provide some background for readers who are unfamiliar with Indian history and institutions. This chapter serves such readers, and may be skipped or glossed over by those who are familiar with the Indian background. We will not attempt to be comprehensive in our treatment, since that would require a book in itself, but hope to provide enough detail to place subsequent descriptions and analysis of the various facets of Indian federalism in context.

The structure of the chapter is as follows. We begin with a rather sweeping overview of developments in the British period, before moving on to a description of the issues concerning federalism as they arose during the period when our Constitution was being drafted, and the resolution of those debates in the Constitution. Next, we summarize the developments in Centre–state relations after the adoption of the Constitution in 1950, particularly focusing on fiscal issues. Finally, we review some of the history of local government in post-independence India, as well as broader developments in governance.

THE BRITISH PERIOD

The British gradually took over a subcontinent that had become politically fragmented and strife-ridden. The imperceptible extension crystallized with the Government of India Act, 1858, by the imposition of direct sovereignty under the British Crown, was reflected in a rather ad hoc mixture of centralized and decentralized administrative structures. Centralization at one extreme was seen in the power of the Secretary of State for India, assisted by a council of fifteen members. The Secretary of State governed through the viceroy, assisted by an executive council. The viceroy, assisted by a small number of district-level British administrators, exercised all the powers. In this centralized system of administration, there was no separation of legislative, executive, and judicial functions. Decentralization at the other extreme was exemplified by the relationship of Indian princely states to the British administration, where their rulers retained discretion with respect to internal matters, while being subject to British control.

As Crown rule was consolidated in the second half of the nineteenth century, the British attempted decentralization based on administrative considerations. In 1874, for example, Assam was separated from the Bengal presidency, with administrative convenience in mind. Administrative decentralization, as we have clarified in our theoretical discussion in Chapter 2, is not the same as federalism. However, political considerations began to affect decisions on government structures with the formation of the Indian National Congress in 1885,[1] formed expressly to press for a greater say for Indians in the governance of India.

The Congress itself developed a somewhat federal structure, being organized on the basis of regional circles, and increasingly on linguistic lines.[2] These linguistic bases for organization foreshadowed post-independence federal structures, reflecting both natural boundaries of governance and sub-national identities. For example, Biharis demanded to be separated from Bengal in 1894, and there was growing nationalism in Bengal. The British responded in 1905 with an east-west partition of Bengal that had to be quickly reversed in the face of massive popular protest. The Congress, on the other hand, created a separate Bihar circle in 1908.

While a national political movement arose and grew, the British continued to develop their fiscal structures, motivated by a continuing interplay of administrative and political considerations. In 1858, the provincial governments depended completely on annual central allocations, since the Centre had authority over all revenue receipts and expenditures. Lord

---

[1] Municipal governments were introduced in the 1860s. The introduction of electoral politics to India, however, may be dated to Lord Ripon's 1886 resolution on local-self government. See Gould (1990).

[2] See Banerjee (1992) for a more detailed discussion of these and other developments in sub-nationalism.

Mayo, in 1870, described his principles for financial decentralization, stating the need to:[3]

... place administration of portions, both of our revenue and expenditure, in the hands of the local Governments ... it will enable the rulers of the country gradually to institute, in various parts of the empire, something in the shape of local self-government, and will eventually tend to associate more and more natives of this country in the conduct of public affairs.

The implementation of Mayo's intent was initially along modest lines. Some expenditure categories (e.g. police, health, education) were assigned to the provincial governments, which received annual lump-sum grants, and had to have separate budgets. In 1877, further expenditure assignments were devolved to the provinces, along with some revenue authority. The year 1881 saw a further development of these arrangements with regard to assignment and revenue sharing.

With the introduction of Morley–Minto Reforms by enacting the Indian Councils Act, 1909, a representative element was introduced for the first time by including elected non-official members. At the same time, the seeds of 'divide and rule' policy were sown by providing a separate representation to the Muslim community. The Government of India Act, 1912 created a new province of Bihar and Orissa and made Assam a new commissioner's province.

In the period until World War I, therefore, there was a gradual, limited decentralization of fiscal matters down to the provincial level. In parallel, however, there was not only the rapid development of a national movement and national identity, especially among the elite, but also of subnational (regional, linguistic, religious) identities. Both these developments were reflected in the operation of the Indian National Congress.[4] The British dealt with this simultaneous rise of sub-nationalism and nationalism in a series of political and administrative responses after the war, that articulated federal ideas to varying degrees.

The period between the wars accelerated the process of British attempts to solve the practical problems of governing India, beginning with the 1918 Montagu–Chelmsford Report on constitutional reforms, which stated:[5]

[O]ur conception of the eventual future of India is a sisterhood of states, self-

---

[3] The quote is taken from Gurumurthi (1995), p. 2. Our brief discussion here draws on his historical summary.

[4] Again, see Banerjee (1992), or his main source on the history of the Congress, Sitaramayya (1969).

[5] The following quote from the report is taken from Ramasubramaniam (1992).

governing in all matters of purely local or provincial interest. Over this congeries of States would preside the Central Government.

The Government of India Act of 1919 based on this report, therefore, devolved some authority to the provinces, and nominally restricted the powers of the Central government over matters assigned to the provinces. While the Indian government remained essentially unitary under the new system, there was relaxation of central control over provinces to some extent by separating the subjects of administration and sources of revenue into Central and provincial jurisdictions. Provinces received unambiguous control over sources of revenue such as land, irrigation, and judicial stamps. In fact, the initial assignment of revenue authority proposed in the Act of 1919 would have required provincial contributions to the Central government. This scheme was quickly modified, including the introduction of the sharing of income taxes into Indian fiscal federalism. The provincial subjects were divided into 'transferred' and 'reserved' categories; the governor administered the former with responsibility to the legislature. In administering reserved subjects, the governor had no responsibility to legislature.

The Indian Statutory Commission of 1928, headed by Lord Simon, marked the next step in British attempts to pave the way for a constitution that would check the growth of nationalism. The proposed scheme for implementation was based on devolution of powers to provincial administrations, and was favoured by the Muslim leadership. The British approach might also have appealed to the princely states, which favoured as loose a federation as possible, but the princes were wary of federal structures that could lead to their being swallowed by an independent India. The Congress, on the other hand, had already developed a model constitution that was considerably more tilted towards the Centre.

The approach of the Simon Commission is clearly illustrated by this statement from its 1929 report:[6]

The ultimate Constitution of India must be federal, for it is only in a federal constitution that units differing so widely in constitution as the provinces and the States can be brought together while retaining internal autonomy.

The reference to the states in this quote is to the princely states, and it was their autonomy that was to be retained.

The Simon Commission report also included a review of India's financial arrangements. Sharing of income tax between the Centre and the provinces was an important part of the new fiscal proposals. Various innovations

---

[6] Again, our immediate source for quote is Ramasubramaniam (1992).

in taxation were also proposed. Subsequently, several committees met to consider the new bases for revenue sharing, particularly the formulas for distributing income tax proceeds between the Centre and the various provinces. While these technical discussions continued, however, they were overshadowed by more pressing political developments.

The beginning of the 1930s was marked by three Round Table Conferences, in which Indian leaders also participated, on the future status of India's governance. These conferences, along with the British government's own deliberations, ultimately led to the Government of India Act, 1935. To quote Banerjee (1992):

The framers of the 1935 Act accepted the logic of the Princely States and denied that of the British Indian delegates and especially of the Congress. By suggesting diarchy at the Centre, the Act denied both Dominion Status and, of course, full independence.

The British clearly wished to have federal structures that would build alliances and support their rule. However, the 1937 elections, where the Muslim League did not fare as well as it expected, pushed the League away from the idea of a single Indian federation. The Congress, in speeches and resolutions in 1937 and 1938, unequivocally rejected the Act of 1935.

While the Act of 1935 provided for the distribution of legislative jurisdictions with the three-fold division of powers into federal, provincial, and concurrent Lists, legislatures, however, did not have the features of a sovereign legislature as their powers were subject to several limitations. The Act also enabled the establishment of a federal court to adjudicate the disputes between units of the federation and was also the appellate court to decide on constitutional questions. On the fiscal front, the Act provided an assignment of tax authorities and a scheme of revenue sharing that, in many respects, laid the foundations of fiscal federalism in independent India. However, the Government of India Act of 1935 failed to satisfy the aspirations of the people. In the meantime, various developments within and outside India pushed the issue of decentralization to the background. The Second World War, in particular, added to the problems of implementing the federation envisaged in the Act of 1935. The war interrupted negotiations over the terms of accession of the princely states. The Congress and the Muslim League pursued their own visions for independence with increased vigour. From 1944 to 1946, some efforts were made to agree to a loose, asymmetrical federation including the Muslim-majority provinces, but all these failed. Ultimately, of course, the Congress implemented its more centralized vision after partition, and the princes' fears were realized.

THE INDIAN CONSTITUTION

The Second World War and the intensification of the Indian freedom movement overtook the implementation of the federal provisions of the Government of India Act, 1935. Yet, the framers of the Indian Constitution, beginning in the Constituent Assembly in 1946, relied heavily on the Act of 1935 for the new constitutional framework. The Act of 1935, the Cabinet Mission Plan of May 1946, and the December 1946 resolution of the Constituent Assembly all were tilted in the direction of a federal system with the provinces or states retaining substantial and residuary powers.

The effect of the planned partition of the country, however, removed any need for the Congress to attempt compromise with the Muslim League, and strengthened the Congress vision of a strong Centre. The actual circumstances of partition only heightened this vision. The Act of 1935 continued to provide a great portion of the detailed provisions of the new Constitution of India, but its more federal structure was rejected, consistent with the Congress's original response to the Act.

Two key individuals supported the more centralized vision for India: Jawaharlal Nehru and B.R. Ambedkar. Nehru's socialist vision was obviously more in line with a unitary governmental system. Even though he had earlier called a unitary state 'a retrograde step both politically and administratively',[7] he presided over the Union Powers Committee of the Constituent Assembly, which stated, in its final report:

Momentous changes have since occurred. Some parts of the country are seceding to form a separate state, and the plan put forward in the statement of the 16th May on the basis of which the Committee was working is, in many essentials, no longer operative. In particular, we are not bound by the limitations in the scope of Union powers .... Now that partition is a settled fact we are unanimously of the view that it would be injurious to the interests of the country to provide for a weak central authority which could be incapable of ensuring peace, of co-ordinating vital matters of common concern and of speaking effectively for the whole country in the international sphere.

If Nehru accepted a more unitary form of government through a mix of circumstances and ideology, perhaps reinforced by his own autocratic temperament, Ambedkar, the chairman of the drafting committee for the Constitution, was always absolutely clear in his preferences. In 1939, he had stated, in a public lecture, 'I confess I have a partiality for a unitary

---

[7] This quote is given in Bhattacharya (1992), p. 96. The quote which follows from Nehru's committee is from the same source.

form of government. I think India needs it.'[8] Later, in the Constituent Assembly debates, he was even more emphatic, 'I like a strong united Centre, much stronger than the Centre we had created under the Government of India Act of 1935.' Ambedkar's conception of federalism was shaped to fit his preferences: a division of powers between Centre and states, but with residuary powers at the Centre, and central ability to impinge severely on the states in special circumstances.

As we have noted earlier, the Congress was strongly in opposition to the decentralizing features of the Act of 1935. Nehru's and Ambedkar's views were more or less shared by the whole party. Perhaps only Mahatma Gandhi provided an articulate alternative position, and his was much more radical than simply greater authority for the states of independent India. Gandhi instead envisaged a nation of village republics. We return to this vision in the 'Federalism and the Common Market' section, in considering the history of local government in India. Here, we may note that Gandhi's ideas were much too far from the reality of post-partition India, and the mood of the Constitution's shapers, to have any substantial or immediate impact on that document.

We can see that the situation facing India at the time of the constitutional debates, as well as the perspectives of the main architects of the Constitution, were quite different from those that faced, say, the United States of America in 1787. Thus, Nehru and Ambedkar were much greater centralizers than, say James Madison, who had argued so eloquently for a strong federation for the United States. There is another, perhaps more striking contrast. Madison was one of those who recognized the problems of incentives in governance. In the Federalist Papers, he argued for checks and balances in a forceful manner absent from the deliberations of the framers of India's Constitution. Men like Nehru and Ambedkar were much more comfortable with the idea of government as benevolent guardian (even *ma-baap sarkaar*), than Madison, who emphasized that men are not angels. This approach also coloured the early, and, to some extent, continuing perception of federalism in India as a cooperative arrangement. Thus, issues of ensuring proper incentives for competing sub-national governments were not really at the centre of any debates. Even though fiscal prudence ('hard budget constraint') might be valued, such concerns were always subsumed to the wisdom of the benevolent guardians at the Centre, who were given escape clauses in almost every case. The example of the common market is described in detail later.

In sum, the Indian Constitution incorporated centralizing features that

---

[8] Again, Ambedkar's quotes are from Bhattacharya (1992), pp. 88–9.

were not present in earlier British legislation, though British practice was more centralized than their ideal for India. In Chapters 4 and 5, we will examine some of the consequences of the politically centralizing features of India's Constitution. The cumulative impact of these features for federal structures is summarized by Bhattacharya (1992):

As one observes the insertion of clear provisions for central dominance such as altering and annihilation of states, central appropriation of the states' legislative field, virtual unitarianization of the nation during the proclamation of emergencies, supersession of state governments on grounds of constitutional breakdown and disobedience of central executive directives, putting impediments to state legislation through a presidential referral system, the federal idea seems, at least formally speaking, untenable.

Despite such strictures, the Constitution did allow for states with elected governments and fiscal authority. And this basic fact has permitted Indian federalism to exist and develop.

While the political structures envisaged in the Act of 1935 were largely superseded in drawing up the Constitution, much of the details of government in the Constitution were taken from the earlier legislation. This characterization applies to the details of assignments of expenditure and revenue authorities, as well as of revenue sharing and grants. The tension that had existed in the British period with respect to assignments and revenue sharing was, to some extent, reflected in the provisions of the Constitution. Chanda (1965, Chapters 2 and 3) has provided an excellent summary of the federal features of India's Constitution. He highlights the power of the Centre to reshape the constituent states and their boundaries. He also discusses the authoritarian features of the Constitution, including the scope of emergency powers available to the Centre, and its ability to suspend a broad range of individual rights in such circumstances. The history and origins of these provisions in British-era legislation, which we have already summarized, have also been analysed by him.

Perhaps the most fundamental federal provision of the Constitution is Article 246, which provides for a three-fold distribution of power, detailed in separate lists in the seventh schedule. These enumerate the specific exclusive powers of the Centre and the states, and those powers that are concurrently held. The three lists are long and close to exhaustive, though residuary powers are explicitly assigned to the Centre. The Constitution is also explicit in exempting the Centre and its property from taxation by the state governments (Article 285). A reciprocal, more limited exemption, of the states from central taxation, is contained in Article 289.

Another centralizing provision noted by Chanda is Article 249, which empowers the Rajya Sabha to transfer legislative jurisdiction from the states to the Centre. While the conditions for doing so are necessity or expediency in the national interest, the transfer requires only a two-thirds majority of members present and voting. In any case, Article 250 allows the central legislature to make laws with respect to matters in the state list. Furthermore, Article 353 (b) authorizes Parliament to make laws on matters not explicitly in the Union list. Finally, Article 354 empowers the president to order the suspension of the provisions of Articles 268 to 279 relating to transfers of revenues from the Centre to the states during a proclaimed emergency. What is most interesting about all these centralizing features (and some additional ones discussed by Chanda) is that they have not been availed of anywhere near to the extent that they might have been in fifty years of the Constitution's existence. We discuss this phenomenon in the next section.

CENTRE–STATE RELATIONS

Perhaps one reason why the most egregious examples of bias in the relative authorities of the Centre and the states have not been exercised is that other methods have sufficed. The Centre has been less concerned about explicit transfer of powers from the states to itself, or temporary suspension of state powers under the provisions noted, because it has been able to exercise political control more directly. During the Nehru era, which covered approximately the first decade and a half of the new Constitution, the prime minister's personal authority and prestige were combined with almost complete legislative control of the Centre and the states. In such circumstances, issues of Centre–state relations were often played out within the ranks of the Congress party.

One of the most striking examples of the substitution of personal relations and party hierarchy for constitutionally mediated federal relations was the 'Kamaraj plan' of the early 1960s. Mr K. Kamaraj, chief minister of Tamil Nadu (then Madras) and a prominent leader of the Congress Party, proposed that all central and state ministers of the party should resign, so that some of the party's leaders could be released for organizational work to revitalize the party. This was accepted by the party high command, with the exception that Prime Minister Nehru's offer to resign was not accepted. Instead, Nehru was given full discretion by the party to decide on the reconstitution of state as well as central ministries. All others 'resigned' en masse. It is commonly accepted that the purpose of this manoeuvring was to solidify the party's political control at all levels, and the control of certain party members, rather than to implement any serious party organizational work. The point is, there was no need for the ruling party at the Centre to resort to any constitutional or other legal avenues made possible by the Constitution's provisions for expansive central authority.

In the above case, the ruling party at the Centre and the states was the same, and the political stature of the prime minister dwarfed that of any other national or regional leader. Both these conditions changed soon after Nehru's death. Lal Bahadur Shastri succeeded Nehru, and was viewed at the time as a relatively weak leader, with substantial power being wielded by regional leaders of the Congress Party such as Kamaraj. This development did not alter the incentive of party leaders to rely on intra-party bargaining, but it certainly reduced the capacity to implement a procedure such as that used by Nehru. When Indira Gandhi succeeded Shastri, she challenged the collective control of regional party leaders at a time when several state legislatures came under the control of parties other than the Congress. This irrevocably moved Centre–state political relations out of the domain of intra-party bargaining, and into the constitutional arena.

The one provision of the Constitution that became the most used (and abused) was Article 356. This allows the governor of a state to advise the president that the government of the state was unable to carry on 'in accordance with the provisions of this Constitution', and allows the president to assume 'to himself all or any of the functions of the Government of the state'. In practice, president's rule means rule by the prime minister and the ruling party at the Centre, and has provided a more direct and blunt means to exercise central political control, bypassing the will of the people expressed electorally at the state level, than that used by Nehru in the 'Kamaraj plan'.[9] Article 356 has proved to be so elastic and powerful that other centralizing provisions of the Constitution have tended to be overshadowed. We return to a further analysis of Article 356 in Chapter 4.

While general central political control in the Nehruvian era was expressed through the internal workings of the Congress Party, specific issues of Centre–state relations did emerge in more formal arenas. Issues of taxation and property rights related to particular provisions of the Constitution did involve explicit disputes between the Centre and the states that had to be adjudicated by the Supreme Court. We briefly discuss two important examples.

---

[9] Nehru did use president's rule against a communist-led state government in Kerala, in 1959, reportedly at the behest of Indira Gandhi.

One dispute involved clause (1) of Article 289, which exempts the property and income of the states from central taxation. In 1951, the Centre attempted to bring business and trading operations of the states under the purview of acts governing customs duties and excise taxes. The states challenged this as an unconstitutional attempt to tax them. From an economist's perspective, the arguments and court decision involved considerable legal hair-splitting, but the net result was a substantial victory for the Centre, reducing 'the immunity of states from Union taxation to minuscule proportions' (Chanda, 1965, p. 89).

A second dispute involved Article 294, which vested control of British Crown property in the pre-independence province of Bengal in the post-independence state of West Bengal. In 1957, the Centre enacted legislation claimed to be derived from an entry in the Union list, empowering Parliament to provide by law for 'the regulation of mines and mineral development to the extent to which such regulation and development under the control of the Union is held to be expedient in the public interest'. The Act of 1957 gave the Centre the power to prospect for coal in lands vested in the state of West Bengal. The state government took its case to the Supreme Court, which undertook an extensive and detailed review of the whole issue of federal relations, sub-national sovereignty, and divisions of powers, including the evolution of the Constitution.[10] Once again, the final judgement came down heavily in favour of the Centre's position and power. While both cases involved some dissent, ultimately the basic centralizing bias of the Constitution can be viewed as having tilted the interpretation of the court against the states in both cases.

We round out our discussion of post-independence Centre–state relations with an overview of the evolution of financial relations. More details on recent and current developments will be found later in the book. At the time of independence, revenue sharing between the Centre and the states was governed by the Act of 1935. In 1947, some adjustments were made in the allocation percentages across provinces as a result of partition. When drafting the Constitution, the Constituent Assembly appointed an expert committee to advise on the financial provisions of the new document. This committee made some specific recommendations on what revenue pools should be shared between Centre and states, as well as percentages for some of these categories. Most importantly, the expert committee recommended the creation of an independent Finance Commission to deal periodically with Centre–state revenue sharing. The Constitution incorporated this latter recommendation, but left it to the

[10] See Chanda, for a detailed discussion of the court's arguments.

new Finance Commission to recommend specific sharing percentages. Since the new commission could not be constituted and could not make its recommendation within a short enough time period after the Constitution was ratified, C.D. Deshmukh, a prominent civil servant and ex-governor of RBI, was asked to make the first revenue-sharing determination. He did this through some further adjustment of the 1947 revenue-sharing scheme, and his award covered two financial years, 1950–51 and 1951–52.

Meanwhile, the problem of integrating the princely states into the financial as well as administrative and political systems of independent India was also being tackled. Another committee, under the chairmanship of V.T. Krishnamachari, was appointed in 1948 to consider financial adjustments that would need to accompany the Centre's assumption of governance responsibilities of the princely states, on both revenue and expenditure sides. The outcome was a recommendation for so-called 'revenue-gap' grants, which were to be fixed for five years, and to be phased out gradually thereafter. A few princely states were actually made better off by the reassignment of responsibilities, and were asked to make some limited contributions to the Centre, which were also to be phased out.

The Constitution assigned various taxing powers to the Centre and the states, some rules for tax revenue sharing, and institutional mechanisms for determining the exact details of revenue sharing. The chief constitutional provision with respect to the last of these was the Finance Commission. Since the assignments of expenditure responsibilities and tax authorities were perceived to imply shortfalls in state revenue without Centre–state transfers, the mechanism for transfers received some attention in drafting the document. The prior experience of other federal countries also shaped the constitutional provisions, which were meant to avoid arbitrariness in distributions made by the Centre to the states.

Some details of the Finance Commission were left to legislation, and the relevant law was passed in 1951, allowing the first commission to be assembled by 1952—in fact, this was done in November 1951. According to this legislation, members of the Finance Commission must have some relevant expertise or experience. The commission has semi-judicial authority and can determine its own procedures of business. Early commissions determined their own scope, within the sometimes ambiguous language of the Constitution. For example, the First Commission held that it had the implicit authority to make recommendations on Centre–state sharing of excise duties, which was explicitly at the discretion of Parliament. It also decided it could make special-purpose as well as unconditional grants; it emphasized 'budgetary need' as a primary principle for grants, identified tax effort relative to tax potential as an important criterion for aid, and considered fiscal economy and efficiency as an important principle. It also laid down low levels of social services, special obligations, and broad purposes of national importance as further principles for determining transfers.

Individually, each one of these principles seems unobjectionable. However, there is clear potential for conflict among them, and, as we shall see in later chapters, the real problems have arisen in translating these disparate principles into a simple, practical, efficient, and effective transfer system. One of the problems in achieving this goal has been that an important recommendation of the First Finance Commission was virtually ignored. This was for the immediate creation of a small permanent organization as a part of the president's secretariat to continuously study the finances of the states, to serve successive commissions. A small cell of this nature was set up, but it was soon transferred to the finance ministry, with very limited functions or resources. It has been speculated that this was a deliberate attempt to restrict the Finance Commission's scope relative to the Planning Commission. We shall discuss this rivalry later in this section as well as in later chapters.

The terms of reference of the Second Finance Commission, appointed in 1956, somewhat enlarged its scope with respect to additional aspects of tax sharing, as well as of grants-in-aid and loans. In particular, the commission had to deal with some thorny issues relating to loans made to those displaced by partition. Most importantly, the Second Commission was to take account of the Second Five-Year Plan in formulating recommendations on grants, but the political realities, whereby the Planning Commission already occupied a favoured position, robbed this possible extension of scope of any force. Problems of discrepancies and conflict between the two commissions' workings were already arising. Overall, therefore, the Second Commission was left to conclude its report by simply suggesting a review of the constitutional provisions dealing with Centre–state financial relations.

A final, smaller difficulty faced by the Second Finance Commission was the timing of its appointment, which required it to hurriedly make an interim report to cover 1957–58. This led to the more timely appointment of the Third Commission, in 1960. The Third Finance Commission was again mandated to consider the requirements of the corresponding five-year plan, and was asked to consider states' tax effort in deciding on grants and on the sharing of some duties and taxes between the Centre and states. This commission's observations on grants were interesting, in that they attempted to move away from the Second Commission, and closer to the

First, in trying to rationalize the assessment of fiscal needs on which grants should be based. However, the Third Commission was not really able to make any practical headway in this matter, and the incentive problems with respect to 'gap-filling' grants have persisted, as we discuss in more detail in later chapters. Neither was the Third Commission able to do more than try to take account of Planning Commission transfers more fully, making some strong recommendations that were, however, rejected by the government. This latter episode marked a clear demarcation of the political (as opposed to constitutional) limits of the Finance Commission's authority, and led to a narrowing of its effective scope.

The government was also slow to act on the Second and Third Commissions' recommendations for an independent commission to look at central–state relations, including an integrated examination of plan and non-plan expenditures and non-financial as well as financial relations. The Third Commission was already concerned about problems of vertical fiscal imbalance, and associated incentive problems for fiscal discipline on the part of state governments. The Administrative Reforms Commission (ARC) in 1969 dealt with some aspects of intergovernmental relations, but the problems of defining the scope and dealing with the incentive structure continued. In response to these problems highlighted by the ARC, the Sarkaria Commission was set up, and submitted its report in 1987. Meanwhile, however, India had gone through many political developments and upheavals that pushed consideration of such institutional reforms well into the future. Many of these issues are still being discussed and grappled with after the turn of the century, when the accumulation of problems has only worsened them.

In particular, the operation of the Planning Commission has continued to raise difficult issues for Centre–state relations. While there was no specific constitutional provision for a planning apparatus, the tenor of the Directive Principles and the ideology of Nehru and many associates were enough to lead to the formation of the Planning Commission through a resolution of the Cabinet. The prime minister has always chaired the Planning Commission, but even then, it has not always succeeded well in coordinating with or among the various ministries. In fact, the finance minister at the time the commission was first formed resigned to protest the unsound encroachment on his ministry's authority implied by the commission. Ministers (including the finance minister) were thereafter appointed to the commission, which has sometimes functioned as an alternative Cabinet. The Planning Commission has, over the decades, expanded in size and control over government resources, with a minister of state for planning, its own building, and hundreds of permanent staff.

Aside from just complicating the work of the finance commissions, the Planning Commission has come into conflict with the individual functional ministries. It has tried to come up with a rational basis for making transfers to the states, but it is not clear whether the Planning Commission has been able to do so. For example, it has not been able to effectively tackle distinctions between current and capital expenditures, and the alternative dichotomy between plan and non-plan expenditures has only muddied the states' budgeting and financial planning waters. In general, India's five-year plans have not been very effective in directing capital to socially efficient uses. Finally, the Planning Commission has not been able to serve as an effective monitor of funds that it has disbursed. While the commission may have achieved some coordination in the functions, it is hard to escape the conclusion that it has served mainly as a convenient avenue for political and financial control of the states by the Centre, especially as internal party mechanisms for this purpose faltered since the 1960s. In many respects, the Planning Commission has illustrated some of the worst problems of the centralizing escape clauses included in an already centralized constitution. It also has represented an important departure from the perspectives of competitive federalism or of MPF. The Planning Commission came about from Nehru's predilection for government holding the commanding heights of the economy, and its continued existence has illustrated the political economy of leviathan government, as articulated by Buchanan (see Chapter 2).

While there are serious economic issues arising from the emergence of Planning Commission as a parallel agency giving Central grants to states, the constitutional validity of plan transfers itself is in serious doubt and needs to be resolved. The Planning Commission makes grants under Article 282, which states, 'The Union or a State may make any grants for any public purpose, notwithstanding that the purpose is not one with respect to which Parliament or the legislature of the State, as the case may be, may make laws'. This has been considered as a miscellaneous provision and plan grants are being given under this. A careful perusal of the article, however, does not permit such a liberal interpretation as was opined by some eminent jurists who gave their written opinion to the Ninth Finance Commission. K. K. Venugopal, who made the detailed analysis was clearly of the view that the positive interpretation of Article 275 shows that all grants, including the plan grants come within the scope of Article 275 (1) itself. Therefore, giving plan grants under Article 282 is unconstitutional (NIPFP, 1993, p. 212). This view is reinforced when we examine Article 282. According to Venugopal, the Administrative Reforms Commission and others have considered Article 282 as a miscellaneous provision mainly because they have interpreted the Article without reading its non-obstante clause. The non-obstante clause is basically meant to lift the bar on the Union or the states from making a grant to subjects on which they do not have legislative competence. Thus, if necessary, the Union government could make grants to the institutions within the ambit of the states and vice versa (NIPFP, 1993, p. 213).

FEDERALISM AND THE COMMON MARKET

In Chapter 2, we briefly discussed the concept of market preserving federalism, which emphasizes the positive role of a common internal market. Interestingly, the framers of the Constitution, although aware of the need to ensure a common market in the federation, were not averse to the idea of placing restrictions if the situation so demanded. Article 301 of the Constitution states, 'Subject to the other provisions of this part, trade, commerce and intercourse throughout the territory of India shall be free'. At the same time, Article 302 empowers Parliament to impose restrictions on this in 'public interest'. This is not surprising because both the general scarcity conditions, and the centralized planning introduced at the time, required restrictions to be placed on the movement of goods as well as allocation of capital to different regions. Unfortunately, several fiscal and regulatory impediments to internal trade have continued even as the objective conditions have changed over time.

An important fiscal impediment to free interstate trade is the levy of interstate sales tax. The tax is levied by the exporting state on interstate sale of goods. Notably, the founding fathers of the Constitution intended that the sales tax system in India should be destination based. According to Article 286 of the Constitution, 'No law of a state shall impose, or authorize the imposition of the tax on the sale or purchase of goods where such sale or purchase takes place (a) outside the state, or (b) in the course of import of goods into, or export of goods out of, the territory of India'. However, based on the recommendations of the Taxation Enquiry Commission (India, 1953), the sixth amendment added clauses (2) and (3) to enable the Central government to levy taxes on interstate transaction. The clauses read:

(2) Parliament may, by law formulate principles for determining when a sale or purchase of goods takes place in any of the ways mentioned in clause (1).
(3) Any law of a state shall, insofar as it imposes, or authorizes the imposition of,
  (a) a tax on the sale or purchase of goods declared by Parliament by law to be of special importance in interstate trade or commerce; or
  (b) a tax on the sale or purchase of goods, being a tax of the nature referred to in

sub-clause (b), sub-clause (c) or sub-clause (d) of clause (29-A) of Article 366; be subject to such restrictions and conditions in regard to the system of levy, rates and other incidents of the tax as Parliament may by law specify.

Under these provisions, the Central government has authorized the states to levy the tax on interstate sale, subject to a specified ceiling rate (4 per cent). Besides creating impediment to free movement of goods (through check posts), this tax on export of goods from one state to another has converted the sales tax into an origin-based tax. The tax has also has caused significant interstate exportation of the tax burden from the richer producing states to the residents of poorer consuming states.

Interestingly, although Article 286 does not impose restrictions on interstate transactions, entry 52 in the state list empowers the states to levy tax on the entry of goods into a local area for consumption, use or sale. In many states, the tax has been assigned to the urban local bodies and the tax is variously called, 'octroi', or 'entry tax'. Thus, taxes are levied not only on the exports from one state to another but also on all imports into local areas, including imports from other states. These taxes have complicated the tax system, created severe distortions, caused severe impediments to inter-regional movement of goods, increased the compliance cost substantially, and have been a source of corruption.

In addition to the fiscal factors, several regulatory policies violate the principles of a common market. These have been introduced as a part of the planned development strategy or as a part of supply management to meet scarcity conditions. While many of the regulations restricting the free flow of goods and factors of production have been removed, the consequences of past policies continue to distort resources as the investment decisions once made cannot be reversed. The policy of freight equalization is a case in point. Besides, some restrictive policies continue to pervade even as they have outlived their utilities. Restrictions on the movement of food grains and restrictions on the export of certain food items are the examples.

The fiscal and regulatory impediments violating the principles of common market are as much a legacy of the development strategy as it is a consequence of political economy. The important issue is that such policies in a globalizing environment are not sustainable. We will review the reform issues relating to these in Chapter 15.

LOCAL GOVERNMENT AND GOVERNANCE

The status and powers of local government in India ebbed and rose throughout the British period. The Government of India Act of 1919 marked the first serious devolution to the local level, with chairmen of district boards (previously provincial officials) becoming elected officials, and municipalities and district and local boards increasing the scale of their activities, though still with relatively narrow expenditure assignments. However, local governments were reluctant to tax, or enforce collections, and revenues came primarily from provincial transfers. Neither hierarchical control nor electoral accountability proved effective for local governments in this period. While municipalities used octroi and personal income taxes, rural boards depended on land revenue surcharges, supplemented by professions and vehicle taxes. In this period, land revenue still represented the major source of provincial revenue, and was seen as a substitute for an agricultural income tax.[11]

Lack of fiscal independence and lack of effective electoral accountability together contributed to the weak effective role of local governments in India. While the Act of 1935 attempted to solidify the institutions governing provincial–central fiscal relations, it did not have much impact on structures of local government. If anything, the main trend was towards centralization, with large-scale infrastructure projects, defence, and transfer payments abroad dominating public expenditure. Typical local responsibilities, such as health and education, received little attention. The Second World War increased centralization of government, and it was only Mahatma Gandhi who continued to press for decentralization to the local-government level. In 1942, he wrote, in a well-known statement of his vision:

My idea of village swaraj is that it is a complete republic ... The government of the village will be conducted by a Panchayat of five persons annually elected by the adult villagers ... this Panchayat will be the legislature, judiciary and executive combined ... Here there is perfect democracy based on individual freedom.

We will reserve detailed discussion of local governments in India until Chapter 11. Here, one might argue that Gandhi's vision of village republic was one of voluntary, cooperative poverty. However, Gandhi was very much in the minority at the time of independence, and immediately afterward. We have earlier seen the centralizing bias of both Nehru and Ambedkar, the two key figures during the period when the Constitution was being drafted. Ambedkar was specifically opposed to Gandhi's vision of local decentralization, given his concerns about village-level power structures, which were perceived as inimical to the welfare of the lower-caste majority. Ambedkar made his own oft-quoted statement during the

---

[11] However, as land revenues declined through the twentieth century, there was no replacement by an agricultural income tax. See Kumar and Desai (1982), pp. 928–30.

Constituent Assembly's debate: 'What is a village but a sink of localism, a den of ignorance, narrow-mindedness and communalism ... ?'[12]

Overall, then, the Constitution drafted in 1950 gave little weight to local governments in India. Nevertheless, Gandhi's perspective received some acknowledgement in the final document. Village self-rule was given a perfunctory nod in Article 40, in the Directive Principles, which requires the government to 'take steps to reorganize village panchayats and endow them with such powers and functions as may be necessary to enable them to function as units of self-government'. This small statement, however, did give the impetus for a variety of Central and state government initiatives to implement the objective of village 'self-government'.

Throughout the period after independence, both Central and state governments appointed a series of committees to examine the functioning of local government, and recommend improvements. In addition, various finance commissions made recommendations on this subject. The Central Council of Local Self-government was created in 1954, under Article 263 of the Constitution, to coordinate urban development issues between the Centre and states. Rural issues remained separate from urban at the state level, but received even greater attention, and states repeatedly passed legislation dealing with the structures of Panchayati Raj. This legislation was often the result of recommendations made by centrally constituted committees.

The genesis of the latest reforms, which began in earnest in the 1990s, lay in the report of the Asoka Mehta committee in 1978. This committee was asked to suggest measures to strengthen Panchayati Raj institutions, allowing them to support more decentralized planning for development. Several states, including West Bengal, Karnataka, and Andhra Pradesh, modified their legislation along the lines of the committee's recommendations, shifting emphasis somewhat from bureaucratic to political control, and generally strengthening rural local government. However, other states continued to have relatively weak Panchayati Raj institutions. Lack of regular elections was a major problem in some states, reducing accountability of local government.

In 1988, another central committee recommended that Panchayati Raj bodies should be given constitutional status. Draft legislation to achieve this had been appended to the Asoka Mehta committee report, and this formed the basis for a constitutional amendment bill introduced in 1989. The motivation for this bill has been called into question, as an attempt to curtail the power of state governments relative to the Centre. While

---

[12] See, for example, Dhavan's introduction to Galanter (1989), p. xi.

political considerations no doubt mattered (it would be exceptional if they did not), it is clear from the historical experience that the bill was the culmination of a long series of steps and the implementation of an ideology that had been evolving since independence. Another criticism of the bill was its imposition of a uniform pattern of local government (for example, three tiers of rural local government) on all the major states, whatever their size, experience, or prevailing institutions. The bill ultimately failed to get the requisite majority in the upper house of Parliament.

A new government in 1990 introduced a revised version of the 1989 bill, dealing with municipalities as well as Panchayati Raj institutions. The government fell before the bill could be discussed in Parliament, but the next government pursued the issue. Finally, in 1991, two separate amendment bills were introduced, covering panchayats and municipalities respectively. It was passed by both houses of Parliament towards the end of 1992, ratified by more than half the state assemblies, and brought into force as the 73rd and 74th amendments to the Constitution in 1993. These amendments required individual states to pass appropriate legislation, since local government is a state subject, and individual states have proceeded to do so.

CONCLUSION

The brief history reported in this chapter is intended to provide some background to the themes that will be examined in more detail in later chapters. In particular, we have identified the centrepetal bias in India's federal structures, and how these have played out in practice. In particular, the Centre has used political discretion through internal party mechanisms, as well as through institutions such as the Planning Commission, to achieve its objectives over conflicting goals of the states. One can understand why these avenues should be preferred to some of the ones that are more explicitly available through constitutional provisions. The latter suffer from being instruments that are too blunt, and also perhaps too obvious and transparent an exercise of Central power.

Of course, there have been cases where the states have explicitly challenged the Centre on specific points of constitutional assignments of authority. Our historical review suggested that the Supreme Court, the arbiter in such matters, has tended to support interpretations that bolster the position most favourable to the Centre, especially in its earlier rulings. The general role of the courts, and other components of government, will be the theme of a later chapter.

The weak position of the states historically translated into an even weaker position for local governments. However, as the states gained more bargaining power in the 1980s, the Centre may have looked to stronger local governments as a counterweight. This interplay may have given a sufficient push to legislation that finally gave local governments separate constitutional status in the 1990s. This ongoing reform will also be taken up in a later chapter.

4

Bargaining, Control, and Commitment

CEMENTING THE FEDERATION

The review of theories of federalism in Chapter 2 provided a synoptic view of political and economic reasons for smaller geographical entities to come together into a union. The political impulse has to be found in issues of freedom, security, and political stability or strength. Similarly, access to a larger common market, reaping economies of scale in the provision of national-level public goods, and availability of wider choice in the bundle of services to meet diverse preferences are economic reasons for smaller units to come together to form a federation. Each federating unit will try to bargain for advantageous terms to join the federation, while the federation will try to attract entry and control exit. Thus, issues of bargaining, control, and commitment are extremely important.

The evolution of federal systems and institutions in India traced in Chapter 3 provides a broad perspective within which issues of bargaining, control, and commitment can be examined in the country's federal arrangements. The historical perspective also provides the background on the relative strengths and weaknesses of the Centre and the constituent units, as well as explanations for asymmetries in the initial arrangements and in the building of conventions. We examine issues related to geography, ethnicity, language, and culture (and sometimes simple bargaining strength), using examples from different parts of the country.

This chapter analyses issues of bargaining, control, and commitment in shaping the structure of the Indian federation and in its working. In particular, it examines the factors that have led to the strong centralizing features of the federal constitution that was crafted after independence. The tension between Centre and states has led to conflicts at the level of 'normal' politics,[1] as well as between the Centre and regional groups outside the electoral process. We develop the observation that centralization plus the diversity of Indian society along the above dimensions have required asymmetric arrangements, which has added to tensions. A more federal or decentralized structure may help to avoid these tensions. At the same time, we analyse the problems linked to fears of secession.

Of course, besides a number of scholars and official reports of the Finance Commission, various bodies, such as the Administrative Reforms Commission, the Committee on Centre–State Relations appointed by the Government of Tamil Nadu (Rajamannar Committee), the Sarkaria Commission and more recently the Constitution Review Commission (M.N. Venkatachaliah Commission) have tried to deal with the problems of Centre–state relations. We review some of these efforts, and re-evaluate them in the context of the analytics of the problems of assignment of tasks and responsibilities to different levels of government. Among the institutional aspects we examine are the nature of bargaining between Centre and states (including issues of credible commitment), and, in particular, the links to fiscal issues such as assignment, overlapping, and fiscal transfers. We examine the non-economic motives for transfers, the special treatment for some states incorporated in the Gadgil formula, special transfers for security, and the process of making and writing off of loans to states.

In our analysis, in this chapter and the next, we adopt very much the economist's view of the role of government, i.e., as a provider of public goods and corrector of externalities, as outlined in Chapter 2. To some extent, the role of the government as a guarantor of civil and political rights, 'valued mainly on non-instrumental grounds' (Elster, 1994, p. 217) is kept in the background, though such rights also have an instrumental component. Similarly, benefits of security and stability can be treated as public goods, very much in line with Riker's and Wheare's views on federalism discussed in Chapter 2. The government is also concerned with equity and distribution. Issues of equity will also be discussed in Chapters 8 and 9, in the context of transfers, and are treated here in the context of the asymmetric treatment of 'special category' states. Furthermore, redistribution by the government may take place not just because of benevolent equity concerns, but also as a response to interest groups. We have discussed issues of rent seeking in Chapter 2, and return to them here.

This chapter is structured as follows. We begin with a discussion of the

---

[1] Manor (1995) defines this term as 'the politics of bargaining, lobbying, relatively peaceful protest and parliamentary niceties' (p. 125).

basic centralizing feature of Indian federation namely, conditions for entry and exit and the rights of the Centre to alter the boundaries of the states. Next, we discuss the arrangements in the Indian Constitution to accommodate special cases, such as Jammu and Kashmir, and the various north-eastern hill states, what has been called 'asymmetrical federalism'. This section focuses on the structural or institutional asymmetries. We combine a discussion of constitutional arrangements with an examination of the role, in this context, of fiscal transfers, which are discussed more broadly in Chapters 8 and 9. Issues of commitment and durability within these structures are discussed next, where these ideas are also applied to Centre–state 'ethnic' conflicts, and to a discussion of legislative structures and interest group politics. Commitment, or the lack of it, is an important idea in analysing federal systems, because the essence of federalism is a binding commitment by the Centre to not exercise its sovereignty fully over constituent governments of the federation. We then briefly review previous recommendations for and attempts at institutional reform of Indian federal structures. The chapter concludes with a summary of our rather wide-ranging arguments.

ENTRY AND EXIT

The centripetal bias in Indian federation is seen in the conditions for entry and exit specified in the basic structure of the Constitution itself. Article 2 of the Constitution enables the federation to allow unfettered admittance. It states, 'Parliament may by law admit into the Union, or establish new states on such terms and conditions as it thinks fit'. Although India is a Union of States (Article 1), the states per se do not have any say in the decision to admit any unit or in forming any state except that the Upper House in the Parliament, the Rajya Sabha, is a council of states, and is supposed to protect their interests. Since India's independence, the only new units to have been added are the state of Sikkim and Goa. The former was a protectorate of India and was formally absorbed into the Indian Union in 1975 as a state. The latter was a Portuguese colony that did not accede to India but was later incorporated, initially as a union territory and in 1987 as a full-fledged state.

Parliament has the powers not only to allow entry of new units, but also to create new states, by altering the areas and boundaries of the existing states. Article 3 empowers the Parliament to:

a) form a new state by separation of territory from any state or by uniting two or more states or parts of states or by uniting any territory to a part of any state;

b) increase the area of any state;
c) diminish the area of any state;
d) alter the boundaries of any state;
e) alter the name of any state.

The only requirement is that the bill for any of the above will have to be introduced in the Parliament after the recommendation of the President and the latter is required to refer the bill to the legislature of that state for 'expressing their views thereon'. It must be noted that the Constitution *does not require the consent* of the state, but only that the views of the state must be obtained. While many instances of creation of states have been the upgrading of Union Territories such as Nagaland, Manipur, and Tripura, in other cases, new states have been carved out of existing ones. In the 1950s, there were substantial redrawings of boundaries as linguistically based states were created. The creation of Haryana out of Punjab in 1966 was the last of these actions. Other examples involved separating out parts of Assam to create new states. Finally, after a long hiatus, in the late 1990s, three significant new states were created from portions of three of the largest states: Uttaranchal from Uttar Pradesh, Jharkhand from Bihar, and Chhattisgarh from Madhya Pradesh. All these cases illustrate the ease with which the Centre has been able to redraw state boundaries within the federation.

As opposed to the creation of new units within the federation, exit has been virtually impossible. Numerous secessionist movements in the northeastern states, as well as in Punjab and in Kashmir, have met with forceful responses, and only the one in Kashmir continues at a level to cause concern to the Central government. We will return to these issues throughout this chapter.

Asymmetrical Structures

We begin with an examination of the origins of some of the asymmetrical features in India's federal structure. In particular, the case of Kashmir is contrasted with the fate of the other princely states in existence at the time of independence. Kashmir is also briefly compared to Punjab, a comparison that is taken up in more detail later. The north-eastern hill states are treated next. The political nature of their implicit 'federal bargain' with the rest of the Indian Union is explored. Together with Jammu and Kashmir and Himachal Pradesh, the eight north-eastern hill states constitute the 'special category states', and we conclude this section with an analysis of the economic consequences for these states of 'asymmetrical federalism'.

Initial Conditions

The Union of India in 1947 began with a major asymmetry, that between British India and the princely states. In almost all cases, the princely states surrendered whatever notional sovereignty they had to the new country of India, in exchange for a guaranteed revenue stream: their 'privy purses'. The nature of this bargain was clear—security and money in exchange for giving up authority or residual control rights. This is close to the standard view of federation as a political bargain, with the difference that the successors of the British in India, the Indian National Congress, were in an extremely strong bargaining position, even relative to the coalition of the princes. This was illustrated in the case of the exceptions to voluntary accession, such as Hyderabad, where military force (the authority over which was also inherited from the British) ensured integration into the new Union.

While many of the former princely states (particularly the larger ones) continued as administrative units after their integration into India, this continuation was not an essential part of the bargain, and reorganization of state boundaries from 1953 onwards, freely permitted to the Centre by the Constitution, gradually eroded this status. The Constitution allowed for sub-state structures for regions closely tied to some former princely states, but this had little practical import, as the states became almost the sole significant sub-national units of governance. Thus, in general, the princely states ceased to matter as geographic entities. In this respect, the outcome was completely different from the standard case of federation, where the constituents of the federation normally retain their identities. Also, the asymmetries present in 1947 with respect to almost all the princely states disappeared from Indian federalism.

The sole exception, of course, was the princely state of Jammu and Kashmir. While this state included several diverse populations and regions, the overwhelming majority of the population of the Kashmir valley was Muslim, and the state bordered the new nation of Pakistan. The history of the conflict over Kashmir has been written about extensively, even though there is no consensus on the interpretation of events in 1947–48. Here, we merely note that the state acceded to the Indian Union under very special terms, which were subsequently incorporated in the famous Article 370 of the Constitution. This article provided the state with a unique position in the Indian Union, with its own constitution, a title interpreted as the equivalent of prime minister for its chief elected official, and a special assignment of functional responsibilities. Specifically, the jurisdiction of the Centre was restricted to foreign affairs, defence, and communications, with the state's legislature having residuary powers.

This was a striking contrast to the situation of all the other states, where the Centre's assignment of responsibilities was much more extensive, and where the Centre retained residuary powers.

The interpretation of this arrangement is straightforward, and well known: it was a consequence of the bargaining strength of the main political forces in the Kashmir valley. Kashmir was the only state that was in this position. Perhaps the only other group that might have bargained for special status in the Union, the Sikhs in Punjab, lacked several of the contributing factors to this bargaining strength. They were not politically unified, they were not in such an overwhelming majority in their region of concentration, they were in disarray as a result of the partition of British India, and, most importantly, their 'outside option' was much less attractive. Joining the Islamic nation of Pakistan was a very reasonable alternative for the Kashmiri Muslims, much less so, if not impossible, for the Sikhs.[2]

Thus, the bargaining strength of the Sikhs was quite negligible, and like the princes, they entered the Indian Union without any special arrangements.[3] Despite the initial dissimilarities in their positions in India's federal structure, conflicts with many similarities and connections developed in these two states, and this development will be analysed later.

The North-eastern Hill States

The process of administrative reorganization of India focused on the creation of new boundaries based on the main principle of language. Typically, separate religious, caste, ethnic or tribal identities within these boundaries were not the basis for further divisions. One major exception to this has been the north-eastern part of India, where there is a distinct difference in ethnicity from the rest of India, and several strong divisions based not only on language, but also on culture and other traditions ('tribal', if one wishes to use that term). This part of India contains the states of Arunachal Pradesh, Assam, Manipur, Meghalaya, Mizoram, Nagaland, Sikkim, and Tripura. Of these, only Assam has a population comparable to other typical Indian states. Most of these states were upgraded from the status of union territories.[4] This reclassification gave

---

[2] While independence has been a longed-for third possibility for many Sikhs and Kashmiri Muslims, it has never seemed like a remotely feasible option, either in economic or political terms.

[3] It should be noted that while the Sikhs did not have any territorial sovereignty as such, there were several Sikh princely states, and the British gave them representation as a religious community at the bargaining table, alongside Hindus and Muslims.

[4] At independence, of course, this entire region was administratively part of Assam

them, at one level, a political status equivalent to large states such as Uttar Pradesh and Bihar: for example, each state carries equal weight in mustering the fifty per cent of states required to ratify an amendment to the Constitution.

However, the above eight states, along with Himachal Pradesh, Jammu and Kashmir, and the more recently included Uttaranchal, are 'special category' states for the purpose of allocation of financial resources by the Centre, as we discuss in the next subsection. Furthermore, there are several constitutional provisions pertaining to the various north-eastern states. These involve various clauses of Article 371, and are discussed in detail in Arora (1995).[5] These provisions have been introduced through amendments, typically at the time of conversion of a union territory to a state, the carving out of one state from another, or, in the case of Sikkim, after its accession to India. They include language designed to protect or respect customary laws and religious practices, restrictions on the ownership and transfer of land, and restrictions on immigration. State legislatures are typically given final control over changes in these provisions.

In practice, the special provisions have reduced tension between the Centre and the north-east, but not eliminated it. The reasons for this are summarized by Arora (1995). While financial transfers from the Centre are weighted in favour of the special category states, as will be discussed later in this section (and also in Chapter 8), the mechanism of transfers accentuates feelings of dependence. Furthermore, the constitutional safeguards are not necessarily explicit enough to be clearly implementable in practice. This is, of course, a general problem with constitutions, which can only provide a broad general framework. The ultimate issue may lie with the broader centralizing features of the constitution, rather than the specific features of various clauses of Article 371, and with the sometimes-attenuated role of the Supreme Court as an impartial arbiter between Centre and states.[6]

---

province, and the union territories themselves were created by separation from Assam. Meghalaya was directly carved out of the state of Assam, while Sikkim was formerly an Indian protectorate. See, for example, Brass (1994) for a chronology.

[5] For example, Article 371A covers special provisions for Nagaland, 371G for Mizoram. These articles required constitutional amendments, but, as in the case of Kashmir, regional movements complain that the constitutional provisions have not been adequately respected in practice.

[6] This goes back to the point made by Wheare, as articulated in Chapter 2, that a federal system creates this additional important role, as adjudicator between different levels of government, for a supreme judicial body, beyond that of checks and balances at the central level itself. These issues are taken up further in this chapter and the next.

An example of conflict between specific and general constitutional provisions in the context of the north-east is provided by Nagaland's concerns with respect to natural resources. As will be discussed in more detail in Chapter 10, natural resources such as minerals appear in both Central and state lists, but with language that gives the Centre the ultimate control over such resources. This control has been exercised by the Centre in practice. As related by Arora (1995, p. 81), Nagaland brought to the attention of the Sarkaria Commission the language of Article 371A, which requires the endorsement of the Nagaland legislature for any Central legislation pertaining to 'the ownership of and transfer of land and its resources', The Nagaland government interpreted this language, reasonably it seems, to cover mines and minerals. The Sarkaria Commission's response in its report was unhelpful: it recommended 'dialogue and discussion'. A bargaining view of federalism would recognize that a transfer of property rights between levels of government cannot be easily achieved through cooperative bargaining, but requires independent arbitration. These issues are examined in detail in Chapter 10, particularly for the case of river waters. Interestingly, Arora points out that 'resources' were omitted from a similar clause introduced for Mizoram twenty-five years after the provision for Nagaland!

As noted in Chapter 2, there are various provisions in the Indian Constitution to protect group rights, and to compensate for initial inequalities in the social system. Thus the Constitution, while recognizing the idea of fundamental human rights at the individual level, does not assume an idealized initial condition of equality, either in pure economic terms or otherwise. Thus there are allowances for separate laws to govern different religious groups, and there are provisions for various kinds of 'affirmative action' for extremely disadvantaged groups. The first kind of provision simply respects diversity (though this can create issues of unequal treatment across subgroups, for example women in two different religious groups). The second attempts to correct specific inequities, recognizing that legislative equal treatment would not achieve desired equity goals where initial conditions are very unequal. Conceptually, at this level of ethical or normative judgement, there is no difference between these provisions and the ones for the indigenous residents of north-eastern states, except that the latter happen to be geographically concentrated into reasonable administrative units. If that is the case, the relationship to federalism is not essential.

However, in the perspective of federalism as a political and economic bargain, geography and demography matter in essential ways. We noted the example of Kashmir and Punjab earlier, and we will now apply a similar analysis to the north-eastern states. In the contrast between Kashmir and Punjab, we noted the strength of the majority of Muslims in the Kashmir valley, their relative unity, and the existence of an alternative country to which the region could accede. This geographical concentration, combined with a feeling of distinctness, makes the idea of political separation seem feasible, even though the economic feasibility of such separation may be questionable. These factors are also present in the north-eastern hill states to a considerable degree, and this makes each of them a significant bargaining unit, beyond what might be the case based on numbers alone. Put another way, a group with a similar size to that of the population of, say, Nagaland, just as distinctive, but scattered throughout the country, would not have the same bargaining position, in terms of obtaining special provisions in the Constitution.

The argument we are presenting therefore downplays a normative explanation of special constitutional provisions ('diversity should be respected'), in favour of one based on bargaining power alone. Note that this does not remove ethical or normative considerations entirely, since those factors presumably do affect the preferences and cohesiveness of the group that bargains. In other words, identity, culture, etc., are valued by the group beyond their instrumental roles.

In making the argument that political bargaining has determined the creation of special constitutional provisions for the north-eastern hill states, one should also examine the argument that the Central government was the driver of the process. In other words, the fact that the northeastern states came into existence on terms favourable to them is a coincidental outcome of a process primarily reflecting central interests. This seems to be the argument of Baruah (1997).

Unlike the reorganization of states in many other parts of India that responded to sustained political mobilization, redrawing boundaries in the North East was much more of a top-down process. This applies even when new states were formed in order to contain or pre-empt separatist insurgencies. The fact that a few of the crucial moves ... took place under a phase of centralisation of power under Indira Gandhi is hardly accidental (p. 27).

We do not agree with the above interpretation. The Naga insurrection was not 'an obscure speck of discontent',[7] and the origins of the problems in what became Mizoram were older than what Baruah recognizes.[8] The creation of Nagaland certainly had demonstration effects encouraging

---

[7] Baruah (1997, p. 28), approvingly quoting a newspaper article by M.S. Prabhakara.
[8] See, in particular, Dua (1990) on the history of the Naga and Mizo movements.

other autonomy movements in the north-east, but this in fact, supports the bargaining power interpretation we have advanced,[9] since such demonstration effects would presumably make the Centre more reluctant to give in.[10] Strategic considerations were certainly paramount for the Central government, with the history of Arunachal Pradesh being the clearest illustration,[11] but again, as argued above, the strategic geographic position of the north-eastern states enhances their bargaining position beyond their political importance in terms of size.

A final point against interpreting the creation of new north-eastern states as a direct expression of centralization comes from examining fiscal transfers to these states. These transfers are relatively large, as we discuss in more detail in the next subsection, and they vary across the different states. The existence of separate states may give the Centre more flexibility in influencing the states through fiscal transfers, but the size of the transfers at least partly reflects the states' bargaining position. We turn now to these fiscal issues.

Economic Asymmetry

The coming together of units with diverse history, resources, policies, and institutions in a bargain to form a federation would certainly entail de facto asymmetry in terms of interstate differences in geography, demography, and economy among twenty-eight states and seven union territories.[12]

The wide differences in the economic characteristics between the states in Indian federation are highlighted in Table 4.1. It is seen that in terms of area the biggest state, Rajasthan is 90 times bigger than the smallest state, Goa. Similarly, in terms of population, Uttar Pradesh, the state with largest population is 308 times bigger than the smallest state, Sikkim. The density of population varies from 13 in Arunachal Pradesh to 901 in West Bengal. Maharashtra has the highest net state domestic product (NSDP),

---

[9] Again, Baruah quotes Prabhakara in favour of the demonstration hypothesis.

[10] In fact, we argue later in this chapter that the case of Punjab illustrates this demonstration problem.

[11] Arunachal Pradesh was originally the North East Frontier Agency, carved out of Assam and brought directly under the control of the Central government. This, however, took place before Indira Gandhi's rule as prime minister contrary to what is mentioned in the quote above from Baruah. A discussion of centralizing and decentralizing tendencies in Indian federal politics is provided in Chapter 10.

[12] Union Territories are governed directly by the Central government. However, two Union Territories namely, Delhi and Pondicherry have their own elected governments and legislatures. Delhi now has a hybrid status as National Capital Territory, and is often treated as a state in policy discussions.

TABLE 4.1
Some Characteristics of States in Indian Federalism

	Area (Sq. Km)	Population (in '000)	Density of Popn	NSDP 1999–2000 Rs million	Per capita NSDP (1999–2000)	Percentage of total area	Percentage of total population	Percentage of total NSDP
High-income States	601,800	194,065	322.5	4,065,770	22,461	18.31	18.90	28.74
Gujarat	196,000	50,597	258.1	896,060	18,685	5.96	4.93	6.33
Goa	3800	1344	353.7	58,620	44,613	0.12	0.13	0.41
Haryana	44,000	21,083	479.2	424,880	21,551	1.34	2.05	3.00
Maharashtra	308,000	96,752	314.1	2,131,510	22,604	9.37	9.42	15.07
Punjab	50,000	24,289	485.8	554,700	23,254	1.52	2.37	3.92
Middle-income States	725,000	302,633	417.4	4,867,930	17,635	22.05	29.47	34.41
Andhra Pradesh	275,000	75,728	275.4	1,117,530	14,878	8.36	7.37	7.90
Karnataka	192,000	52,734	274.7	862,980	16,654	5.84	5.13	6.10
Kerala	39,000	31,839	816.4	569,260	17,709	1.19	3.10	4.02
Tamil Nadu	130,000	62,111	477.8	1,143,090	18,623	3.95	6.05	8.08
West Bengal	89,000	80,221	901.4	1,175,070	14,874	2.71	7.81	8.31
Low-income States	1,409,300	458,682	325.5	4,022,290	9013	42.87	44.66	28.44
Bihar	94,000	82,879	881.7	383,260	4813	2.86	8.07	2.71
Chhattisgarh	135,100	20,796	153.9	213,310	10,405	4.11	2.02	1.51
Jharkhand	79,700	26,909	337.6	232,270	9223	2.42	2.62	1.64
Madhya Pradesh	308,000	60,385	196.1	677,780	11,626	9.37	5.88	4.79
Orissa	156,000	36,707	235.3	311,950	8733	4.75	3.57	2.21

(contd)

(*Table 4.1 contd*)

	Area (Sq. Km)	Population (in '000)	Density of Popn	NSDP 1999–2000 Rs million	Per capita NSDP (1999–2000)	Percentage of total area	Percentage of total population	Percentage of total NSDP
Rajasthan	342,000	56,473	165.1	710,200	13,046	10.40	5.50	5.02
Uttaranchal	53,500	8480	158.5	NA	NA	1.63	0.83	0.00
Uttar Pradesh	241,000	166,053	689.0	1,493,520	9323	7.33	16.17	10.56
General Category States	2,736,100	955,380	349.2	12,955,990	14,476	83.23	93.02	91.59
Special Category States	540,500	55,182	102.1	639,300	12,339	16.44	5.37	4.52
Arunachal Pradesh	84,000	1091	13.0	14270	13,352	2.56	0.11	0.10
Assam	78,000	26,638	341.5	2,533,300	9720	2.37	2.59	1.79
Himachal Pradesh	56,000	6077	108.5	106,570	17,786	1.70	0.59	0.75
Jammu & Kashmir	222,000	10,070	45.4	121,820	12,373	6.75	0.98	0.86
Manipur	22,000	2389	108.6	28,580	12,721	0.67	0.23	0.20
Meghalaya	23,000	2306	100.3	29,040	12,063	0.70	0.22	0.21
Mizoram	21,000	891	42.4	12,880	14,909	0.64	0.09	0.09
Nagaland	17,000	1989	117.0	23,300	12,594	0.52	0.19	0.16
Sikkim	7000	540	77.1	7580	14,751	0.21	0.05	0.05
Tripura	10,500	3191	303.9	41,930	13,195	0.32	0.31	0.30
All States	3,276,600	1,010,562	308.4	13,595,290	14,359	99.67	98.40	96.11
UTs	10,974	16,453	1499.3	549,870	31,211	0.33	1.60	3.89
Total	3,287,574	1,027,015	312.4	14,145,160	13,778	100.00	100.00	100.00

Notes: NA — Not Available. All State NSDP figure does not include SDP from Uttaranchal.
NSDP figure of UTs excludes SDP from Dadra and Nagar Haveli, Daman and Diu, and Lakshadweep.

Sources: 1. Finances of State Governments, 2001–02; Reserve Bank of India; 2. CSO, Ministry of Planning, Government of India.

284 times that of the state with the lowest (Sikkim). There are significant variations in per capita incomes as well. In 2000–01, Goa, a small state on the western coast had the per capita NSDP of Rs 44,613, which was almost 9 times that of Bihar with Rs 4813.

For the sake of analytical convenience, the states may be classified into special category states and non-special category states. The former are given a special status in dispensing plan assistance by the Central government. The non-special category states, in turn, are classified into high-income, middle-income, and low-income states based on their per capita NSDP.[13] It is seen from the table that special category states with 14 per cent of geographical area of the country have only 5 per cent of the population and generate 4 per cent of the NSDP. The importance of non-economic factors in determining the structure of federalism is underscored by the fact that most of the special category states are not economically viable. Even among non-special category states, there are states that are too large like Madhya Pradesh, Bihar, and Uttar Pradesh even after carving out the three new states of Chhattisgarh, Jharkhand, and Uttaranchal respectively from the territories of these states in 2000.

Within the non-special category states, there are wide variations in area, population, and income levels. The high-income states with about 18–19 per cent area and population generated 29 per cent of NSDP whereas the low-income states with 43–45 per cent of geographic area and population accounted for only 28 per cent of income. There are wide variations in the sizes and income levels within each of the categories of states as well. On the whole, among the non-special category states, the most populous state (Uttar Pradesh) had 123 times the population of Goa, the least populous state, and the income differences between the highest- and lowest-income state was 36 times.

The above discussion brings out that economic viability has never been a consideration in demarcating the states in India. Nor has it been a factor in reorganization of the states despite the fact that the Constitution empowers the Central government to reorganize them. Thus, to begin with, intergovernmental relationships are placed on an uneven economic keel. Naturally, uniform assignment system in an unevenly endowed federating system results in large differences in fiscal capacities. Varying sizes of states in terms of area and population, demographic compositions, different terrain and topography cause significant variations in the unit cost of providing public services, with varying expenditure needs, and

[13] The states with per capita NSDP more than 15% of the average are classified as high income states and those with less than 10% of the average are classified as low income states.

places a heavy burden of equalization on the intergovernmental transfer system.

The implications of interstate differences in economic conditions and fiscal variables of the states are shown in Table 4.2. The table brings out some important fiscal features of Indian federalism. First, variations in economic characteristics has resulted in significant differences in revenues collected in different states, partly due to differences in the capacity to raise revenues and partly due to differences in their collection efficiency. By and large, the ratio of revenues to state domestic product (SDP) is positively related to the level of per capita. The low-income states had lower revenue ratios than the middle-income states, which in turn had lower ratios than the high-income states. Second, the ratio of revenues to NSDP was much lower in special category states than general category states even when the latter had comparable levels of NSDP. The singular exception to this is the case of Sikkim, which had retained the power to levy income taxes while acceding to the country. Thus, unlike in other states, Sikkim has the power to levy income tax and federal income tax cannot extend to Sikkim. Third, the small size of jurisdictions in these states implies that they cannot reap economies of scale in providing services. Besides, the hilly and inhospitable terrain in these states means that the unit cost of providing public services will be higher than in other states. It is thus not surprising to see over-whelming dependence of special category states on central transfers. Thus, in 2001–02, non-special category states on an average raised revenues to finance over 50 per cent of their current expenditure whereas in special category states it was just about 20 per cent. Thus, central transfers financed more than 80 per cent of the expenditures of special category states. In per capita terms, transfer to special category states is more than four times that of the average transfer received by general category states.

The different position of the special category states is reflected not only in structural asymmetries in the constitutional framework, but very importantly in the methods and the patterns of fiscal transfers from the Centre to these states. In some respects, the small size of these states is an advantage in this dimension. Transfers that are large in per capita terms for these states (Table 4.2) may not place a significant cost on the rest of the nation. In fact, even the entire group of these states has a population share of only 5.4 per cent. This is important, since otherwise the group of states as a whole might place a burden if large per capita transfers were made to each member of the group. Also, this small size encourages these states to combine politically for some purposes, in councils that allow them to coordinate policies, or to collectively negotiate with the Centre. This is in contrast to the insignificance of zonal councils for other states.

TABLE 4. 2

Revenues and Expenditures of the States—2000–01 (RE)

States	Per capita SDP (Rupees)	Poverty ratio (per cent) 1999–00	Per capita own revenue (Rupees)	Own revenue as percentage of SDP	Per capita transfers	Per capita current spending (Rupees)	Percentage of own revenue to current spending
High-income States	22,461	17.83	2931.6	13.1	500	4386.6	66.8
Gujarat	18,685	14.07	2684.6	13.2	863	5167.6	52.0
Goa	44,613	4.4	14,310.3	15.8	588	11,904.8	120.2
Haryana	21,551	8.74	3209.7	12.1	502	4107.9	78.1
Maharashtra	22,604	25.02	2741.3	11.1	448	3852.6	71.2
Punjab	23,254	6.16	3333.2	10.2	494	4712.7	70.7
Middle-income States	17,635	20.3	1868.8	10.6	658	3400.4	55.0
Andhra Pradesh	14,878	15.77	1930.2	10.7	713	3320.2	58.1
Karnataka	16,654	20.44	2148.1	11.3	686	3580.9	60.0
Kerala	17,709	12.72	2295.8	10.2	690	3689.4	62.2
Tamil Nadu	18,623	21.12	2342.5	11.3	658	3594.3	65.2
West Bengal	14,874	27.02	1091.0	5.5	576	3092.7	35.3
Low-income States	9013	34.28	846.8	9.4	673	2243.4	37.7
Bihar	4813	42.6	338.2	8.9	724	1515.5	22.3
Chhattisgarh	10,405	NA	1264.0	4.9	NA	2455.2	51.5
Jharkhand	9223	NA	1128.0	9.0	NA	2229.4	50.6
Madhya Pradesh	11,626	37.43	1061.9	11.5	624	2695.5	39.4

(contd)

For Rakesh (1968–2017)

(Table 4.2 contd)

States	Per capita SDP (Rupees)	Poverty ratio (per cent) 1999–00	Per capita own revenue (Rupees)	Own revenue as percentage of SDP	Per capita transfers	Per capita current spending (Rupees)	Percentage of own revenue to current spending
Orissa	8733	47.15	900.5	9.3	969	2785.3	32.3
Rajasthan	13,046	15.28	1297.2	10.4	693	2864.2	45.3
Uttaranchal	NA	NA	1295.5	NA	NA	4912.7	26.4
Uttar Pradesh	9323	31.15	791.2	8.1	598	2135.6	37.0
General Category States	14,476	25.97	1594.0	11.0	660	3045.3	52.3
Special Category States	12,339		1155.9	9.4	2896	5715.4	20.2
Arunachal Pradesh	13,352	33.47	1067.8	5.3	7985	9992.3	10.7
Assam	9720	36.09	798.7	7.2	1216	3317.0	24.1
Himachal Pradesh	17,786	7.63	1660.5	7.8	3070	7420.6	22.4
Jammu & Kashmir	12,373	3.48	1150.4	7.9	4602	6080.0	18.9
Manipur	12,721	28.54	406.0	3.1	3971	6032.3	6.7
Meghalaya	12,063	33.87	1066.8	6.3	3149	5878.4	18.1
Mizoram	14,909	19.47	679.0	3.8	9602	12,845.6	5.3
Nagaland	12,594	32.67	506.8	3.7	6332	7291.0	7.0
Sikkim	14,751	36.55	5998.1	15.9	7945	12,200.6	49.2
Tripura	13,195	34.44	729.6	4.8	3376	5838.9	12.5
All States	14,359	26.1	1570.1	10.9	768	3191.1	49.2

Notes: NA — Not Available.
Sources: 1. Finances of State Governments, 2001–02, Reserve Bank of India; 2. CSO, Ministry of Planning, Government of India.

Table 4.2 brings out some important fiscal features of special category states. It is seen that, for the special category states as a group, per capita own revenues are quite low on average, being comparable to the average for the low-income major states, although per capita incomes are higher than the average for the low-income states. This difference is captured in the lower revenue effort numbers for the group of special category states. There are considerable variations within the group itself, from a high of 15.9 per cent own revenue as a percentage of SDP for Sikkim[14] to a low of 3.1 per cent for Manipur. Another way to see that transfers for the special category states are high is by noting that for most of the sates in this group (except Assam, Himachal Pradesh, and Sikkim) the percentage of own revenue to current spending is lower than the lowest figure for the major states (22.3 per cent for Bihar).

Several explanations are possible for these transfers. They may simply reflect equity concerns, since the costs of providing certain public goods and services may be much higher in remote, mountainous areas. They may reflect higher costs of providing the goods due to diseconomies of scale and scope, due to the small size of these states, and their internal diversity. Thus, although the average per capita spending for the special category states is higher than the average for the high-income states, it may not imply larger service levels but simply reflect higher costs of provision. The high transfers may also be the result of special expenditures, such as higher levels of security, which are not required in other states. Thus, these states may to some extent be acting as agents of the Centre in the provision of the national public good of strategic stability and defence.

Finally, the large transfers may also be a consequence of the political bargain that brought these areas firmly into the Indian Union, and keeps them there. This kind of reasoning is particularly clear for such formal, separate induction into the Union as Sikkim, and for the case of Kashmir, which is analysed further in the next subsection, but it also applies to cases such as Nagaland, where a long insurgency after Indian independence was finally brought under control through the granting of statehood with special provisions, and where an implicit political bargain may require continuing transfers beyond the average.[15]

[14] However, the high figure for Sikkim is largely driven by the fact that it has the power to levy its own income tax.

[15] One other possible reason also involves strategic motives. For strategic reasons, the Central government may wish to restrict private investment, particularly, but not restricted to, foreign investment into these regions. Thus, public spending may be a compensation for this restriction. To some extent, this is also a consequence of features of the political bargain that restrict non-residents of the state from certain kinds of ownership of property in the state, thus acting as a restriction on investment.

Contents

Tables, Images, and Figure

Tables

Images

Figure

This last reason may be contrasted with the idea that transfers may be made due to the political strength of a state. In both cases, higher transfers are hypothesized to be associated with higher bargaining strength, but the source of the bargaining advantage is different. In the case of a large or rich state, it is the potential for enhanced political support for the ruling party or coalition at the Centre. For the special category states, however, their bargaining power comes from their strategic importance for defending the boundaries of the nation, from the threat of insurgency (exit), and from their small size, which reduces the aggregate cost of raising their per capita state government spending.

In this context, the figures for Assam in Table 4.2 are somewhat revealing. While Assam is a special category state, the per capita transfers it receives, and its per capita spending are low relative to the rest of the group. In some sense, since the other north-eastern states are strategically more important, and smaller, the Centre is able to target transfers to them to achieve its objectives, without having to make large per capita transfers to Assam. This point is particularly illustrated by the contrast in transfers between Assam and Meghalaya, which was carved out of Assam. Since Assam is possibly not large or rich enough to have bargaining strength in the other category,[16] its low per capita transfers and spending (though not out of line with the general category states at similar income levels) are consistent with the hypothesis of a political bargaining explanation of actual transfers.

Other Issues of Asymmetry

Kashmir and the north-east do not exhaust examples of issues of asymmetric arrangements. Tribal areas in some states received constitutional recognition and special provisions, but these rarely translated into meaningful implementation, since this depended on the discretion of state governments—a similar but stronger version of issues that have plagued Centre–state relations. Examples of such special provisions are the Fifth and Sixth Schedules of the Constitution, created in Article 244.

The Fifth Schedule deals with tribal areas in the relevant states ('scheduled areas'). Since scheduled tribes are provided with reserved constituencies in the national parliament as well in state legislatures, the provisions of this schedule build on this provision to mandate advisory councils, and articulate special responsibilities of the state governor and the Central

---

[16] This assertion must be qualified by noting that the state does have a larger tax base than the other special category states. In particular, it receives significant revenue from tea plantations through an agricultural income tax.

government towards these areas. In practice, these have had little effect. In the predominantly tribal region of Jharkhand, in Bihar, a similar advisory council was also ineffective, and demands for greater autonomy continued, until their recent recognition in the current government's proposal to carve out several new states, based on ethnic (and to some extent linguistic) criteria, in Jharkhand, Chhattisgarh in Madhya Pradesh, and Uttaranchal in Uttar Pradesh.

Other recent examples of sub-state councils of varying effectiveness also exist. They include the Darjeeling Gorkha Hill Council in West Bengal, the Bodo Autonomous Council in Assam, and the Autonomous Hill District Council in the Ladakh region of Jammu and Kashmir. These bodies have been created by state-level legislation in response to pressures from ethnic groups that perceive advantages in greater autonomy. To some extent, they represent improvements over prior arrangements, but have run into problems because financial autonomy has not complemented the institutional creation.[17] Also, this kind of limited decentralization has the potential to be subsumed by the much more significant decentralization embodied in the local government reforms discussed in Chapters 11 and 12. This is as it should be, since as discussed in Chapter 2, regional interests or preferences for public goods can be better served with decentralization, irrespective of whether they are articulated by organized interest groups or not, and irrespective of whether the group has a particular ethnic identity or not.

Returning to the original constitutional provisions (with subsequent amendments), the Sixth Schedule—now covering Assam, Meghalaya, Tripura, and Mizoram—provided a more elaborate structure of autonomous district councils in those states than the provisions of the Fifth Schedule. This was motivated, of course, by the greater ethnic and linguistic diversity in the north-eastern region. However, state–district relations in these cases were subject to the general problems of state–local relations throughout the country, as discussed in greater detail in Chapter 13. As listed by Arora (1995), these were 'limited powers, inadequate finances, insufficient autonomy and ... gubernatorial intervention'. Again, the more sweeping general reforms of local government may overtake such special provisions.

The conclusion to draw from the above discussion is that many of the asymmetrical features of federalism below the state level may be dealt with more comprehensively in the broader local government reforms. In some cases, however, the state boundaries do not seem to work, even with

---

[17] See Arora (1995) for further details and references on the formation of these bodies.

such decentralization, in terms of respecting diversity of preferences and identities. This has been reflected in the creation of various new states in the past, and in the current proposal for three new states in tribal or hill areas. It should be noted, as we have discussed above in considering fiscal asymmetries, that tribal or hill areas often have significantly different economic structures, and so the economic reasons for such separate states may reinforce, or even outweigh, reasons based on non-instrumental factors such as 'recognition' of identities.[18]

DURABILITY AND COMMITMENT

By their nature, laws are meant to be somewhat durable, that is, they are expected to last for some time. In practice, of course, informal social norms may have greater durability. Here, we focus on codified laws, whether written down in statutes and regulations, or established by formal judicial precedents. Within this category, there may deliberately be different degrees of durability. Constitutions are meant to be more durable than most laws, and are relatively difficult to amend. Within the particular constitutional framework, specific laws may be changed more easily, by legislative action. Administrative rules and ordinances are the least durable. The durability of judicial precedents is less clear. Ideally, we would expect precedents to make the interpretation of laws more durable than simple administrative procedures.

We begin with a broad discussion of the rationale for durability. We then briefly consider the role of constitutions, as a prelude to a fairly detailed examination of the conflicts in Punjab and Kashmir, whose origins were briefly considered in the previous section. Next, we examine general issues of legislation and administration, topics dealt with in more detail in Chapter 5. We conclude with a summary of arguments.

Rationale

The rationale for durability is two-fold, involving the usual economist's dichotomy of equity and efficiency. The kind of durability built into constitutions involves both. There are protections of individual and—in the case of India and many other countries—group rights against future attack. This may be justified on ethical grounds, rooted in equity considerations. Provisions to protect property rights, such as requiring government compensation for taking private property, may be seen as

---

[18] However, as an example of a case that does not seem to fit this statement, the division of Punjab in 1966 was driven purely by linguistic and religious factors, and not by any obvious differences in economic structure between what became Punjab and Haryana.

enhancing efficiency by reducing investment-inhibiting uncertainty. In practice, any constitutional aspect can have implications for both equity and efficiency. For example, protecting some minority rights may be necessary for their acceptance of the constitution, avoiding either a less efficient composition of the country without the minority, or the costs of future conflict if minority concerns are ignored. Or, in the case of protections for private property, these may be seen in terms of fairness, and a particular attitude towards the status quo distribution of property. Thus, equity and efficiency considerations are not separable in practice.

The efficiency rationale for durability may also be seen in terms of the benefits of pre-commitment (i.e. the ability to publicly stick to some predetermined course of action) to avoid the problem of 'time inconsistency' (Kydland and Prescott, 1977). This term refers to the problem whereby a government or other economic actor may announce a policy, but then have incentives to modify it once others have responded to the policy. If all eventualities can be anticipated, ex ante, having pre-commitment will be better than not having it. If, in some eventualities, there is the likelihood of ex post renegotiation of contracts, laws, rules or agreements, this, too, can be anticipated ex ante. In such cases, some degree of flexibility, by allowing renegotiation, may improve ex post efficiency in some states at the expense of ex ante efficiency. If all eventualities cannot be anticipated, pre-commitment is de facto incomplete. In practice, therefore, the optimal degree of durability is impossible to prescribe in general. Perhaps the only possible, rough generalization is that there should be a trade-off in practice between specificity of laws and their durability, as measured by the difficulty of changing them. We will use this idea to examine the durability of laws in the Indian experience.

The economic literature on governance and on federalism also recognizes the importance of durability and commitment. Thus, Buchanan explicitly distinguishes between constitutional and ordinary legal provisions. Breton (2000) speaks about inextinguishability of units and ownership rights in federalism as compared to a mere decentralized set up. The theory of market preserving federalism, in its emphasis on a common market and hard budget constraints, implicitly assumes some kinds of constitutional commitments to maintain these conditions, though these institutional arrangements are not necessarily spelled out in detail. The rationale for both these approaches is the presumption that ex post incentives for government decision makers will be different than ex ante incentives, and that ex post, government decision makers may be subject to temptations that they would choose to bind themselves against ex ante. Of course, self-interested constitution makers could choose to give

Preface

This book is a partially revised version of my PhD thesis submitted to the University of Delhi. My doctoral work had started more than a decade ago with three counts of dissatisfaction with the existing state of historiography in the field normally referred to as 'medieval India'. The first of these was the fact that the fifteenth century in north India was, with only the rare exception, a barely addressed period. In fact, even these exceptions did not exist at the time when I started thinking about the area of my research. The second point of dissatisfaction issued from the fact that a major chunk of the historiography of this period in North India appeared to have become synonymous with Persian studies. The 'mainstream' histories of 'medieval' North India rarely bothered to consult the large corpus of extant materials in Sanskrit, thus catering lazily to the popular and hugely problematic equation of medieval = Persian = Muslim = foreign. The third point had to do with the disappearance of the regions falling in the present province of Bihar from 'histories of medieval India'. This absence was especially hurtful as I spent the first seventeen years of my life in Jamshedpur, a part of the then undivided Bihar. Under the circumstances, a close study of some of Vidyapati's works came in very handy, since he was a Sanskrit scholar and poet of the fifteenth century, who spent most of his life in north Bihar. Since the inception of my work, there has been some exciting new work in the area, and I discuss some of it in the second chapter of the book. This book, I hope, will add further force to the gathering momentum.

At a time when we are exhorted 24 × 7 to understand politics as the game played by those who occupy the offices of the state and those who aspire to replace them, it is important to recover a slice of history when intellectual ferment, dissemination of ideas, ethical regimes, and cultivation of certain skills, such as those of documentation, seem to have had substantive political consequence in the long term. While this is probably true of all times, it is more starkly visible in a period during which readymade histories and master-narratives of imperial formations were not produced. North India in the 'long fifteenth century' is a case in point when we do have this unusual silence.

When I made the fateful journey from a humble Hindi-medium school to Ramjas College, Delhi, it was a huge task to cope with the heat, dust, English language, and cultural alienation in a metropolitan city. Unfortunately, neither of the two factors that helped me survive and grow in spite of the material hostilities has survived. It was the 'leisurely' pace of the annual system that allowed 'slow-wits' like me to adjust to the demands of the academic rigours of University of Delhi. Come 2010, and that leveller of the academic field was forced to give way to a ruthless system of six-monthly examinations and continuous assessment, with no space to make mistakes and learn on the go.

One of my first companions in the college campus, hardier and more sincere than most of us, was Rakesh. His raw humility, desi humour, extraordinary generosity, and candid affections steadied many wayward souls like myself. He is no more. He would have taken personal pride in this book. I dedicate it to his memory.

Pankaj Jha
September 2018
Delhi

themselves more freedom to act ex post in ways that will benefit them. In the Indian case, the escape clauses in the constitution were more likely to have been motivated by a certain kind of myopia or different perspective on human nature, rather than by any narrow self-interest. Thus, as we have discussed in Chapter 3, the constitution makers saw themselves as benevolent guardians who would continue in that role, or be succeeded by similar noble beings. This was far from, for example, James Madison's views at the time of the framing of the US Constitution, warning that men are not angels.

Constitutions

One may argue that India's Constitution, while avoiding the problem of being over-specific (a charge that has been made about Brazilian constitution-making efforts), has been insufficiently durable. This is because it is too easily amended. The erosion of Kashmir's special constitutional status and its effects on the development of violent conflict in that region illustrate this proposition. This is not directly an economic inefficiency, though the economic costs of such conflicts are great.

If one examines other key amendments to the Indian Constitution, they, too, have tended to have more political than economic consequences, limiting individual rights in some cases, or enhancing the power of the Central government vis-à-vis the states. The efficiency consequences of this lack of durability are not clear. The past and present working of the Indian economy have not necessarily been significantly affected by the lack of constitutional durability, but the consequences for conflict between Centre and states have been more apparent, as is illustrated by the cases of Punjab and Kashmir.

Conflict in Punjab and Kashmir

The conditions for potential conflict between the Centre and groups in Punjab and Kashmir also existed to some extent in other Indian regions. There, too, the result has often been violent conflict. Yet the two cases studied here stand out in terms of the length and persistence of the problems. Despite their initially different characteristics, the nature of the two conflicts has become somewhat similar. Several reasons may be adduced for this development, as we discuss below. The continued, and increasingly salient attempt to define a more exclusively Hindu identity for India also makes these two cases very important.

To the extent that the disagreements involve groups that are avowedly different from the Hindu majority, there is less accommodation on both sides. This is true even though Hinduism itself is an amorphous entity, and there are significant cultural overlaps among different religious groups in the same region, but great differences across regions. What is significant is not only that Sikhs and Muslims stand out as different, but this difference makes it harder for any Central government to make concessions to them, as this is seen as appeasing a group that emphasizes its separateness. This is a theme that is continually harped on by Hindu groups that have been attempting to redefine a 'Greater' Hindu identity. In this respect, the conflicts in Punjab and Kashmir have an important common thread.

Another, related phenomenon has reinforced this commonality. Whereas earlier leaders, for Sikhs and Kashmiris, looked to Western models such as the British colonists or the Soviet revolutionists for ideologies that would provide coherence to their communities, more recent models have been non-European. In particular, the Iranian revolution clearly must have had some impact on the style and consciousness of dissident leaders in Punjab and Kashmir. For Kashmiri Muslims the connection was obvious. What is striking is how the Sikh leader, Bhindranwale, spoke of Sikhism in terms that emphasized its similarity to Islam (as well as Judaism and Christianity) and distinction from Hinduism.

A final parallel in the two conflicts is the impact of exogenous geopolitical events. In particular, the Soviet invasion of Afghanistan clearly had a major impact on the two conflicts. It took place in December 1979, capping a period of several years of instability in that country. The invasion increased Pakistan's strategic importance in the region, since it became the haven for Afghan rebels and conduit for American arms and supplies to them. Many of these arms, as well as some captured from the Soviets, found their way into Punjab and Kashmir. Pakistan also became aggressive in promoting dissidence in the two Indian states. These geopolitical changes help explain why Punjab and Kashmir erupted more in violence than other parts of India, even though other preconditions for conflict could have been present in those other parts.

Economic growth may help ameliorate conflict, to the extent that it allows the Centre to more effectively bribe away dissidence. It pursued this strategy de facto in Punjab, despite the overall pressure on Central government finances, as one part of its response to insurgency. In that respect, there was some similarity between large payments made to Punjab for security expenditures, and the more institutionalized payments received by the special category states, which, as we argued earlier in this chapter, reflect a mix of concerns about cost disabilities and carrots to accept peaceful existence within the Indian Union. Since Punjab is relatively more populous than almost all the special category states, one might speculate that the increasing inability of the Centre to do this in the 1980s, as government finances came under greater pressure, and as statutory transfers were made more progressive, may have made it more difficult to use financial carrots to manage internal unrest. In some respects, the proliferation of subsidies to special interest groups defined by occupation or class (university students, middle-class consumers, farmers, etc.) competes with the use of financial carrots for sub-national units where conflict needs to be controlled. The use of money is rather an obvious and easy way out, if feasible. If the Central government controls more resources it can more easily respond with carrots than sticks to interest group pressures. A subtler lesson also emerges from the above two and other cases of Centre–state conflict in India. In each of the cases, we suggest that the inability of the Centre to credibly commit itself to courses of action has produced conflict. In the case of Kashmir this is a process that began right after the Constitution was framed. A constitution may be viewed precisely as a device for achieving credible commitment: it makes it hard to change agreements that have constitutional status. But in the case of Kashmir, its special status guaranteed in the Constitution was rapidly chipped away through amendments and through gap-closing ordinances and legislation. Punjab, despite Sikh efforts soon after independence, was not able to achieve such special constitutional status, but later negotiations between Sikh political leaders and the Centre illustrate a similar problem of commitment. These were typically negotiations outside any legal framework, in the sense that agreements reached could not be enforced by any court. This effectively removed ex post incentives for the Centre to implement the agreements, since electoral incentives were also not significant: Punjab elects only a little over two per cent of the seats in India's parliament.

Thus, one can argue that the problem in India that has exacerbated conflicts between the Centre and regions such as Punjab and Kashmir is partly an institutional one. First, the constitution is too easily amended. Second, the courts have a very limited jurisdiction vis-à-vis the legislative/executive branch of the government. In either case, the inability of the Centre to make credible commitments reduces the range of mutually beneficial agreements that can be achieved, and exacerbates the potential for conflict. Therefore, one might argue that institutional reform that strengthens the courts and reduces the mutability of the Constitution might help to reduce the likelihood of violent conflicts at the sub-national level. Another way of thinking about this is that groups will invest in violence if they think that the expected payoff from more peaceful ways of pursuing their interests is relatively low. More effective mechanisms for negotiation and enforcement of agreements between a sovereign Central government and constituent governments will improve this trade-off towards less violence.

An opposing, more pessimistic view would be that what matters is not what is on paper, but the ability and desire to implement written-down laws and rules. Taking this position, one can argue that the Indian legal framework was quite strong, with checks and balances incorporated, but actual political practice based on traditions of patron–client relationships was what effectively mattered, so that tinkering with laws would do no good unless social norms were also altered. There is much to be said for this cautionary position, but we believe one can offer examples of specific reforms that might ameliorate conflict, or improve efficiency more generally in the Indian context. In the context of Punjab, for instance, a mechanism for third-party arbitration by the judiciary might have been more effective than the repeated informal negotiations between the Central government and various Sikh political groups from 1985 onwards, which resulted in repeated broken agreements and increased mistrust and violence. Such arbitration would be more in the spirit of actual federalism, rather than informal negotiations between the Centre and regional groups, which undercut the formal federal institutions.

We may summarize our argument based on the two cases studied in this subsection. In India, as in many countries, religious identities are often salient. When they overlap strongly with language, class, geographical contiguity and other dimensions of identity, that bundle is easily activated. It becomes a tool for political mobilization simply because enough dimensions of material and non-material interests coincide. We would argue that the role of leaders in such a process is merely instrumental, in that they effectively package and sell grievances, but cannot do so unless they have a sufficient number of concerns to work with.

Since much collective action is about access to resources, the key question is why such demands may more likely become violent than others. Here we would suggest that this will occur when institutions for bargaining are weak, and this may apply more to such regional groups than, say, to other groups organized on principles such as employment, where well-defined rules for collective bargaining may exist. It is also possible that the strength of identification with one's fellow workers is unlikely to match that created by religion, language, and ethnicity, so that worker groups are less likely to resort to violence. Well-developed social norms, with punishment for transgression, may be more operative for ethnic rather than employment groups, especially in developing countries. Finally, labour groups may also not be able to muster sufficient numbers within a specific region. However, none of these factors is necessarily compelling.

Perhaps more important for the weakness of bargaining institutions are two other factors which make it difficult for the Central government to negotiate such demands. First, reputational effects may be stronger: Kashmiris may push harder if Sikhs succeed, and be more accommodating if they see Sikh militancy crushed, but this may be less likely to apply for two different trade unions in India, unless they are in similar industries or regions.[19] Second, the potential for complete territorial loss and consequent material losses for the rest of the country is obviously greater when a group is concentrated geographically and in a border position. Punjab and Kashmir fit this description well. For both these reasons, the government may not be able to 'give in', and violence is then perceived as the only instrument for pursuing goals.

What may also matter in such cases is economic growth that allows the Centre to more effectively bribe away dissidence. Economic liberalization that increases growth also goes hand-in-hand with a reduction in central political control with respect to matters such as industrial investment. Reducing central power in such dimensions may complement the achievement of more effective bargaining mechanism between the Centre and the states. Changes in effective bargaining power may even substitute for institutional changes that make it easier to enforce commitments.

Legislation and Administration

If we turn to ordinary legislation and administrative regulations, the issue of durability seems more important directly for economic efficiency. However, the problem in the Indian case seems not to have been the one that would be suggested by theory. Much of the legislation and administrative rules that have governed India's economy have been remarkably durable. Despite concerns raised as far back as the 1960s about the basic regime of controls, it was only in the 1990s that any significant changes were made. In terms of the theoretical framework discussed above, investment or other economic actions in India have not been inefficiently

---

[19] Reputational effects also seem to have been at work in the north-east, discussed in the previous subsection. Beginning with Nagaland, there has been a sequential elevation of union territories to statehood, or the creation of new states out of parts of existing ones, with consequent greater autonomy. In these cases, the perception of the north-east as a special region has limited the political impacts on the rest of the nation, though movements for greater autonomy within Uttar Pradesh, Bihar, and Madhya Pradesh were somewhat similar to those of hill peoples in the north-east. These movements took a long time to succeed, but ultimately did lead to the formation of the states of Uttaranchal, Jharkhand, and Chhattisgarh.

inhibited by the lack of durability of the day-to-day laws and rules governing such actions. Indeed, one could argue that economic actors in India have operated very efficiently in this context: knowing that the domestic market was protected and regulated, entrepreneurs, bureaucrats, and politicians behaved accordingly, often making long-term investments in things that mattered, such as relationships with politicians, or political careers. The inefficiency has been, therefore, in the particular laws themselves, not in their lack of durability. However, this inefficiency raises the question of its origins, and its persistence.

Suppose that we adopt the position, suggested by an optimal contracting view of legislation, that particular laws or administrative regulations were ex ante efficient when introduced. Why were they not reversed or modified when ex post inefficiencies became apparent? The general answer, which we attribute to Bardhan (1984), is that enough groups with sufficient political influence were deriving benefits from the current system to block changes in legislation (a 'multiple veto system'). This view suggests that durability of laws is not just dependent on formal legislative rules, such as majority voting to pass legislation, but also the microeconomics of the organization of the legislature.

Inman and Rubinfeld (1997), for example, distinguish between two types of legislatures: minimum winning coalition (MWC) and universalistic (U), as we have discussed in Chapter 2. Policies chosen in the MWC legislature would reflect the preferences of the winning majority. With multidimensional policies, this would, in turn, depend on factors such as agenda rules, to overcome preference-cycle problems. In U legislatures, such problems are overcome by adherence to an informal norm of deference (mutual back-scratching). Empirical research for the United States (Weingast and Marshall, 1988; Hall and Grofman, 1990), suggests that U legislatures lead to higher allocations of public goods. However, to the extent that the government not only provides public goods but also makes redistributive transfers, these will also be higher with U-type legislatures.

We conjecture that the Indian context seems to fit the U legislature model, and the proliferation and persistence of interest group subsidies in India, including indirect or in-kind subsidies involved in the protections provided by legislation such as the Industrial Disputes Act (see Datta-Chaudhuri, 1994, and Menon and Debroy, 1995, Chapters 1 and 2), can be explained by this reinterpretation of Bardhan's analysis. Note that in this application of the idea to India, geographically based local public goods, the focus of Inman and Rubinfeld, are replaced or supplemented by interest group benefits. Clearly the states constitute an important class of such interest groups.

A further point also needs to be made. Inman and Rubinfeld's discussion assumes that legislators are acting on behalf of their median constituents. In practice, especially in the Indian case (and no doubt in other countries also), legislators may be substantially influenced by direct and indirect payments from beneficiaries of legislation. If rent creation leads to such rewards for legislators, legislation that creates rents is likely to come about, and to endure, due to the sharing of those rents by legislators. This is, of course, a well-known observation in the Indian context. This point, unlike the one about the organization of the legislature, also applies to bureaucrats, and the implementation and durability of rules and regulations that create rents is likely to be biased by this process.

Thus, the issue of the optimal degree of durability of laws (how hard are they to change?) is not simple, in that there is no single answer. For protecting individual rights and freedoms, the Indian Constitution seems to have been too easy to amend. But the efficiency consequences of that lack of durability are only indirect, through the effects of conflict. In other contexts, everyday laws and regulations, things have been often too hard to change, owing to the creation of rents, and interests in protecting those rents. Starting from a discussion of durability, we have thus come to the public choice position of Buchanan, Olson, Tullock, and many others, outlined in Chapter 2. Their answer to the problem of 'Leviathan' government is political competition, both through decentralization, and through effective democracy. We shall see that rent-seeking crops up again in the discussion of enforcement of laws in the next chapter. Decentralization is discussed in Chapter 13.

Institutions Governing Centre–state Relations

Responding to continued concerns about the nature of Centre–state relations, in particular, the perception of states that the balance of power in the Indian Union was inordinately tilted toward the Centre, the Central government appointed a commission, to examine Centre–state relations under the chairmanship of Justice R.S. Sarkaria of the Supreme Court. The mandate of the Commission was broader than that of previous bodies including the Administrative Reforms Committee of the late 1960s.[20] The 'Sarkaria Commission' submitted its report in 1988 in two volumes with numerous recommendations, many of which remained unaddressed by the Centre.

[20] To some extent, the 1983 Commission picked up the ball from the report of the Rajammanar Committee that was appointed by the Tamil Nadu government in the 1960s to investigate issues of Centre–state relations.

The conceptual framework that has driven the Sarkaria Commission and other attempts to smoothen Centre–state relations has been which goes within the rubrik of 'cooperative federalism'. Policy recommendations that emerge are often then simply exhortations to get along with each other, as already discussed with respect to the Sarkaria Commission's response to Nagaland's concerns about mineral rights. As we argue in Chapter 10, in the context of water resources, the difficult problems are often ones where the conflict is over the assignment of rights, and one party in a dispute can gain only at another's expense. This is not to say that situations where there are potential mutual gains are always ones where they are achieved. The issue is really one of appropriate institutions for bargaining.

Inman and Rubinfeld, as discussed in Chapter 2, and earlier in this chapter, do try to interpret cooperative federalism as a particular institutional arrangement, involving veto power by any constituent of the federation. In this interpretation, cooperative federalism has never been, and can never be, an accurate description of the Indian arrangement.

Staying with the issue of different types of bargaining games, we may note that measures such as the creation of an Inter-State Council in 1990 (recommended by the Sarkaria Commission in its report) can be viewed as attempts to improve the protocols for potential bargaining games, so that information flows more effectively and cooperative outcomes are more likely to be attained where Pareto improvements are indeed possible. In practice, the Inter-state Council has been ineffectual, and Parliament remains the primary forum for raising concerns about Centre–state issues. This is in keeping with the approach taken by Inman and Rubinfeld, where the organization of the central legislature is the key institutional arrangement of federalism. In this context, it is worth noting that Arora highlights proposals (in particular, by Singh, 1991) for strengthening the role of the Rajya Sabha as a true 'Council of States', a role that has been played effectively in the United States, for example, by the Senate.[21]

The ineffectiveness of the Inter-state Council was presaged by the failure of previous zonal councils to achieve anything significant. The Sarkaria Commission recommended that these zonal councils be part of a grid or hierarchy, with the Inter-state Council at the apex, but this recommendation was not adopted. The zonal councils, in any case, were ineffective because they were viewed as control instruments of the Centre. States cooperate in dealing with the Centre when they perceive the need, as in joint memoranda to the central finance commissions.

---

[21] See, for example, Wheare (1953) for a very positive appraisal of the US Senate.

In many respects, previous commentaries on institutional reform of the federal system have not addressed the heart of the issues. In our view, these issues lie with the relationships between different branches of government and different components of the bureaucracy, and with the nature of an assignment of revenue and expenditure authority that creates large vertical fiscal imbalances. The latter question will be taken up in subsequent chapters.

CONCLUSIONS

This chapter has discussed a wide range of issues related to control and commitment. Control reflects the desire of the Centre to maintain the federation intact, as well, perhaps, as the desire to increase its power within the existing federal structures. The former motive may be possessed both by benevolent and by self-interested government decision makers while the latter motive is clearly driven by self-interest. In any case, control cannot be absolute, and, in particular, a constitution, however centralizing its features, does in general provide some checks on the Centre's powers. Thus, the problem of control is a problem of bargaining, and the Indian Constitution has special structures to accommodate variations in initial conditions with respect to bargaining games. Kashmir was in a particularly special position at the time of Indian independence, while the various north-eastern hill states established similar special positions as the Indian nation evolved. The resulting special constitutional provisions illustrate what has been generally referred to as 'asymmetrical federalism': asymmetries in characteristics, if great enough,[22] are reflected in constitutional asymmetries.

While political scientists have often highlighted institutional asymmetries, we have also, in this chapter, explored, in this context, the role of fiscal transfers. Vertical fiscal transfers, so important in India, become a major way to back up or supplement constitutional provisions. Thus, asymmetries in characteristics drive asymmetries in initial assignments as well as asymmetries in fiscal transfers from the Centre to the states. The difference between the two reflects not just dimensions of resources, but also degrees of commitment.

Issues of commitment and durability have been broadly discussed in terms of Centre–state political conflicts. The degree and nature of

---

[22] Another well-known example of this phenomenon, from outside India, is Quebec in Canada. Note that, Punjab has been analysed in this chapter as a case where there were asymmetries, but not of a nature or degree sufficient to generate special structures at the constitutional level.

commitment, as emphasized in the discussion on the basic nature of federalism (as well as the special case of market preserving federalism) in Chapter 2, is important because the essence of federalism is a binding commitment by the Centre to not exercise its sovereignty fully over constituent units. Issues we explored in this section were the absence of certain kinds of commitment in the Indian Constitution—essentially commitments by the Centre not to exercise certain kinds of control, the weakness of other institutional structures for achieving commitment—checks and balances of the kind that will be explored further in Chapter 5, and the problem of non-durability of initial commitments through amendment of the constitution. While various committees on Centre–state relations have tried to come to grips with these issues in the past, we have offered here what we hope is a clearer analytical framework for discussion of problems of Centre–state relations.

5

☒

Dimensions of Federal Governance

INTRODUCTION

In this chapter, we continue the themes of Chapter 4, and examine more closely the different institutions of governance, paying particular attention to their interaction with federal structures. We examine the conduct of electoral politics and the federal structures of India's political parties, as well as of the judiciary, police, and bureaucracy. These governance structures must be examined in order to understand the actual workings of the constitutional assignment of functions and revenue sources to be discussed in Chapters 6–8, and to gain better insight into the issues of commitment raised in Chapter 4.

This chapter continues our examination of the functioning of India's institutions of governance. We use the term 'governance' somewhat broadly. Williamson (1994), following Davis and North (1971), for example, distinguishes between the institutional environment ('the set of fundamental political, social, and legal ground rules') and institutions of governance ('arrangements between economic units that govern the ways in which these units can cooperate and/or compete'). This distinction is hard to draw in practice. In fact, it seems that the institutional environment in India deserves scrutiny, as it affects governance in practice. Therefore, we focus attention on some aspects of the legislative and executive branches of government, the judiciary, and the bureaucracy, as well as the role of non-governmental organizations. Thus our use of 'governance' is close to that of Manor (1995), who uses the term to mean 'both the political system and relations between state and society'.[1] In exploring these themes, we will focus on the structures of Indian federalism.

---

[1] Lewis (1995), in a definition similar in scope describes governance more picturesquely

One may view the question of governance as being, ultimately, about the making and enforcing of laws. While classical economic models took the assignment and enforcement of property rights, and other laws affecting economic exchange, as given and exogenous, much recent work has focused on endogenizing these aspects, and analysing the institutions of legislation and enforcement. While the political process is about the making of laws, their refinement and implementation lies with the bureaucracy, and enforcement is the responsibility of the police and judiciary, acting in complementary fashion. The police monitors, investigates, and prevents immediate violation where possible. The judiciary examines evidence and it rules on innocence, guilt, and punishments. It is this possibility of punishment that acts as a deterrent to violating the law. We treat each of these dimensions of governance in turn, in the context of India's federal system.

The structure of the chapter is as follows. We begin with an examination of political parties followed by the bureaucracy, the judiciary, and the police. Next, we briefly discuss the issue of 'checks and balances' versus 'multiple vetoes'. The chapter includes a consideration of the possible roles of non-governmental action and of civil society, as well as alternative structures of institutions of governance, leading to the analysis of local government in Chapter 11. We conclude with an assessment of the different dimensions of government in Indian federalism.

POLITICAL PARTIES

To the extent that the essence of federalism is based on democratic politics, the role of political parties, in particular the interactions between central and state-level politics, are crucial aspects of federal structures. To illustrate this importance, consider the extreme case where government powers are notionally decentralized, with residuary powers residing at the state level, but the national and all state governments are all controlled by a single, rigidly hierarchical political party. In such a case, the outcome will effectively be the same as in a centralized, unitary system.

In this section, we go from an overview of trends towards decentralization of party politics in India, to a consideration of the role and functioning of regional parties, and a discussion of issues of heterogeneity that links back to the discussion in Chapter 4. We then examine the question of what happens when state-level political competition becomes unstable,

---

as the politics, but, even more, the texture and machinery of government, the bureaucracy, and its interactions with politicians and interests'.

in particular the role of Article 356 of the Constitution that allows the imposition of president's rule. A summary of our arguments concludes the section.

Decentralizing Trends

As described in Chapter 2, Riker and Schaps's measure of the degree of centralization in a federation is based on the level of political harmony, measured in turn by an index of concordance between which party is in power at the Centre, and which parties are in power at the various constituents of the sub-national, here state level. While this is clearly not the only relevant aspect for measuring centralization—fiscal control being equally if not more important, as we have argued—it is certainly a key measure for assessing this dimension of governance.

Riker (1975) noted the increasing decentralization of Indian federalism, measured according to this sort of index, after the Nehru era. Events after he wrote this represented a period where this trend was resisted by the Centre, in the increased use of Article 356 of the Constitution to remove elected state governments and impose direct central rule, and, in an extreme manifestation, in the Emergency imposed by Indira Gandhi in 1975. However, the last decade has seen a resumption of the decentralizing trend, with regional parties becoming more significant, and diversity in the composition of governments at the Centre and in the various states becoming an ordinary situation.

Brass (1994) also reached the conclusion that political decentralization has been increasing, arguing that the increased use of Article 356 to impose president's rule (P.R.) in the states was a response to the trend, rather than an indicator of a movement in the other direction. In fact, comparing the later period with the Nehruvian approach, Brass states:

The increased frequency of its [P.R.] use represents less an increase in centralizing tendencies than a shift in the instruments of central intervention and the arenas of center-state relations. The principal instrument of central intervention has become the central government and administration rather than the Congress organization. The arenas of center-state relations have also shifted from the Congress organization to the state legislatures and the electoral process.

Given the reduced importance of the Congress party in various dimensions, including geographic, this shift in instruments is unsurprising.

Even as the Bhartiya Janata Party (BJP) has built up a national constituency to rival that of the Congress, the importance of regional parties has not diminished. The days when regional groups operated only within national parties seem to be over, and most states have significant parties whose bases are *only* regional. In some cases, parties with only regional presences are organized on the basis of ideology (the CPM in Kerala and West Bengal in particular), but parties such as the DMK, AIADMK, Telugu Desam, and Akali Dal have regional interests as their raison d'etre.[2] This situation will clearly persist. Hence, Centre–state political competition will remain very much out in the open, rather than take place within party organizations. We next consider regional political parties in more detail.

Regional Parties

Manor (1995) provides a recent analysis of the role of regional parties in India's federal system. The key elements of his analysis are the following. First, of the three main elements of the national party system—the Congress, the BJP, and a 'centre-left bloc'—only the third of these involves regional parties as such. These regional parties are each typically strong in one state only, though they may play significant roles in national-level coalitions.[3] Second, the Congress has always tended to encompass regional alliances, and has therefore had a federal structure within the party organization. The tendency under Indira and Rajiv Gandhi to try to overcome this through centralization of the party structure and personal loyalty did not and could not become a permanent arrangement, given the heterogeneity of interests of the components of the party. Third, the BJP itself, as it strives to become more of a national party, and not one just based in the Hindi heartland, has had to become more decentralized in nature, if not quite federal. The consequence of these first three points, in our view, is to recognize that India's formal federal structures are well reflected in its party politics. The states, because they command significant resources, because they are often large relative to the Centre, and finally because they are relatively homogeneous linguistic units, are bound to be important political arenas, and political competition at the state level will have a life of its own.

Manor's tripartite division may be somewhat oversimplified, to the extent that regional parties do not necessarily have an ideology that places them in the 'Centre-left' of the spectrum. Brass (1994, Chapter 4) analyses regional parties in greater detail. The conclusion that the states will remain significant arenas of political competition is unchanged by such an analysis. Brass does add another point worth considering. He comments

---

[2] This is not to say that religion, caste, and class do not matter—these do come into play, and restrict such parties' appeal to regional subgroups.

[3] It is interesting to note that Manor was writing before, and somewhat presciently about, the 1996 elections which brought the United Front government to power at the Centre.

on the nature of institutionalization of regional political parties, and notes that some are rather ephemeral, more in the nature of the factions so common within parties, factions defined solely by loyalty to a particular individual. To some extent, this is true even of parties that have long histories, such as the DMK and its descendants. Charismatic leaders are able to define combinations of political followers in ways that are rare in, say, Britain or the US. While this phenomenon may be stronger at the regional level, it is also present at the national level, and in the last analysis, it does not seem to significantly affect the fact of decentralization, along regional and state lines, of political parties.

Dimensions of Heterogeneity

Manor (1995) makes another significant observation with respect to state-level politics. A central point of his analysis, based on a recognition of the various dimensions of heterogeneity in identities (language, religion, different forms of tribal allegiance, caste, and so on), is that there is not obviously a single fault line along which conflict can become concentrated and persist. As a consequence, he also notes that states with boundaries based on language have not become the basis for secession because of the heterogeneity of identities that exist within each state. Exceptions to Manor's observation exist, of course: we have discussed the cases of Punjab, Kashmir, and the north-eastern states in Chapter 4. In such cases, different dimensions of identity coincide enough to lead to concentrated, persistent conflict, exacerbated by inappropriate Central government responses. In fact, one might argue that unfettered electoral political competition at the state level is likely to ameliorate such conflicts *whatever* the fault lines that exist.[4]

With some caveats, therefore, Manor's analysis also has favourable implications for extending party politics more firmly down to the local level, as is envisaged in the recent legislative changes to strengthen local government: these issues are taken up in Chapter 13. It is also possible to relate Manor's observation to the discussion in Chapter 2: federal political structures allow the provision of a greater diversity in local (or, more generally, sub-national) public goods, by improving accountability and

---

[4] There are clearly many subtleties to be considered here. The statement made implicitly assumes something like a median voter model, where the median voter does not benefit from secession. It is also possible that, given a set of central policies, the median voter would prefer secession. This still might be resolved by Centre–state bargaining within the realm of normal politics, rather than violent conflict, if bargaining is permitted to proceed within the appropriate institutional framework for achieving durable agreements. These issues were discussed in Chapter 4.

incentives at this level. They also allow an unbundling of this provision from that of national public goods, and to that extent they make complete separation, to enjoy the benefits of local diversity, unnecessary. Thus, Tamil Nadu, where a regional party has been continuously in power for long periods of time (though often in coalition with the Congress) can enjoy considerable autonomy in many spheres, without having to give up the benefits of defence being provided at the national level. Such an argument assumes, of course, that a regional party provides certain benefits that cannot be delivered by the state-level organization of a national party. For example, a Tamil party may appeal to constituents per se, even if the public goods provided by it are no different from those provided by a national party.[5]

State-level Politics and Article 356

A discussion of political parties at the state level is perhaps an appropriate place to consider the issue of Article 356 and president's rule in more detail. We earlier noted Brass's views on how to interpret the increased use of president's rule in analysing decentralizing trends. Here we look more carefully at the rationale for such use. In doing so, we foreshadow some of the discussion of the judiciary's role, and of the issue of checks and balances, later in this chapter. Manor's analysis again provides a useful take-off point.

Manor views Article 356 of the Constitution as having the positive potential to allow the Centre to 'cool off' regional conflicts, by suspending normal party politics at the state level, and acting as an impartial negotiator. While this echoes Breton's view of the monitoring and regulatory role of Central governments in a federal system, applied not just to interstate but also intra-state competition that is potentially inefficient or destructive, it does seem to rely on, as Manor says, 'enlightened central leaders'. The problems here are not only with impartiality and enlightenment.[6] There is also a problem of commitment, as highlighted in the previous chapter, where a sovereign Centre may not have an ex post incentive to follow through on informal agreements. In the case of Article 356, the Centre has a difficult time in committing not to use it liberally: the conditions under which it may be properly applied are subject to varied interpretations.

[5] In practice, an independent regional party is better able to credibly commit to certain policies—the state wing of a national party might, in the minds of voters, and in practice be subject to national-level control.

[6] Leaders are self-interested, and this problem will be heightened when the ruling party at the Centre has a stake in forming a government at the state level.

If we discard the assumption of benevolence, as we have suggested is appropriate in our own analysis, the question remains as to what can be done when normal politics, including party competition at the state level, no longer works. One possible answer lies in a stronger system of checks and balances at the central level, which will constrain the legislative branch at the Centre. First, it should be more difficult to extend central rule in a state: firm deadlines for negotiation between the Centre and the state concerned are likely to reduce the hazard of applying Article 356 inappropriately. Second, there should be some method of enforcing agreements. For this to be achieved for a sovereign Centre, the two possibilities are a stronger role for the judiciary at the Centre, that is, the Supreme Court, and a stronger executive, that is, the president.[7]

We consider the judiciary first, and make two observations. First, the suggestion of judicial checks raises the issue of the benevolence of the judiciary. We must put this off to the subsection that deals with that institution. Second, the Supreme Court, as interpreter of the Constitution, has ruled that the use of Article 356 is subject to judicial review. However, the Court can decide only after the event is over, and there is no mechanism to bring the situation to the status quo ante. Finally, the exercise of this power by the Court raises the issue of conflict between the two branches of government. Ultimately, of course, the legislative branch may win this conflict. But if the benefits of such a win are tested by the process of electoral accountability, the conflict between the two branches has the virtues of being rule-bound and transparent, which are ultimately missing from the Centre's negotiation with the state government outside of any formal institution.

Turning to the executive branch, the Indian reality has tended to be one where the national executive (the president and governors)[8] has been subsidiary to the legislative branch, with an executive-style prime minister. However, in recent times the president has used his advisory powers to turn back an attempt to use Article 356 in a situation where, in the past, the state government (in this case, Uttar Pradesh) might have been dismissed with impunity. This may be a transitory phenomenon, involving an independent president and a very weak Central government, with the

---

[7] In many respects, the president is only a nominal executive, with the prime minister and cabinet playing that role in fact. However, this is not entirely fixed by the Constitution, and the present president has demonstrated the possibilities of exercising real authority precisely in the context of the use of Article 356. See below.

[8] Governors are appointed on the advice of the prime minister, and this has made them politically subservient to that office. While we do not pursue their role in detail here, we note that the suggestion that they be elected at the state level has merit.

structural weakness of the executive remaining. However, if coalitions at the Centre become more the norm, and the Supreme Court is assertive, the president's role may continue to be more significant than in the past.[9]

Conclusions

To sum up, national political parties in India have incentives to be federal in the nature of their organizations, following the federal structure of Indian government itself. At the same time, purely regional parties may have certain advantages over state-level units of national parties, when regional identities are strong. Issues of commitment and control may arise in political party structures, just as they do in the case of different levels of government, as analysed in Chapter 4. The question of how to manage breakdowns in state-level party politics raises issues of checks and balances among different branches of government. These issues will be explored further later in this chapter. We turn from political parties to a discussion of the component of government that actually implements the will of politicians, namely, the bureaucracy.

THE BUREAUCRACY

If elected politicians act as agents of constituents or voters, bureaucrats in turn act as the agents of elected officials. Bureaucrats are partly insulated from political whims and pressures, but ultimately in a democracy must be subordinate to the people's elected representatives. This means that a unitary, hierarchical bureaucracy cannot by itself negate a federal political structure in the same way that a powerful, centralized, national political party might. However, a centralized bureaucracy can act as the agent of such a political party, in acting against the requirements of a federal system. There are elements of such action in the workings of Indian bureaucracy, but the story is also a more complicated one.

In this section, we first provide an overview of the Indian bureaucracy and its structure, then examine the incentive conflicts that arise as a result of this structure, and the efficiency consequences that have sometimes followed. We conclude with a discussion of the bureaucracy's role vis-à-vis federal political structures.

[9] Although the president is required by the Constitution to sign if the proposal to dismiss a state government is sent back to him, such an action by the president has enormous significance for two reasons. First, the aggrieved party at the state level would really have a more favourable case in the Supreme Court because even the president was not convinced that the law and order situation has broken down. More importantly, this could have a very adverse electoral impact for the party ruling at the Centre, given its weakness and the likelihood that the neutral electorate would disapprove the partisan move by the Centre.

Overview

The bureaucracy in India has played a crucial role in the country's governance since independence, and this role has been an important aspect of the conflicts over the degree of centralization or federalism. The bureaucracy has not only enforced myriad regulations in the realm of industry and trade, simply by its power to say 'no', but some of its members have also acted directly in judicial roles. This has been through the magistrate's role accorded to members of the Indian Administrative Service (IAS), in direct descent from pre-independence governance structures, particularly in rural areas.[10] What is particularly noteworthy in understanding Indian bureaucracy is that it is provided constitutional recognition. The central and state-level tiers of the 'public services' are given shape through the provisions of part XIV of the Constitution.

Of course, any bureaucracy in a federation will have a federal character in the sense that each layer of government requires its own administrative apparatus to accompany the political structures. In particular, state governments must be able to appoint (and dismiss) bureaucrats to implement state-level policies: this would seem to be an essential consequence of a federal structure of government. This is certainly the case in India, where there is a central bureaucracy as well as an independent bureaucracy in each state, as indicated by the Constitution.

However, the federal structures of Indian bureaucracy are complicated—some might say muddied—by the dual allegiance of key components of the central bureaucracy, in particular the IAS.[11] The IAS is an all-India bureaucratic hierarchy, in the sense that its members are chosen by a central process, and trained together in a national academy. However, they are then assigned to particular states, and become, technically as well as in most practical matters, members of a state-level bureaucratic hierarchy as well. This structure is an ingenious one, which has performed a reasonable job of succession to the British-era 'steel frame' of administration, the Indian Civil Service (ICS). It has coped with demands placed on it that far exceeded those made on the ICS, including not just daily administration and law and order, but also the implementation of a formal process of development planning that was completely absent in the colonial period. We shall restrict our focus to its interaction with India's federal political institutions.

---

[10] The police and the formal judiciary remain important, of course, as a back-up, if decisions of administrators are not respected.

[11] The Indian Police Service (IPS) also has this structure. We take up the police later.

Incentive Conflicts

As noted, the key feature of the IAS is its dual structure of allegiance, to the Centre and to the member's 'home' (more accurately, assigned) state. While all of an IAS member's early career is spent within the home state, and while senior-level appointments at the state level carry considerable power and prestige, the most prestige and power, and the greatest attraction as a result, lie with appointments within the Central government. Thus, while the structure of the IAS was designed as a compromise between, on the one hand, the desire to have an effective administrative apparatus at the governmental level to which most of the tasks of day-to-day administration, development, and law and order were assigned by the Constitution (i.e. the state level), and, on the other hand, the fear of promoting regional loyalties over national ones (with the further fear of disintegration of the nation), this compromise has been inherently problematic. Essentially, a bureaucracy in a democratic system is the administrative tool of elected politicians, and a lack of clear lines of authority creates difficulties for incentives. To some extent, of course, the incomplete decentralization of the IAS simply mirrors or parallels the ambiguities inherent in the political structures of Indian federalism. However, it seems that the last decade has seen federalism in the operation of electoral politics, as discussed in the previous subsection, outstrip the more rigid structures of the bureaucracy. As long as the most important positions in the state-level bureaucracies are held by members of an organization with political masters at two different levels, incentive conflicts will continue to arise.

This is not to say that greater decentralization of the bureaucracy will remove all such problems. There are, of course, hierarchies and levels within each state. And the differing incentives of bureaucrats and elected politicians will always lead to conflicts. B. Sivaraman, a member of the ICS, whose members continued alongside the new IAS after independence, provides many examples of the distortion of supposedly impartial administrative decision-making by political pressures in his (1991) memoirs. In one case, in Orissa in 1959, a village panchayat refused permission to construct a temple in a particular location. The thwarted village group petitioned the state government to overrule the panchayat. Sivaraman, as chief secretary (the highest administrative post in the state) made a recommendation upholding the panchayat's decision, supported by the relevant state minister. The chief minister, from a different party in the coalition government in the state, was forced to accept this advice, because of prior agreement among the coalition members to govern such situations, despite a direct appeal to him by the pro-temple group. A victory for rules and transparency and checks and balances? Not quite: shortly thereafter, Sivaraman reports, he was transferred by the chief minister! In his concluding chapters, Sivaraman notes the increasingly widespread use of transfers of administrators and bureaucrats as a means of exercising political control, especially in the last two decades. Wade (1988), in his studies of south Indian irrigation systems too, has detailed similar phenomena.

To some extent, the problem for the bureaucracy is unavoidable, since it must be subordinate to the elected representatives of the people in a democracy.[12] As long as the incentives of politicians are not addressed, not much can be done about providing appropriate incentives to the bureaucracy. This suggests that too much judicial power should not be vested in the bureaucracy, either in rural magistrates, or in those who implement and enforce administrative rules and regulations. Such power will always be susceptible to distortion by political influence. On the other hand, there is no reason for the regular judiciary to be as subordinate to the political system as it has become in India. Politicians have come to use their powers of appointment and transfer over the judiciary in heavy-handed ways as well, but the judiciary in its basic concept is more independent of politicians than is the bureaucracy. While politicians will always control the purse strings, within this constraint, the Indian judiciary can be strengthened in ways that enhance its ability to enforce the law.

Efficiency of Bureaucratic Interventions

The above argument for constraining the bureaucracy, lest it become corrupted, is worth further analysis. Sivaraman—not surprisingly—emphasizes the positive role in Indian development played by the bureaucracy of which he was a part, especially when it was not subject to arbitrary political control. He, in fact, did play an important role in initiating the Indian 'Green Revolution'. Case studies and discussions of the experience of Punjab, the state that was at the leading edge of this revolution, buttress this view with accounts of the positive part played by state-level bureaucrats and technocrats. Bureaucratic governance has also been suggested as a positive factor in East Asia's growth. In both these cases, politicians and bureaucrats seem to have collaborated effectively. In both Punjab and East Asia, one can explain this as a case of politicians

[12] We should note, however, that a variety of arrangements could exist within this constraint. In particular, checks and balances between the legislature and executive may affect the functioning of the bureaucracy. Manor (1992) provides contrasting examples of Indian states. In Haryana in 1982, bureaucrats were browbeaten by individual state legislators, while in Karnataka, they were protected from such pressure by a strong chief minister.

having appropriate incentives flowing from their constituents (e.g. middle peasants in Punjab), though, in East Asia, this would require an indirect argument, appealing to factors beyond electoral pressures.

In contrast to these successful bureaucratic interventions, we may note the relative failure of bureaucratic governance in Indian industry and trade. The erstwhile Soviet Union and its former satellites provide other examples of bureaucratic inefficiency. Shleifer (1994), in discussing these cases, and their difficulties of transition from central planning, provides a thoughtful analysis that points to where the differences may lie, in addition to the discipline of the electorate. Shleifer's argument is based on inefficient control structures or property rights, and is as follows. According to Grossman and Hart (1986), property rights are residual control rights over assets. Shleifer further distinguishes between physical and legal rights, the latter being protected by the courts. If there is a divergence between the two types of rights, so that bureaucrats or politicians have extensive physical control rights, final allocations after Coasian bargaining are not enforceable by the courts, so Coasian bargains, and hence efficiency, cannot necessarily be achieved. The focus on property rights points out how to resolve the puzzle of different qualities of bureaucratic interventions.

The answer we give is a very conventional one. If the scope of bureaucratic control extends too heavily to physical property rights, then rent seeking, corruption, and inefficiency are a likely result, as discussed by Shleifer and others. However, where bureaucratic interventions are limited to providing public goods, such as information on new technologies or seed varieties; or correcting externalities, such as by subsidizing credit or inputs; or doing both, such as by creating appropriate institutional forms, there is a greater likelihood of positive effects. This seems to fit well with the Indian case, where farmers did not have to get permission to sow more land, or switch crops, whereas industrialists needed bureaucratic approval to expand capacity or switch product lines.

Bureaucracy and Federalism

The issues of the efficiency consequences of the scope of governance are, to some extent, independent of the structures of federalism. They point to guidelines for constraining bureaucratic interventions at any level, whether national or sub-national. However, it should be noted that the consequences of mistakes in assignment with respect to bureaucratic authority are more likely to be felt in a centralized structure. In other words, competitive federalism is more likely to lead to corrections than in a unitary state, to the extent that electoral monitoring and incentives are more effective in a federal system, as discussed in Chapter 2. While competition among sub-national jurisdictions may lead to a race to the bottom in tax rates or environmental regulations, it also puts more pressure on politicians to correct mistakes in bureaucratic decision making than may exist in a centralized system.

In the final analysis, the structural questions of bureaucratic organization in a federal political system remain important ones for India. The need for members of the IAS to explicitly or implicitly serve two masters—state and central-level politicians—has contributed to the attenuation of state government autonomy in the Indian context, since politicians rely on bureaucrats for policy implementation. Decentralization of political competition, analysed earlier, increases the potential for conflict in this regard. A similar issue arises with the constitutional creation of a third tier of Indian government, at the local level. Even if local governments are able to effectively hire and fire bureaucratic employees at this level, such employees will have neither the official nor the de facto status possessed by central and state-level bureaucrats. If the latter's scope of authority is not properly circumscribed local governments may themselves be hampered.[13]

THE JUDICIARY

The judiciary is, in some respects, a specialized bureaucracy, but one with a potential degree of independence that is not possessed even by the IAS in India. The IAS and other branches of the bureaucracy act as agents of elected officials in implementing policies that are in theory designed to meet the wishes of constituents. As such, the bureaucracy is part of the legislative and/or executive branches of government. On the other hand, the judiciary is conceptually more separate, constituting a distinct branch of government at its higher levels. While much judicial activity involves judging whether the law was broken and who broke the law in particular cases, in which capacity the judiciary acts as a specialized agent of elected officials who frame laws, the higher levels of the judiciary also act as judges of the laws themselves within the context of the overarching legal and constitutional framework. Furthermore, the judiciary in theory can check

[13] These issues are discussed in Chapter 11. We may also briefly relate this issue to the perspective of earlier chapters. The essence of federalism is the nature of the assignment of tax and expenditure authorities. In order that formal assignments are translated into real ones, the capacity for collecting taxes and making the right expenditures must be present. Bureaucrats are essentially specialists with this capacity, acting as agents of politicians, who are in turn agents of constituents.

the actions of politicians in ways that may be difficult for bureaucrats: 'no one is above the law'. Practice diverges from ideals, of course, and the how and why of this divergence make up this section.

We begin with an overview of judicial structures in India, then turn to a specific discussion of the judiciary at the local level. A fairly detailed examination of the efficiency of judicial processes in India is followed by an overall assessment.

Overview

The Supreme Court of India stands at the top of the judicial hierarchy. Its powers include broad original and appellate jurisdiction and the right to judge the constitutionality of laws passed by Parliament. In practice, there has been conflict between the Supreme Court and the legislature, or more exactly, the prime minister acting as executive, over the scope of these powers, and their boundaries remain subject to bargaining. At times, such as during the Emergency, the Supreme Court seemed to be overawed by the prime minister, while more recently it has reasserted its powers. Justices of the Court are appointed by the president, in consultation with the prime minister. In practice, this has given the prime minister a major say in appointments, and Indira Gandhi in particular used this power to try to control or influence the Supreme Court.

At the state level, below the Supreme Court, are the high courts. Each high court's justices are appointed by the president again, this time in consultation with the chief justice of the Supreme Court and the state's governor. Paralleling the situation at the Centre, the state's chief minister is in a position to strongly influence the governor's advice. High courts also have both original and appellate jurisdiction. In addition, they super-intend the work of all courts within the state, including in particular the district courts, and also various courts subordinate to the district courts. These subordinate courts are specialized, with smaller civil matters being separated out from criminal cases, for example. Criminal cases are dealt with in magistrates' courts. As we noted, bureaucrats may fulfil such magisterial roles also.

The formal judiciary, then, constitutes a well-defined hierarchy, with a relatively clear assignment of tasks. This assignment and hierarchy appear to be overly centralized, in the sense that not enough matters are disposed of at lower-level courts. This partly reflects a lack of resources devoted to lower-level courts (though, as we discuss below, the resource problem exists at all levels), but also simply a centralized assignment of the scope of jurisdictions. The problem is compounded by the nature of the appeals process, and by the failure of higher-level courts to control appeals. Note also that judges below the state level are typically not appointed by local government officials, representing a significant departure from a federal system below the state level. This is taken up in detail in Chapter 11, though we briefly review local judicial functions next.

Local-level Judiciary

In practice, in many cases in India, the formal judiciary does not directly control or enter into the legal process. Several examples of alternative enforcement structures exist in India. We have noted the importance of the bureaucracy in India, as regulators and as direct judicial decision makers, particularly in rural areas. Also in rural areas, traditional local councils (panchayats) have had effective judicial authority over a range of matters. The existence of multiple layers and levels of judicial authority is not unique to India, nor are the problems associated with its particular structures.

The judicial role of panchayats has been given some policy attention in the past. Since Article 50 of the Constitution requires separation of the judiciary and the executive, an attempt was made, especially after 1959, to create *nyaya* or *adalati* panchayats (NPs) to handle local judicial matters, separating this traditional activity from the panchayats that had per-formed it in the past. This arrangement was also meant to parallel the decentralization of developmental functions to panchayats, while avoid-ing overburdening them. However, delays and arrears, ultimately attributable to a lack of adequate funding of the NPs, led to the effective failure of the system. The decentralization of government structures, through recent constitutional changes strengthening local government in other dimensions, has raised these issues again, and they are revisited in Chapter 11.

Judicial efficiency

Here we note that the use of local councils and rural magistrates for handling a wide range of legal violations makes sense in terms of effi-ciency. In particular, it economizes on the scarce resource of the formal judiciary. This scarcity is, in fact, one of the fundamental problems for India, because by creating lengthy delays, it severely undermines enforce-ability of laws. One of the most striking features of the state of India's judiciary is the degree of delay.

Siwach (1985) estimated that by 1980 there were approximately 30,000 cases pending with the Supreme Court, up from about 2000 twenty years previously, a rate of increase far exceeding the population growth rate. With the Supreme Court receiving considerable attention, this number, after increasing further, was actually brought down in the 1990s, and stands at about 20,000 currently.[14]

Mookherjee (1993) reported data from the Malimath Committee Report (1990) which provided estimates from 1989 of over 1.4 million cases pending at the high court level. This figure represented a quadrupling since 1971, again much greater than the growth rate of the population. The latest estimates put the figure at over three million, with a total of twenty-five million cases pending at all levels. Table 5.1 gives a breakdown of pending cases by high courts, and indicates two significant points. First, the worst problems are in civil cases, in terms of total numbers (and possibly also length of delay). Second, there are variations across the high courts, indicating that there are implementation problems as well as systemic issues. We discuss both these sources of inefficiency further in this section.

TABLE 5.1
Backlog of Cases, High Courts (1997)

State/location	Civil	Criminal	Oldest case
Allahabad	690,666	125,366	1961
Andhra Pradesh	127,047	8518	1972
Bombay	260,165	24,098	1968
Calcutta	268,342	37,356	1955
Delhi	152,308	18,593	1966
Gauhati	33,034	5003	1978
Gujarat	105,403	16,129	1973
Himachal Pradesh	9345	2583	1974
Jammu & Kashmir	69,917	2034	1968
Karnataka	78,128	4359	n.a
Kerala	87,015	9888	1977
Madhya Pradesh	63,121	40,699	1950
Madras	323,712	33,383	1973
Orissa	105,242	9306	1971
Patna	66,962	15,950	1966
Punjab/Haryana	148,837	29,160	1971
Rajasthan	97,720	21,778	1971
Sikkim	170	33	1985
Total	2,687,074	404,236	n.a

Source: www.palpaponline.com/lawyer/topnews/backlog.htm

[14] This figure, and other recent Indian data on judicial cases pending, is from http://www.palpaponline.com/lawyer/topnews/backlog.htm.

Mookherjee notes the failure of the number of judges to grow sufficiently quickly over this period, both in terms of total positions and their rate of being filled. According to his calculations, the number of judges would have had to be doubled in 1989 to deal with existing pendency at the high court level over five years. Obviously this did not happen.

The problem of insufficient judicial strength has several causes: 'Insufficient financial outlays of State governments, lack of proper manpower planning in response to workload increases, and undue exercise of influence by the Executive (i.e. the Home Ministry, the Chief Minister of the concerned state, or the Law Ministry)'. The influence is, of course, for the purpose of distributing patronage. Mookherjee notes the cumbersome procedure for appointment of judges, which permits this influence to be exercised, and which delays appointments. A further negative consequence of this is the erosion of quality of appointed judges.

Given the number of judges, what matters for delay is the rate of disposal. Mookherjee notes substantial variation in effective management of caseloads among chief justices of different high courts. He (quoting the Malimath Committee) and Siwach also list other factors influencing disposal rates: antiquated procedures such as long oral arguments or the method of writing judgments, the length of the workday, lax codes of conduct for lawyers (leading to frequent lawyers' strikes), and norms for classification and allocation of cases among judges.

Reductions in delays could also be achieved by reducing the number of cases that have to be considered at this level. Measures to do this include reassigning jurisdictions between lower level and high courts, better scrutiny of appeal petitions, and the development of alternative mechanisms for dispute resolution. The first of these, in particular, stands out as a solution recognizing the 'federal' character of the judicial system, both at the level of Centre and states, and within the states. There is a strong argument for having many kinds of routine local legal disputes at the lowest level consistent with fairness and efficiency. The second of these, if it results in fewer appeals being heard, also constitutes effective decentralization. The third suggestion is an example of what Rondinelli calls 'delegation'.[15]

The effects of delays in the judicial system are manifold. A major one is that they can increase uncertainty as to final resolution, and discourage

[15] Note that giving magisterial powers to bureaucrats, which we have cautioned against, is also an example of this form of delegation. The issue is therefore the incentives of the dispute resolution agents. Presumably, fifty years ago, bureaucrats were the best choice, and they may still be for certain rural milieus. But many kinds of commercial and other urban disputes may better be referred to specialized arbitration bodies.

investment. Delays also mean that dispute resolution may become a question of 'might is right': using extralegal force to settle a dispute that is stuck in the judicial system becomes attractive since the use of force itself may not be punished swiftly. This further undermines the credibility of the judicial system.

In practice, what seems to have substituted for the creaky judicial system is the workings of the political system. Those in political power may not only influence the working of the judicial system through patronage appointments, but also take over its functions. Disputes may be resolved by each side appealing to different politicians or political factions. Resolution of disputes is then a function of the relative political influence of the disputants and the relative political strength of the politicians. While the judicial system may also be subject to these effects, and litigation is costly, resolution of ordinary legal disputes by political means sacrifices fairness, transparency, and certainty, since there are no rules, only discretion.

A particularly pernicious side effect is that politicians become above the law, since they control its enforcement. Not only are they free to engage in illegal activities without deterrent, but those who are already lawbreakers have a strong incentive to enter politics. All the anecdotal evidence points to the pervasiveness of these developments in India. Note that these effects are self-reinforcing: politicians self-selected by a system that protects them from punishment have an incentive to weaken the judicial system, and the pervasiveness of a norm may affect the number of people who adhere to it.

Assessment

The microeconomic inefficiencies of the judicial system in India, while partly reflecting inadequate decentralization along the lines of deconcentration and devolution within the judiciary itself, ultimately are a consequence of inadequate delegation of powers by the legislative/ executive branch. In turn, this is partly a constitutional problem, in that this delegation is absent in some of the particulars of that document, though the Indian Constitution does contain some ideas of checks and balances. We earlier discussed these issues in the context of the conflation of the legislative and executive branches. If these two were more separate, or if the notional executive had more powers, one might have seen a greater balancing role played by the national judiciary, and greater influence by its higher levels in solving some of the microeconomic inefficiencies.

While a weak Central legislature may allow the national judiciary, particularly the Supreme Court, to play a more effective checking role, it is not clear how this will solve the problems associated with resource allocation that must ultimately be corrected to allow a smoother working of day-to-day judicial functions. One is tempted to suggest that again, the pressure will come from competition among sub-national jurisdictions pursuing commercial motives: this may lead to a correction of some of the worst inefficiencies in legal processes. In other words, as states and localities try to attract investment and commercial activity, they will be under pressure to provide judicial systems that support commercial activity. It should be noted that this argument applies in particular to areas such as contract enforcement, or property rights enforcement more broadly, rather than the criminal justice system. Hence, this possibility does not by itself predict enhancement of the basic justice, particularly the general criminal side of the judicial system.

THE POLICE

The role of the police is special, because it involves both the bureaucracy and the judicial system in an intimate way. Ideally, the police are impartial investigators and monitors, preventing violations of law where possible. Their role complements that of the judiciary in enforcement. However, the police are also organized as a bureaucracy under the control of politicians, just as are other branches of administration, but unlike the case of the judiciary, which has a notional independence. The actual functioning of the police in India therefore becomes subject to the kinds of influences discussed above in the context of relations between bureaucrats and politicians. One important aspect of this politicization has been the encroachment of the Central government into law and order, constitutionally a state subject.

An additional complication with respect to the police is the relationship between it and the IAS. As emphasized by Bayley (1969), whose analysis of the Indian police still remains one of the best, the police establishment is responsible at two levels to IAS officials, one at the district level, where the collector, a member of the IAS, is the single executive officer with responsibility for the jurisdiction, and the second at the level where the state inspector general of police reports to the state home secretary. We will return to these aspects after noting the basic organizational structure of the police.

Organizational Overview

The Indian Police Service (IPS), which is the superior officer cadre for the police in India, is organized on similar dual lines to the IAS, that is, centralized recruitment and bureaucracy, but without the same key role in the Central government that belongs to the IAS. This latter difference, of course, reflects the fundamental difference between the generalist IAS and the functional specialization of the IPS. However, it remains true that among the various branches of the bureaucracy, the IPS follows only the Indian Foreign Service and the IAS in prestige. Furthermore, the fact that the IPS is a central bureaucracy, as in the case of the IAS, puts its members on a different footing than members of state police forces, that is, those recruited directly by state governments, even though IPS officers are assigned to particular states.

While each state has its own police force, the Union government possesses several police forces also. The Central Reserve Police Force was created by legislation in 1949, before the division of powers assigned by the Constitution in 1950. It is to be used for assisting states in times of large-scale public disorder, and for guarding frontiers. It is directed by an inspector general in the Central home ministry. The Central Bureau of Investigation was set up in 1963, and plays the role implied by its name. There are also the Border Security Force, the Railway Protection Force, and other centrally controlled enforcement agencies. All these together give the Central government considerable power over policing, well beyond what might be suggested by the constitutional assignment of powers. In practice, therefore, the Centre has taken a substantial role in the maintenance of law and order.

Police and IAS

While there are jurisdictional conflicts between the Centre and the states in policing, conflicts also exist between different branches of the bureaucracy, particularly the IAS and the IPS. Bayley (1969) describes the peculiar relationship in rural areas between the district superintendent of the IPS and the district collector of the IAS, where the superintendent is responsible both to the collector for law and order, and to his uniformed superiors for internal management.

The lack of clear lines of accountability and control tends to adversely affect incentives and efficiency. Though it is argued that the check of civilian administration, at as many levels as possible, on a police force that is distrusted or inefficient, is a necessary safeguard, it is not clear that the present arrangement is the best possible institutional structure. Ultimately, both the police and the IAS are subject to political control, and this is where the key to restructuring lies.

Political Influence and Accountability

The problem of political influence is nowhere more potentially fraught with controversy than in the case of the police, which embodies the government's role in monopolizing violence in internal matters.[16] In a democracy, it is impossible to free administration completely from politics. The issue is the separation of proper from improper political influence. One of the problems perceived in the Indian case is the great degree of improper political influence. The solution to the resultant problems of enforcement—inconsistency, corruption, uncertainty, delays—may be to strengthen the organizational independence of the police vis-à-vis politicians, and possibly other bureaucrats, but allow greater control by a stronger judiciary. This line of reasoning may seem naïve—after all, why should the judiciary provide an effective monitor of the police, especially since judges do not have to be responsive to electorates?

One answer might be that a strengthened judiciary, at least at the local level, might be made subject to election, somewhat along the lines of the United States model.[17] Another possibility is that power and prestige may lead to the opposite of short-term self-interested behaviour. The persistence of the Indian armed forces as an institution with relatively high integrity and efficiency, without obvious abuses of power, yet without direct control by the electorate, is worth considering in this respect. Of course, the interests of the armed forces may be less in conflict with those of politicians than would be the interests of a strengthened judiciary.

An alternative is suggested by trends in countries such as the United States and Britain: a greater role for citizens' organizations, in the form of police review commissions, as a direct democratic check on police behaviour. However, this may be more effective in dealing with sins of commission, rather than of omission. It should be noted that in the United States in particular, much policing is handled at the local level, and local elected officials provide a fairly direct check on the operation of police, ensuring some measure of responsibility and accountability. Some of the pitfalls in local policing in India are similar to those of decentralization in general: lack of resources, training, and equity. These pitfalls are

---

[16] Of course, the army, the other component organization of the government's monopoly of violence, can be turned from its external role to use on a country's citizens.

[17] In the past, this idea would have been almost unthinkable, due to the power of rural oligarchs. In many states, however, the situation has changed enough that local elections of panchayats, as mandated in the 73rd Amendment, are becoming routine. Local judicial functionaries are not necessarily in a different category. These issues are taken up again in Chapter 11.

illustrated by the workings of the traditional village police, as described in Bayley (1969, Chapter 15), where all three are in short supply.

However, there is no reason that a carefully planned and executed decentralization cannot overcome some of the current problems created by divergence between the interests of citizens and of individuals engaged in law enforcement. Such decentralization would, of course, have to include attention to the organizational structures within which the police operate. In particular, the assignment of tasks to different levels of police would have to be done carefully: economies of scale and scope are likely to be quite important, and overlapping of assignments may create confusion.[18] Decentralization in local government is discussed more broadly in Chapter 11, but here we may note that the argument for decentralization of the police is based on the general idea of improving accountability and incentives, and cannot work without progress in that direction for local government more broadly.

CHECKS AND BALANCES VERSUS MULTIPLE VETOES

In discussing durability and commitment in Chapter 4, we referred to India's 'multiple veto' legislature which prevents changes in inefficient existing laws. This concept was also referred to in the context of the inefficiency of India's bureaucracy above. This kind of reasoning might seem to indicate that the idea of checks and balances which we suggest in the context of the judiciary and the legislative and executive branches is misplaced.

One possible reconciliation of the two positions is to say that there is some optimal degree of checks and balances, and it has been too great within different components of the governance structure in India, but not sufficient across these components. Within the bureaucracy or legislature, it has often proved hard to get anything done, because it would hurt some group relative to the status quo. On the other hand, the de facto executive branch of government in India (the prime minister) has come to dominate governance in practice when it is able to overcome these internal constraints and to act. Therefore, multiple vetoes within the legislative branch of government serve as an excessive form of checks on government action.

[18] Bayley (1969, p. 405) makes the point as follows: 'Under the proposed scheme *panchayats* would have responsibility for and control of their own police. To be sure, their functions would have to be spelled out by state legislatures so as to avoid conflicts with state police authority. Village police would have to remain primarily a guarding and reporting agency. America's mistake with a multiplication of autonomous local police jurisdictions must certainly be avoided.'

The dominance of the executive suggests another possible difference between the ideas of multiple vetoes and checks and balances. Multiple veto powers have mattered particularly for specific decisions in specific circumstances. The concept of checks and balances applies more at the level of rules rather than specific decisions. Hence, checks and balances are captured in concepts such as the Supreme Court's powers of review of legislation in general, or the legislature's power to ratify or reject executive legislative proposals.[19] Multiple vetoes, on the other hand, are reflected more in the powers of interest groups defined by particular pieces of legislation.

GOVERNANCE VERSUS GOVERNMENT

In this chapter we have focused exclusively, so far, on the structures of government. We now turn to governance more broadly, which brings us to consider issues related to the concepts of self-governance, civil society, social capital, and non-governmental organizations (NGOs) as embodiments or expressions of these concepts.

We begin with a brief overview of civil society and NGOs in India, bringing out the importance of governmental frameworks. We then discuss the nature of effective government, emphasizing accountability. The dual roles of NGOs as alternative providers of collective goods and as direct accountability mechanisms are examined. Finally, these issues are tied to our main theme of examining Indian federalism.

Civil Society and Voluntary Action

If we interpret civil society to be the entire gamut of NGOs and collective institutions, we do not necessarily see any lack in India. Voluntary organizations, interest groups, and social welfare associations seem to be multiplying, alongside and overlapping with traditional occupational and religious groupings or organizations. To some extent, these can be substitutes for lack of effective government: in Delhi, middle-class neighbourhood residents' associations finance and carry out the provision of basic local services such as garbage collection, which are supposed to be performed by local government, but are not, at least not effectively enough. One can view this as an improvement over nothing at all.

---

[19] Persson, Roland, and Tabellini (1997) formalize the concept of checks and balances as a system where there is a conflict of interest between legislature and executive, but requiring both to agree on policy. This formalization is closer to our first interpretation, of checks and balances and multiple vetoes as different types of the same phenomenon, distinguished merely by whether their effects are good or bad.

However, it is important to remember that the rationale of government comes from the publicness of public goods, and the sub-optimality of voluntary provision due to free rider problems, as noted in Chapter 2. Voluntary membership in neighbourhood associations at rates of 40–50 per cent may be less efficient than more effective taxation and public provision of some services. Issues of economies of scale are also relevant in cases such as these, since non-rivalry of a good and the presence of economies of scale due to fixed costs are conceptually closely related.

A counter argument may be that if government is ineffective, self-governance is better. This also seems to be the tenor of detailed studies of self-governance in areas such as local irrigation institutions (Ostrom, 1992; Tang, 1992). However, even here, it is recognized that such institutions are ultimately feasible only in a system where laws and rules at a broader level are enforced clearly and consistently by government. In a wider perspective, any collective action on a large scale will involve some specialization and delegation of functions. Government is just one aspect of this fact. In a democracy, individuals agree to be ruled by laws made by elected representatives, who are themselves subject to those laws. Voting is only one of several ways that constituent preferences can be articulated. While self-help and voluntary collective action to achieve certain ends are extremely important at the micro level, ultimately, government is the main institution of governance. It must be shaped to serve this role effectively.

Governance and Effective Government

The idea that the effectiveness of NGOs ultimately flows from effective government, albeit with significant feedback mechanisms, must be considered in more detail. In particular, the structure of what constitutes effective government deserves attention. Lewis (1995), for example, describes 'pluralism', or 'delegating sideways' as a 'logical companion theme to decentralisation', and supports this strongly. He explains these terms as the delegation of authority to agencies outside the official hierarchy, including private enterprises, cooperatives, development corporations, and voluntary public associations. These organizations can provide checks and balances outside the apparatus of government.

Lewis notes the boom of NGOs in recent years, and their frequent virtues, but goes on to point out that 'NGOs, whether externally based or indigenous, are often incomplete or awkward substitutes for legitimate official bodies'. For Lewis, the danger is one of persistent dependence on external benefactors, whether official or not. This brings him back to the need for local self-government and the issue of accountability of local government to its citizenry. To summarize, effective rules or laws, with a reasonable degree of durability and enforceability, are essential whatever the degree of decentralization of government. This is a theme we have pursued in this chapter and the previous one. Therefore, decentralization must be accompanied by more efficient organization of the primary institutions that make, interpret, and enforce laws. Of these, the judicial system may be the immediate place to start. Given a smoothly operating and independent judiciary, democracy—which gives constituents the ability to replace their representatives routinely and easily—will be more effective than if it is only a revolving door for opportunism. Accountability requires the law and democracy to work together.

NGOs and Accountability

In a broader institutional framework, therefore, the role of NGOs and other non-official institutions is two-fold. First, any collective group, whether a firm or a voluntary organization, may be engaged in producing something of value, ranging from purely private to purely public goods. For each such institution there are issues of efficient internal organization. These include taking advantage of any economies of scale or scope, having a system of corporate governance, and providing incentives to individual members of the organization.

The second aspect of any such group (and in some cases the primary, or even only role) is its interaction with government in pursuing its goals. This is typically thought of as lobbying. It can be hidden and corrupt, trying to circumvent laws or rules, or it can be open and righteous, trying to enforce existing laws, or change them to make them better. Society ideally controls and condemns the former, but encourages acceptable forms of the latter. Political action by consumer or other public groups (outside the electoral process) is, therefore, potentially an additional means for achieving accountability of government.

At the same time, issues of accountability and responsiveness arise for non-official bodies as well. We think this is what makes government the key aspect of governance, and resolves the potential 'chicken and egg' problem—do we need effective non-governmental action to ensure a responsive and efficient government? Therefore, the place to start when thinking about institutional reform, to complement recent economic reforms that have partly redefined the role of government, is the rule of law. Creating more effective governmental and judicial structures, with an efficient assignment of tasks, and the power to raise resources and enforce laws at every level, is likely to have a significant payoff. These ideas are examined in more detail in Chapter 11, in the context of local government reform.

Federalism and Self-governance

The discussion of NGOs, voluntary collective action, and self-governance typically focuses at the local level, as we have done above. This focus is driven by conceptual as well as pragmatic reasons. Conceptually, there is an ideological preference for local issues and local action. Pragmatically, the difficulties of large-scale voluntary action tend to restrict the locus of such efforts. The absence of effective local government structures heightens the importance of such local voluntary action, but as we have noted above, NGOs cannot be substitutes for effective local government, and are often best viewed as complements.

Even though the primary locus of self-governance and voluntary action is local, it is not exclusively so. NGOs and other voluntary associations can also operate at the state and even national level, particularly in their role as monitors of government; NGOs may be able to expand beyond their initially local activities by growing directly, merging, or federating. A larger-scale organization gains in political clout, and can possibly take advantages of economies of scale in information, management, and financing. Potentially, therefore, NGOs can have structures that parallel the layers of federal government along all the dimensions discussed in this chapter.

There is no unique or right answer concerning the structure and role of voluntary action. Even in a decentralized federal system, NGOs of many kinds will have a role. However, we think it is reasonable to assert that more effective federal structures of government, in the sense that they are able to better deliver local public goods, will reduce the need for and role of voluntary collective action in these dimensions.

CONCLUSIONS

The broad theme of this book is that neither economic nor political aspects of federalism can be looked at in isolation, if one wishes to gain a proper understanding of the workings of a federal system. In this chapter, we have tried to unpack the political side of federalism by discussing the various dimensions of government and governance. Governance involves a complex of tasks, and government has different components to handle different aspects, just as would any large organization. Elected officials in theory act directly as agents of constituents to decide policies, and bureaucrats in turn act as the agents of elected representatives, advising on and implementing these policies. The judiciary and police are, in the abstract, special bureaucracies assigned the fundamental task of monitoring and enforcing law and order in general, and the protection of corporate and individual property rights as well as other individual rights.

The existence of different dimensions of governance implies that a federal political system cannot exist simply through a constitutional assignment of responsibilities to different layers of government. Each level of government in a federal system must not only have authority to raise revenues (the theme underlying our next four chapters), but it also has to have the authority to carry out decisions made at that level. In India, the IAS, the IPS, and the judiciary are all perhaps more centralized than they need to be, or should be, given the current federal political system. While independent India began with a relatively circumscribed federal model, independent political competition at the state government level has thrived, as we have outlined above. This decentralization has not necessarily been matched in the other dimensions of government, but may need to be for a more effective federal system to operate.

To some extent, the failure of federalist principles to permeate the different dimensions of government has given an impetus to non-governmental forms of collective action, particularly at the local level. This is an important positive development, both for improving the accountability of government and for the provision of some collective goods, but it cannot, in our view, fully substitute for greater decentralization, such as the creation of effective local governments. Nor can NGOs take the place of sideways delegation or unbundling of government at every level to improve the accountability and efficiency of government.

PART II

ECONOMICS OF INDIAN FEDERALISM

6

Assignment of Taxes and
Expenditures

FISCAL DECENTRALIZATION: THEORETICAL CONSIDERATIONS

Fiscal federalism has two fundamental facets: (i) the assignment of functions and sources of revenue to finance them and (ii) layers, numbers, and morphology of jurisdictions that constitute the governmental system delivering public services. One could take the structure of government and jurisdictions as given and determine the equilibrium assignment of powers or alternatively, establish an efficient jurisdictional organization or structure for the given set of functions. As the objective of this study is to examine the federal fiscal issues within the framework of the given governmental structure, we take the governmental structure as given and analyse the division of powers.

This chapter deals with the assignment of functions and sources of finance to undertake the assigned functions. Division of powers among different governmental units vertically between different levels of government and horizontally between different jurisdictions within each level is the starting point for the examination of efficiency in the delivery of public services. Mapping of benefits across jurisdictions cannot be perfect; overlapping tax powers can create problems of fiscal disharmony and create incentive for free-riding; nor will the assigned finances match the functions at sub-national levels. These problems of fiscal spillovers, disharmony, and imbalances have their roots in assignments and therefore, this issue warrants a careful analysis.

The earlier layer-cake models of assignment of governmental functions assumed that public services could be aggregated unambiguously into Musgravian tripartite categories—allocation, distribution, and stabilization. Under this scheme, primary responsibility for macroeconomic stabilization and redistribution of income and wealth should lie with the Central government (Oates, 1972, 1977). It is difficult for local governments with small, open economies to pursue independent stabilization policies. They cannot be given the power to vary money supply and the effectiveness of fiscal policy for stabilization at the sub-central levels is limited by the spillover of effective demand to areas outside their jurisdictions. Similarly, potential mobility of economic agents places limits on the ability of sub-central governments to pursue serious redistributive policies. Sub-central governments have serious disincentives to pursue vigorous redistribution. In undertaking the allocative functions, however, decentralized provision promises the greatest gains. The decentralization theorem demonstrates that provision of public services by sub-central governments, in the absence of scale economies, can result in significant welfare gains as compared to the centralized solution of uniform supply.[1] The more varied the demand for public services across different jurisdictions, the larger the welfare gains from fiscal decentralization. Decentralized provision of local public goods can cater to the varying preferences of people better and thus enhance social welfare. It is also demonstrated that the welfare gains from decentralization are inversely related to the price elasticity of demand for public services (Oates, 1977). Welfare gains can also accrue from the wider choice implicit in the different tax–benefit packages offered by different jurisdictions. When the choice set is wider, individuals can vote on their feet for the preferred communities. Further, the wider choice reduces the welfare cost implicit in the bundling (provided on take it or leave it basis) of public services. However, when there are significant economies of scale or when sub-central provision of public services involves transaction and organizational costs,[2] the assignments should be done so as to maximize the net welfare gains.

In the real-world situation, however, assignment of the responsibility of providing *goods and services* in terms of the three *functional* branches of the government would be impossible. At the same time the three functions are not independent contrary to what was assumed in these models. Even more important, the sub-national governments are found to have legitimate redistribution and stabilization roles in all multilevel fiscal systems. Pauly (1973) and Tresch (1981) have argued that redistribution may be considered a local public good and when population is not mobile across jurisdictions, local initiative in redistribution may be desirable.

---

[1] On the attempt to measure welfare gains, see Bradford and Oates (1974). The price elasticity of demand for local public services is estimated by Bergstrom and Goodman (1973).

[2] Breton and Scott (1978) identify four kinds of transaction costs namely, mobility, signalling, administration, and coordination.

Similarly, sub-central fiscal policies can and do play a role, albeit limited, in managing local unemployment and hence, stabilization (Inman and Rubinfeld, 1992; Gramlich, 1987).

When the assignment question is formulated in terms of *goods and services* instead of functional *branches* of government, three broad approaches may be discerned, namely: (i) Breton–Olson–Oates models of efficient management of spillovers; (ii) Breton–Scott model of minimizing costs including transaction and administrative costs; and (iii) competitive federalism model which effects assignments according to comparative advantage.

The first approach views assignments as an outcome of managing benefit spillovers from various public goods. This has been discussed in some detail in the context of economic theories of federalism and it may not be out of place here to recapitulate important strands of the approach. The approach was first developed by Breton (1965) and later by Olson (1969) and Oates (1972). In this approach, broadly all public services are assumed to pure Samuelsonian (1954) type, but with varying regional benefit 'spans'. To minimize spillovers, the public goods with different benefit spans will be hierarchically ordered into local, metropolitan, regional, provincial, national, and international public goods (Breton, 1965). In Olson's (1969) scheme, the perfect matching of benefits with geographical boundaries or 'fiscal equivalence' would warrant as many governmental levels as the number of public goods. In Oates's approach, with stabilization and redistribution functions assigned (mainly) to the Central government, decentralization is relevant only in the allocation function. In undertaking the allocation function, however, welfare maximizing necessarily implies that sub-national governments have a predominant role. According to the 'decentralization theorem', sub-national units have greater advantage in providing the Pareto-efficient levels of public services as they can cater to the diversified preferences of people in different jurisdictions unless there are offsetting gains from economies of scale due to centralized delivery of public services. In the case of public services with scale economies, public 'provision' of the good can still maintain the advantage and private 'production' can help to reap economies of scale. In this case, wherever feasible, the local governments can provide the privately produced services by purchasing them in the market. However, in cases of services requiring public production, optimal assignment and jurisdictional size are arrived at by maximizing net welfare gains.

Thus, the crux of the Breton–Olson–Oates approach is that an efficient design of jurisdictional boundaries or assignment of functions results from the scheme, which manages the spillovers efficiently. However, when the exogenously given jurisdictional boundaries do not exactly coincide with the benefit spans, the spillovers will have to be internalized through a system of Pigovian grants administered by the higher-level government. The problem with this approach as pointed out by Weldon (1966) is that it requires an omniscient Central government to accurately calculate the spillovers, and if the Central government has so much information to accurately estimate spillovers, supply-side reasons for decentralization simply disappear (Breton, 1995, p. 185).

The second approach takes optimal assignments as a consequence of minimizing transaction costs. According to the decentralization theorem discussed above, optimal assignments result from maximizing net welfare gains. This implies that a function should be decentralized so long as welfare gains from decentralized provision exceeds the additional cost disadvantages if the good in question is subject to increasing returns to scale. A clearer theory of assignment resulting from cost minimization was proposed by Breton and Scott (1978). In this, optimal assignments are achieved when transaction or organizational costs of providing the services are internalized into the decision-making framework. These include the costs of mobility, signalling, administration, and coordination. While analytically attractive, this approach too, to be operational, requires an *omniscient* decision maker who can model the cost functions and minimize them to achieve equilibrium assignments.

Both the above approaches are normative in the sense that they implicitly assume welfare-maximizing government behaviour. In contrast, the 'competitive federalism' approach is positive and is based on the self-interest axiom. Nor does it require an omniscient Central government or planner to arrive at efficient assignment. Assignment leads to intergovernmental competition and, over time, competition determines assignments as well. In this approach, the guaranteed assignment system in a federation enables the hierarchically ordered governmental units to compete with one another in providing public goods, and in the equilibrium. Competition will force the governmental units to specialize in the supply of public services in which each unit is relatively more efficient. At the same time, constitutional division is the consequence of the competitive advantage of different jurisdictions. This however, does not mean that constitutionally entrenched assignments are irrelevant. One way to look at this issue is to make the Brennan–Buchanan (1980) distinction between constitutional changes and in-period changes. While intergovernmental competition can influence assignments in the medium and long term through constitutional amendments and evolution of conventions, the in-period or short-run intergovernmental relationships are conducted in the framework of the existing constitutional arrangements. Another way to look at the issue is to consider the existing constitutions as a constraint on competition in evolving equilibrium assignments.

A common thread in all the three views is that optimal division of functions is achieved when the assignment to different levels of government corresponds to its comparative advantage. Comparative advantage may be in terms of provision of public services according to varying preferences or considerations of local choice, or in terms of cost efficiency by reaping economies of scale or transaction costs or in terms of competitive ability of different levels of government.

EXPENDITURE AND TAX ASSIGNMENTS

The major responsibility of the Central government according to these principles will be (i) to provide public and merit goods and services with benefits spanning across different states and, (ii) to monitor inter-jurisdictional competition among sub-central governmental units. In the provision of public services it would have a predominant role in macroeconomic stabilization, poverty alleviation (poverty anywhere is a concern everywhere in the country), and in providing public services with national spillovers like defence and those with interstate ramifications. As regards cost consideration, transaction and coordination costs can still be an important issue in determining the division of functions; however, the possibility of accessing private supply for public provision in many cases reduces the role of the Central government from the viewpoint of economies of scale.

One of the important functions of the Central government is to monitor inter-jurisdictional competition. An efficient monitoring mechanism is an essential prerequisite for securing stability in horizontal competition. This requires the Central government to formulate rules to prevent 'beggar thy neighbour' policies such as predatory pricing of goods and services, erection of trade barriers and impediments to mobility of factors, and exportation of tax burden to non-residents. The Central government has to secure stability in competition because voluntary cooperation among the sub-national governments does not work in situations of pure conflict.[3] The Central government can secure stability in horizontal competition by setting the rules of competition and enforcing them to achieve (i) competitive equality of jurisdictions and (ii) correspondence of

---

[3] For details, see, Breton (1995), pp. 240–5.

costs of benefits of public services in each of the jurisdictions. The Central government can achieve these preconditions for stable intergovernmental competition by employing three instruments individually or in conjunction with others namely, the use of prohibitions and standards, the use of regional policies, and the implementation of intergovernmental transfer programmes (Breton, 1987).

First, the use of regulations, prohibitions, and standards is aimed at preventing the sub-national governments from undertaking measures advantageous to them, but inimical to the economy as a whole. Erecting barriers to prevent free movement of resources and goods across boundaries, indulgence in unhealthy tax competition—'race to the bottom'—and according of liberal fiscal and financial incentives by sub-national governments to attract capital into their jurisdictions are examples of this. Such policies segment the factor and commodity market, distort the pattern of resource allocation, rob the advantages of a common market, cause significant interstate tax exportation and bring about non correspondence between taxes and public services, and redistribute resources in favour of more 'powerful' jurisdictions which is necessarily inequitable. Thus, regulations are called for to bring about cost–benefit appropriability, prevent diversion of trade and capital from their natural locations, and to ensure a common market for the country.

Second, competition among sub-national governmental units, to be stable and beneficial, calls for 'competitive equality' and this can be achieved by appropriate regional policies or intergovernmental transfer system. This is analogous to the firms in a competitive industry where no single firm is in a position to dominate the scene and influence prices. A necessary condition for equalizing the competitive strength of different regions (states) within a country is to enable them to provide equivalent levels of social and economic infrastructure at a given tax-price through Central transfers or through the Centre's direct investments. This ensures that larger/stronger units cannot continually dominate, coerce or prevent the smaller/weaker units from making independent decisions, nor can they inflict disproportionate damage on them (Breton, 1987). The Central government can ensure equality in the competitive powers of sub-national governments either by employing its own expenditure priorities and allocations to achieve the intended pattern of regional benefit spread, or through regionally discriminating regulations or intergovernmental transfer systems.

Thus the Central government does not have comparative advantage in providing most public services except those which have national jurisdiction or are international in scope. In contrast, state and local governments are better placed to provide most public services including many social services like education, preventive and curative health care, water supply, and social security and welfare, and economic services like building physical infrastructure.

The broad generalizations made above, help us to draw three principles of tax assignment: (i) sub-national governments should only levy 'residence-based' (as against resources-based) taxes and user charges; (ii) the non-benefit taxes needed to be levied particularly for redistributive purposes should be levied by higher-level (Central) governments; (iii) to the extent sub-central governments have to levy non-benefit taxes, they should employ taxes on bases which are relatively immobile across jurisdictions. These principles place the Central government at a distinct advantage in levying taxes on broad based and mobile bases, because taxes on such bases if levied by sub-national governments could result in significant evasion and avoidance. Besides, the mobility of the tax bases in search of tax havens can cause serious resource distortions (Musgrave, 1983; Breton, 1995). Similarly, they have distinct advantages in borrowing from the market or creating resources through seignorage.

Thus, in general the assignment system results in 'vertical fiscal imbalance'. While the Central government has a distinct advantage in raising revenues, the state and local governments are better placed to provide public services. This calls for another reason for the transfer of resources, besides intergovernmental transfers given to offset relative fiscal disabilities arising from shortfall in the capacity to raise revenues and excessive cost disadvantages. At the same time, divergence between revenue and expenditure decisions can have adverse efficiency consequences and in the ultimate analysis the equilibrium assignment should weigh the trade-off between welfare gains from efficient revenue and expenditure assignments with the efficiency loss due to the divergence of revenue and expenditure decisions. Linking expenditures on public services with prices (user charges or tax payments) tends to preserve incentives and accountability, makes the system transparent, and enhances consumers' choice.

How then should the assignment of taxes and expenditure functions between different levels of government be sequenced? In the literature, it is suggested that the assignment of spending responsibility should precede division of tax powers (Shah, 1994). This is because, division of tax powers, besides being based on the principles of tax assignment, should be determined by the requirement of different spending agencies. Devolution of tax powers based on expenditure responsibilities is desired so that subnational governments do not have to rely exclusively on intergovernmental transfers to finance their expenditures. The linking of revenue and expenditure decisions is considered important to preserve the incentive and accountability. Excessive recourse to intergovernmental transfers to finance sub-national expenditures severs the linkage between revenue–expenditure decisions as explained above and can have adverse effects on the fiscal management at sub-national levels. Even when the tax powers assigned to sub-national governments have distortions, it may be preferable to do so if it results in more cost-effective public service provision. Thus, the choice between assigning tax powers and providing transfers to sub-national governments to finance their services depends upon the trade-off between the additional efficiency loss due to sub-national taxation and efficiency gains from cost-efficient spending by them and consideration of regional equity.

While the broad principles of assignment expounded above are helpful in designing expenditure and tax assignments, it is necessary to recognize that actual assignments do not always follow the theoretical ideal. This is because, actual fiscal arrangements are determined by historical, political, and other non-economic factors, besides economic considerations. For example, though customs duty theoretically should be a Central levy, in Malaysia, local governments administer it. Similarly, property tax which should theoretically be a local levy, is a Central tax in Indonesia, and a provincial tax in Pakistan. Income tax, given the mobility of the tax base, should be a Central levy, but in Canada and the United States of America, the state or provincial governments can levy the tax concurrently with the Central government. In many countries, revenues from natural resources, particularly minerals, accrue to the Centre, but in Canada, it is a provincial domain. Such examples of deviation of actual assignments from the principles abound. Some of them may create distortions and inequities, but that must be taken as the cost of political compromises in determining assignments.

TAX AND EXPENDITURE ASSIGNMENTS IN INDIA: IMPORTANT ISSUES

The discussion on economic principles in the preceding section provides us the benchmark for evaluating the actual assignment of tax and expenditure powers to different levels of government in the Indian federation. Briefly stated, these principles are:

(i) Assignment of taxes and expenditures should be according to the principle of comparative advantage. In the case of expenditures, this would imply provision of public services conforming to the diverse preferences; minimization of mobility, signalling, and coordination costs;

and avoiding the scope for free-riding. In the case of tax assignment, comparative advantage is determined by the enforceability of taxes, and neutrality with regard to location decisions.

(ii) The assignment should not adversely affect incentives and accountability for both Central and sub-central governments. It should preserve a strong link between revenue and expenditure decisions to avoid disincentives in fiscal management at all levels of government.

(iii) The assignment should ensure not only efficient provision of public services, but also pave the way for overall allocative efficiency. Specifically, the assignment of taxes and expenditures should not promote 'free-riding' among the sub-national governments and should minimize market segmentation and impediments to the free movement of factors and commodities across the country.

In India, the first systematic attempt at defining the roles of Central and state governments was done as far back as 1918, when the Montague–Chelmsford reforms were implemented. However, it was the Government of India Act, 1935, which clearly demarcated the roles of the two levels of government, and in many respects, the present constitutional assignment closely follows that demarcation. The Constitution, in its seventh schedule, assigns the powers and functions of the Centre and the states. The schedule specifies the exclusive powers of the Centre in the Union List; exclusive powers of the states in the State List; and those falling under the joint jurisdiction are placed in the Concurrent List. All the residuary powers are assigned to the Centre.

The functions of the Central government can be classified as those required to maintain macroeconomic stability, international trade and relations, and those having implications for more than one state, for reasons of economies of scale and cost-efficient provision of public services. Issuing currency and coinage, dealing in foreign exchange, foreign loans, the operation of the central bank of the country (Reserve Bank of India or RBI), international trade, banking, insurance, and operation of stock exchanges are some of the major functions assigned to the Central government to maintain macroeconomic stability. Functions like the operation of railways, posts and telegraphs, national highways, shipping and navigation on inland waterways, air transport, atomic energy, space, regulation and development of oilfields and major minerals, interstate trade and commerce, and regulation and development of interstate rivers are the major functions assigned to the Centre for reasons of economies of scale and spillovers in respect of services with benefits spanning more than one state.

The power of the Central government has been further strengthened by placing a number of additional items in the Concurrent List and vesting it with overriding powers in regard to these subjects. The important items included in the Concurrent List are: economic and social planning (which embraces virtually all items under economic and social services), commercial and industrial monopolies, trade unions, social security, employment and unemployment, welfare of labour, price control and trade and commerce in and production of certain basic goods such as foodstuffs, cotton and any other goods if the Parliament decides to bring it into this category.

The major subjects assigned to the states comprise public order, police, public health, agriculture, irrigation, land rights, fisheries, and industries and minor minerals. As mentioned earlier, the states do have jurisdiction over concurrent items and can take initiatives with regard to these subjects. However, in the event of conflict between the Centre and the states, the former's decision will prevail. Subjects like public health, agriculture and irrigation involve considerable governmental intervention and expenditures. Even with regard to the subjects in the Concurrent List like education and transport, social security and social insurance, the states would be compelled to assume a significant role given their proximity to the people in a democratic polity.

The assignment of tax powers, however, is based on the principle of 'separation', and the tax handles are exclusively assigned either to the Centre or to the states. Most of the broad-based and productive tax handles have been assigned to the Centre, perhaps for reasons of stabilization and redistribution stated earlier. These include, taxes on income and wealth from non-agricultural sources, corporation tax, taxes on production (excluding those on alcoholic liquors, opium, hemp and other narcotics) and customs duty. A number of tax handles are assigned to the states as well. These include taxes on agricultural income and wealth, taxes on the transfer of property (stamp duties and registration fees), taxes on motor vehicles, taxes on the transportation of goods and passengers, sales tax on goods, excises on alcoholic beverages, entertainment tax, taxes on professions, trades, callings and employment, property tax, and taxes on the entry of goods into a local area for consumption, use or sale (Octroi). However, from the viewpoint of revenue productivity, only the tax on the sale and purchase of goods is important. The Centre has also been assigned all residual powers which implies that the taxes not mentioned in any of the lists automatically fall into its domain. The division of tax and expenditure powers as placed in Central, State, and Concurrent lists of the seventh schedule to the Constitution is given in Table A6.1.

The Constitution also recognizes that the states' tax powers are inadequate to meet their expenditure needs and, therefore, provides for the sharing of revenues from Central taxes. Prior to the enactment of the Constitution (Eightieth Amendment) Act 2000, taxes on incomes other than non-agricultural incomes and Union excise duty were shared with the states. Considering the potential adverse incentives of sharing of taxes from individual sources for the Central government, based on the recommendations of the Tenth Finance Commission, the Constitution was amended to include proceeds from all Central taxes in the divisible pool. In addition to tax devolution, the Constitution provides for giving grants-in-aid to the states as well (Article 275). Both tax devolution and grants-in-aid have to be determined by the Finance Commission, an independent body appointed by the president every five years (Article 280).

The shares of Central and state governments in revenues and expenditures summarized in Tables 6.1 and 6.2 bring out their respective roles.[4] The states, on an average, raise about 34 per cent of revenues and incur 58 per cent of expenditures. In 1998–9, revenues from exclusive Central taxes constituted 23 per cent of the total; those from exclusive state taxes was 30 per cent; the shareable sources constituted 24 per cent; and the remaining 23 per cent was from non-tax revenues. Since 2000–1, there are no exclusive Central taxes as the Finance Commission recommended that all tax revenues collected by the Centre excluding the surcharges levied for specified purposes are shareable with the states.

The states' share in spending, however, is about 58 per cent and it is broadly the same in both current and capital expenditures. As about 15 per cent of total expenditures is incurred on centrally sponsored schemes which have matching requirements, their flexibility with regard to expenditure is less than that indicated in the expenditure shares. In fact, states' expenditures on these schemes increased from 7 per cent of the total in 1985–6 to about 15 per cent in 1997–8.

The pattern of expenditures shown in Table 6.2 indicates that the Central government plays a major role in defence and provision of large physical infrastructure facilities. On the other hand, the states have a high share of expenditures on internal security, law and order, social services, and economic services like agriculture, animal husbandry, forestry, fisheries, irrigation and power, and public works. The states' share in expenditure on administrative services is about 38 per cent; on social services they spend about 82 per cent; and on economic services their share is about two-thirds. Their role in providing social services like education, public health, and family is particularly predominant, close to 90 per cent.

---

[4] The data pertain to the period prior to the constitutional amendment and hence, refer to tax on personal income and union excise duty as shared taxes. After 2000–01, revenue from all Central taxes is kept in the divisible pool.

Table 6.1

Revenue Receipts of the Central and State Governments: 1995-6

Items of Revenue	Revenue Share 1985-6		Revenue Share 1990-1		Revenue Share 1999-2000		Revenue Share 2000-01 (RE)		Per cent of total revenue 2000-01
	Centre	States	Centre	States	Centre	States	Centre	States	
A. Tax Revenue (a+b)	49.00	51.00	48.10	51.90	46.70	53.30	45.20	54.80	76.10
a. Central Taxes	100.00	–	100.00	–	74.70	25.30	72.80	27.20	47.20
1. Corporation Tax	100.00	–	100.00	–	100.00	–	72.80	27.20	9.20
2. Personal Income Tax	100.00	–	100.00	–	35.60	64.40	72.80	27.20	8.40
3. Custom Duties	100.00	–	100.00	–	100.00	–	72.80	27.20	11.90
4. Union Excise Duty	100.00	–	100.00	–	56.50	43.50	72.80	27.20	16.80
5. Others	100.00	–	100.00	–	100.00	–	72.80	27.20	0.90
b. Exclusive States Taxes	–	100.00	–	100.00	–	100.00	–	100.00	28.90
1. State Excise Duties	–	100.00	–	100.00	–	100.00	–	100.00	3.90
2. Sales Taxes	–	100.00	–	100.00	–	100.00	–	100.00	16.60
3. Taxes on Transport	–	100.00	–	100.00	–	100.00	–	100.00	2.20
4. Others	–	100.00	–	100.00	–	100.00	–	100.00	6.30
B. Non-tax Revenue	62.10	37.90	55.10	44.90	62.40	37.60	58.20	41.80	12.50
1. Net Contribution from Public Enterprises	–868.70	968.70	–288.70	388.70	128.80	–28.80	118.30	–18.30	3.10
2. Administrative Receipts	59.20	40.80	36.50	63.50	27.50	72.50	26.10	73.90	1.90
3. Interest Receipts	66.60	33.40	59.60	40.40	47.60	52.40	39.50	60.50	4.00
4. External Grants	100.00	–	100.00	–	100.00	–	100.00	–	0.20
C. Grants to States	–	100.00	–	100.00	–	100.00	–	100.00	11.40
D Total Revenue Accrual	45.20	54.80	43.50	56.50	44.60	55.40	41.60	58.40	100.00
E. Total Revenue Collections	69.50	30.50	67.80	32.20	65.90	34.10	65.90	34.10	100.00

Source: Public Finance Statistics, Ministry of Finance, Government of India.

TABLE 6.2
Share of State Governments in Total Expenditures*

Expenditure Item	1985–6			1990–1			1999–2000			2000–01 (RE)			Percentage of total expenditure
	Current	Capital	Total	Current	Capital	Total	Current	Capital	Total	Current	Capital	Total	
A. Interest Payment	34.60	–	34.60	35.50	–	35.50	41.10	–	41.10	44.00	–	44.00	21.41
B. Defence	–	–	–	–	–	–	–	–	–	–	–	–	9.46
C. Administrative Service	85.20	0.80	78.00	76.40	1.80	73.40	64.20	13.30	62.50	64.90	17.50	63.80	15.98
D. Social and Community Services, of which:	94.80	67.00	92.70	78.90	74.10	78.70	83.80	73.40	83.20	83.40	83.10	83.40	21.56
i. Education	84.80	79.50	84.70	84.50	61.70	83.90	89.40	90.90	89.40	89.60	93.10	89.60	11.94
ii. Medical and Health	92.50	94.80	92.80	90.30	95.30	90.70	88.30	95.50	89.20	87.50	98.20	89.30	4.57
iii. Family Welfare	93.40	90.40	93.10	92.20	100.00	92.70	80.20	100.00	80.40	78.40	100.00	78.80	0.60
iv. Others	98.10	40.70	88.20	61.10	64.00	61.40	59.60	49.30	58.20	61.00	61.60	61.10	4.46
E. Economic Services, of which	78.10	46.30	62.90	50.20	53.10	51.10	59.50	68.50	62.00	60.20	76.60	65.00	22.99
i. Agri. and Allied Services	99.90	52.10	96.70	77.80	94.80	78.60	65.10	91.00	67.00	68.70	98.40	71.70	6.88
ii. Industry and Minerals	36.70	9.80	18.10	40.70	44.10	41.90	14.00	42.70	16.20	16.70	56.40	20.60	2.99
iii. Power, Irrigation and Flood Control	94.70	65.40	73.90	86.20	62.90	69.10	88.80	83.00	86.00	90.40	86.80	88.80	6.58
iv. Transport and Communication	68.30	68.30	68.30	70.40	32.10	47.30	55.70	60.60	57.90	44.30	71.50	55.80	4.10
v. Others	24.90	18.00	23.90	16.60	51.30	19.70	79.20	36.60	59.80	56.20	46.60	52.20	2.45
F. Others	80.00	14.70	33.20	57.20	–	57.20	55.10	–	55.10	61.70	–	61.70	6.90
G. Loans and Advances @	–	51.70	51.70	–	51.10	51.10	–	79.50	79.50	–	73.20	73.20	1.70
H. Total	55.20	43.00	52.10	55.00	44.50	52.90	56.40	56.70	56.50	57.80	59.70	58.00	100.00

* Revised Estimates ** Includes Food and Fertilizer Subsidies @ Excludes appropriation for redution and avoidance of debt

Source: Public Finance Statistics, Ministry of Finance, Government of India.

The analysis of constitutional assignment in India brings out the following features:

(i) *Centripetal bias:* The delegation of responsibilities between the Centre and the states shows an inherent 'centripetal' bias. The constitutional assignment closely follows the division of powers made in the Government of India Act, 1935, which was designed to keep a firm administrative control of the country from the Centre. Thus, like in administrative and political spheres,[5] the constitutional assignment of economic functions vests the Centre with powers to impose its will on the states if such an action, in its view, is warranted in the 'national interest'. Therefore, commentators have characterized the Indian Constitution as 'quasi-federal'.

Centralization of economic power can be clearly seen when we analyse the constitutional assignments. In the Constitution, as already pointed out, the Central government enjoys both overwhelming and overriding powers. Assignment of major broad-based taxes to the Centre (except the sales tax), vesting it with residuary and overriding powers, and the restrictions on the states' power to borrow are some of the examples of this.

Article 293 of the Constitution does allow the states to borrow from the market. However, it is stipulated that when a state is indebted to the Centre, it has to seek and obtain the Centre's permission for exercising its borrowing powers. As all state governments are indebted to the Centre, states have little leeway in determining their market borrowing. Actually, the Planning Commission, in consultation with the Union finance ministry and the RBI, simply determines the total quantum of states' borrowing and allocates the shares of each of the states. The details of states' borrowings are discussed in Chapter 7.

In effect, unless additional Central transfers are given, the states' ability to increase their expenditures depends merely on their capacity and

---

[5] The concentration of power in political and administrative spheres has been subject matter of a number of scholarly works on the Indian federation. Article 2 of the Constitution, which assigns the Centre with powers to redefine state boundaries, negates the very concept of federalism. More importantly, there has been considerable discussion on the legitimacy of the use of Article 356 by the Centre. Large number of instances can be cited where the Centre has used the powers to dismiss elected state governments to meet the partisan ends of the political party in power at the Centre (Guhan, 1995). In fact, the entire constitutional machinery in the country was trampled with and the federal principle in the policy was brought to nought when the then Prime Minister Indira Gandhi acquired emergency powers for the Central government, merely to keep herself in power in the wake of the Allahabad High Court judgement setting aside her election. Also, the role of all-India services and the absence of federal features in the national political parties seem to have contributed to the unitary bias in the Indian political federalism (Chelliah, 1991).

willingness to enhance revenues from the tax and non-tax sources assigned to them. Although in each of the states the overall transactions in a year should match revenues and expenditures, there are bound to be variations in daily and monthly positions. The cash balance position or the 'ways and means' position of the states is maintained by the central accounts section of the RBI. The cash balances of the states are invested by the RBI as per states' instructions and the states can also take overdrafts up to the limits stipulated by the RBI, by agreement with the respective state government. Any borrowing beyond this limit is called 'unauthorized overdraft'. Until 1985, the states could resort to this means rather liberally. To that extent, Central control over macroeconomic policy was less effective. Further, when the overdraft position reached very high levels, from time to time, the Centre simply cleared the overdrafts by converting them into medium-term loans. In January 1985, however, a overdraft regulation scheme was introduced, which stipulated that if the states continue to have overdrafts with the RBI for more than seven continuous working days, the RBI is not obliged to honour the cheques of such states.[6] This measure has vested the Centre with more effective control of money supply and borrowing powers (and therefore, macroeconomic management of the economy), and at the same time has introduced harder budget constraints on the states. However, as will be shown in Chapter 7, the states have found a variety of ways to soften their budget constraints.

The centralization of economic power in India is not merely an outcome of constitutional assignments. The public sector was expected to reach the commanding heights of the economy in the planned developmental strategy adopted after independence. The heavy-industry-based import-substituting industrialization strategy with a dominant public sector necessarily augmented the economic power of the Centre. Entry 20 in the Concurrent List ('Economic and Social Planning') enabled the Centre to direct resource allocation, and by virtue of the powers conferred by Entry 52 in the Union List, the Industrial Development and Regulation Act was passed to give control over almost all important industries to the Centre. The Planning Commission became a pivotal agency to determine resource allocation. While the investment pattern and its regional distribution in the private sector was sought to be influenced through industrial licensing and other policy measures, the public sector allocation was determined by the Planning Commission. Of course,

---

[6] The states have reacted to this measure by taking resort to short-term borrowing from the private sector or from their own enterprises. Thus, there has been an attempt by the states to soften the budget constraint. The West Bengal government, for example, took short-term loans from Peerless Insurance Company, a private sector financial firm.

the states were allowed to prepare their plans but this was judged and appraised in terms of the national objectives and norms. In addition, the states' priorities were also influenced through a multitude of centrally sponsored schemes—shared cost programmes which at present number as many as 179.

(ii) *Separation of tax powers:* The constitutional assignment of tax powers follows the principle of 'separation' in contrast to that of 'concurrence' followed in federations like USA and Canada. The clear demarcation of the tax handles of the Central and state governments has been prescribed to avoid tax overlapping and concurrency. However, tax separation in a system where the tax bases overlap can only be done in a de jure sense, and de facto overlapping cannot be avoided as the tax bases of the Centre and states are interdependent. First, the splitting of the power to levy taxes on incomes and capital between the Centre and the states on the basis of whether they are derived from agricultural or non-agricultural sources has led to distortions, tax evasion and avoidance, besides violating the principle of horizontal equity or equal treatment of equals (Chelliah, 1991). This has not only created some problems of tax enforcement, but also led to adverse economic consequences. Similarly, the Constitution assigns the states the power to levy sales taxes but, only on goods and not on services. There was no separate mention of taxation of services in any of the lists until the 95th Constitutional amendment when it was put in the central list, but the Centre has continued to buy on selected services. However for evolving a coordinated tax structure in the country, the taxes on goods and services should go together. Besides, the states cannot levy a broad-based and less distortionary value added tax because they do not have the power to extend the tax on services.

Second, although in a legal sense the Central and state levies are separate, they levy taxes on virtually the same base. Consequently, the problem of vertical tax overlapping has continued to plague the Indian tax system. The Central government is empowered to levy manufacturing excises. The states levy sales taxes on the excise duty paid value of commodities.[7] In addition, the tax on the entry of goods into a local area for consumption, use or sale, or 'octroi' (contained in the State List and delegated to the local bodies), too falls on the same tax base. This is a clear example of vertical tax overlapping. Such a levy of tax on tax and margins on taxes in a mark-up pricing situation creates divergence between the

---

[7] In an economy where the producers are protected from both domestic and foreign competition, mark-up pricing may be an appropriate characterization. Of course, this general characterization may not be applicable to particular industries.

producer and consumer prices much more than the tax element. The extent of distortions caused and the welfare cost of this overlapping tax system remains unknown.

At the Central level, some progress has been made in extending input tax credit in the case of excise duties. Some of the states too extend concessional tax treatment to input purchases by manufacturers in the case of sales taxes. However, the scope of these concessions is limited and procedures involved in availing them cumbersome. Thus, input taxation has continued to persist. In the event, tax burden on different commodities and the extent of cascading remains unknown. Thus, existence of parallel and overlapping domestic indirect tax systems and the Centre–state and interstate commodity tax competition has resulted in a complicated, distorting, and inequitable domestic commodity tax system. As the report of the NIPFP study team states:

...the system that is operating at present is antiquated, complex—according to the knowledgeable experts, the most complex in the world—and injurious to the economy in many ways. It follows no rational pattern ... and violates all time-honoured canons of taxation—certainty, neutrality and equity.[8]

The Indian experience with separation of tax powers clearly contrasts with the assignments prevailing in a number of federations, where the Constitution itself assigns concurrent powers of taxation of some broadbased taxes. In Australia, the problem arising from such concurrency has been minimized as all major taxes are assigned to the Commonwealth government. This has helped to ensure that the tax system is relatively more harmonious, but at the same time, leads to undue dependence of the states on intergovernmental transfers. In the USA and Canada, the federal and state (provincial) governments have concurrent powers to levy income taxes, but as many of the states levy the taxes on the base determined by the federal government, the disharmony has been minimized to a great extent. In Canada, the arrangement essentially is one of piggybacking. In the USA, in a majority of the states the tax bases are not identical to that of the federal government in respect of both individual and corporate income taxes but the differences are not significant enough to cause major distortions.

As regards domestic consumption taxes, a considerable degree of vertical coordination between the federal and state (provincial) levels has been achieved to make the tax system relatively simpler and more transparent. In the United States, the federal government does not levy any broadbased internal indirect tax and the states have the exclusive right to levy

[8] NIPFP, 1994, p.1.

the sales tax. In Canada, both federal and provincial governments can levy consumption taxes.[9] Thus, while the federal government levies a value added tax (goods and services tax or GST), the provinces levy a retail sales tax (RST). The nature of RST, however, varies among the provinces. The eastern provinces levy RST on the GST-inclusive value of goods sold to consumers. Ontario levies the tax on the value excluding the GST. Alberta does not levy RST at all. Quebec, however, has harmonized its tax fully with the GST and it collects the tax for the federal government as well. Of course, the GST in Quebec has significant differences with the GST levied by the federal government in other parts of the country. There is, thus, some degree of vertical overlapping of indirect taxes. In Switzerland, the Constitution allows for a significant degree of tax over-lapping between the federal and the cantonal governments, but, historical developments have ensured that the federal government collects most of the indirect taxes and direct taxes are collected mostly at the cantonal level (ACIR, 1981). In Germany too, income taxes, customs and excises, and important business taxes including the value added tax are leviable by the federal government, but the elaborate system of legislated sharing of taxes has ensured adequate resource flow to the states while achieving a high degree of vertical harmonization (ACIR, 1981).

Thus, many of the developed federations have, to a large extent, resolved vertical tax overlapping either through tax assignment or tax coordination. Of course, this is not to say that there is a perfect tax harmony between different levels of government in these federations. But surely, the degree of disharmony is nowhere as much as it is seen in India. In India, tax assignments have a large area of concurrency in indirect taxes, and because mutual understanding and trust between the Centre and states is inadequate, attempts at coordination have not been serious enough to minimize distortions in the tax system.[10]

The Indian experience brings out three important lessons. First, tax assignment should not be done merely on legal considerations; economic

[9] The Constitution allows the levy of all direct taxes by both federal and provincial governments, and the courts have interpreted retail sales tax to be a direct tax.

[10] Some degree of coordination was achieved in 1956 when the states surrendered the right to levy sales tax on sugar, textiles, and tobacco in lieu of which, the Central government agreed to levy additional excise duties on the three groups of commodities, the proceeds of which were to be assigned to the states. However, over the years, the states have been dissatisfied with this arrangement and the recommendations of the Committee extending the arrangement to five more groups of commodities were unanimously rejected by the states (Government of India 1983). Again, the decision taken in at the National Development Council to levy the sales tax at uniform rates on twenty-nine groups of commodities as a measure to contain tax competition has not been acted upon.

consequences of such assignments must be taken account of. Second, avoidance of concurrency in a de jure sense does not prevent de facto overlapping. Finally, while overlapping exists in all federations, often in the assignment of the tax itself, like in the USA and Canada, the success of the federation lies in how effectively the adverse effects of tax overlapping are resolved through tax coordination and harmonization. Unfortunately, the attempts at tax coordination in India have not been successful enough to minimize distortions in the tax system.

(iii) *Internal trade barriers:* A major advantage of a federation over a balkanized system is the existence of a unified market not encumbered by any form of impediment to the free movement of and trading in factors of production as well as products. The Constitution recognizes this in Article 301, which reads, 'Subject to other provisions of this part, trade, commerce and intercourse throughout the territory of India shall be free'. However, Article 302 states, 'Parliament may by law impose such restrictions on the freedom of trade, commerce or intercourse between one State and another or within any part of the territory of India as may be required in the public interest'. What is more, Entry 92A (inserted by constitutional amendment in 1956) in the Union List allows the Centre to levy 'taxes on the sale or purchase of goods other than newspapers, where such sale or purchase takes place in the course of inter-State trade or commerce'. Under this provision, the Centre has allowed the states to levy taxes on interstate sale subject to the specified ceiling rate. This has resulted in each state creating a tariff zone by levying a tax on its exports to other states. Although there is a ceiling on the interstate sales tax, the cascading nature of the sales tax system renders the effective tax rates on interstate sales much higher, varying with the stage of processing of the goods sold in the course of interstate trade (raw material, intermediate good, or finished good).

An even more serious impediment to the free movement of goods is caused by the levy of a tax on the entry of goods into a local area for consumption, use or sale, commonly known as 'octroi', which is permitted under Entry 52 in the State List. Presently, among the major states, Gujarat, Haryana, Maharashtra, Orissa, and Rajasthan levy octroi. Some states abolished the levy, but instead imposed entry tax, an account-based tax on purchase of goods from outside the local area.

Octroi has been variously described as 'obnoxious', 'vexatious', 'wasteful', and 'distorting' (Rao, Pradhan, and Bohra, 1985). Important shortcomings of the levy are the production loss arising from hindrance to smooth traffic flow, rampant corruption and harassment to taxpayers, perfunctory assessment of the tax based on trust rather than on actual books of accounts, efficiency loss resulting from the collection of revenue predominantly on inputs and capital goods, multiple taxation of the same goods in different urban local bodies, and exportation of the cost of urban development to rural areas.

In spite of its known disadvantages, collection from octroi forms a predominant proportion of the revenues of urban local bodies in many states. In fact, the standard of urban local services in the states where octroi is not levied is abysmally low.[11] What is more, the day-to-day collections from the tax help in the liquidity of the local bodies. Due to the difficulty in finding a suitable alternative, the tax has continued to be levied in spite of its shortcomings.

Both interstate sales tax and octroi (and other similar forms of taxes) violate the principle of free internal trade and a unified common market. In fact, these taxes have tended to create several tariff zones within the country, causing distortions in resource allocation, and perverse transfer of resources from poorer to richer regions (Rao, 1993).

(iv) *Free-riding and interstate tax exportation:* As already mentioned, a desirable principle of tax assignment is to entrust relatively less mobile tax bases to states and local governments so that they do not indulge in 'free-riding' by exporting the tax burden to non-residents and thereby distort the tax system. The motivation behind the constitutional amendment to allow taxation of interstate trade was to provide a safeguard against the evasion of sales tax by camouflaging local sales as interstate sales. The Taxation Enquiry Committee (India, 1953), therefore, recommended an interstate sales tax at a low rate of one per cent. However, this was used as a revenue-raising measure to finance developmental plans and over the years the rate was increased to 4 per cent.[12] The tax is collected by the exporting state and although the rate cannot exceed four per cent, the actual rate of tax exportation can be much higher, for, the cascading taxes on inputs and capital goods also may be shifted forward to the consumers. This has distorted relative prices, created impediments to the free movement

---

[11] The Rural Urban Relationship Committee (1963) estimated the expenditure needs of the urban local bodies. Employing these norms, the gap between desired expenditures and existing revenues of the municipal bodies was estimated. For details, see Rao, Pradhan, and Bohra (1985).

[12] The CST is levied at 4 per cent or at the tax rate prevailing in the exporting state, whichever is lower, when the interstate sale is made to a registered dealer. If the goods are sold to an unregistered dealer, the lower of 10 per cent or the local sales tax rate in the importing state will apply.

of goods across the nation, and caused inequitable resource transfers from poorer consuming states to the richer producing states (Rao and Vaillancourt, 1994). These will be discussed in greater detail in the next chapter.

SUMMARIZING MAJOR ISSUES IN FISCAL ASSIGNMENT IN INDIA

The analysis of constitutional assignment in India brings out the following:

(i) The Constitution exhibits a clear centripetal bias in the distribution of fiscal powers. In addition to the expenditure functions assigned, the Centre can also influence the expenditure decisions of the states. The assignment of most of the broad-based taxes and residuary tax powers to the Centre, its overriding powers in regard to the functions in the Concurrent List, and domination through economic planning and control over virtually the entire financial sector are only some instances of the Centre's dominance in the economic sphere.

(ii) The assignment of tax powers follows the principle of 'separation' in contrast to that of 'concurrence' followed in federations like the USA and Canada. This, however, could not avoid de facto overlapping. The demarcation of tax powers in the legal sense has not prevented actual concurrency. This has prevented the Centre from levying income tax on a comprehensive base, hindered the development of neutral and broad-based sales taxation, and has given rise to overlapping consumption tax systems at central, state, and local levels which is distorting and iniquitous. The most important adverse consequence of 'separation' is the assignment of the right to levy taxes on services only to the Centre under the residual entry. Unless the states too are empowered to levy taxes on services by amending the Constitution, they will not be able to transform the prevailing cascading-type sales taxation to the destination based VAT.

(iii) The Constitution allows levy of some taxes which can create severe impediments to interstate trade. The levy of tax on interstate sale of goods by the exporting state (subject to a ceiling rate of 4 per cent), besides creating resource distortions, has caused perverse transfer of resources from the poorer consuming states to the more affluent producing states. Similarly, the states can levy a tax (octroi) on the entry of goods into a local area for consumption, use, or sale. This has created impediments to the free movement of goods and also erected a number of tariff zones coinciding with the localities in the country (Rao, 1993). The tax on interstate sale of goods has not only posed impediments to the movement of goods across the country, but has also been a serious source of inefficiency and inequity. Enabling the states to export the tax burden has led to widespread free-riding, and as the ability to free-ride depends on the level of development of the state, this has caused inequitable resource transfers.

(iv) It was alleged that assignment of tax powers was a source of disincentives to the Central government. It was suggested that devolution of a very high proportion of income tax and excise duty is alleged to have robbed the Central government of the incentive to collect revenues from these sources and concentrate on non-shareable taxes like customs duty, causing distortions in the tax structure. However, the recent initiative of giving the states a fixed share (29 per cent) of the total tax revenue would remedy the situation to a large extent.

APPENDIX

Table A6.1

Taxation Heads Assigned to the Centre and the States in the Constitution
(As Listed in the Seventh Schedule of the Constitution)

Centre		States	
Entry in List I of the Seventh Schedule	*Head*	*Entry in List II of the Seventh Schedule*	*Head*
82	Taxes on income other than agricultural income	45	Land revenue, including the assessment and collection of revenue, the maintenance of land records, survey for revenue purposes
83	Duties of customs including export duties	46	Taxes on agricultural income
84	Duties of excise on tobacco and other goods manufactured or produced in India except: a. alcoholic liquors for human consumption; b. opium, Indian hemp and other narcotic drugs and narcotics; but including medicinal and toilet preparations containing alcohol or any substance included in sub-paragraph (b) of this entry	47	Duties in respect of succession of agricultural land
85	Corporation tax	48	Estate duty in respect of agricultural land
86	Taxes on the capital value of the assets, exclusive of agricultural land of individuals and companies; taxes on the capital of companies	49	Taxes on lands and buildings
87	Estate duty in respect of property other than agricultural land	50	Taxes on mineral rights subject to any limitations imposed by Parliament by law relating to mineral development
88	Duties in respect of succession to property other than agricultural land	51	Duties of excise on the following goods manufactured or produced in the state and countervailing duties at the same or lower rates

Centre		States	
Entry in List I of the Seventh Schedule	Head	Entry in List II of the Seventh Schedule	Head
			on similar goods manufactured or produced elsewhere in India: a. alcohol liquors for human consumption; b. opium, Indian hemp and other narcotic drugs and narcotics; but not including medicinal and toilet preparations containing alcohol or any substance included in sub-paragraph (b) of this entry.
89	Terminal taxes on goods or passengers carried by railway, sea or air; taxes on railway fares and freights	52	Taxes on the entry of goods into a local area for consumption, use or sale therein
90	Taxes other than stamp duties on transactions in stock exchanges and future markets	53	Taxes on the consumption or sale of electricity
91	Rates of stamp duty in respect of bills of exchange, cheques, promissory notes, bills of lading, letters of credit, policies of insurance, transfer of shares, debentures, proxies and receipts	54[1]	Taxes on the sale or purchase of goods other than newspapers, subject to the provisions of entry 92A of List I
92	Taxes on the sale or purchase of newspapers and on advertisements published therein	55	Taxes on advertisements other than advertisements published in the newspaper[2] and advertisements broadcast by radio or television
92A[3]	Taxes on the sale or purchase of goods other than newspapers, where such sale or purchase takes place in the course of interstate trade or commerce	56	Taxes on goods and passengers carried by road or on inland waterways
92B[4]	Taxes on the consignment of goods (whether the consignment is to the person making it or to any other person), where such consignment takes place in the course of interstate trade or commerce	57	Taxes on vehicles, whether mechanically propelled or not, suitable for use on roads including tramcars, subject to the provision of entry 35 of List III

Centre		States	
Entry in List I of the Seventh Schedule	*Head*	*Entry in List II of the Seventh Schedule*	*Head*
97	Any other matter not enumerated in List II or List III including any tax not mentioned in either or both the lists	58	Taxes on animals and boats
		59	Tolls
		60	Taxes on professions, trades, callings, and employments
		61	Capitation taxes
		62	Taxes on luxuries, including taxes on entertainments, amusements, betting, and gambling
		63	Rates of stamp duty in respect of documents other than those specified in the provision of List I with regard to rates of stamp duty

[1] Substituted by the Constitution (Sixth Amendment) Act 1956, s.2 for entry 54

[2] Inserted by the Constitution (Forty-second Amendment) Act, 1975, s.57 (w.e.f. 31.1.1977)

[3] Inserted by the Constitution (Sixth Amendment) Act, 1956, s.2

[4] Inserted by the Constitution (Forty-sixth Amendment) Act, 1982, s.5

Extracts from the *Report of the Commission on Centre–State Relations* (Justice R.S. Sarkaria), 987.

TABLE A6.2

Illustrative List of Developmental Subjects (Other than Financial Subjects)
Included in Centre, State, and Concurrent Lists in
The Seventh Schedule of the Constitution

(A) Centre List

S. No.	Entry No.	Subject
1.	6	Atomic energy and mineral resources necessary for its production
2.	22	Railways
3.	23	Highways declared by or under law made by Parliament to be national highways
4.	24	Shipping and navigation on inland waterways, declared by Parliament by law to be national waterways; as regards mechanically propelled vessels the rule of the road on such waterways
5.	25	Maritime shipping and navigation including shipping and navigation on tidal waters provision of education and training for the mercantile marine and regulation of such education and training provided by states and other agencies
6.	26	Lighthouses, lightships, beacons, and other provision for the safety of shipping and aircraft
7.	27	Ports declared by or under law made by Parliament or existing law to be major ports, including their delimitation and the constitution and powers of port authorities therein
8.	28	Port quarantine, including hospitals connected therewith seamen's and marine hospitals
9.	29	Airways aircraft and air-navigation provision of aerodromes; regulation and organization of air traffic and of aerodromes; provision for aeronautical education and training and regulation of such education and training provided by states and other agencies
10.	30	Carriage of passengers and goods by railways, sea or air, or by national waterways in mechanically propelled vessels
11.	31	Posts and telegraph: telephones, wireless, broadcasting, and other form of communications
12.	41	Trade and commerce with foreign countries; import and export across customs frontiers; definition of customs frontiers
13.	42	Interstate trade and commerce
14.	52	Industries, the control of which by the Union is declared by Parliament by law to be expedient in the public interest
15.	53	Regulation and development of oilfields and mineral oil resources; petroleum and petroleum products; other liquids and substances declared by Parliament by law to be dangerously inflammable
16.	54	Regulation of mines and mineral development to the extent which such regulation and development under the control of the Union is declared by Parliament by law to be expedient in the public interest

S. No.	Entry No.	*Subject*
17.	56	Regulation and development of interstate rivers and river valleys to the extent to which such regulation and development under the control of the Union is declared by Parliament by law to be expedient in the public interest
18.	57	Fishing and fisheries beyond territorial waters
19.	65	Union agenda and institutions for:
		a. professional, vocational or technical training including the training of police officers; or
		b. the promotion of special studies or research; or
		c. scientific or technical assistance in the investigation or detection of crime
20.	66	Coordination and determination of standards in institutions for higher education or research and scientific and technical institutions
21.	68	Survey of India, the geological, botanical, zoological, and anthropological surveys of India, meteorological organizations

(B) State List

1.	5	Local government, that is to say, the constitution and powers of municipal corporations, improvements trusts, district boards, mining settlement authorities and other local authorities for the purpose of local self-government or village administration
2.	6	Public health and sanitation; hospitals and dispensaries
3.	9	Relief of the disabled and unemployable
4.	13	Communications, that is to say, roads, bridges, ferries, and other means of communication not specified in List I: municipal tramways; ropeways; inland waterways and traffic thereon subject to the provisions of List I and List II with regard to such waterways; vehicles other than mechanically propelled vehicles
5.	14	Agriculture, including agricultural education and research, protection against pests and prevention of plant diseases
6.	15	Preservation, protection, and improvement of stock and prevention of animal diseases; veterinary training and practice
7.	17	Water, that is to say, water supplies, irrigation and canals, drainage, embankments, water storage and water power subject to the provisions of entry 56 of List I
8.	18	Land, that is to say, rights in or over land, land tenures including the relations of landlord and tenant, and the collection of rents; transfer and alienation of agricultural land; land improvement and agricultural loans; colonization
9.	21	Fisheries
10.	23	Regulation of mines and mineral development subject to the provisions of List I with respect to regulation and development under the control of the Union
11.	24	Industries subject to the provisions of entries 7 and 52 of List I
12.	25	Gas and gas-works

S. No.	Entry No.	Subject
13.	26	Trade and commerce within the state subject to the provisions of entry 33 of List III
14.	27	Production, supply, and distribution of goods subject to the provisions of entry 33 of List III
15.	32	Cooperative societies
16.	35	Works, lands, and buildings vested in or in the possession of the state

(C) Concurrent List

S. No.	Entry No.	Subject
1.	17A	Forests
2.	20	Economic and social planning
3.	20A	Population control and family planning
4.	23	Social security and social insurance; employment and unemployment
5.	25	Education, including technical education, medical education and universities, subject to the provisions of entries 63, 64, 65 and 66 of List I; vocational and technical training of labour
6.	27	Relief and rehabilitation of persons displaced from their original place of residence by reasons of the setting up of the dominions of India and Pakistan.
7.	31	Ports other than those declared by or under law made by Parliament or existing law to be major ports
8.	32	Shipping and navigation and inland waterways as regards mechanically propelled vessels, and the rule of the road on such waterways, and the carriage of passengers and goods on inland waterways subject to the provisions of List I with regard to national waterways
9.	33	Trade and commerce in, and the production supply and distribution of: a. the products of any industry where the control of such industry by the Union is declared by Parliament by law to be expedient in the public interest and imported goods on inland waterways subject to the provisions of List I with regard to national waterways b. foodstuffs, including edible oilseeds and oils; c. cattle fodder, including oilseeds and other concentrates; d. raw cotton, where ginned or unginned and cotton seed; and e. raw jute
10.	36	Factories
11.	37	Boilers
12.	38	Electricity

Extracts from the *Report of the Commission on Centre–State Relations* (Justice R.S. Sarkaria), 1987.

7

Fiscal Overlapping, Concurrency, and Competition

SETTING

The theoretical rationales for assignment of functions and sources of finance to hierarchically ordered governments were discussed in the previous chapter. It was argued that in real-world situations, even in the best assignment system, perfect mapping between functions and geographical boundaries cannot be achieved, and overlapping in functions is unavoidable. In this chapter, we discuss an important aspect of imperfect mapping, namely overlapping jurisdictions, and their consequences.

Fiscal overlapping can occur due to concurrent assignments, interdependence of fiscal revenue bases and expenditure functions, and competition among hierarchically ordered governmental layers (vertical) and jurisdictions within each layer (horizontal). Fiscal overlapping can occur both in tax and expenditure functions. Vertical and horizontal interdependence between different layers of government arises because of overlapping jurisdictions or due to intergovernmental transfers designed to offset vertical fiscal imbalances. In fact, intergovernmental transfers are both a cause and consequence of fiscal interdependence between different layers of government. Overlapping jurisdictions impact on fiscal efficiency and equity due to: (i) imperfect mapping; (ii) policy interdependence between governmental units; and (iii) strategic interactions between governmental units.

Imperfect mapping is an important reason for ambiguity and fiscal overlap—both vertical and horizontal. The problem arises not because of concurrency in assignments but due to ambiguity in the role of different jurisdictions. Absence of clear assignments can lead to free-riding on the one hand and underinvestment in the sector on the other. We will return to this later in the chapter.

Another reason for overlapping in functions is policy interdependence. Macroeconomic stabilization and redistribution policies implemented by the Centre can require microeconomic adjustments at the sub-national levels. Similarly, the sub-national fiscal imbalances have serious macroeconomic implications. The policies on wages, interest rates, prices, and incomes implemented at one level can have repercussions on others. The problem is not confined to vertical overlapping. At the sub-national level also, fiscal, regulatory, and investment policies impact on other subnational units.

Overlapping assignment and policy interdependence accelerate the impact on fiscal harmony when combined with strategic interaction by participating/affected governmental units. In terms of vertical interactions, the strategy could be to maximize fiscal transfers in response to a given transfer formula or scheme, or maximize the gains from payment of dues to Central government departments, or minimize fiscal losses arising from a policy change. Similarly, in the case of horizontal interactions, the strategy could be to operate the fiscal system to maximize the gains to the different agents of the government or to the residents of the jurisdiction. Attempts to attract trade and industry and attempts to export the tax burden to residents of other states are the examples of the latter.

The principal reason for fiscal overlapping is intergovernmental competition. A system of cooperative federalism may overcome these problems, but in a situation where the players adopt non-cooperative strategies, this may not be feasible. On the other hand, collusion can blunt intergovernmental competition.[1] In competitive federalism, intergovernmental competition works mainly through the 'Salmon mechanism'. According to this, the voters as well as opposition parties in a governmental unit benchmark the supply performances of competing governmental units and affect the decisions of the unit to provide comparable standards of public service-tax mixes either by influencing the decisions of the government or voting it out of power (Salmon, 2002). Of course, it is possible to visualize a situation where the Salmon mechanism results in 'competitive' populism rather than efficient public service provision depending on the time horizon of the political parties and the nature of institutions in the economy.

Considering that fiscal overlap can occur due to competition, it would

---

[1] Breton (1987, p. 277), goes as far as stating, 'Co-operative federalism, if it came to pass, would deny federalism itself. Those who seek co-operative federalism and labour for its realization, seek and labour for a unitary State, disguised in the trappings of federalism, but from which competition would have been reduced to a minimum or even eliminated'. We do, however, think that there is a role for co-operative federalism in certain spheres.

not be appropriate to infer that this would necessarily be either beneficent or harmful. Often, in developing economies, competition can be unstable and welfare reducing, given that there exist a variety of reasons for decentralization failure (Breton, 2002). An important precondition for benign intergovernmental competition is that there should be a mechanism to bring about stability. For this, it is necessary to formulate rules to prevent predatory pricing of public services, exportation of tax burdens to non-residents, spillovers of negative externalities across jurisdictions, erection of trade barriers, and any drive towards a race to the bottom to attract trade and investment. Therefore, it is important to institute an effective mechanism to monitor competition by having checks and balances in the system.[2] This implies that no governmental unit should be in a position to exploit others and if it does, there should be an effective mechanism to counter it. Exploitation can be minimized when there is 'competitive equality' or equality of the power of the competing entities. It is also important to see that no jurisdiction is able to 'free-ride' on others or provide public services to its residents by passing on the burden of financing them to non-residents.

Concurrency and competition can cause fiscal overlapping and disharmony, resulting in inefficiency and inequity in the delivery of public services.[3] In order to ensure that competition is beneficent, it is important to understand the sources of instability. The objective of this chapter is to analyse the sources of disharmony and instability in the delivery of public services and in raising revenues to finance them, both vertically between different levels of government, and horizontally between different jurisdictions, and to suggest ways and means to resolve the disharmony and restore stability to intergovernmental competition.

VERTICAL FISCAL DISHARMONY: MAJOR ISSUES

It must be mentioned that in all constitutionally assigned governmental systems, no matter how carefully the assignments are worked out, some disharmony in the functioning of vertical intergovernmental units is inevitable. This is because, first, constitutional assignments are determined by a number of historical, political, and social factors besides economic considerations[4] and second, even when economic considerations

---

[2] For details, see Breton (1995) pp. 240–62.

[3] According to Oates (1972, p.145), fiscal disharmony enhances excess burden and yields undesirable pattern of incidence.

[4] As stated by Breton (1981, p. 253), '… political scientists, who know better, have in their

are important, this has been driven by the eagerness to forge cooperation by suppressing competition. Finally, in a hierarchically ordered governmental system, unless the monitoring mechanism is effective, higher-level governments can suppress competition by appropriating the powers to themselves through various means.

In the Indian context, vertical disharmony between the Centre and the states in fiscal and regulatory functions arises for a variety of reasons. The first and foremost is the interdependent nature of fiscal operations of the Central and state governments. Both policies and strategic responses to policies by the Centre and states contrive to create vertical fiscal disharmony. The second source of vertical fiscal disharmony is to be found in the centripetal bias implicit in the assignment system and the intrusion of the Central domain over that of the states in the course of development planning. The problems caused by the lack of clarity in assignments, particularly in respect of areas under concurrent jurisdiction, also contributes to vertical disharmony.

(i) Interdependence of policies and vertical fiscal overlap: There are many ways in which the Central policies affect the fiscal operations of states and vice versa. In a system where many prices and quantities are determined by administrative fiat rather than by market forces, and where the public sector controls a significant proportion of production and distribution activities, the cost of public service delivery at each level of government will be affected by the policy changes in others. Here, no attempt is made to comprehensively record the interdependence but some examples will suffice to place the issue in proper perspective. Thus, administered price changes at the Centre can affect the ability to provide public services by state and local governments and vice versa. The policies on interest rates and lending to the states affect their ability to finance infrastructure and debt servicing. Similarly, wage increases at the Centre raise the demand for pay revisions in the states. Increases in administered prices of coal escalate the cost of generating power by state electricity boards (SEBs). Similarly, increase in administered price of petroleum products increases the cost of providing public services in states. More importantly, the levy of Union excise duties by the Central government at high rates reduces the tax room for the state governments.

The policies and actions of state governments affect efficiency in the delivery of public services by the Centre as well. Despite the Constitution placing restrictions on the states' borrowing powers to ensure proper

more generous moments treated economists as poor souls with a model in need of an application.'

macroeconomic management, the states have found several ways to soften the constraints. Borrowing from public accounts, particularly small saving loans, borrowing through public enterprises, and creating large contingent liabilities can create serious macroeconomic stability concerns to the Central government.

(ii) Centripetal bias: while the centripetal bias in the constitutional assignment has led to concentration of powers with the Central government, the working of the constitution over the years has led to a steady erosion of the authority of state governments. The single most important issue that has caused this is item 20 in the Concurrent List in the Seventh Schedule to the Constitution, which reads, 'Economic and Social Planning'. The instrumentality of planning has been used by the Centre to expand its activities even in areas clearly demarcated to the states. The Central government could bring in any of the subjects in both State List and Concurrent List and influence policies through the Central sector and centrally sponsored schemes. While programmes in the Central sector are funded entirely by the Centre and employ the state governments merely as implementing agencies, the centrally sponsored schemes are in the nature of shared cost programmes. There were as many as 262 centrally sponsored schemes a decade ago, accounting for about 10 per cent of states' expenditures. Even in 2000–01, there were more than 210 schemes and their share in states' expenditures has increased steadily to about 15 per cent. The large number of these programmes is also indicative of the role of political factors in determining the transfer system. This will be discussed in greater detail in Chapters 9 and 11.

(iii) Ambiguity in assignments: Lack of clear assignment can be a source of overlap between the Central and state functions. This is not a necessary outcome of concurrent assignments. It is possible to clarify the roles of different levels of government, even when a particular function is concurrently assigned. At the same time, even when a function is specifically assigned, there may not be clarity, because often it is not clear whether a function should be undertaken by the government or left to the market.

Assignment of functions to a government can be seen as analogous to assignment of property rights. It is only when the property rights are clearly assigned that the owner has an incentive to make the investments needed to develop it. Lack of clarity in assignment, therefore, can result in under provision of the service in question. We may cite three examples of ambiguity in assignment resulting in the under provision of services. The first is the case of agricultural research. This is in the concurrent domain, and both Central and state governments want that the other level should make the investment and consequently, the service is under provided.

Second is the case of the generation of electric power. Over the years, state governments have shown a tendency to reduce investments in this sector even as the Central government has increased its spending through the National Thermal Power Corporation. However, fiscal difficulties have constrained the Centre also from making the required level of investment. The third example is that of river water disputes. Lack of clear assignment has resulted in the non-resolution of the dispute. The issues relating to the problems in sharing of river water are discussed in Chapter 10.

In the case of tax powers, an apparently clear assignment actually involves concurrency and inefficiency. As discussed in the previous chapter, although in a legal sense the assignment of taxes on production (excise duty) to the Centre and sales tax to the state is in accordance with the principle of separation, in effect the two taxes are on the same base, resulting in concurrency. Each level of government attempts to levy the tax to maximize its revenues while ignoring the effect of the tax levied at the other level. There has been no attempt at developing a coordinated system of consumption taxation. Thus, it is not surprising that at both Central and state levels, domestic taxes on production and consumption predominate, and have been on the increase. Given that both Union excise duty and state sales taxes are characterized by multiplicity of tax rates, plethora of exemptions, and given further that there is no mechanism to relieve taxes on inputs and capital goods particularly in the case of sales taxes, it is virtually impossible to determine the effective rate of consumption tax levied at the two levels. This also makes it difficult to limit the overall tax burden and the relative tax rooms for the Centre and states in imposing taxes on different commodities.

Three alternative approaches have been suggested to reform domestic trade taxes. The first is to transfer the power to levy domestic trade taxes to the Centre. A variant of this is to allow the Centre to levy the value added tax up to the retail stage and allow the states to piggyback on the Central levy (Government of India, 1992). This would require a constitutional amendment to allow the Centre to extend taxation up to the retail level. In the latter case, it is necessary to vest concurrent powers to the two levels of government. Of course, this might not be acceptable to the state governments as it removes their autonomy to determine the tax base. The second solution may be to allow the states to levy the VAT (Burgess, Howes, and Stern, 1993; Joshi and Little, 1996). Therefore, the study team on domestic trade taxes, after a detailed examination, concluded that the solution to reforming domestic trade taxes lies in having a dual VAT—converting the prevailing excise duties into a manufacturing-stage VAT and levying destination-based retail-stage VAT by the states (NIPFP, 1994).

The Centre–state coordination and bargaining required in reforming domestic trade taxation to evolve the dual VAT in India is considerable. First, it is important to take a view on the overall tax burden from domestic trade taxes and determine the relative tax room for the Centre and the states. Next, there is the problem of relieving the taxes on interstate sale and consignment transfers.[5] The alternatives suggested are of zero-rating the taxes at the point of interstate sales or introducing a clearing-house mechanism.[6] Whatever the solution, it is important to note that the Central government has to coordinate reform in this area. A major problem in carrying out this reform is the fear of loss of revenue by the state governments. Perhaps, the Central government should bargain the reform implementation with the states in the interest of larger welfare gain by giving them concurrent powers to levy sales tax on services. This will also help to evolve the state sales taxes as full-fledged, destination-based value added taxes on goods and services.

INTER-JURISDICTIONAL TAX COMPETITION AND ALLOCATIVE EFFICIENCY

In the literature on fiscal federalism, horizontal fiscal competition and overlapping has received considerable focus. The mobility models where the consumer–voter chooses her residence among the competing suppliers of public services, the practices of sub-national governments to divert trade and attract industry by giving fiscal and financial incentives, political scientists' preoccupation with the need to evolve 'cooperative federalism', and the discussions on tax harmonization are some of the examples which recognize the competitive nature of horizontal intergovernmental relationships.

However, as mentioned earlier, horizontal intergovernmental competition can be beneficial only if the competition is 'stable'. Instability in horizontal competition can arise when there are significant competitive inequalities among the jurisdictions, or when the jurisdictions are allowed to 'free-ride', or when they erect trade barriers to protect trade within their jurisdictions or when the competition to attract trade and industry results in a 'race to the bottom' in terms of reduction in tax rates and giving fiscal and financial incentives. Ensuring stability necessitates

---

[5] The traders tend to send goods on consignment transfers to the state where the goods will be sold and then sell them as local sale to avoid Central sales tax. This also causes interstate tax exportation as the goods sent on consignment carry input taxes in a cascading system of sales taxation. For details, see Rao and Vaillaincourt (1994).

[6] For details, see NIPFP (1994).

monitoring competition—ensuring that competition is governed by set rules which are properly enforced, with violations penalized. A major role in monitoring competition has to be borne by the Central government which will employ regional policies and intergovernmental transfers to ensure 'competitive equality' and form rules and enforce them to prohibit inter-jurisdictional exportation of tax burdens and negative externalities, and erection of trade barriers to ensure 'cost–benefit appropriability' of jurisdictions.

In a developing-country federation like India, however, there are several reasons for intergovernmental competition can be unstable. Acute interstate inequalities in the levels of development and the consequent variations in the ability and 'power' of different states violate the basic precondition for stability namely, 'competitive equality'. Instability is accentuated when each state attempts to attract trade and investments through fiscal and financial incentives, tax competition, and by erecting trade barriers. Further, as a high degree of vertical imbalance, and predominance of non-benefit, particularly 'origin'-based domestic trade taxes, severs the Wicksellian connection (tax and expenditure decisions are not effectively linked), costs and benefits of public services provided by the states are not clearly perceived and they can pass the burden of financing public services to non-residents.

Interstate Tax Disharmony in Indian Federation

In this section, we analyse the salient features of the states' tax systems in India and identify the sources of instability in states' tax systems causing interstate tax disharmony. The analysis shows that major sources of instability and disharmony in the states' tax systems are caused by 'beggar-my-neighbour' policies followed by the states to attract trade and industry, 'free-rider' behaviour by exporting the tax burden through levying 'origin'-based consumption taxes, and erection of trade barriers through fiscal instruments. The analysis helps to highlight inefficiencies and inequities caused by the strategic behaviour of the states.

States' Taxes in India—Salient Features

States play an important role in raising tax revenues in Indian federalism and therefore, structure and operation of their tax systems have a significant impact on economic efficiency and equity. Together, states raise almost 35 per cent of total tax revenues. As a ratio of the SDP, revenue from state taxes showed a steady increase from a little over 6 per cent in the mid-1970s to almost 8.5 per cent in 1990–1 and declined thereafter to 7.3 per cent in 1999–2000 (Table 7.1). Although the ability of the states to finance expenditures from their own taxes has shown a steady decline over the years, they still finance over 40 per cent of current expenditures of the states. It is also seen that there are wide variations in the level of taxes raised as well as the share of tax revenues in expenditures among the states and these variations have shown a steady increase over the years.

TABLE 7.1
Importance of States' Tax Revenue

Year	Share of States' Own Tax Revenue in State domestic Product (SDP)		Share of States' Tax Revenue in States' Current Expenditure		
	Mean	Coefficient of variation	Median	Mean	Coefficient of variation
1975–6	6.3	19.7	6.8	53.5	20.8
1980–1	6.9	23.5	7.6	47.9	25.9
1985–6	8.2	26.8	8.4	47.8	24.6
1990–1	8.5	26.9	7.6	45.3	27.7
1995–6	7.3	26.0	7.1	45.3	32.7
1999–2000	7.3	22.4	7.7	40.3	30.0
2000–01 (RE)	7.7	25.4	8.5	40.9	29.8

Note: Estimates relate to fourteen major states and they constitute 93 per cent of total population. The hill states of the north-east and the small state of Goa are not included in the analysis.

Sources: 1. Budget documents of the state governments.
2. Central Statistical Organization, Ministry of Planning, Government of India.

As in the case of the Central government, political economy considerations have dominated the evolution of state tax systems. The inability of the states to raise direct taxes on land and agricultural incomes has resulted in the predominance of indirect taxes (Table 7.2). The revenue from indirect taxes has steadily increased over the years from about 85 per cent of states' tax revenues in the 1950s to almost 97 per cent in 2000–01, with the sales tax alone contributing over 60 per cent of total tax revenues. The pattern is broadly similar across states with the share of sales tax varying from 44 per cent in Punjab to over 70 per cent in Bihar. The other major state taxes are state excise duties on alcoholic beverages (14.7 per cent) and stamp duties and registration fees (8.4 per cent).

Given that revenue from sales taxes predominates in the states' fiscal operations, the structure and operation of sales taxes have an important bearing on allocative efficiency and equity in the economy. Interstate competition in levying consumption taxes introduces additional issues having implications not only on allocative efficiency and equity but also on the very stability of the competition itself.

TABLE 7.2

Composition of State Taxes

Taxes		1975–6	1980–1	1985–6	1990–1	1995–6	1999–2000	2000–01 RE
A.	Direct Taxes on Land and Income	8.00	4.10	4.30	4.10	3.50	2.80	3.00
B.	Indirect Taxes, of which	92.00	95.90	95.70	95.90	96.50	97.20	97.00
B.1	Sales Tax	51.00	55.50	55.30	54.70	55.60	60.70	61.80
B.2	Stamps and Registration	6.10	6.40	5.90	6.90	9.20	8.30	8.40
B.3	State Excise Duty	12.40	12.60	14.20	15.90	13.30	14.70	13.40
B.4	Others	21.70	21.40	20.30	18.40	18.40	13.40	13.40
Total State Tax		100.00	100.00	100.00	100.00	100.00	100.00	100.00

Source: Public Finance Statistics, Ministry of Finance, Government of India (various years).

Whether interstate competition in taxation leads to inefficient resource allocation or it is a beneficent force is a controversial issue. Break (1967, pp. 23–4) almost three and a half decades ago argued, '....(A)ctive tax competition ... tends to produce either a generally low level of State–local tax effort or a State–local tax structure with strong regressive features'. More recently, Rivlin (1992) has argued for the replacement of state taxes with tax-sharing arrangements to avoid disruptive interstate competition. In contrast, Oates and Schwab (1988) show a Pareto efficient outcome in a formal model of inter-jurisdictional competition in which states provide two public goods—one local consumption good and another public input that enhances the productivity of capital and finances the public goods through benefit taxes. However, if the states deviate from the basic assumption of the model and levy non-benefit taxes, particularly taxes on capital, the state taxes can be a source of allocative distortions. Another critical assumption is, like in the case of atomistic competition, the states are assumed to be 'small', essentially 'price-takers'. Finally, like all neo-classical models, Oates and Schwab assume a benevolent public decision maker. If the elected state officials have their own objective function, contrary to the objective function of the state population, the resulting tax system could be distorted. Thus, it would seem that the interstate tax competition could produce beneficial results only when there is a monitoring mechanism to ensure that competition is stable.

The analysis of interstate competition in India shows that often, it has been a source of distortions and inequity and this is particularly true of the sales tax. The adverse consequences have been caused by (i) divergence in tax rates, tax competition, and irrational tax system; (ii) incentive to 'free-ride' resulting in significant interstate tax exportation; and (iii) erection of trade barriers. These issues deserve to be analysed in detail.[7]

(i) Divergence in sales tax rates and tax competition: A major consequence of sales tax competition is the minute differentiation in the nominal rates. Although originally rate differentiation was introduced on equity grounds or for raising additional resources or for efficiency reasons (lower tax rates on inputs and capital goods), in recent years, tax competition among the states has contributed to this outcome in no small a measure. The desire to attract cross-border purchases has led to reduction in tax rates on commodities with high price elasticity of demand and to increased rates on price inelastic commodities, which are predominantly exported out of a state. Thus, there are quite a few instances where motor cars and consumer electronics are taxed at the same or lower rates than food grains and edible oils, neutralizing the very objective of equity for which rate differentiation was introduced in the first place.[8]

The problems with the sales tax system and the contribution of interstate competition to its irrationality has been brought out clearly in the report of the study team on domestic trade taxes appointed by the ministry of finance (NIPFP, 1994). Analysis of interstate competition brings out a number of problems to the fore in sales tax systems. First, the competition, instead of converging the tax rates, has led to significant divergence in exemptions, and nominal tax rates. Second, attempts to conceal the tax burden have led to taxation of inputs and capital goods, resulting in tax on tax, mark-up on tax, and tax on mark-ups. Fourth, interstate competition, besides significant cascading, has caused distortions in relative prices to inequity. Interstate competition in India has also led to reducing tax rates with higher price elasticity and vice versa for

---

[7] For detailed analysis of the sales tax systems in different states and its adverse efficiency and equity consequences, see, NIPFP (1994).

[8] In Punjab, for example, the tax rate on motor cars is 3.5 per cent whereas food grains are taxed at 4 per cent and edible oils at 8 per cent. Of course, the equity objective in the design of tax rates itself has been taken account of on the basis of the judgements about income elasticity of demand for various commodities without considering the general equilibrium effects of such a tax design.

those with lower price elasticity. This, besides minute differentiation in tax rates has led to inequity in the tax system. The rate of tax on motor cars in Kerala and Rajasthan was the same as that on bicycles, but was lower in Gujarat, Punjab, and Uttar Pradesh. Medicines are taxed at rates higher than on motor cars in eight out of fourteen major states. Electronic goods are taxed at lower rates than items such as bicycles in a number of states.

Exemptions and differences in nominal tax rates are not the only cause of differences in effective tax rates among states. First, there are notable differences in the sales tax systems in different states. While most of the states levy the tax at the point of manufacture or import into the state for administrative reasons and because it is more acceptable to the traders, some states have tended to conceal the effective tax rates by spreading the tax burden at different stages of sale transactions in respect of some commodities. In addition, most states levy additional sales tax, or a surcharge on sales tax over and above the general sales tax, on sales tax dealers above a specified turnover limit. Second, the standards of tax administration and enforcement vary widely across states, resulting in wide differences in the effective tax rates. The third source of variation in effective rates of tax is the interstate competition in providing sales tax concessions to attract new investments. This 'beggar my neighbour' policy, besides causing significant loss of revenue to the states' exchequer, has distorted the relative prices across both commodities and regions.[9] All these factors have tended to cause minute differentiation in effective tax rates on commodities within and between different states.

A notable feature of the interstate competition is the role of Union Territories. As their expenditures are underwritten entirely by the Central government, they are under no compulsion to raise revenues from the tax handles assigned to them. At the same time, this provides incentive for them to reduce tax rates in order to attract investments and trade. Thus, they have kept their tax rates at abysmally low levels, particularly in commodities with high price elasticities. As a result, the tax system in Daman and Diu has impacted the system in Gujarat and Maharashtra; tax competition by Chandigarh has impacted the tax system in Punjab and Haryana, and Pondicherry has adversely impacted the southern states. The effect of this has not only been to distort the tax structures but also to render the tax system unstable. The attempt by the ministry of finance to discipline the Union Territories to adhere to the floor rates fixed by the empowered committee has tried to remedy the situation to some extent,

---

[9] For analysis of cost and efficacy of sales tax incentives, see Tulasidhar and Rao (1986).

but much remains to be done to achieve this. The reluctance of the Central government to discipline the Union Territories is a major stumbling block in the development of a coordinated system of consumption taxation in India.

(ii) 'Free-riding' and Interstate Tax Exportation: Another worrisome consequence of interstate competition arises from the attempts by the states to pass the tax burden to non-residents. As already mentioned, in India the states levy sales taxes predominantly on the basis of origin, at the stage of manufacture or import. Further, for revenue reasons, given their constraint on tax handles and narrow tax bases, the states have tended to tax raw materials, intermediate inputs as well as capital goods. Further, the states can levy the tax on interstate sale subject to the ceiling rate of 4 per cent.[10] In an imperfect market characterized by 'mark-up' pricing in many sectors, where consumption taxes are fully shifted forward, the taxes on inputs and capital goods cascade on to interstate sales tax and the effective tax rate on interstate exports would be much higher than the 4 per cent nominally levied. Further, it is seen that the exports of more developed states are larger than their imports and the proportion of final goods in their exports too is higher. Thus, the residents of poorer states end up paying taxes on a larger volume of imports and at higher effective tax rates. Absence of information on interstate transactions in goods makes it impossible to estimate the extent of interstate tax exportation with any degree of accuracy. Based on the available information we have worked out some crude estimates and these are detailed in Chapter 9. At this stage, it is sufficient to mention that the volume of interstate exportation in India seems to be very high and these transfers have been very inequitable as the exports are predominantly from the richer producing states to the poorer consuming states.

(iii) Sub-national Tax System and Impediments to Internal Trade: A major advantage of a federal system as opposed to a Balkanized economy is the availability of a common market. The common market enables the producers to reap optimal production scale and achieve cost-efficient production of goods and services. However, this is possible only when there are no impediments to free trade and movement of factors of production and goods and services throughout the federation. When certain minimum levels of social and economic infrastructure are provided across the federation, free mobility of capital and labour tends to

---

[10] The ceiling rate is applicable only when the transaction takes place between the registered dealers. If the sale is from a registered dealer, in the exporting state to a non-registered dealer in the importing state the ceiling rate applicable is 10 per cent.

equalize marginal productivities across different regions, thus realizing the maximum possible output in the economy. The inter-jurisdictional competition among different states in providing varying public expenditure–tax mixes to attract capital could provide an accommodating environment for innovations. Thus, fiscal federalism helps in not only ensuring efficient utilization of resources (operating on the production possibilities frontier) but also in technological progress (shift in the frontier) to result in higher economic growth than in a balkanized economy.

On the other hand, impediments to free trade and movement of factors and products can seriously misallocate resources. Each state would be interested in preventing the outflow of capital and inflow of labour to jurisdiction, but such self-interest of regions would not be in the interest of the country as a whole. Similarly, there would be attempts to regulate the free movement of commodities across the states or local bodies. In a scarcity-hit economy, regulatory impediments are placed to prevent speculation and profiteering and to ensure fair distribution of the commodity across regions and persons at a reasonable price (rationing). Though this has adverse effects on resource allocation in the long run, it could be justified in the short run as a measure to manage the fair distribution of the scarce commodity. The restrictions on the movement of food grains even when the country has a food surplus situation are a case in point. However, when a jurisdiction erects fiscal or non-fiscal barriers to provide for local protection, it could have serious distortionary effects on resource allocation.

Barriers can be erected either as a measure to protect local trade and industry, simply to collect the tax in that jurisdiction, or merely to export the burden of providing public services to non-residents. These could take the form of placing restrictions either on the exports out of a state or imports into a state. The restrictions may be placed on either the inputs or the outputs and this could take the form of fiscal impediment or physical restrictions. The restriction can be placed on interstate movements or on intrastate movements.

There are several regulatory impediments imposed by different state governments. Most of these are informal and non-transparent. Most state governments have the knowledge of local language as a precondition for employment in the state government. Preference given to the enterprises owned by the state government in the purchase policy even when there is a price disadvantage is not uncommon. Some state governments even require that non-residents cannot conduct trade and commerce in the state unless they have a local partner with them. Some states restrict the sale of raw materials on interstate sale to ensure that the value addition takes place inside the state. The restrictions on the interstate sale of oilseeds in Gujarat, raw cashewnuts in Kerala and monopoly procurement of cotton in Maharashtra are cases in point. Even the regulation against the closure of financially unviable firms acts as an impediment. Also, some states insist on the employment of local personnel as an eligibility condition for getting concessions and incentives. The industrial policy of Karnataka, for example, stipulates that 80 per cent of additional employment opportunities created by the industry should accrue to the local people. Similarly, in Kerala, government and state's public enterprises give price preferences of 15 per cent on the purchases made from the small-scale units and 10 per cent on the purchases made from the medium- and large-scale industries located in the state.

The non-fiscal impediments mentioned above are of lesser consequence as compared to the fiscal impediments on interstate and intrastate trade. The two most important fiscal impediments are the levy of tax on interstate trade in goods, and octroi or tax on the entry of goods into a local area for consumption, use, or sale. Until recently, the states having large deposits of coal like Bihar, Madhya Pradesh, Orissa, and West Bengal used to impose a cess on the royalty rate at very high rates. However, this had to be abolished after the Supreme Court disallowed it. The extent of adverse economic consequences of all these levies, though unclear, is significant and hence deserves discussion in greater detail.

TAXATION OF INTERSTATE TRADE: MAJOR ISSUES

In Chapter 3, we have referred to the issue of constitutional status relating to the maintenance of common market and the problems arising from the levy of central sales tax (CST) and it may be useful to briefly refer to the discussion here. Article 301 of the Constitution states, 'Subject to the other provisions of this part, trade, commerce and intercourse throughout the territory of India shall be free'. However, Article 302 imposes restrictions on this freedom if this is necessary in 'public interest'. Using this provision, entry 92A was inserted in the Union List, enabling the Centre to levy the taxes on interstate sale and purchase of goods. The Centre rented the power to levy the CST to the states subject to a ceiling rate specified, which increased from the initial one per cent to four per cent over the years. Thus, although the Constitution originally envisaged that the sales taxes levied by the states should be destination based, the levy of CST has transformed it to predominantly an origin-based tax.

The CST was initially imposed on the recommendation of the Taxation Enquiry Commission (1956) as a measure against evasion of sales tax by misdeclaration of intra-state sales as interstate sales. Though initially levied at the ceiling rate of one per cent, over time, this became important as in stages the rate was increased to four per cent and thus it became a significant revenue instrument, with revenues constituting about 20 per cent of sales tax revenues, or about one per cent of GDP. This has become a major instrument of interstate tax exportation with adverse consequences on efficiency and equity. In a sales taxation in which inputs, outputs, and capital goods are taxed, the tax burden exported to non-residents includes not only the CST but also the input taxes that are included in the products. The tax exportation is from the richer producing states to poorer consuming states which has led to inequitable resource transfers.[11] The analysis of invisible transfers due to CST is discussed further in Chapter 9.

Other Fiscal Impediments

Another major hindrance to inter-regional trade and commerce is the tax on the entry of goods into a local area for consumption, use, or sale. Presently, among the major states, Gujarat, Haryana, Maharashtra, Orissa, and Rajasthan levy octroi. Karnataka and Madhya Pradesh have abolished this levy, but in lieu of it, an entry tax is levied.

The disadvantages of the octroi have already been discussed in chapter 6. Despite these disadvantages, this tax continues to be levied in the absence of suitable alternatives.

Karnataka and Madhya Pradesh have replaced octroi with an entry tax. In principle, this is also a tax on the entry of goods, but as it is account based, the hindrances, delays, and harassment arising from the check posts and physical verification can be avoided if the administration is backed by adequate information systems. However, the proceeds of the entry tax have been found to be inadequate to completely offset the loss of revenue from octroi and, given the states' reluctance to make larger devolutions, this has had an adverse effect on urban infrastructure in these states. It must also be noted that the entry tax, like octroi, is a tax on the entry of goods and hence has similar economic effects. In some cases, this has tended to shift the production and distribution centres to outside municipal limits, necessitating needless movement of consumers to these distribution centres. A more serious issue, however, is that, in many cases, as the metropolitan areas are centres of entrepôt trade, the goods necessarily have to pass through these centres. In such cases, the additional protection

---

[11] For a more detailed discussion on allocative and distributional consequences of CST, see Rao (2003).

accorded to manufacturing units located within the urban areas due to the levy of octroi or entry tax exerts a strong gravitational pull into these areas with attendant problems of congestion, slums, and environmental pollution.

The search for new resources driven by the increasing need to finance ever expanding expenditure requirements of the states have led them to levy highly distorting taxes. In particular, mention must be made of the recent trend in the states of levying taxes on the entry of all commercial vehicles into their jurisdictions (*path kar*). This tax, like octroi and entry tax, causes significant resource distortion due to the delays caused by the check posts as well as the inefficiencies arising from the additional tariff barriers. Similarly, the levy of market fees and cesses on the sale of agricultural commodities in organized markets, applied in a number of states, causes significant inefficiencies by discouraging trading in orga-nized markets and altering relative prices of commodities in unintended ways. Though not yet important in terms of their contribution to the exchequer, the inefficiencies caused by these taxes could be considerable.

The above analysis shows that interstate fiscal competition in the Indian context has caused significant resource distortions and inequities. This also implies that the Central government has not effectively carried out the function of monitoring interstate competition either in terms of formulating the rules of competition or in implementing them. Rather than preventing inefficient competition, there are instances where the Centre has actively prompted the states to create it. The most glaring instance is the 'race to the bottom' indulged by the Union Territories, whose policies are decided by the Union home ministry.

The analysis of intergovernmental competition in India points towards serious vertical and horizontal disharmony in the tax systems. Vertical disharmony arises because of the overlapping commodity tax systems by three levels of government. The levy of Union excise duties by the Centre, sales taxes by the states, and octroi by local bodies has made the tax system non-transparent and rendered the pursuit of the objectives of tax policy difficult. In such a tax system, the incidence of taxes on commodities remains unknown and multiple taxation of commodities by different levels of government creates greater variation between producer and consumer prices. This is particularly true as the Centre levies the tax at the manufacturing stage and the states levy the sales tax predominantly at the first point of sale—on the excise duty paid value. In respect of commodi-ties which have high price elasticities of demand, the levy of commodity taxes at high rates by higher levels of government leaves very little tax room for lower levels of government. While in the past, the market— sheltered as it was from both foreign and domestic competition—could sustain such a tax system, it may not be sustainable when the import of consumer goods is liberalized.

The problem of vertical overlapping of taxes is compounded by the levy of cascading-type consumption taxes. Although Union excise duties has broadly acquired the character of a manufacturers' value added tax, the levy at the first point of sale, and input and capital goods taxation in the states' sales tax systems combined with the manufacturers' excises levied by the Central government has caused high degree of cascading, thereby creating greater divergence between producers and consumer prices than the tax element. This alone can cause large distortions in relative prices. As mentioned in the previous section, there are several serious sources of horizontal tax disharmony as well. Interstate competition has led to minute differentiation in the structure of tax rates. The strategic actions of the states also have led to significant 'free-riding' in terms of interstate tax exportation, predatory pricing of goods and services, erection of trade barriers, and under-pricing of capital by varying degrees through fiscal and financial incentives. In an economy where the spread of production structure and infrastructure facilities are largely the consequence of history, and where the ability (power) of different states to play this strategic game is not equal, intergovernmental competition cannot be expected to improve economic welfare.

There have been significant attempts at reforming taxes separately at the level of the Centre and states, but coordinated development of the tax system at Central and state levels has not received much attention. These issues are discussed in greater detail in Chapters 13 and 14.

8

Intergovernmental Transfers
Rationale and Design

INTRODUCTION

In this chapter, we review the rationale for intergovernmental transfers as discussed in the literature, examine the design of transfers to fulfil alternative objectives and, in the light of this conceptual framework, analyse various forms of intergovernmental transfers in India. A large branch of literature on intergovernmental transfers deals with their economic rationale. This branch takes economic objectives as the sole determinant and discusses the design of the transfer system based on normative criteria, but typically downplaying political constraints. However, even economic objectives have political elements and, often, the design and implementation of transfers reflects political compromises. Therefore, to be useful for policy, this approach must identify and analyse the political implications, while keeping the economic objectives in mind. The emphasis on economic objectives helps to focus the analysis on benchmark transfer schemes, and departures from this can then be analysed in terms of various non-economic objectives. In this chapter, we present the economic rationale for transfers, analyse their appropriate design to fulfil the stated economic objectives and, within this conceptual framework, evaluate the prevailing transfer systems in India.

INTERGOVERNMENTAL TRANSFERS: ECONOMIC RATIONALE

The main economic arguments for intergovernmental transfers have been made in terms of (i) offsetting fiscal imbalances or closing fiscal gaps; (ii) establishing horizontal equity across the federation; and (iii) offsetting inter-jurisdictional cost and benefit spillovers or for merit good reasons.

In addition, transfers may also be given to carry out some agency functions for the Central government.

Intergovernmental Transfers to Offset Fiscal Imbalances

An important reason for giving transfers arises from fiscal imbalances or mismatch between revenues and expenditures of different governmental units. Fiscal imbalances can be 'vertical' or 'horizontal'. Vertical fiscal imbalance refers to the difference between expenditures and revenues at different levels of government, while horizontal fiscal imbalance refers to the differences between revenue and expenditure levels within a particular level of government. Although these two concepts are identifiable by themselves, they are, except under very special circumstances, related.

Vertical Fiscal Imbalances

Vertical fiscal imbalance is a feature common to all multilevel fiscal systems. Even when functions and revenue powers are efficiently assigned, imbalances are bound to occur. As discussed in Chapter 2, expenditure assignment typically does not match tax assignment if done efficiently. The Central government has a comparative advantage in raising revenues whereas sub-central governments are better placed to provide public services efficiently corresponding to varying preferences of people of different jurisdictions (Breton, 1987, 1995). Therefore, assignments according to comparative advantage result in vertical fiscal imbalance. Of course, actual assignments are done not necessarily on the basis of economic considerations and many non-economic factors enter into the determination of the assignment system. These, too, could contribute to vertical fiscal imbalances. Vertical fiscal imbalances can also be caused by factors other than assignments. At sub-national levels, intergovernmental tax competition can result in lower tax rates, but competition to provide public services can enhance expenditure levels, thereby accentuating vertical fiscal imbalance. In addition, differential fiscal performances can also be a cause of variations in revenues and expenditures.

Vertical fiscal imbalance essentially measures fiscal dependence of sub-national governments on the Central government. The usually employed indicator of vertical fiscal imbalance measures the share of expenditure of sub-national governments financed from their own sources of revenue. Thus, Hunter (1977) has three alternative measures of 'coefficient of vertical balance', depending upon three different concepts of independent revenue sources of sub-national governments.[1] In the first, only the sub-national

---

[1] Thus, Hunter's measures of coefficient of vertical fiscal imbalance can be shown as:

governments' own revenues are taken, the second also includes shared taxes, and the third includes both shared taxes and unconditional grants, in addition to own revenues.

Although the concept is intuitively clear, estimation of the coefficient of vertical fiscal imbalance is beset with conceptual and measurement problems. This is because it is difficult to make judgements about the degree of independence of various sources of revenue in different countries. Nor are any of the measures of vertical fiscal imbalance independent of the nature of fiscal management of governmental units. In other words, the vertical fiscal imbalance will be higher if sub-national levels put in lower tax effort or are fiscally profligate or, conversely, if there is higher tax effort and better fiscal management at the Centre. As noted by Bird (1986, p. 402), there is '... no useful shortcut by which analysts can avoid the painstaking work really needed to understand the federal fiscal system of any one country'.

Vertical Fiscal Imbalance in India

In this study, we measure vertical fiscal imbalance in India by taking only the own revenues in the current account as the states' independent source of revenue. The analysis shows a clearly increasing trend in vertical fiscal imbalances. Thus, the ability of the states to finance current expenditures from their own revenues has declined from 69 per cent in 1955–6 to less than 50 per cent in 2000–1 (Table 8.1). Interestingly, during this period, states' shares of current expenditures as well as current revenues have remained broadly constant and yet, their dependence on transfers has increased. This apparent paradox is because an increasing proportion of government expenditures of Central and state governments over the years have been financed from borrowings. Thus, the declining share of states' own revenues to their current expenditures shown in column 4 actually reflects an increasing tendency to divert capital receipts to meet current expenditures. As the states do not have much manoeuvrability in regard to capital receipts, this implies increasing vertical imbalance.[2]

$V = 1 - G/E$, where, V is the coefficient of vertical balance, G is the amount of state expenditures determined by Central government, and E is the total state expenditures.

[2] According to Article 293 of the Constitution, if the states are indebted to the Centre, they have to seek the permission of the latter to borrow from the market. As all the states are indebted to the Centre, the amount each state can borrow from the market is decided by the Union finance ministry in consultation with the Planning Commission and Reserve Bank of India. Thus, the states have no manoeuvrability to determine either the Central loans or the market borrowing.

TABLE 8.1
Trends in Vertical Fiscal Imbalance

Year	Per cent of states' own current revenues to total current revenues	Per cent of states' current expenditure to total current expenditure	Per cent of states' own current revenues to states' current expenditure	Per cent of states' expenditure* to total expenditure*
1955–6	41.20	59.00	68.90	61.70
1960–1	36.60	59.90	63.90	56.80
1965–6	32.60	55.60	63.50	53.30
1970–1	35.50	60.20	60.60	53.90
1975–6	33.50	55.10	70.40	47.60
1980–1	35.60	59.60	60.10	56.00
1985–6	35.50	56.00	57.70	52.60
1990–1	35.20	54.60	53.10	51.70
1995–6	39.20	57.00	58.60	55.80
1999–2000	38.60	56.40	49.80	56.00
2000–01 RE	38.10	57.80	48.70	57.10

* Current + capital expenditures; RE: Revised Estimates.
Source: Public Finance Statistics, Ministry of Finance, Government of India (relevant years).

Increasing centralization and imbalance are not entirely reflected in the quantitative indicators detailed above. In fact, there has been significant erosion of states' control over expenditure decisions also because the component of specific-purpose transfers with matching requirements has increased steadily over the years. Analysis shows that the share of Central sector and centrally sponsored schemes in total state expenditure has increased particularly after the transfers for plan purposes were determined on the basis of a formula determined by the National Development Council.[3] Thus, the proportion of specific-purpose transfers in total transfers increased from 12 per cent in the Fifth Plan (1969–74) to 18 per cent in the Seventh Plan (1985–90), while presently, almost 15 per cent of states' expenditures are spent on these schemes, up from about 9 per cent in the Fifth Plan period. Such transfers not only change the expenditure priorities of the states in the short run, but also have an effect in the longer

[3] A detailed discussion of the various types of intergovernmental transfers in India is taken up in the next chapter. However, it should be noted that the transfers referred to above amounted to more than 17 per cent of the total current transfers from the Centre to the states in 1992–3, and thus are not insignificant quantitatively.

term, when transfers under the schemes are no longer available, as the states may get locked into many such schemes, having started them with financial backing from the Centre.[4]

While there is a clear evidence of increasing vertical fiscal imbalance in Indian federalism, that by itself would not provide a justification for intergovernmental transfers. In fact, a vertical fiscal imbalance rationale for such transfers is tautological, because growth of the vertical fiscal imbalance itself could be due to (i) increases in revenue capacity at the state level not keeping pace with growing expenditure needs and (ii) slackening fiscal management at the state level resulting in lower tax effort and increased expenditure profligacy. Further, giving transfers to fill the gaps between actual revenues and expenditures of the states can also create serious disincentives for states' fiscal management.

Horizontal Fiscal Imbalance

The 'filling the "fiscal gap"' rationale for intergovernmental transfers extends to horizontal fiscal imbalances as well. Horizontal fiscal imbalances refer to the mismatch between revenues and expenditures of governmental units within a level of government. In the Indian context, they refer to an excess of expenditures over revenues of different state governments. From the national point of view, it has been considered improper to allow the persistence of large horizontal imbalances both for political and economic reasons, and these have been sought to be corrected through equalizing transfers from the Centre. Note that this situation automatically implies the existence of some degree of vertical imbalance as well.

Horizontal fiscal imbalances can arise due to revenue or expenditure differences between the states. Revenue differences can be either due to differences in fiscal capacity or in effort. Similarly, expenditure differences between states may be due to differences in the quantity or quality of public services provided, or differences in the unit cost. Again, cost differences can be due to factors beyond the control of the states or due to differences in fiscal management.

Table 8.2 presents differences in per capita incomes, revenues, and expenditures as well as poverty levels among the twenty-five states in India. To facilitate meaningful comparisons, the states have been classified first in terms of fifteen *relatively* homogeneous ones (though stratified by per capita SDP) and ten 'special category' states (seven north-eastern

---

[4] The question of why state government decision makers would allow this to happen is easily answered by consideration of the short-term electoral motives that often guide acceptance of intergovernmental aid with strings attached.

TABLE 8.2
Revenues and Expenditures of the States—2000–01 (RE)

States	Per capita SDP (Rupees)	Poverty ratio (per cent) 1999–2000	Per capita own revenue (Rupees)	Own revenue as percentage of SDP	Per capita transfers	Per capita current spending (Rupees)	Percentage of own revenue to current pending
High Income States	22,461	17.83	2931.6	13.1	500	4386.6	66.8
Gujarat	18,685	14.07	2684.6	13.2	863	5167.6	52.0
Goa	44,613	4.4	14,310.3	15.8	588	11,904.8	120.2
Haryana	21,551	8.74	3209.7	12.1	502	4107.9	78.1
Maharashtra	22,604	25.02	2741.3	11.1	448	3852.6	71.2
Punjab	23,254	6.16	3333.2	10.2	494	4712.7	70.7
Middle Income States	17,635	20.3	1868.8	10.6	658	3400.4	55.0
Andhra Pradesh	14,878	15.77	1930.2	10.7	713	3320.2	58.1
Karnataka	16,654	20.44	2148.1	11.3	686	3580.9	60.0
Kerala	17,709	12.72	2295.8	10.2	690	3689.4	62.2
Tamil Nadu	18,623	21.12	2342.5	11.3	658	3594.3	65.2
West Bengal	14,874	27.02	1091.0	5.5	576	3092.7	35.3
Low Income States	9182	34.28	858.5	9.3	673	2261.3	38.8
Bihar	4813	42.6	338.2	8.9	724	1515.5	22.3
Chhattisgarh	10,405	NA	1264.0	4.9	NA	2455.2	51.5
Jharkhand	9223	NA	1128.0	9.0	NA	2229.4	50.6
Madhya Pradesh	11,626	37.43	1061.9	11.5	624	2695.5	39.4
Orissa	8733	47.15	900.5	9.3	969	2785.3	32.3

(contd)

174

(*Table 8.2 Contd*)

States	Per capita SDP (Rupees)	Poverty ratio (per cent) 1999–2000	Per capita own revenue (Rupees)	Own revenue as percentage of SDP	Per capita transfers	Per capita current spending (Rupees)	Percentage of own revenue to current pending
Rajasthan	13046	15.28	1297.2	10.4	693	2864.2	45.3
Uttaranchal	NA	NA	1295.5	NA	NA	4912.7	26.4
Uttar Pradesh	9323	31.15	791.2	8.1	598	2135.6	37.0
General Cat. States	*14,605*	*25.97*	*1606.3*	*11.0*	*660*	*3060.9*	*52.5*
Special Cat. States	*10,695*		*1032.2*	*9.7*	*2896*	*5126.7*	*20.1*
Arunachal Pradesh	13,352	33.47	1067.8	5.3	7985	9992.3	10.7
Assam	9720	36.09	798.7	7.2	1216	3317.0	24.1
Himachal Pradesh	17,786	7.63	1660.5	7.8	3070	7420.6	22.4
Jammu & Kashmir	12,373	3.48	1150.4	7.9	4602	6080.0	18.9
Manipur	12,721	28.54	406.0	3.1	3971	6032.3	6.7
Meghalaya	12,063	33.87	1066.8	6.3	3149	5878.4	18.1
Mizoram	14,909	19.47	679.0	3.8	9602	12,845.6	5.3
Nagaland	12,594	32.67	506.8	3.7	6332	7291.0	7.0
Sikkim	14,751	36.55	5998.1	15.9	7945	12,200.6	49.2
Tripura	13,195	34.44	729.6	4.8	3376	5838.9	12.5
Uttaranchal	NA		1295.5		NA	4912.7	26.4
All States	*14,359*	*26.1*	*1570.1*	*10.9*	*768*	*3191.1*	*49.2*

Note: NA — Not Available, Revenues and expenditures are net of lotteries; SDP—State Domestic Product.
Source: 1. Reserve Bank of India Bulletin, December 2000; 2. Public Finance Statistics, Ministry of Finance, Government of India, 1994–5.

states, Sikkim, Jammu and Kashmir, and Himachal Pradesh). As discussed in Chapter 4 the 'special category' reflects a combination of strategic, ethnic, and geographic differentials.

In Chapter 4, we brought out the heterogeneity of states in Indian federalism in economic and fiscal aspects and even at the cost of repetition, it may be useful to highlight some important aspects here, which have a bearing on the design and implementation of the transfer system. We noted the wide interstate differences in revenues and expenditures presented between special and non-special categories of states as well as among the states within each category, in both per capita terms, and as a ratio of net state domestic product (SDP) (Table 4.2). Second, these variations indicate both interstate differences in revenue capacity and efforts. Thus, it is seen that the variation in per capita taxes is much higher than that of per capita SDP. Among the non-special category states (excluding the small state of Goa), the richest state (Punjab) has more than four times the per capita income of the poorest state (Bihar), but the state with the highest per capita revenues (Haryana) has 6.1 times the per capita taxes of Bihar. It is also seen that some of the richer states have revenue–SDP ratios lower than middle- and low -income states in spite of the fact that the high-income states have greater advantage in exporting the tax burden to poorer states, as argued in Chapter 7. Third, per capita expenditure variations among the non-special category states are lower than the variations in per capita SDP. Fourth, the tax–SDP ratio in the special category states is lower than that in the non-special category states in spite of their higher per capita SDP. This is partly because in these states SDP is derived mainly from government administration and does not reflect the tax base. Fifth, although per capita revenue bases in special category states were lower than the average by 7 per cent, their per capita expenditures were higher on an average by almost 62 per cent.[5] Finally, the fiscal dependence of the states on the Centre was not only high, but also varied inversely with per capita SDP.

An important consequence of the horizontal imbalances is the skewed distribution of social and physical infrastructure among the states. The richer states were able to incur higher expenditures on social and economic services due to their better ability to raise resources. Consequently, the composite index of infrastructure estimated by the Eleventh Finance Commission was higher than the average by 56 per cent for high-income states and lower than by about 13 per cent for low-income states (Table 8.2).

[5] The higher than average per capita expenditures in special category states should be attributed largely to their cost disabilities though this can also be due to their poor fiscal management.

TABLE 8.3

Coefficients of Variation in State Government Expenditures for 14 Major States

Expenditure/ NSDP Items	1975–6	1980–1	1985–6	1990–1	1993–4	1999–2000	2000–01 (RE)
General administration	23.40	21.90	25.00	29.30	31.10	38.51	33.50
Education	32.90	31.70	26.40	20.30	26.90	50.88	41.60
Health	23.80	24.30	27.60	25.80	22.60	44.72	39.00
Total social services	35.20	29.60	31.10	26.00	24.70	44.21	33.10
Total economic services	37.40	34.00	41.00	36.70	31.60	44.34	26.60
Total current expenditure	26.00	23.50	24.80	23.20	27.10	37.61	26.00
Total capital expenditure	38.70	28.10	54.30	40.20	43.10	56.58	31.70
Total expenditure	26.60	23.00	28.30	24.20	28.10	38.44	25.60
Total Per Capita NSDP	29.90	31.70	31.70	34.10	36.20	38.90	41.50

Source: Budget Documents of State Governments (Relevant years).

177

A similar pattern is seen in the case of the human development index (HDI) estimated by the Planning Commission.

Wide interstate disparities and horizontal imbalances existed when the country achieved independence and over the years, there is no evidence of any significant convergence. Historical factors, inherent biases in the strategy of development and the pattern of infrastructure distribution have been important in determining regional differences in development.[6] However, in spite of over four decades of planning and repeated rhetoric on 'balanced regional development', interstate disparity in India has accentuated. As may be seen from Table 8.3, the coefficients of variation in per capita SDP as well as per capita revenues increased over the period 1975–6 to 1999–2000. The coefficient of variation (CV) in the expenditure–NSDP ratio showed a sharp increase in 1999–2000 over 1993–4 in respect of every expenditure category. This was also true of the variations in revenue-raising capacity as indicated by the per capita NSDP. As equalizing federal transfers did not entirely offset the increase in the variations in per capita revenues, the coefficients of variation in per capita expenditures, particularly capital expenditures have shown increases.

While persistent horizontal imbalances do indeed cause unequal spread of infrastructure across states, and can accentuate interstate inequalities in income levels, they cannot, by themselves provide a rationale for inter-governmental transfers. This is because, like vertical fiscal imbalance, horizontal fiscal imbalance is not exogenous to the states' fiscal management. In other words, revenue–expenditure mismatch in the states can occur not only because they have inadequate resource base in relation to their expenditure requirements, but also because their fiscal management in terms of effort at mobilizing revenues and exercise economy in spending is not satisfactory.

Fiscal Equity Arguments for Intergovernmental Transfers

The argument for intergovernmental transfers on equity grounds has been made either in terms of ensuring horizontal equity of individuals residing in the states across the country, or simply to ensure inter-regional equity (Musgrave, 1962). Both the approaches build a case for unconditional or general-purpose transfers from the Centre to the states to offset the fiscal disabilities arising from low revenue capacity and high expenditure needs. Interstate differences in the capacity to raise revenues and differences in

---

[6] There are a number of studies examining the issue of interstate differences in the pattern of development. For details, see Ahluwalia (2002), Singh and Srinivasan (2002), and Rao, Shand, and Kalirajan (1999). We take up this issue in Chapter 12.

the unit cost of providing public services due to factors that are beyond the control of the states can create inequity and therefore, transfers have to be given to offset these inequities. In the literature, the efficiency and growth implications of equitable transfers have also been discussed at considerable length, though the issue of efficiency versus equity consequences of intergovernmental transfers has never been satisfactorily resolved (Scott, 1964; Wiseman, 1992).

The natural starting point for this analysis is the horizontal equity rationale for federal transfers (Boadway and Flatters, 1982; Buchanan, 1950; Bradbury et al., 1984). The horizontal equity criterion states that two persons equally well off before the introduction of the fiscal system should also be so afterwards. Boadway and Flatters (1982) present equity arguments for intergovernmental transfers in a formal stylized model of the economic system with a number of simplifying assumptions. For simplicity, a federation is assumed with two states. It is also assumed that income is generated from labour, land, and capital. Labour is assumed to be mobile within states but immobile between them. Capital, on the other hand, is assumed to be mobile between the states. The states levy three kinds of taxes: a 'residence-based' proportional income tax on all incomes, 'source-based' taxes on capital income, and land rents. The taxes collected by the states are used entirely to provide public services of a private nature only to residents. Prices are assumed to be identical in the two states.

Taking comprehensive income—which includes current private consumption, net accretion to wealth, and current benefits from the public services—as the index of well-being, it has been shown that even when the fiscal systems of the Centre and individual states treat equals on an equal footing, nationwide horizontal equity may be violated. This is because fiscal activities of state governments result in differential net fiscal benefits (NFB)[7] to individual equals and the Central income tax as is presently structured cannot take account of the real income from differential NFBs. Thus, even when the states levy proportional income taxes at uniform *rates*, the revenue *collections* and therefore, *per capita* expenditures in richer states will be higher, and if public services are assumed to be a perfect substitute for private goods, the residents in these states will get higher benefits from public services for the same tax rate payment.[8]

---

[7] NFB in a state is measured as per capita expenditure incurred by the state minus per capita taxes collected by it.

[8] This implies two things. First, the state government provides completely a private good and second, the productivity of the state government is equivalent to that of the private sector. In other words, the state government merely replaces the private sector in providing

The differences in NFBs arise from the fact that the states cannot levy benefit taxes. Specifically, 'free-riding' behaviour among the states induces them to levy resource-based taxes or origin-based consumption taxes, and this can cause significant interstate tax exportation. The ability to export taxes differs among the states, causing significant differences in NFBs. In addition, the states may have their own redistributive policies and this, too, can cause variations in NFBs. Variations in NFBs can also arise when the services provided by the states have 'public good' characteristics.[9] In these cases, equalization of NFBs would either call for discriminating Central tax rates, which may not be feasible, or giving equalization grants to poorer states.

According to Boadway and Flatters (1982), the degree of equalization depends on the view one takes on horizontal equity. There are two alternative ways in which horizontal equity is defined. According to the *broad* view, the fiscal system should be equitable nationwide vis-à-vis the action of all governments and two persons equally well off before federal and states' action must also be so afterwards. To fulfil this concept of horizontal equity, it is necessary to give transfers so that each state is enabled to provide the same level of public services at a given tax rate or, as in a unitary country, the NFBs in the two states should be completely equalized. Full equalization of NFBs is also justifiable on efficiency grounds because differences in NFBs due to interstate tax exportation or redistributive policies of the state governments affect migration decisions and prevent the marginal productivity of labour from being equalized among different provinces. Thus, equalization payments are called for on grounds of both equity and efficiency.[10]

In contrast, the *narrow* view of horizontal equity takes the actions of state governments as a given datum. In this scheme, Central fiscal action will be directed to ensure horizontal equity after the state fiscal system has been established. Two persons equally well off after the state budgets should be equally well off after the Central government fiscal activity. The Central budget need not offset the inequities introduced by the

---

the service. However, the argument is strengthened when the services provided by the state governments have public good elements as the larger *total* outlay (as against *per capita* outlay) will yield higher benefits, because of the non-rival nature of the benefits.

[9] The level of public services (g) is assumed to depend on a 'congestion' technology: $g_p = G_p/L_p^\alpha$, where G_p is the public expenditure, L_p is the number of residents, and α is the congestion elasticity, bounded between 0 in the case of pure public goods and 1 in the case of pure private goods. *Ceteris paribus,* the lower the value of α, the higher is the value of g_p and therefore, NFB.

[10] For a detailed examination of efficiency implications of horizontal equity transfers, see Courchene (1984).

operation of the state budgets per se, but take account of the income distributional effects of the states' fiscal operations (Boadway and Flatters, 1982, p. 20.)

The Central income tax as presently structured (and as is the case everywhere) taxes only wage and property incomes and not the real income accruing to residents in the form of higher public expenditures due to source-based taxes collected by the states from non-residents. For the same reason, such source-based taxes or state taxes on resource rents prevent the attainment of horizontal equity because Central taxes are paid only on market income and not real income, which includes state spending on public services financed from source-based taxes. Similarly, when we relax the assumption of identical individuals, the redistribution from the states' budgetary activity will cause the NFBs to differ across the states, in a manner which cannot be captured in the prevailing structure of Central income tax. The simplest example is to consider the typical case of individuals within a state receiving equal benefits from a state's public expenditures financed by a proportional income tax. When the income levels in the two states are different, a person who is otherwise equal, residing in a higher-income state would have a higher NFB than the one residing in low-income state.

So far we have restricted our analysis to the case in which the states levy only personal income tax or taxes on factor incomes at source. Instead, when the states get revenue from indirect taxes, the equity case depends on the degree to which the taxes are shifted forward in terms of higher prices and the proportion of the taxes shifted forward to non-residents. If market imperfections cause a significant degree of forward shifting of the indirect taxes, and if the tax is predominantly origin based, it is reasonable to expect that a significant portion of the taxes collected by a state would be exported to non-residents. The equity case thus depends on the degree of shifting of the tax burden to non-residents through interstate tax exportation.

The preceding analysis assumes that the functioning of the states' fiscal system is the only source of inequity and inefficiency. In economies where many prices and outputs are determined or regulated by government policies rather than by the market mechanism, there can be other sources of inequity. Often, these 'invisible' sources of inequity can be very significant, and as the intergovernmental transfer system fails to offset them, the inequities and inefficiencies in such federations continue to persist. An obvious source of interstate variations in NFBs in developing countries is the subsidized loans given to the states by either the Central government or the public sector financial and banking system. Such implicit transfers may create further inequities and the transfer system in such cases has the additional task of offsetting them. We will discuss these issues further in the next chapter.

While the horizontal equity argument for transfers is intuitively appealing, it is possible to argue that these are neither necessary nor are they sufficient to establish horizontal equity. It must be noted that fiscal actions of the sub-national governments violate horizontal equity only when they actually undertake redistribution. If the sub-national governments levy simply benefit taxes, the NFBs will be identical across jurisdictions and therefore, transfers are not *necessary*. Besides, equalizing NFBs does not mean that equals in different jurisdictions are placed at the same *welfare* level. Individuals with identical incomes (including benefits from public services) can be at different welfare levels depending on their preferences for public vis-à-vis private goods. Transfers are not *sufficient* to ensure horizontal equity because they only ensure *potential* and not *actual* equality of equals (Musgrave, 1962).

Intergovernmental Transfers to Correct Spillovers

In the mainstream literature, intergovernmental transfers are seen as a device to resolve the problem of mismatch between benefit spans from various hierarchies of public goods and exogenously given spatial jurisdictional domains. When the benefits of public services provided by a state spill over outside its jurisdiction, it ignores the benefits accruing to the non-residents while deciding the amount of the service provided. The jurisdiction equates the marginal benefits from the public service with the marginal cost of providing it, and as it ignores the part of the benefit accruing to the non-residents, the result is non-optimal provision of the public service. Optimal provision of the service in question can be ensured through Coasian bribes or voluntary action of the jurisdictions to compensate for the spillovers (Gramlich, 1993). However, such solutions are infeasible and, therefore, spillovers have to be arbitrated through Central grants akin to 'Pigovian' subsidies to offset the spillovers. These transfers must necessarily be specific purpose, requiring matching contributions from the states and the exact matching rate should depend upon the size of spillovers. This implies that the matching rate should vary with the degree of externality generated by various public services. Further, a uniform rate of matching transfers would have non-uniform responsiveness in different states depending on their level of development, as complete equalization in fiscal capacities is never achieved in any federation. This calls for varying the matching rates itself in favour of the poorer states (Feldstein, 1975; Rao and Dasgupta, 1995).

Intergovernmental Transfers to Ensure Competitive Equality

The competitive federalism literature (Breton, 1995), however, brings out three basic assumptions of the welfare-economics-guided spillover rationale for intergovernmental transfers. First is the existence of a body that would correctly decide the division of powers. As the division of powers is exogenously given, we simply ignore the motivation for the existence of spillovers, but simply concentrate on its effects. Second is an omniscient Central government which can assess and accurately estimate interstate spillovers and make intergovernmental transfers based thereon. If indeed the Central government is omniscient, it would probably be preferable to have it provide such public services rather than design the grants to the states corresponding to the degree of spillovers. Finally, the model assumes away any role for intergovernmental competition in determining the division of functions or jurisdictional tiers altogether.

If the existence of vertical and horizontal intergovernmental competition is recognized, both assignments and intergovernmental transfers may be seen as outcomes of competition rather than decided exogenously. Competition, as mentioned in Chapter 7, results in vertical imbalance because the higher levels of governments have a comparative advantage in collecting revenues and lower-level governmental units have a comparative advantage in spending. The higher-level governments are relatively better placed to minimize tax avoidance and evasion due to the mobility of tax bases, lower cost of assessing the size of the tax base, and ability to stand political pressures (Breton, 1995), and this results in revenue centralization. The lower governmental units have a cost advantage in obtaining information on demand for most of the services, particularly congestible services. This would necessitate intergovernmental flow of funds or 'revenue payments' (Breton, 1995, p. 258).

In addition to these 'revenue payments', the Central government has to give unconditional grants to 'stabilize' horizontal competition as well. Besides providing the public services in which it has a comparative advantage, the Central government has the responsibility of monitoring both vertical and horizontal competition, with a view to securing stability. Inefficiency in competition may be caused by the fact that individual rationality differs from collective rationality. Thus, it is perfectly rational for an individual sub-national jurisdiction to resort to beggar-thy-neighbour policies through measures like predatory pricing of goods and services, exportation of tax bases, dumping externalities, erection of trade barriers, and incentives to attract capital flows. When there are significant differences in the ability of the jurisdictions to compete, the stronger ones can dominate to the detriment of the political stability of the federation. The Central government can, if it chooses, employ a variety of instruments to enhance efficiency of horizontal competition. Setting the rules through the use of prohibitions and standards helps to prevent beggar-thy-neighbour policies. Regional policies help to achieve equitable spread of infrastructure and Central government investments. Intergovernmental transfers complement the regional policies to achieve 'competitive equality' of jurisdictions. The transfers given to enable 'competitive equality' of jurisdictions are called 'stabilizing grants'. As already mentioned, these are in addition to the 'revenue payments' given to offset competitively determined mismatch between revenue and expenditure assignments.

Economic Rationale for Intergovernmental Transfers: A Synoptic View

The economic rationales for intergovernmental transfers discussed above have an intuitive appeal and probably explain why transfers are in fact given in most federations. Yet, a careful scrutiny of the arguments reveals that each rationale has very limited explanatory power. As already mentioned, the fiscal imbalance argument does not exclude the actual fiscal behaviour of the states. Designing of transfers to offset fiscal imbalances could, in fact, encourage fiscal laxity. Similarly, as argued above, transfers are neither necessary nor are they sufficient to ensure horizontal equity. Transfers to ensure competitive equality are appealing, but it is difficult to equate competitive 'power' with the amount of transfers. Finally, designing of transfers to offset spillovers would require an omniscient Central government, and if there is such a Central government, it is not certain whether there would be gains from decentralization at all.

The foregoing discussion did not consider the non-economic objectives of intergovernmental transfers. In a federal polity, transfers may be given to induce the units to be a part of a federation or simply, a bribe paid to the reluctant participant. They may also be an instrument through which the Central government intends to alter states' allocations in favour of its own preferred sectors. Bureaucrats and politicians may employ transfers to favour some regions over others to gain political support as discussed in Chapter 2.

THE DESIGN OF INTERGOVERNMENTAL TRANSFERS

The precise design of the transfer system depends upon the particular rationale underlying it. The rationale determines the objectives, and transfers are then designed to fulfil them. Thus, transfers given to offset fiscal imbalances or to ensure horizontal equity or stabilize intergovernmental competition ought to be unconditional. However, to avoid the moral hazard of states viewing such transfers as 'blank cheques' from the Central government, the amount of such grants can be tied to the tax efforts of the states. Grants given to offset spillovers, or those given to ensure minimum outlays on specified services (merit good reasons), must be purpose specific, with matching requirements from the states. There is also a case for having matching ratios varying inversely with the level of development of the states to ensure uniformity in the responses of all the states to these transfers (Feldstein, 1975).

Thus, intergovernmental transfers can be designed in a variety of ways and the effect of transfers depends on the way they are designed (Wilde, 1971; Gramlich, 1977). While the theoretical rationale helps them justify the objectives of transfers and provides broad guidance on their design, in actually designing the transfer system, a number of judgements have to be made. This in turn, would have efficiency and equity consequences. Naturally, each country has developed its own system of transfer design depending upon various political, historical, and economic compulsions. In what follows, we discuss the designs of unconditional and specific-purpose transfers which minimize disincentive effects on recipients.

General-purpose Transfers

General-purpose transfers are given to enable sub-national governments to offset the fiscal disadvantages arising from a lower revenue capacity and/or a higher unit cost of providing public services. This is achieved by giving unconditional transfers in a variety of ways, but the least distorting way is to give transfers equivalent to their 'need–revenue' gap (Bradbury, et al., 1984). The 'need–revenue' gap measures the difference between what a state ought to spend to provide specified levels of public services and the revenue it can raise at a given standard level of tax effort.

Thus, the need–revenue gap for the ith state can be taken as:

$$G_i = \bar{Q}C_i - \bar{t}B_i \qquad (8.1)$$

where G_i is the gap (per capita), $\bar{Q}$ is the desired (normative) level of composite public service provided by the state per capita, C_i is the unit cost of the public service (reckoned at justifiable costs), $\bar{t}$ is the standard tax effort, and B_i is the per capita tax base. C_i in turn, consists of two components: (i) unit cost within the control of the state governments, (C_{1i}); and (ii) that beyond the states' control, (C_{2i}). For need calculations, the unit cost within the control of the state governments (C_{1i}) would also have to be reckoned at justifiable levels (Ci). Thus,

$$G_i = \bar{Q}(C_i + C_{2i}) - \bar{t}B_i \qquad (8.2)$$

The fiscal disadvantage of the state (D_i) is determined on the basis of the difference between a state's need–revenue (G_i) gap and the normative gap (G^*) or the gap of the baseline state. That is,

$$D_i = G_i - G^* = Q(C_i + C_{2i}) - tB_i - G^* \qquad (8.3)$$

A state with a disadvantage $(D_i > O)$ is eligible to receive aid, whereas one without $(D_i < O)$ is not. If the Central government sets apart 'M' amount to be distributed to the eligible states on the basis of their fiscal disadvantage, the amount of funds the ith eligible state would receive is given by:

$$S_i N_i = [(D_i N_i)^a / S_i (D_i N_i)^a] M \text{ for all } D_i > 0 \qquad (8.4)$$

where S_i represents per capita transfers received by the ith state and N_i its population. First, whether or not a state is eligible to receive aid depends on the normatively chosen G^*. It is possible to select G^* such that even the state with the lowest G_i (or the state with the highest fiscal strength) is also eligible to receive aid. Second, the states may not be given grants to fill the entire gap, $G_i - G^*$; the share of individual states in such a case is determined by the exponential 'a' of the gap to be equalized, the total amount of funds available for transfer (or perceived vertical fiscal imbalance), and gap of the state in relation to the total gap. The degree of equalization achieved, thus, depends upon the normatively chosen (G^*), the value of the exponential (a), and the amount of funds available for transfer (M).[11]

Specific-purpose Transfers

Specific-purpose transfers are intended to set the prices right to ensure optimal provision of sub-central services having spillovers. Under such a scheme, the additional per capita outlay (A_{ij}) required to ensure a minimum level of the public service 'j' in the ith state would be the difference between the justifiable cost of providing the required minimum level of the service per capita $(\bar{Q}^*_j C_{ij})$ and the justifiable cost of the actual per capita service level provided in the state $(Q_{ij}^* C_{ij})$. That is

---

[11] For a similar formula, see Ahmad and Thomas (1997), pp. 363–4.

$$A_{ij} = \bar{Q}_i.C_{ij} - Q^*_{ij}.C_{ij} \qquad (8.5)$$

The per capita grant to be given to each state to ensure the minimum standard of service is given by,

$$S_{ij} = r_c \, [\bar{Q}^{*j} \, C_{ij} - Q^*_{ij} \, C_{ij}] \qquad (8.6)$$

such that

$$r_c + r_s = 1 \qquad (8.7)$$

where 'r_c' is the proportion of additional outlay the Central government bears and 'r_s' is the matching proportion the state government contributes. As the response to a given r_c is lower in poorer states, to obtain a given uniform impact, r_c should vary inversely with the per capita incomes. Similarly, to ensure the specified level of service, r_c should be inversely related to the price elasticity of demand for the service. If the price elasticity is zero, to ensure the minimum level of service it would be necessary for the Central government to transfer the entire quantum of expenditure required to provide the prescribed level of the public service.

RATIONALE FOR INTERGOVERNMENTAL TRANSFERS SUMMARIZED

Ideally, the design and implementation of transfers should consider three important things. First, besides being equitable, the formula must be simple and transparent. Second, it should not have incentives for 'free-riding' or fiscal laxity or profligacy. Finally, the method of making transfers should not only be, but also appear to be objective. Combining all these elements in the design of the transfer system is by no means an easy task, but is nevertheless essential for achieving the objectives of transfers in an efficient manner and infuse confidence in the transfer scheme by all the concerned players and ensure its acceptability.

An important element in the design of the transfer system is the degree of progressivity of the transfers. The ideal situation is the one in which the state with the lowest need–capacity gap is chosen as the baseline state and fiscal disadvantages of the others are completely offset. The choice of baseline and the extent to which the fiscal disadvantages are offset will depend upon the volume of resources available for transfer and the value judgements made on the degree of progressivity. The most common practical judgement made is to estimate the need–revenue gap using the 'average' behavioural parameters. Another alternative may be to use the Rawlsian 'maximin' rule whereby, successively, the need–capacity gap of the most disadvantaged state is brought down to the level of the next most disadvantaged state and so on until the resources available for transfer are exhausted. Clearly, additional strategies are also possible. However, while these theoretical constructs are useful signposts, the actual design of transfer system is influenced as much by political bargaining and other non-economic factors as by economic rationality. We provide some evidence for this assertion in Chapter 12.

While the objectives of intergovernmental transfers are important to determine the volume of transfers and the degree of progressivity, it is important to take account of a number of additional considerations in designing transfer systems. The first and foremost is the need to avoid arbitrariness and impart objectivity. This will minimize the political influence and infuse confidence with the Central government as a monitoring agency. For this reason alone, formula-based transfers are preferred over discretionary transfers. It must however be noted that a formula-based system should not degenerate into a rigid mechanical exercise; it should have sufficient flexibility to take into account the changing situations and complexities in intergovernmental fiscal relationships.

Even when the transfer system is formula based, it may not subserve the objectives if, as already mentioned, the design of transfers creates perverse incentives. Thus, if the transfers are designed to perform 'fiscal dentistry', they can only induce larger budgetary cavities; designing transfers to fill the budgetary gaps of the states can only encourage fiscal mismanagement. Avoiding perverse incentives in designing transfers and imparting objectivity and flexibility to the transfer systems are as important as targeting the transfers to fulfil the economic objectives in the design of transfer systems.

To summarize the main issues involved: (i) even in the ideal transfer design, value judgements are unavoidable; (ii) estimation of fiscal parameters required to design an ideal transfer system requires further adjustments and judgements;[12] (iii) there is a trade-off between ideal design and simplicity in transfer formulas. The most practicable approach is to have a simple design incorporating the basic objectives of transfers which would be easy to understand and, therefore, more easily acceptable to the states.

Nor do ideal transfer systems exist in practice. This is because, however much economic objectives are important, historical, political, and cultural factors probably play more important roles in the actual design of transfers. Thus, even though economic considerations warrant a radical

[12] See Rao and Sen (1997) for details.

redistribution, it may be possible to implement this only incrementally. Similarly, whatever be the economic rationality, a reform plan cannot be implemented unless it is politically acceptable to the parties concerned. Thus, the extent to which these non-economic factors sway the polity constrains the design of intergovernmental transfers in achieving economic objectives. This issue is taken up in the next chapter.

9

✡

Explicit and Implicit
Intergovernmental Transfers

INTRODUCTION

As discussed in Chapter 8, intergovernmental transfer has a variety of objectives in a federation. It is also seen that a number of factors should be taken into account in designing and implementing the transfer system to fulfil the overall objectives of fiscal and political federalism. The ideal transfer system should have some important properties. First, the transfer system should have a mix of general-purpose and specific-purpose transfers. Second, it should be equitable. Third, a good transfer system should be mainly formula based and not discretionary. Fourth, formula-based transfers should be simple and transparent, and should not have adverse incentives on fiscal management for both donor and recipients. Finally, the mechanism for designing and implementing the transfer system should be clear, transparent, and objective, and should be capable of adjusting to changing economic situations.

Much of the discussion on equalization or regional equity in a federal system is confined to explicit intergovernmental transfers. In the setting of a developing country, explicit intergovernmental transfers are not the only channel for influencing inter-regional resource flows. There are a number of sources of invisible transfers. First, in all countries, the Central government, in pursuit of regional policies evolves its policy frame to include the regional pattern of its direct expenditure allocation. In addition, in developing countries, making a transition from central planning to market-based resource allocation, involves a variety of controls and regulations that can cause significant inter-regional resource flows. In India, there are also controls introduced to implement its centralized plan strategy, and to meet the requirements of an economy with perceived shortages. Finally, another important source of regional resource allocation is the existence of origin-based consumption taxes.

The problem of invisible transfers is particularly important in the Indian federation, where many prices and outputs are still administratively determined and the origin-based consumption tax system causes significant interstate tax exportation. While there are many sources of invisible interstate resource flows, in this chapter, we look at three important sources. The first is interstate tax exportation, which was qualitatively analysed in Chapter 7. The second is subsidized lending to the states from the Centre, as well as through market allocation of states' borrowings. While this source has dried up after interest rates on states' borrowings were aligned to market rates, other form of bail-outs can contribute to invisible transfers. Bailouts such as writing off of loans contracted by state governments or enterprises by the Central government or its agencies are another form of implicit transfer.[1] Another major source of invisible transfers pertains to regional allocation of subsidized loans through the financial sector. These include distribution of seignorage by the Reserve Bank of India by means of refinancing and regional allocation of priority sector loans. The analysis is only illustrative and by no means are these the only sources of implicit transfers.

This chapter analyses inter-regional transfers in India. This includes analysis of the design and implementation of transfers from the Finance Commission, the Planning Commission, and through various central ministries for Central sector and centrally sponsored schemes. This is followed by the analysis of the implicit inter-regional resource flows. The analysis shows that such subterranean transfers significantly offset the progressivity of explicit transfers.

EXPLICIT CENTRAL TRANSFERS TO STATES

Volume and Composition

Transfers from the Central government contribute a significant part of state finances (see Table 9.1). In per capita terms at constant (1981–2) prices, Central transfers to the states increased by over 2.5 times from Rs 77 in 1975–6 to Rs 194 in 1993–4 and declined marginally thereafter owing to greater fiscal compression (Table 9.1). It is also seen from the table that until 1993–4, growth of transfers was faster than both the

---

[1] Writing off of loans can be an important source of invisible transfer. Similarly, the accelerated power development scheme introduced recently is a form of bail-out involving interstate resource transfers.

Centre's and the states' own revenues. In fact, during the period since the mid-1970s, while the annual average rate of growth of states' own revenues was just about 15.3 per cent and that of Central revenues was even lower at 14.8 per cent, Central transfers to states increased at 16.4 per cent. In the latter half of the 1990s, however, these transfers have decelerated to grow slower than both Central and state revenues. Thus, the share of transfers in Central revenues increased from 32 per cent in 1975–6 to 44 per cent in 1997–8 and declined thereafter to 33 per cent in 1999–2000. Similarly, their share in state revenues increased from 39 per cent in 1975–6 to 45 per cent in 1997–8 and declined to 36 per cent in 1999–2000. Of course, state expenditures increased at a much faster rate during this period and, therefore, the share of transfers in state expenditures declined steadily. Yet, they finance almost a third of state expenditures.

TABLE 9.1
Trends in Central Transfers to States

Years	Per Capita Transfers (1993–4 Rupees)	Percentage of transfers to GDP	Percentage of transfers to Central Revenues	Percentage of transfers to State Revenues	Percentage of transfers to State Expenditure
1975–6	198.2	3.67	31.80	38.64	44.80
1980–1	272.2	4.84	34.80	43.81	47.50
1985–6	381.0	5.55	40.98	45.62	46.42
1990–1	449.9	4.66	39.06	38.37	30.85
1995–6	450.8	4.28	36.53	38.61	31.07
1996–7	487.0	4.28	36.35	39.97	31.83
1997–8	578.0	4.86	43.66	44.91	35.33
1998–9	469.9	3.73	34.46	37.69	26.29
1999–2000	504.1	3.80	32.62	36.46	25.05
2000–01	580.1	4.41	35.38	37.41	26.92
2001–02*	633.1	4.49	35.80	38.02	28.30

Note: * Revised estimates; ** GDP estimated to increase by 13% in current prices.
Source: Indian Economic Statistics; Public Finance Statistics; Ministry of Finance, Government of India.

A notable feature of the federal fiscal arrangements in India is the existence of multiple channels of transfers from the Centre to the states. First, there is a constitutional mechanism to devolve tax shares and give grants. Second, the Planning Commission gives grants and loans for implementing development plans. Finally, various ministries give grants to their counterparts in the states for specified projects either wholly funded by the Centre (Central sector projects) or requiring the states to share a proportion of the cost (centrally sponsored schemes).

The constitutional mechanism for Central transfers consists of devolving the tax shares (Article 270) and providing grants-in-aid to the states in need of assistance (Article 275).[2] Until the Eightieth Amendment of the Constitution in 2000, the Central government was required to compulsorily share proceeds from individual income tax (Article 270) and optionally share revenue from Union excise duties (Article 272). After the amendment, however, revenue from all Central taxes is shareable with the states under the new Article 270, and Article 272 has been omitted. To ensure an impartial and objective arrangement, the tax devolution and grants are required to be made based on the recommendations of a semijudicial body, the Finance Commission, to be set up by the president of India every five years (or earlier), under Article 280. However, with development planning gaining emphasis, the Planning Commission became a major dispenser of funds to the states by way of both grants and loans. As there is no specific provision in the Constitution for plan transfers, the Central government channelled the transfers under Article 282, the legitimacy of which has been seriously questioned.[3] Prior to 1969, plan assistance was scheme based but since then, the distribution has been done on the basis of a consensus formula arrived at in the National Development Council (NDC).[4] However, after the introduction of a formula-based transfer system, various Central ministries have attempted to influence states' allocation either by entirely funding specific programmes (in which case states are being used as agencies) or through specific-purpose transfers with matching requirements. The matching ratio varies between the programmes but is uniform across states. Thus, at present, there are three major channels of Central transfers to states, namely, (i) tax devolution and grants given by the Finance Commission, (ii) grants and loans given by the Planning Commission, and (iii) transfers for various Central sector and centrally sponsored schemes devolved by various Central ministries, but monitored by the Planning Commission.

The relative shares of the three channels of Central transfers to states

---

[2] The Constitution, under 275 (1) also provides for giving Central grants to the states for promoting the welfare of scheduled tribes in a state or for raising the level of administration of scheduled areas.

[3] Some constitutional experts argue that transferring funds to states under Article 282 is unconstitutional. Others consider that though this is permissible, channelling large amounts under this Article is not in keeping with the spirit of the Constitution (see NIPFP, 1994).

[4] The NDC is chaired by the prime minister, and its members include all cabinet ministers at the Centre, chief ministers of the states, and members of the Planning Commission.

TABLE 9. 2
Composition of Central Transfers to States

Rs Billion

Plan periods /years	Finance Commission transfers			Plan grants			Other grants	Total
	Tax devolution	Grants	Total	State plan scheme	Central scheme	Total		
Fourth Plan (1969–74)	45.60 (54.35)	8.60 (10.25)	54.20 (64.60)	10.80 (12.87)	9.70 (11.56)	20.50 (24.43)	9.30 (11.08)	83.90 (100.00)
Fifth Plan (1974–9)	82.70 (50.21)	28.20 (17.12)	110.90 (67.33)	29.10 (17.67)	19.30 (11.72)	48.40 (29.39)	5.40 (3.28)	164.70 (100.00)
Sixth Plan (1980–5)	237.30 (56.97)	21.40 (5.14)	258.70 (62.11)	73.80 (17.72)	69.00 (16.57)	142.80 (34.29)	15.10 (3.63)	416.50 (100.00)
Seventh Plan (1985–90)	494.60 (54.17)	62.70 (6.87)	557.30 (61.04)	155.20 (17.00)	165.10 (18.08)	320.30 (35.08)	35.20 (3.85)	913.10 (100.00)
Annual Plan 1991–2	172.00 (52.22)	34.50 (10.47)	206.50 (62.66)	57.20 (17.36)	55.40 (16.82)	112.60 (34.15)	10.20 (3.10)	329.40 (100.00)
Eighth Plan (1992–7)	1318.50 (55.56)	147.20 (6.20)	1465.70 (61.76)	483.40 (20.37)	364.70 (15.37)	848.10 (35.75)	58.40 (2.46)	2373.10 (100.00)
1997–8	404.11 (62.52)	16.80 (2.60)	420.91 (65.12)	120.08 (18.58)	67.56 (10.45)	187.64 (29.03)	37.80 (5.85)	646.35 (100.00)

(contd)

(Table 9.2 contd)

Plan periods /years	Finance Commission transfers			Plan grants			Other grants	Total
	Tax devolution	Grants	Total	State plan scheme	Central scheme	Total		
1998–9	394.20 (62.29)	14.20 (2.24)	408.40 (64.54)	132.70 (20.97)	71.10 (11.24)	203.80 (32.21)	20.60 (3.26)	632.80 (100.00)
1999–2000	441.21 (59.03)	19.88 (2.66)	461.09 (61.69)	163.16 (21.83)	82.03 (10.98)	245.19 (32.80)	41.14 (5.50)	747.42 100.00
2000–01 RE	518.27 (52.28)	121.69 (12.28)	639.96 (64.56)	157.59 (15.90)	136.76 (13.80)	294.35 (29.79)	56.99 (5.75)	991.30 100.00
2001–02 BE	603.50 (55.41)	95.34 (8.75)	698.84 (64.17)	190.67 (17.51)	152.52 (14.00)	343.19 (31.51)	47.04 (4.32)	1089.07 100.00

Note: Figures in parentheses are percentages to total transfers.
Source: State Finances—A Study of Budgets (various years); Reserve Bank of India Bulletin.

since the Fourth Five Year Plan presented in Table 9.2 bring out some important features. First, there has been a steady increase in the *discretionary element* of transfers. The proportion of transfers recommended by the Finance Commission or statutory transfers in total current transfers declined from 65 per cent during the Fourth Plan (1969–74) to less than 60 per cent during the Eighth Plan (1991–5) and thereafter increased to about 67 per cent in 2000–01. On the whole, formula-based transfers from Finance and Planning Commissions have shown large fluctuations from one plan period to another. These transfers claimed about 85 per cent of total transfers in the Fifth Plan period and during the Seventh Plan period, the share was lower at 78 per cent.

Of the discretionary transfers, specific-purpose transfers for Central sector and centrally sponsored schemes, constitute the bulk. The share of these transfers increased steadily from less than 12 per cent in the Fourth and Fifth Plan periods to about 20 per cent by the end of 1990s. Most of these schemes require matching contributions from the states. Thus, there is a clear evidence of increase in the discretion element in the transfers. The increase in the discretionary element is one of the most significant political economy features of intergovernmental transfer system in India.

Second, within statutory transfers, the proportion of tax devolution has been extremely high, and has steadily increased until 1998–9. Thus, even as the share of statutory transfers declined from about 67 per cent during the Fifth Plan to about 59 per cent in 1999–2000, tax devolution increased its share. Tax devolution constituted 84 per cent of statutory transfers during the Fourth Plan period, but increased to almost 90 per cent during the Eighth Plan. In fact, much of the increase in per capita transfers at constant prices over the years shown in Table 9.1 was from the increase in tax devolution. This may be explained by the fact that while the finance commissions since the Seventh Plan attempted to impart greater progressivity in tax devolution, this was done only by protecting the transfers of the better-off states in absolute terms (at constant prices). In the event, both tax devolution and overall per capita transfers showed a significant increase. Thus, even when the transfers are formula-based and determined by a supposedly impartial and non-political institution, the actual transfers given are based on some sort of a compromise solution between states.[5] We will return to these issues later in the chapter. It

[5] We will not go into the political aspects involved in the manner of appointments to the finance commissions (see Rao and Sen, 1997). The important issue is that even in formulating their recommendations, finance commissions take into consideration political acceptability by states. The extreme example is the sharp criticism and pressure by a state government, ruled by one of the coalition partners at the Centre, forcing the Central government to include additional terms of reference to the finance commissions.

would be instructive to discuss the three major channels of Central transfers to states in some detail.

The Finance Commission Transfers

The terms of reference: Under Article 280 of the Constitution, the president of India appoints the Finance Commission every five years or earlier to make recommendations on:

(a) the distribution between the Union and the states of the net proceeds of taxes which are to be or may be divided between them and the allocation between the states of the respective shares of such proceeds;

(b) the principles which should govern the grants-in-aid of the revenues of the states, out of the consolidated fund of India and the sums to be paid to the states which are in need of assistance by way of grants-in-aid of their revenues under Article 275 of the constitution;

(i) the measures needed to augment the consolidated fund of a state to supplement the resources of the panchayats in the state on the basis of the recommendations made by the Finance Commission of the state;

(ii) the measures needed to augment the consolidated fund of a state to supplement the resources of the municipalities in the state on the basis of the recommendations made by the Finance Commission of the state;

(iii) any other matter referred to the Commission by the president in the interest of sound finance'.

So far, eleven finance commissions have made recommendations and, barring a few exceptions, these have been accepted by the government.[6] Yet, the working of these commissions, the design of the transfer system, and the approach and methodology adopted by them has come in for severe criticisms. The main criticisms are (i) those relating to attempts to restrict the scope of the finance commissions through the presidential terms of reference; (ii) those on the approach and methodology employed by the commissions and its consequences on the design of the transfer scheme evolved by them in terms of equity and incentives.

(*i*) *Restrictions on the scope of the Commission*: The adoption of a planned developmental strategy with a pronounced socialist bias led to the concentration of economic powers in the hands of the Centre and even within

---

[6] A notable exception is the rejection of the majority recommendation of the Third Finance Commission on the inclusion of 75 per cent of plan revenue expenditures in the assessment. Another exception is the rejection of unanimous recommendation of the Seventh Finance Commission to treat the small saving loans given to the states as 'loans in perpetuity'.

the Central government, the Planning Commission. The increased dominance of the Planning Commission in allocative decisions and its empowerment to dispense assistance to the states to finance their developmental activities substantially curtailed the role of the Finance Commission in making intergovernmental transfers. Although the Constitution does not make any distinction between plan and non-plan sides of the budget and channels the transfers under Articles 270 (income tax), 272 (excise duty), and 275 (grants) entirely within the jurisdiction of the finance commissions, presidential terms of reference have restricted the finance commissions to confine themselves to making transfers only to meet the non-plan requirements of the states. The conflict in the jurisdictions of the two commissions surfaced for the first time when the Third Finance Commission made its recommendations. Although the majority recommendation of the Finance Commission was to take account of 75 per cent of the plan requirements of states, the Central government rejected this recommendation and accepted the recommendation of the member-secretary to stay clear of the plan side of the states' fiscal requirements altogether. For the subsequent commissions (until the Ninth) the terms of reference itself excluded the plan sides from their scope. This did provoke the chairman of the Fourth Commission to state, ' ... there is nothing to exclude from its purview, grants for meeting revenue expenditures on the plan schemes nor is there any explicit bar against grants for capital purposes' but nevertheless excluded it '... as it would blur the entire division of functions between the (Finance) Commission and the Planning Commission'.[7] In fact, even when the terms of reference did not impose any restrictions as in the case of the Ninth Finance Commission, the convention of assessing the non-plan side separately from the plan side was continued, as the Commission could not break the shackles imposed by precedent.

The restriction placed on the finance commissions to confine themselves to the non-plan side of the budget has led to a number of problems. First, this has constrained the role of the Finance Commission. The transfers by the Planning Commission and various Central ministries constrains its ability to effect intended redistribution. Second, it prevented comprehensive periodic review and precluded taking a holistic view of state finances. Third, conceptually, plan and non-plan distinction is unsound. This artificial classification has, on the one hand, created a craze for large-sized plants leading to proliferation of expenditure and, on the other, led to inadequate provision for maintenance of the existing assets. Finally, it is not even clear whether the practice of giving transfers under

[7] India, 1965, p. 12.

Article 282 of the Constitution for plan purposes is constitutionally valid. K. K. Venugopal's careful interpretation of the provisions of Constitution shows that, 'Article 275 ... comprehends within its scope the entirety of grants by the centre to the states ... in which both Plan and Non-Plan expenditure would be covered' (p. 227) and 'Article 282 has nothing whatsoever to do with the making of grants exclusively in derogation of the powers of the Finance Commission under Article 175' (p. 228).

(*ii*) *Methodology—the gap-filling approach*: The approach of the Finance Commission to federal transfers consists of (i) assessment of overall budgetary requirements of the Centre and states to determine the volume of resources available for transfer with the Centre and required by individual states and during the period of recommendation; (ii) projecting of states' own revenues and non-plan current expenditures; (iii) distributing assigned taxes,[8] broadly on the basis of origin; (iv) distributing shareable taxes—the personal income tax and Union excise duties between the Centre and the states and among the states inter se; and (v) filling the gap between projected expenditures and revenues after tax devolution with grants.[9] This is popularly known as the 'gap-filling' approach.

Assigned taxes are distributed according to the principle of origin and there are no serious problems associated with them. Of course, the states contend that the Centre has not exhausted the potential of Article 269 taxes, which are to be levied by the Centre, but the proceeds to be assigned to the states. As regards shared taxes, the basic issue is that as the Centre gives away large shares to states, it concentrates on non-shareable revenue sources which not only creates horizontal inequities and relative price distortions, but also distorts the tax structure.

In the evolution of tax devolution over the years, some important features are notable. First, states have always preferred tax devolution to grants due to its inherent responsiveness to changes in prices and incomes. Second, the finance commissions, in response to the criticism that the grants recommended by them have disincentives for fiscal management in the states, have preferred to increase tax devolution rather than 'gap-filling'

---

[8] These are additional excise duties in lieu of sales tax, estate duty in non-agricultural land (abolished since 1985), wealth tax on agricultural property (abolished since 1982), and grants in lieu of repealed tax on railway passenger fares.

[9] The grants (G_i) receivable by the ith state is given by,

$G_i = E_i - (R_{oi} + R_{ai} + R_{si})$. $G_i \geq O$

E_i denotes projected non-plan current expenditures of the ith state.

R_{oi} = Projected own revenues of the ith state; R_{ai} = Projected share of assigned revenues of the ith states; and

R_{si} = Projected shared taxes of the ith states.

grants. Thus, tax devolution has shown a significant increase both in absolute terms, and in relation to grants over the years.

After estimating the gap between projected revenues (including assigned taxes) and non-plan expenditures within the revenue accounts of the states, the finance commissions determine tax devolution to cover bulk of the gap and the remainder is through grants under Article 275. Tax devolution is made mainly on the basis of general economic indicators like population, per capita SDP in its inverse or distance form,[10] other indicators of backwardness, and tax effort. The criteria and relative weights for tax devolution (see Table 9.3).

An examination of the criteria for the distribution of tax shares recommended by the Eleventh Finance Commission brings out some notable features. First, as already mentioned, tax devolution was made on the basis of general economic indicators like population and backwardness and not on the basis of fiscal disadvantages per se. Until 1989–90, tax devolution was not linked to the fiscal needs of the states as measured by the finance commissions at all; the Ninth Finance Commission, however, felt the need to link tax devolution to the estimated deficits but assigned only 5 per cent, which was followed by 7.5 per cent weight by the Tenth Finance Commission. Of course, all the commissions have assigned significant weights to population, which broadly represents expenditure need, but even in doing this, they are mandated to use the 1971 population figures, ostensibly to provide incentive to states for family planning. In the process, even states with higher population growth due to immigration of people, and not just higher fertility, are penalized. Second, while the objective of basing transfers on general economic indicators was to keep the devolution package simple and transparent, the purpose was lost when the finance commissions used a number of factors which included multiple variables and the same variable was used with different exponential powers as was done in the case of inverse and distance forms of per capita SDP. Again, the 'backwardness' criterion sometimes included a number of variables. The Fifth Finance Commission considered a list of five variables. The Ninth Commission in its second report took into account three overlapping variables namely, scheduled caste and scheduled tribe population, agricultural labourers, and people below the poverty line. In the first report of the Ninth Finance Commission, only the poverty ratio

---

[10] The inverse formula is given by $\dfrac{P_i/Y_i}{\Sigma_i \; P_i/Y_i}$, and the distance formula is given by

$(Y_h - Y_i)P_i/\Sigma_i \; (Y_h - Y_i)P_i$, where Y_i and Y_h represent per capita SDP of the ith and the highest per capita SDP state, P_i – the population of the ith state; $(Y_h - Y_i)$ for the 'h' state is taken to be the distance between the highest and the next highest per capita SDP.

was taken to the benefit of high-income states with high poverty ratio like Maharashtra, much to the consternation of middle- and low-income states with relatively low poverty ratios.

TABLE 9.3

Criteria and relative weights for tax devolution

Criterion	Weight (per cent)
1. Population	10.00
2. Income (Distance Method)*	62.50
3. Area	7.50
4. Index of Infrastructure	7.50
5. Tax Effort**	5.00
6. Fiscal Discipline***	7.50

Notes: * The distance method is given by: $(Y_h - Y_i)Pi/\Sigma(Y_h - Y_i)P_i$ where, Y_i and Y_h represent per capita SDP of the ith and the highest income state, respectively and P_i is the population of the ith state.

    ** Tax Effort (η) is estimated as $(\eta) = (T_i / Y_i) / (0.5/Y_i)$ where, T_i is the per capita tax revenue collected by the ith state and Y_i is the per capita state domestic product of the ith state.

    *** Estimated as the improvement in the ratio of own revenue of a state to its revenue expenditures divided by a similar ratio for all states averaged for the period 1966–99 over 1991–3.

Soruce: Authors' calculation.

Grants recommended by the finance commissions (Article 275), on the other hand, are determined on the basis of projected gaps between non-plan current expenditures and post-tax devolution revenues. In this sense, the finance commissions have acted as 'fiscal dentists' filling in 'budgetary cavities'. Of course, some of the commissions moderated the 'gaps' by taking account of normative growth rates of revenues and expenditures in projections, and taking the returns from public undertakings on a normative basis. Some of the commissions (particularly after the Sixth) also attempted to enhance outlays on specified services in the states by making closed-ended specific-purpose non-matching grants. However, these attempts were selective and, by and large, it would not be incorrect to characterize their approach as 'gap-filling'. The Ninth Finance Commission was the first to attempt and comprehensively adopt the normative approach, and determined the gap between revenue capacities and expenditure needs of the states. However, the relevance of the approach was lost to a great extent when the bulk of the transfers was given by way of tax devolution based on general economic indicators and not the fiscal need as assessed. The Tenth Finance Commission reverted to the old methodology on the plea that it was not mandated to follow the 'normative' approach in its terms of reference.

(iii) *Evaluation of transfers by the Finance Commission*: The approach adopted by the Finance Commission does not consider the economic objectives of the transfer system discussed in Chapter 8. The transfer system seems to have been influenced more by political economy considerations rather than economic objectives as may be seen from a number of shortcomings in their design and implementation. First, none of the finance commissions assessed the overall resource position of the Centre and the proportion of the resources required to meet its commitments on any objective basis, although the terms of reference explicitly required them to do so. They merely made judgements about the proportion of Central taxes to be shared. In fact, the commissions have found it difficult to evolve any objective criteria for evaluating the Centre's needs. On the other hand, continuously raising states' share in shareable taxes implicitly meant that the Centre had more resources than its own needs, or that it was the Centre, which should or could raise more resources. With the deterioration in the Centre's own fiscal position in the 1980s, larger devolution meant higher fiscal imbalance at the Centre and the exercise of distributing transfers became merely one of distributing deficits.

Second, the prevailing practice of dealing with plan and non-plan requirements of the states separately by the Planning and the Finance Commission has not only prevented a holistic view on the fiscal needs of the states, but has also compartmentalized the assessment of interdependent components of states' fiscal needs. The expenditures on completed plan schemes are classified as non-plan. The interest payable on plan loans is a non-plan item. On the other hand, there are several instances when new expenditures of a developmental nature are undertaken on the non-plan side. In fact, whether or not a particular developmental scheme should be included under the plan is left to the discretion of the state concerned. Besides poor coordination, the compartmentalized treatment of plan and non-plan expenditure needs, and emphasis on having large-sized plans has led to inadequate provision for maintenance of assets created under previous plans. From the states' point of view, separate plan and non-plan assessments gave them the opportunity to submit different projections to the two commissions—an overestimated non-plan budgetary gap to the Finance Commission and overestimated saving in the non-plan account to the Planning Commission. Even the presence of a common member in both the commissions has not made any difference to this tendency.

The third weakness of the Finance Commission's transfer scheme is the lack of clear purpose in them. These transfers have not been designed to meet the major objective of unconditional transfers discussed in Chapter 8, namely, offsetting fiscal disadvantages of the states. The tax devolution was decided on different considerations from those of the grants-in-aid, and, even in the case of the former, the criteria for distributing income tax were different from those for excise duties. The earlier commissions recommended tax devolution mainly on the basis of population but, and as later commissions substantially increased devolution, better targetting had to be done by assigning greater weightage to the backwardness factor so as to contain the cost of transfers to the Centre. Even so, a predominant proportion of transfers continued to be given as tax devolution distributed on the basis of general economic indicators, of course, with high weights being assigned to the backwardness factor but not designed to offset fiscal disadvantages of the states per se.

Fourth, although successive commissions assigned higher weights to backwardness in the tax devolution formula, their methodology has had an inherent bias against poorer states. As existing revenues and non-plan expenditures with some minor modifications are firmed up as bases for making projection, prevailing tax levels and standards of services implicitly became the most important determinant. In the event, any change in the transfer system could only be marginal and incremental. Further, as the bulk of the transfers—the tax devolution—was distributed on the basis of general economic indicators, even the states with low fiscal disabilities in the commissions' own reckoning received substantial amounts. Thus, the states with greater means ended up with high levels of estimated per capita non-plan surpluses after the award of the finance commissions. Given this unequal starting position, the richer states could make larger plan investments, resulting in the imbalances in the pattern of development itself.

Fifth, there has been a considerable concern at the finance commissions following the 'gap-filling' approach and its possible disincentives on fiscal management in states. This was the reason for modifying the terms of reference of the Ninth Finance Commission to follow a 'normative approach'. However, the Commission did not fully make use of the estimate of fiscal capacities and needs of the states in formulating its recommendations. The Tenth Finance Commission simply abandoned the approach. The Eleventh Finance Commission in the additional terms of reference given to it just before the finalization of its recommendations was asked to '... draw a monitorable fiscal reforms programme aimed at reduction of revenue deficit of the state and recommended the manner in which the grants to the states to cover the assessed deficit in their non-plan revenue account may be linked to progress in implementing the programme'.

The Eleventh Commission worked out a scheme by pooling 15 per cent of revenue deficit grants and adding an equal amount to it to create an incentive fund to be allocated among the states based on fulfilment of targets of growth of tax and non-tax revenues and expenditures on salaries, interest payments, and subsidies, as set in the fiscal restructuring plan detailed by the Commission. The incentive fund has been allocated to the states according to their population shares. A state will get the full amount if it fulfils the specified targets of the monitorable measure evolved for the purpose and the amount will vary depending on the degree of achievement of monitorable targets. If a state does not get the full amount during the first four years it will continue to be available in subsequent years, but if by the fifth year the targets are not achieved, the funds will lapse. To implement the scheme a monitoring agency is supposed be set up by the Government of India. The ministry of finance has implemented the recommendation and the states have signed the Medium Term Fiscal Reform Programme (MTFRP) with the Centre, which is monitored by a committee comprising representatives of the finance ministry, Planning Commission, power ministry, and independent economists.

The ministry of finance has set up a committee to monitor the MTFRP. For operational purposes, it has evolved a single monitorable measure, revenue deficit as a percentage of total revenue receipts of the states. Each state is required to reduce this percentage by five points so that by the end of five years covered by the finance commission's recommendation, the revenue deficit of the states is completely eliminated.

However, there are a number of problems with the proposed scheme and some of them have been alluded to. Conceptually, the scheme has serious shortcomings as pointed out by the note of dissent of Amaresh Bagchi, one of the members of the commission (Government of India, 2000, pp. 9–13). In terms of volume of transfers, the amount earmarked under the incentive scheme is so negligible that it can hardly make any difference. On the one hand, the entitlement of general transfers to each state is worked out on the basis of projected fiscal gaps, and, on the other, a small portion is earmarked for incentives. Second, the design of the monitorable measure itself leaves much to be desired. The measure— revenue deficit as a percentage of revenue receipts—has inherent bias against the states with large dependence on transfers. In the case of small and poorer states, the fiscal dependence is large and the measure is biased against them. In fact, in some of the states, Central transfers constitute over 80 per cent of revenues. Reduction in Central transfers adversely impacts on both the numerator and the denominator and the states are penalized for no fault of theirs when the Central transfers decline. The issue is not merely of academic interest for, during the last decade, the Central transfer to states as a percentage of GDP has declined by over one percentage point. Third, the adjustment path given in the MTFRP is different from the path specified in the medium-term fiscal plan adopted by some of the states that have taken adjustment loan from the multilateral lending agencies. Finally, there are so many incentive schemes that have been introduced in recent times that the whole thing has resulted in segmented incentivizing without much impact. The Accelerated Power Development Scheme, Accelerated Irrigation Development Scheme, incentives for voluntary retirement scheme, besides multiple centrally sponsored schemes provide enough scope for softening the budget constraint to the states.

Plan Transfers

Plan assistance to the states comprises grants and loans. Prior to 1969 these were distributed largely on a schematic basis in which both the quantum of transfers and its loan-grant components were discretionary. However, since 1969, plan assistance has been distributed on the basis of the 'Gadgil formula' approved by the National Development Council (NDC) modified from time to time. The latest modification in the formula was done in December 1991. According to this, at present 30 per cent of the funds available for distribution are kept apart for the special-category states. Assistance to them is given on the basis of plan projects formulated by them and 90 per cent of the transfer is given by way of grants and the remaining as loans. The 70 per cent of the funds available to the major states is distributed with 60 per cent weight assigned to population, 25 per cent to per capita SDP, 7.5 per cent to fiscal management, and the remaining 7.5 per cent to special problems of states. Of the 25 per cent weight assigned to per capita SDP, 20 percentage points worth is allocated only to the states with less than average per capita SDP on the basis of the 'inverse' formula and the remaining is assigned to all the states according to the 'distance' formula. For the non-special category states, assistance is given by way of grants and loans in the ratio of 30:70. The transfers given to the states for plan purposes are not related to the required size or composition of plan investments (see Table 9.4).

The Planning Commission works out five-year plan investments for each of the sectors and the states. Keeping this in the background, and based on estimated resource availability, which includes the balance from current revenue, the contribution of public enterprises, additional resource mobilization, plan grants and loans, market borrowings and other miscellaneous capital receipts, the states work out their respective annual plans for each year, which are then approved by the Planning Commission.

TABLE 9.4

Formula for Distributing State Plan Assistance

Criteria	Share in Central plan assistance (per cent)	Share of grants and loans	Distribution criteria non-special category states
A. Special-category states (10)	30	90:10	
B. Non-special category states (15)	70	30:70	
(i) Population (1971)			60.00
(ii) Per capita income, of which			25.00
(a) According to 'deviation' method covering only the states with per capita income below the national average			20.00
(b) According to the 'distance' method covering all the fifteen states			5.00
(iii) Fiscal performance, of which			7.50
(a) Tax effort			2.50
(b) Fiscal management			2.50
(c) National objectives			2.50
(iv) Special problems			7.50
Total			100.00

Notes: (a) The formula as revised in December 1991.

(b) Fiscal management is assessed as the difference between states' own total plan resources estimated at the time of finalizing annual plan and their actual performance, considering latest five years.

(c) Under the criterion of the performance in respect of certain programmes of national priorities the approved formula covers four objectives, viz. (i) population control, (ii) elimination of illiteracy, (iii) on-time completion of externally-aided projects, and (iv) success in land reforms.

Source: Gadgil formula (NDC modified).

Thus, in the final analysis, given that the Central assistance to the states is determined by the Gadgil formula, the states have some degree of freedom to alter the plan size only by changing their own resource position.

Interestingly, plan assistance has no relationship with the investment requirements of the states. The transfers are not directly related to the shortfall in states' resources, given the required volume of plan investments and own resources reckoned at a standard performance level. The plan assistance given to the states, as also its grant-loan components are not related to the required plan investments, their sectoral composition, resources available with the states or their fiscal performances. In fact, the grant component of Central plan assistance has been kept at 30 per cent because, at the time the Gadgil formula was introduced, the current component of plan outlay was approximately 30 per cent. Of course, there were considerable variations in the ratio of current plan expenditures among individual states, but the grant-loan component for plan assistance for the major states has been kept constant though, for the special-category states the grant portion has been kept at 90 per cent. The constancy in the grant portion to all the major states does not take into account the differing repayment abilities of the states; besides, this inherently results in bias against the states with strategies for development through human capital formation, as against those with emphasis on physical capital formation. In the former, the current expenditure component according to the prevailing budgeting practices would be higher. Further as the return on expenditure in the medium term would accrue to the individual rather than the government, the states with larger current component of plan expenditures would have as much of interest liability as the states with larger share of capital expenditures, but with much lower levels of revenue-yielding assets. There is certainly a case for varying the grant component of Central plan assistance depending on the repayment capacity of individual states.

Assistance for Central Sector and Centrally Sponsored Schemes

Assistance given to states via central sector and centrally sponsored schemes, constituting about 20 per cent of total transfers, is the most controversial component of transfers. These are neither based on the recommendations of the Finance Commission nor are determined by the Gadgil formula, but are discretionary. The Central government ministries initiate a number of national programmes either by themselves or at the request of the relevant ministries at the state level. The central sector schemes are assisted entirely by the Central government; the states merely execute these programmes. The centrally sponsored schemes, on the other hand, are shared cost programmes and central assistance is given by way of grants or loans decided for each of the programmes. The rationale for introducing these programmes is ostensibly to finance activities which have a high degree of interstate spillovers or are in the nature of merit goods (poverty alleviation and family planning).

The central sector and centrally sponsored schemes have attracted the sharpest criticism because of their arbitrariness and discretion implicit in them. Although major programmes on family planning and rural development are well designed, and the transfers are given according to the formula devised by the administering ministries, bureaucratic and political discretion plays an important role in introducing and designing most of the programmes. Most schemes are designed at the Central level, applied uniformly to all the states without taking account of their institutional realities. Most schemes require that new employees be created for implementing the schemes and this leaves the states with a new burden. There are also instances when the prime minister announces the programmes in public meetings, leaving the Planning Commission and the relevant ministries to work out details. When even a few such programmes are determined in an arbitrary and non-transparent manner, some of the well-formulated programmes under central sector and centrally sponsored schemes also become subject to serious doubts about their objectivity and transparency.

These programmes have provided the Central government an instrument to interfere with the states' allocations. Until 1969, when the volume and pattern of assistance to state plan schemes were decided for each project, the Central government did not find the need for these transfers. But once plan assistance was given according to the 'Gadgil' formula, the Central government took recourse to these specific-purpose transfers and expanded them significantly.

Thus, these schemes have grown in both volume and number over the years. In spite of the states' objection to the proliferation of such schemes and the decision of the NDC in 1970 to roll the assistance to one-sixth of the Central assistance for state plans, the volume of transfers amounts to about 40 per cent. Politicization of the schemes is illustrated by the fact that there are over 225 such schemes and despite several attempts by the Planning Commission to consolidate them, it has achieved little success. Besides the discretion and arbitrariness implicit in these transfers, conditionalities imposed by the Centre including those on staffing pattern tend to distort the states' own priorities and programmes. While in any federal system, and more so in India, there is certainly a case for specific-purpose transfers, it is important to ensure that these are well designed to ensure minimum standards of public services. Choosing the programmes on political considerations and spreading the resources thinly across multiple schemes without a proper monitoring mechanism may serve the political objective of dispensing political patronage to groups and parties, but does not help to fulfil the economic objectives of such transfers. Furthermore, political and administrative discretion may be necessary in any system, but it is important that these are transparent and based on consensus.

CENTRAL TRANSFERS TO STATES AND INTERSTATE EQUITY

Strict adherence to economic rationale would require that transfers be designed to offset revenue and cost disabilities. However, actual transfer systems fall short of this ideal, as historical and political factors are also important in determining them. Thus, the volume and design of transfers and the degree of progressivity in their distribution are determined as a compromise between economic considerations and the constraints placed by non-economic factors. However, the extent to which the economic objectives of intergovernmental transfers policy are met is important and needs to be analysed. In what follows, an attempt is made to analyse the equity implications of Central transfers to states in India.

Analysis of intergovernmental transfers shows a fair degree of inter-state redistribution. Central transfers vary inversely with the level of per capita NSDP (Figure 9.1). The cross-section income elasticity of aggregate transfers in 1998–9 was –0.194 (Table 9.5). However, equalization in the transfer system was entirely due to the redistribution in Finance Commission transfers. The elasticity of Finance Commission transfers with respect to GSDP in 1997–8 was –0.26. In contrast, plan grants and grants for centrally sponsored schemes did not have significant equalization. These transfers did not achieve significant equalization. Thus, by and large, the transfer system may be considered equitable. Nevertheless, it should be noted that the absolute value of elasticity is low. On an average, per capita transfers were higher by 0.19 per cent when the per capita SDP was lower by one per cent. This shows that although the transfer system on the whole has an equalizing impact, it is not designed to offset shortfall in fiscal capacity and cost disabilities fully.

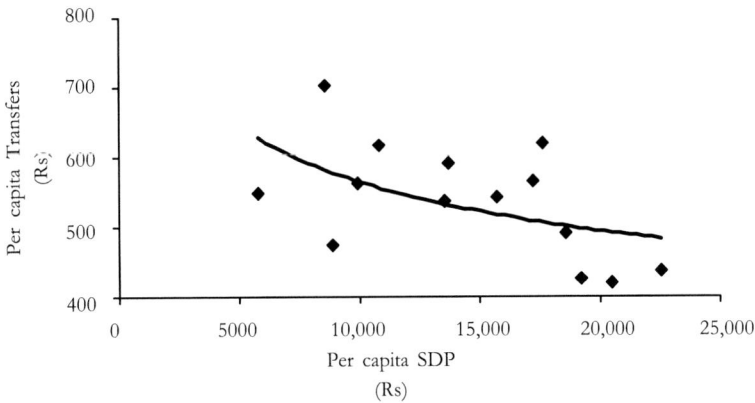

Figure 9.1: Equalization in Intergovernmental Transfers 1998–9

TABLE 9.5

Per capita Current Transfers to States from Centre 1998–9

State	Finance Commission	Planning Commission			Total Transfers
		State plan schemes	Centrally sponsored	Total plan transfers	
1. Major States					
Intercept	8.383	5.859	–2.819	3.848	8.124
T value	8.943	3.527	–0.760	2.011	9.180
Co-efficient	–0.260	–0.171	0.736	0.115	–0.194
T value	–2.638	–0.978	1.891	0.573	–2.087
R^2	0.349	0.068	0.216	0.025	0.251
2. Special-category States					
Intercept	8.031			16.241	12.546
T value	1.502			2.003	1.907
Co-efficient	-0.081			–0.932	–0.467
T value	-0.141			–1.075	–0.664
R^2	0.002			0.104	0.042
3. All States					
Intercept	12.956		3.911	14.652	14.616
T value	3.087		0.606	2.071	2.768
Co-efficient	–0.679		0.101	–0.916	–0.798
T value	–1.531		0.148	–1.226	–1.431
R^2	0.089		0.001	0.059	0.079

Soruce: Authors' calculation.

Despite the somewhat progressive distribution of intergovernmental transfers, per capita revenue accruals and, therefore, per capita expenditures across states continue to be significantly higher in states with higher per capita SDP as may be inferred from Figure 9.2. Thus, the distribution of per capita revenue accruals as well as per capita expenditures across the states has a positive slope when they are plotted against per capita SDP. It is also seen that the slope of revenue accruals, which includes the Central transfers, is only marginally different from that of the states' own revenues.

INSTITUTIONAL MECHANISM FOR INTERGOVERNMENTAL TRANSFERS

Keeping in view the need to evolve a transparent and an impartial system of transfers to ensure that the financial strength of the Centre and the

Equalization in Indian Fiscal Federalism 1999–2000

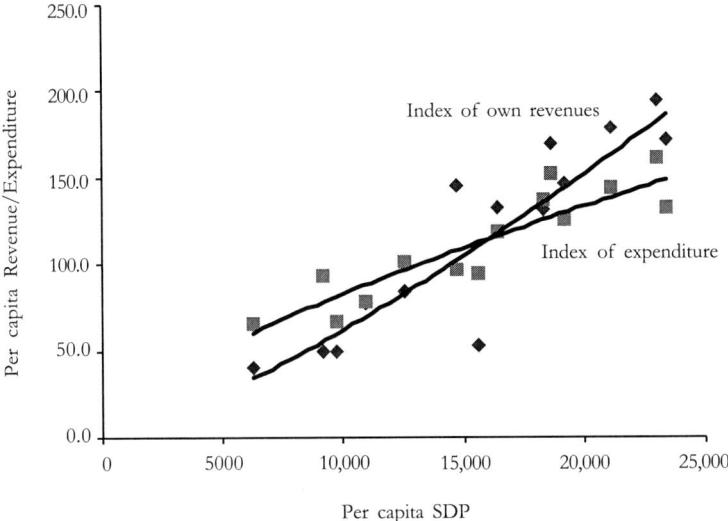

Equalization in Indian Federalism

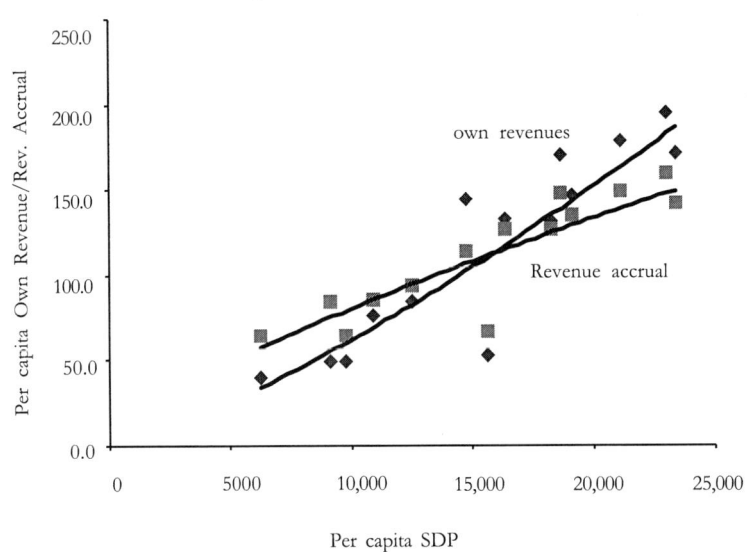

Figure 9.2

states are on an even keel, the Constitution provided for the appointment of the Finance Commission. As the Commission was to be appointed every five years, the mechanism provided for taking account of the changing needs and norms of the Centre and the states. The Finance Commission (miscellaneous) Act also lays down qualifications of the chairman and members of the Commission and the presence of a judicial member/chairman in the Commission is supposed to give it a semi-judicial status. The provision for setting up the Finance Commission has been on the lines of the Commonwealth Grants Commission in Australia, though there are important differences both in their status and working.

Despite the provision of a specialized independent and semi-judicial agency, it is difficult to pronounce that the intergovernmental institutions have helped to evolve a satisfactory system of fiscal transfers. The short-comings of the institutional mechanism are seen in a number of ways. First, as already mentioned, although the Constitution envisaged rule-based transfers on the recommendation of the finance commissions, developments have contrived to reduce the constitutional body to a minor role and a major proportion of transfers lies outside its purview. The multiple agencies giving transfers in an uncoordinated manner cannot be expected to singularly pursue economic objectives of intergovernmental transfers. Besides, while the Finance Commission is expected to be a non-political body, the Planning Commission is not. The Gadgil formula used for distributing plan assistance is determined by consensus in the National Development Council where all the states are members and it would be unrealistic to expect targeted transfers to offset fiscal disadvantages in such a system. The centrally sponsored schemes in any case are discretionary, designed by the Central ministries where many non-economic consider-ations enter into the distribution mechanism.

Although the Finance Commission is expected to be a non-political body, political considerations play an important role in the appointment of the chairman and members of the Commission, in specifying their terms of reference and in the functioning of the commission itself (Rao and Sen, 1997). In selecting the chairman and members of the Commission and specifying its terms of reference, the Central government, more particularly the Union ministry of finance plays a leading role, and this raises questions about their objectivity and fairness in the minds of the states. This is particularly true when the appointment of chairman and members of the commission is done on political considerations or politi-cal personalities are appointed to the Commission. In addition, the mem-ber-secretary/secretary is always a senior bureaucrat belonging to the IAS, who is appointed not because of his expertise or interest in the subject, but merely because he qualifies to be appointed as a secretary to Government of India. Often, midway through the Commission's tenure, the member-secretary secures transfer to regular posting as the secretary in an important ministry.[11] The staff of the Commission, by and large, also comes on deputation from various Central ministries and most of them are not familiar with the technical requirements of determining intergovernmental transfers and understanding of finances of Central and state governments. In short, the whole approach to the appointment of the Finance Commission and its functioning has not been very professional. Thus, not surprisingly, and unlike the Australian Commonwealth Grants Commission, their contribution to the development of an objective and scientific approach and methodology to satisfactorily resolve fiscal imbalances and infuse confidence to cement stronger intergovernmental relationships has left much to be desired. In the event, the very objective of establishing an independent semi-judicial body to recommend intergovernmental transfers has been defeated.

Lack of coordination between the Planning Commission and the Finance Commission is another important issue. The whole exercise is based on the incorrect assumption that the plan and non-plan sides of the budget are independent and exclusive. Parallel assessment of state finances by the two agencies results not merely in duplicating the work; there are instances where the Planning Commission has gone about filling the non-plan gaps of the states in the current account, resulting from the non-compliance of the norms set by the Finance Commission. The states on their part, submit different projections of revenues and expenditures to the two commissions; the projection submitted to the Finance Commission attempts to magnify the gap in the revenue account in order to get larger assistance whereas the one submitted to the Planning Commission exaggerates the availability of resources to have larger plan size. The presence of a common member in both the commissions has resolved this issue to a considerable extent, but the issue of independent treatment of interdependent plan and non-plan sides remains.

The important issue emanating from the above is that political elements enter into fiscal transfer decision in all federal countries. To that extent, actual transfer system deviates from the ideal either in its design or implementation. Politics matters and we do not live in the world of benevolent state. The agents—be they politicians or bureaucrats—are self

---

[11] The member-secretaries of both the Ninth and Tenth Finance Commissions were changed midway through the Commissions' deliberations as they were transferred to administrative departments.

interested and yet it is possible to enhance objectivity and evolve a scientific approach when the ideas of commitment and delegation discussed in chapters 4 and 5 are satisfied and the system of checks and balances is allowed to function.

INTERGOVERNMENTAL TRANSFERS IN INDIA: IMPLICIT TRANSFERS

The foregoing analysis demonstrates that even when there is a constitutional mechanism to effect formula-based transfers, the political system may not allow evolving a simple, equitable, objective, and rule-based system of transfers as demonstrated in the Indian federation. Even if such a system is developed, there can be a number of implicit and invisible ways in which the more powerful states can effect resource transfers in their favour to offset the effect of explicit transfers. Besides the pattern of distributing Central government's own expenditures and its regional policies in terms of locating Central public enterprises, we can identify at least three important sources of resource transfers:

(i) Interstate tax exportation;

(ii) subsidized lending by banking and financial institutions to the private sector. This includes lending by All-India Financial Institutions[12] (AIFI) at below market interest rates subsidized by the refinancing facility extended by the Reserve Bank of India, and priority-sector lending by commercial banks for specified activities like agriculture and rural development, industrial promotion, small-scale industry, and exports; and

(iii) Subsidized borrowing by the states from the Central government and the banking system. The main source of inter-regional transfers from lending to the governments comes from the stipulation to the banking system on the extent of their lendable resources to be held in government bonds at regulated interest rates (statutory liquidity ratio), stipulation on the quantum of assistance to be given to the 'priority sector', and the distribution of seigniorage or the profits of the Reserve Bank of India through the refinancing facilities given to AIFI. We discuss the three sources of invisible transfers in some detail.

---

[12] All-India Financial Institutions refer to All-India Development Banks (Industrial Development Bank of India, Industrial Finance Corporation of India, Industrial Credit and Investment Corporation of India, Small Industries Development Bank of India, Industrial Reconstruction Bank of India, Shipping Credit and Investment Company of India Ltd), specialized financial institutions (Risk Capital and Technology Finance Corporation Ltd, Technology Development and Information Company of India Ltd.), Travel Finance Corporation of India Ltd), and investment institutions (LIC, UTI, GIC).

Interstate Tax Exportation

In Indian federalism, states raise almost 35 per cent of the total tax revenue or about 5.8 per cent of GDP and, therefore, structure and operation of their tax systems have a significant impact on economic efficiency and equity. An overwhelming proportion (over 90 per cent) of state tax revenue accrues from indirect taxes, and sales tax alone contributes to 53 per cent.

Given that revenue from sales taxes predominates in the states' fiscal operations, the structure and operation of sales taxes and interstate tax competition have important implications on allocative efficiency and equity. The analysis of the Indian experience shows that interstate tax competition can be a source of serious allocative distortions and regressive interstate transfers.[13] Distortions are caused by excessive and irrational form of rate differentiation as well as the erection of trade barriers across different jurisdictions (Rao and Vaillancourt, 1994). Regressive interstate resource transfers are caused by the states attempting to 'free-ride' by exporting the tax burden to non-residents.

'Free-riding' and Interstate Tax Exportation

Interstate tax exportation arises from the levy of origin-based cascading-type sales taxation along with the taxation of interstate sale of goods. The sales taxes levied by the states are predominantly on the basis of origin, at the stage of manufacture or import. They also levy taxes on raw materials, intermediate inputs, and capital goods. In addition, interstate sale is also taxed subject to the ceiling rate of 4 per cent. In an economy where there is only a limited internal and external competition the tax is fully shifted forward, input taxes cascade on to interstate sales tax and consequently, effective tax rate on interstate sales would be much higher than the four per cent nominally levied. This results in the exportation of the tax burden from more affluent producing states to the consumers in poorer consuming states. When the exports of more developed states are larger than their imports, and the proportion of final goods in their exports too is higher as in the Indian case (Rao and Sen, 1997), the residents of poorer states end up paying taxes on larger volumes of imports and at higher effective tax rates.

Non-availability of data on interstate trade makes it difficult to esti-mate interstate tax exportation accurately. However, our analysis pre-sented in Table 9.6 shows that in more-than-average per capita income

---

[13] For detailed analysis of the sales tax systems in different states and its adverse efficiency and equity consequences, see NIPFP (1994).

TABLE 9.6

Consumption Shares, Tax Shares, and Effective Tax Rates (1999–2000)

	Household consumption (Rs Crore)	State government purchase of goods (Rs Crore)	Total consumption (Rs Crore)	Percentage of total consumption	Sales tax collections (Rs Crore)	Percentage of total sales tax collections	Difference between sales tax shares and consumption shares	Effective sales tax rates (per cent)	Tax exported (Rs Crore)	Per capita tax exportation (Rs)
Andhra Pradesh	48,723	1033	49,756	8.16	6172	10.60	2.44	12.40	150.88	20.32
Bihar	45,936	973	46,909	7.69	2280	3.92	−3.77	4.86	−86.03	−8.83
Gujarat	34,647	772	35,419	5.81	5134	8.82	3.01	14.50	154.73	32.74
Haryana	17,762	414	18,176	2.98	1967	3.38	0.40	10.82	7.87	4.05
Karnataka	35,862	700	36,562	5.99	4683	8.04	2.05	12.81	96.05	18.78
Kerala	26,990	620	27,610	4.53	3854	6.62	2.09	13.96	80.67	25.32
Madhya Pradesh	43,521	1046	44,568	7.31	2555	4.39	−2.92	5.73	−74.53	−9.58
Maharashtra	74,091	1387	75,478	12.37	10,509	18.05	5.68	13.92	596.78	66.55
Orissa	17,665	554	18,219	2.99	1108	1.90	−1.08	6.08	−12.01	−3.39
Punjab	21,076	596	21,672	3.55	1977	3.40	−0.16	9.12	−3.09	−1.32
Rajasthan	34,212	740	34,952	5.73	2425	4.16	−1.56	6.94	−37.94	−7.26
Tamil Nadu	47,541	1394	48,935	8.02	7024	12.07	4.04	14.35	284.06	46.55
Uttar Pradesh	100,272	2117	102,389	16.78	5099	8.76	−8.03	4.98	−409.23	−24.81
West Bengal	48,210	1167	49,376	8.09	3429	5.89	−2.20	6.94	−75.59	−9.75
All Major States	596,509	13,514	610,022	100.00	58,216	100.00	0.00	9.54		

Source: Authors' calculations.

states, tax shares are systematically higher than comparison consumption shares (household consumption plus state government purchase of goods). Of course, it is possible that the difference could also be due to better tax performances and not tax exportation. However, there is no reason to assume that tax performances are related to per capita SDP. On the contrary, there is reason to believe that total volume of exports would be higher in producing states with higher per capita SDP than consuming states with lower SDP. In addition, richer states export a higher proportion of finished goods, whereas the exports of poorer states comprise mainly primary products and raw materials. Thus, the input tax element in the exports of states with higher per capita SDP is higher. Analysis of states' data shows that, by and large, sales tax shares were higher than the consumption shares in states with higher per capita SDP. This indicates that richer states collect substantial revenues by exporting the tax burden to the residents of poorer states. It is seen that Gujarat, Maharashtra, Kerala, and Tamil Nadu have substantially higher sales tax shares than their consumption shares whereas Uttar Pradesh, Bihar, Madhya Pradesh, Rajasthan, and Orissa are in the opposite situation. If the entire difference is attributed to tax exportation, Maharashtra exported about Rs 597 crore to the rest of the country whereas Uttar Pradesh paid almost Rs 500 crore to the rest of the country.

Inter-regional Transfers From Subsidized Lending by Financial Institutions

The pursuit of planned development strategy required the use of controls on prices and quantities. Important among these has been the distribution of credit to the specified activities in the private sector by the banking and financial system at below market interest rates. This includes credit given by the banking system to 'priority sector' activities such as agriculture, small-scale enterprises and exports, and refinancing provided by the AIFI at subsidized rates. Priority-sector lending constituted about a third of total bank credit in 1995–6, and the subsidy element in these advances is significant. For example, interest rate on priority-sector borrowing in 1993–4 was 5.5 to 6.5 per cent as compared to the SBI long-term lending rate of 19 per cent. The quantum of subsidy implicit in the assistance given by AIFI was significant in earlier years, as much of the profits of the Reserve Bank of India (seigniorage) were used for refinancing these institutions, but the subsidy has declined since 1992–3 as the Centre has been appropriating the profits of the RBI entirely.

Table 9.7 presents the distribution of priority-sector credit and the financial assistance given by the AIFI. It is seen that the distribution of

TABLE 9. 7
Explicit and Implicit Transfers in Indian Federation

States	Per capita SDP 2000–01 (Rs)	Infrastructure index 1997–8	Per capita revenue accrual 2001–02 (Rs)	Per capita own revenue 2001–02 (Rs)	Per capita transfers 2001–02 (Rs)	Per capita all financial institution assistance 2001–01 (Rs)	Per capita priority sector lending 1999–2000 (Rs)	Per capita bank lending 1999–2000
High-income States	22,461	156.32	3537.00	2931.60	605.40	1637.25	2886	5038
Gujarat	18,685	200.57	15,755.40	14,310.30	1445.10	957.20	2743	4724
Goa	44,613	124.31	3522.10	2684.60	837.50	1583.50	1651	2997
Haryana	21,551	137.54	3757.90	3209.70	548.20	823.00	2198	3971
Maharashtra	22,604	178.68	3220.00	2741.30	478.70	2069.40	3542	6033
Punjab	23,254	187.57	3962.50	3333.20	629.40	772.20	3459	6280
Middle-income States	17,635	109.43	2771.70	1868.80	902.90	612.66	1824	3175
Andhra Pradesh	14,878	103.30	2925.00	1930.20	994.90	499.30	1672	2925
Karnataka	16,654	71.46	3020.10	2148.10	872.00	948.10	2107	3644
Kerala	17,709	104.89	3132.20	2295.80	836.40	351.00	2162	3529
Tamil Nadu	18,623	149.10	3056.20	2342.50	713.60	755.20	2687	4798
West Bengal	14,874	111.25	2100.30	1091.00	1009.20	492.70	968	1690
Low-income States	9013	87.33	1851.80	846.80	1005.00	162.95	750	1255
Bihar	4813	81.30	1232.90	338.20	894.70	20.70	399	666
Chhattisgarh	10,405		2278.90	1264.00	1014.90	278.00		
Jharkhand	9223		2266.80	1128.00	1138.70	51.90		
Madhya Pradesh	11,626	76.79	2083.00	1061.90	1021.10	192.10	885	1525

(contd)

218

(Table 9.7 contd)

States	Per capita SDP 2000–01 (Rs)	Infrastruc-ture index 1997–8	Per capita revenue accrual 2001–02 (Rs)	Per capita own revenue 2001–02 (Rs)	Per capita transfers 2001–02 (Rs)	Per capita all financial institution assistance 2001–01 (Rs)	Per capita priority sector lending 1999–2000 (Rs)	Per capita bank lending 1999–2000
Orissa	8733	81.00	2209.30	900.50	1308.80	286.40	675	1121
Rajasthan	13,046	75.86	2242.70	1297.20	945.50	300.40	1021	1825
Uttaranchal	NA		3326.90	1295.50	2031.40	102.40		
Uttar Pradesh	9323	101.23	1668.50	791.20	877.30	156.00	824	1324
General Category States	14,476		2485.50	1594.00	891.50	604.88		
Special Category States	12,339	78.25	4855.10	1155.90	3699.20	225.25	663	1075
Arunachal Pradesh	13,352	69.70	12,042.20	1067.80	10,974.30	51.40	289	510
Assam	9720	77.70	2488.60	798.70	1689.90	83.10	469	755
Himachal Pradesh	17,786	95.03	6053.10	1660.50	4392.50	1161.60	1170	1936
Jammu & Kashmir	12,373	71.46	6810.40	1150.40	5659.90	185.90	1182	1902
Manipur	12,721	75.39	5994.10	406.00	5588.00	93.30	442	736
Meghalaya	12,063	75.49	5888.50	1066.80	4821.70	61.80	358	574
Mizoram	14,909	82.13	12,390.80	679.00	11,711.80	95.60	362	564
Nagaland	12,594	76.14	7519.40	506.80	7012.60	56.20	427	747
Sikkim	14,751	108.99	19,598.30	5998.10	13,600.20	1075.30	581	835
Tripura	13,195	74.87	5842.30	729.60	5112.80	26.90	394	632
All States	14,359	100.00	2614.90	1570.10	1044.80	584.15	1600	2669

Notes: NA—Not Available

Source: Authors' calculations.

both sources of lending is disproportionately in favour of high-income states. In the aggregate, these states with just about 19 per cent of population received 35 per cent of priority-sector lending, and their share of assistance from AIFI was 43 per cent. In contrast, the low-income states with almost 44 per cent of population received just about than 15 per cent and 22 per cent of assistance from AIFI. Thus, the distribution of subsidized credit by the banking system and AIFI has been to confer disproportionate benefits to more advanced states.

Invisible Transfers from Subsidized Lending to States

The most important source of implicit transfers, however, is subsidized lending to the states. Loans from the Central government alone contribute to almost 68 per cent of states' liabilities, a bulk of which was given for plan purposes under the Gadgil formula. The market borrowings constitute another 22 per cent, which is subscribed mainly by the banking system so as to fulfil the statutory liquidity ratio (SLR) requirements.[14] The extent and nature of intergovernmental transfers from this source depends upon the pattern of interstate allocation of when loans to state governments or public enterprises run by the states are rescheduled and written off, implicit transfers do arise. The recent attempt to bail out the state electricity boards by providing a one-time settlement of their dues to Central public sector undertakings (PSUs) is a case in point. The scheme was evolved on the basis of the recommendation of an expert group. The scheme envisaged the securitization of outstanding dues through fifteen-year tax-free bonds issued by respective state governments. It also envisaged 50 per cent waiver of the outstanding surcharge as an incentive for the states to take up the scheme of securitization. The scheme that was finally adopted was even more liberal. However, the nature of this restructuring could be construed as creating moral hazard for future payments to the Central PSUs.

Until the rate of interest on states' borrowings was aligned to market rates, lending to states did involve significant implicit transfers. These were analysed in detail in Rao (1997). The implicit transfers were estimated by taking long-term lending rate of the State Bank of India as the benchmark rate of interest and comparing with actual rate of interest paid by the state governments. The analysis concluded that implicit transfers arising from subsidized lending to states was significant and that these

---

[14] At present, the SLR stipulation requires the commercial banks to keep 25 per cent of their demand and time liabilities in eligible assets like Central and state government bonds. In fact, the financial sector reforms brought down the SLR from 38.5 per cent in 1991–2 to 25 per cent in 1996–7.

implicit transfers had a regressive impact and, therefore, they offset the progressivity of the explicit transfer system significantly. As shown in Table 9.8, the implicit transfers had a positive and significant income elasticity, and were responsible for reducing the overall progressivity of the explicit transfer system during the period 1981–94. Of course, this estimate of implicit transfers from this source is an underestimate as the loans written off to states were not considered in the analysis.

Another important invisible source of inter-regional resource flows arises when the nationalized banking and financial system gives subsidized lending to the different sectors of the economy in a non-neutral manner. Important sources of subsidized lending with inter-regional implications include priority-sector lending by the banking system and non-neutral distribution of refinancing facilities for lending by AIFIs. Subsidized lending by AIFIs such as IDBI, ICICI, IFCI, NABARD, and SFCs to different sectors in different states involves inter-regional transfers. Transfers

TABLE 9.8

Progressivity of Explicit and Implicit Transfers from
Subsidized Lending to States

Year	Income elasticity of explicit transfers	Income elasticity of implicit transfers from states' borrowing
1981–2	−0.3855*	0.2506**
1982–3	−0.4877*	0.3149**
1983–4	−0.3817*	0.3711**
1984–5	−0.3754**	0.3951**
1985–6	−0.4617**	0.3073**
1986–7	−0.5056*	0.5165
1987–8	−0.6910*	0.4845**
1988–9	−0.5692*	0.6481
1989–90	−0.8171*	0.5641**
1990–1	−0.7410*	0.7348**
1991–2	−0.8248*	1.1138
1992–3	−0.6640*	0.6188@
1993–4	−0.6669*	0.3837

Notes: Income elasticities are estimated by regressing per capita transfers across states on their per capita SDP; * Significant at one per cent level; ** Significant at 5 per cent level; @ Significant at 10 per cent level.

Soruce: Authors' calculations.

from this source are particularly significant when they are unable to recover the loans advanced by them (resulting in increase in their non-performing loans).

CONCLUDING REMARKS

While the economic objectives of the transfer system are clear, the transfer system actually represents a political compromise. Thus, political elements necessarily enter into the determination of intergovernmental transfers. In this sense too, the transfer system performs the nation-building role. Perhaps, it is difficult to find a perfect equalization system in any federation, even if such a system were to be desired by economists. The degree of equalization achieved in a federation will be determined by political compromises made. Nevertheless, it is important to keep in mind the economic objectives because that serves as the benchmark for reforming the transfer system.

Analysis shows that the transfer system in India has not been successful in fulfilling overall objectives of offsetting revenue and cost disabilities and ensuring minimum standards of services provided. The existence of multiple channels, lack of clarity in the objectives to be achieved by them, and their inability to design a transfer system geared to these objectives are the important reasons for this outcome.

Elements of political economy have impacted on the transfer system in a variety of ways. While the Constitution envisages only the Finance Commission as the all-important institution to determine the transfer system, it is the political elements that have resulted in the emergence of Planning Commission and individual ministries as important dispensers of transfers. This has made it easier for the political executive to bring in its discretion in the determination of the transfer system. Notably, the analysis has also brought out that a statutory body like the Finance Commission is not immune from political influences. In fact, political elements have played important roles in the selection of the chairmen and members of the Finance Commission, in formulating their terms of reference, and in their own functioning and recommendations. In fact, the functioning of the commissions does not always infuse confidence in the transfer system playing a nation-building role.

It must also be noted that the inter-regional resource allocation is achieved also by other instruments such as regional policies. More importantly, an economy with the legacy of central planning of financial policies and the various regulations and controls introduced by the Central government can also have significant implications on regional resource allocation. In this chapter, we have identified a few such sources of implicit transfers. Often, they can work at cross-purposes and can dilute the pursuit of objectives by the explicit transfer system.

10

✖

Natural Resources

INTRODUCTION

An important dimension of federalism is the sharing of the power to own and manage natural resources. Both from the viewpoint of principles and contemporary practices, it is difficult to discern an ideal arrangement in regard to the assignment of ownership and management of natural resources in a federation. Given that distribution of natural resources across regions can be uneven and further that they can be a source of significant economic activity, distributional considerations dictate against assigning management of natural resource to sub-national governments. Exploitation of important natural resources also involves significant interstate externalities and assignment of such resources to the states could lead to inefficient allocation of resources. It could also cause significant differences in the tax effort as a state with significant natural resources may decide to use origin-based natural resource revenues rather than destination-based taxes.[1] At the same time, transaction cost of utilizing natural resources is lower at sub-national levels. For this reason, the Constitution of India assigns the right to exploit major minerals to the Centre while, the exploitation of minor minerals is placed in the state list.

The issues arising from the assignment of natural resources are much broader than the assignments of mineral resources. In particular, the exploitation of water resources involves many unconventional issues. If the right to exploit such natural resources is assigned to sub-national governments, the existence of high degree of externalities necessitates proper assignment of property rights and the institution of a proper bargaining mechanism. Unfortunately, the externalities involved in the

---

[1] The province of Alberta, in Canada, for example, gets much of its revenues from oil resources and does not impose the retail sales tax on its citizens.

management of water resources are not of a conventional variety. Externality involved in the flowing waters in a river can be negative or positive and it can vary not only from one year to another but also from season to season. Further, upper riparian states always have a certain degree of control over the extent of externality that can accrue to the lower riparian states. The problems when there is abundance of water is different from those that arise out of scarcity. The issue gets complicated the greater the number of parties to the dispute. Similarly, externalities involved in the exploitation of forest resources are based on the sustainability of nature and future generation. Assignment of the task of managing natural resources to the Central government will not necessarily solve the problems and may sometimes create additional inefficiencies.

The chapter analyses federal issues in the utilization of natural resources. A particular focus is on the process of resolving interstate water disputes. Settlement mechanisms for water disputes are ambiguous and opaque in India. The problems are compounded by the entanglement of interstate water disputes with more general Centre–state conflicts and with everyday political issues. We argue that these impacts can be reduced by a more efficient design of mechanisms for negotiating interstate water disputes. We present some of the possibilities, including a national water commission independent of daily political pressures, a federated structure incorporating river basin authorities and water user associations, and fixed time periods for negotiation and adjudication.

We begin with a general overview that motivates the main concern of this chapter, the federal institutions governing the allocation of water. Next, we examine India's federal institutions governing water allocation and interstate water disputes in particular, as well as previous policy recommendations, especially those of the Sarkaria Commission. Three cases are discussed in some detail, to give a flavour of the issues that have arisen in recent persistent disputes. Analytical issues such as distinguishing between reallocation of water starting from well-defined initial rights— including mechanisms for compensatory transfers—from cases of contests over the allocation of rights themselves are also discussed. We also address the important aspect of investments that affect the productivity or the availability of water, and issues of cooperation in this dimension. From our analysis and case studies we provide an assessment of the issues and make recommendations. We examine federal issues related to minerals, before summarizing some of the federal aspects of environmental regulation pertaining to forests and to pollution.

SHARING THE RIVER WATER—AN OVERVIEW OF ISSUES

Because large areas of India are relatively arid, mechanisms for allocating scarce water are critically important to the welfare of the country's citizens. Water contributes to welfare in several ways: health (e.g. clean drinking water), agriculture (e.g. irrigation), and industry (e.g. hydroelectric power). Because India is a federal democracy, and because rivers cut across state boundaries, constructing efficient and equitable mechanisms for allocating river flows has long been an important legal and constitutional issue. Numerous interstate river-water disputes have erupted since independence. In the mid-1990s, a dispute involving the Yamuna River, and the states of Delhi, Haryana, and Uttar Pradesh, provoked thousands of women from Haryana to march to Delhi's busiest intersection, carrying earthen pitchers. In a dramatic protest they smashed the pitchers, demanding that their government stop supplying water to Delhi.

This particular dispute was resolved by conferences involving three state chief ministers, as well as the Central government, after prior intervention by the Supreme Court had failed. Not all disputes have happy endings, however: the larger dispute between Karnataka and Tamil Nadu over the waters of the Cauvery rages on. Interstate water disputes are a persistent occurrence in India.

The phenomenon of interstate water disputes in India is still relatively less understood. Part of the difficulty is the plethora of actors and the complexity of the institutional environment within which the various parties reach (or fail to reach) agreement. Actors include state governments (which in turn are influenced by professional politicians, political parties, and interest groups), the national parliament, Central ministries, the courts, and ad hoc water tribunals. These actors negotiate within a rich institutional setting. In general, river-water disputes have involved state and Central politicians, as well as the courts and special tribunals and commissions set up to arbitrate. Although fairly explicit constitutional provisions govern interstate river waters, it is unclear whether existing mechanisms for adjudicating interstate water disputes are efficient. Indeed, there is growing consensus that existing institutions are increasingly unable to generate acceptable outcomes that contribute to economic growth and national welfare.

The critical role of water for Indian development is obvious. Unfortunately, water is becoming scarcer thanks to population growth, urbanization, and rising incomes. As with any scarce resource, conflicts can be expected to arise over how the resource is used. Accordingly, designing mechanisms for the efficient allocation of water is an increasingly important task.

Disputes arising out of sharing and uses of river water are costly and burden the courts, distract politicians, foment popular discontent, stimulate interstate conflict, foster the inefficient use of water, and, as we show, encourage inefficient, non-cooperative investments in dams, irrigation, etc. Such investments—rational from the viewpoint of a state that has failed to reach an agreement with another state—divert scarce investment resources and thereby retard economic growth.

Why do these disputes persist even as they have proved costly? Why have the existing dispute resolution mechanisms often failed to reach efficient and equitable agreements? We argue that the answer lies in the flawed design of settlement mechanisms, which are ambiguous and opaque. A cooperative bargaining framework suggests that water *can* be shared efficiently, with compensating transfers as necessary, *if* initial water rights are well defined, and *if* institutions to facilitate and implement cooperative agreements are in place. Our analysis also emphasizes the role of complementary investments, and the need to expand the scope of bargaining to include these where feasible.

We also distinguish between situations where cooperation is possible and situations where the initial allocation of rights is at stake, and consequently the parties face a situation of pure conflict rather than one of potential gains from trade. In the pure conflict situation, which seems very relevant for Indian interstate disputes, a search for a negotiated solution may be futile, and quick movement to arbitration or adjudication may be more efficient. However, in the Indian case, not only is this process slow, but also effective binding arbitration does not exist. As a result, in several major disputes there has been no agreement, leading to the costs described above.

WATER AND INDIAN FEDERALISM: THE 'RULES OF THE GAME'

Indian institutions for resolution of disputes pertaining to water are ambiguous and opaque. State governments dominate the allocation of river waters. The Interstate Water Disputes Act of 1956 was legislated to deal with conflicts, and included provisions for the establishment of tribunals to adjudicate where direct negotiations have failed. However, states have sometimes refused to accept the decisions of tribunals, so arbitration is not binding. Significantly, the courts have also been ignored on occasion. The Centre has sometimes intervened directly, but in the most intractable cases, such as the sharing of the Ravi-Beas waters among

Haryana, Jammu and Kashmir, Rajasthan, and Punjab, Central intervention, too, has been unsuccessful. In short, an unambiguous institutional mechanism for settling interstate water disputes does not exist.

The relevant provisions of the Indian Constitution are included in Entry 17 in the State List, Entry 56 in the Union List, and Article 262. The first provision makes water a state subject, but qualifies it by Entry 56 in the Union List, which states: 'Regulation and development of interstate rivers and river valleys to the extent to which such regulation and development under the control of the Union is declared by parliament by law to be expedient in the public interest'. Article 262 explicitly grants parliament the right to legislate over the matters in Entry 56. As documented by Iyer (1994a, b), parliament has not made much use of Entry 56. Various river authorities have been proposed, but not legislated or established as bodies vested with powers of management. Instead, river boards with only advisory powers have been created.

The 'rules of the game' of Indian federal governance shape the opportunities and strategies of parties to water disputes. India has been characterized as having a 'quasi-federal' structure, because of the large degree of Central discretion and control permitted by the Constitution. Such a structure, whatever its other benefits, does little to ensure swift resolution of interstate water disputes.

Essentially, Indian federalism, while marked by a relatively powerful Centre, has consistently involved coalition building to create such a Centre. This has meant a high level of explicit or implicit 'horse-trading' among the Centre and states that are potentially key elements of a central coalition. One possible interpretation, therefore, is that the Centre wishes to preserve a system which allows it flexibility or discretion in bargaining over Center–state issues in general, with water being one of them. A related feature of Indian political economy is the problem of multiple vetoes (Bardhan, 1984; see also Singh, 1997), which would help explain why, with discretion preserved, it may not be used decisively. This, too, seems relevant to the case of water, where negotiations have dragged on, and where the Central government has sometimes prolonged them by failing to speedily appoint a tribunal, even when asked.

Disenchantment with the adjudication process of interstate river disputes led to several attempts at change. First, the National Water Development Agency (NWDA) was created in July 1982, to 'carry out the water balance and other studies ... for optimum utilization of water resources ...' (National Water Development Agency, 1992). This agency is a Government of India society in the ministry of water resources, and lacks any statutory backing. Furthermore, its scope is technical, and separate from the institutional realities of water allocation. Second, in 1983, the National Water Resources Council (NWRC) was created by a Central resolution. Its composition includes chief ministers of states, lieutenant governors of union territories, several Central ministers, and the Prime Minister as chairman. This group met first in October 1985, and adopted a National Water Policy in 1987. This policy emphasized an integrated and environmentally sound basis for developing national water resources.

Unfortunately, however, it provided no specific recommendations for institutions to achieve this. Though the NWRC was created out of disenchantment with the adjudicative process for interstate river disputes, it has neither provided any concrete proposals to improve that process, nor offered any alternative mechanism.[2] We analyse the reasons for this failure later.

Finally, how—and when—are tribunal decisions enforced? The Sarkaria Commission noted that Section 6 of the ISWD Act of 1956 provides that 'the Union Government shall publish the decision of the Tribunal in the Official Gazette and the decision shall be final and binding on the parties to the dispute and shall be given effect by them' (Government of India, 1988, chapter 17.4.18, p. 491).

The Commission's report goes on to suggest that the Centre cannot enforce the tribunal's decision if a state government refuses to implement the award. It notes that the amendment of the act in 1980, inserting section 6A, which provides for an agency to implement a tribunal award, is not sufficient because such an agency cannot function without the cooperation of the states concerned. The Sarkaria Commission's recommendation was, therefore, that 'a water tribunal's award should have the same force and sanction behind it as an order or decree of the Supreme Court. We recommend that the Act should be suitably amended for this purpose' (Government of India, 1988, chapter 17.4.19, p. 491).

This has not been done. Water tribunals have powers equivalent to that of a court for a narrow range of issues, including gathering of information, requiring witnesses to testify, and recovering the costs of the tribunal (Section 9 of the ISWD Act, reproduced in Ramana, 1992, p. 60), but they lack the most important power: the knowledge among litigants that the court can enforce its decisions.

Furthermore, the ISWD Act, Section 11, states that 'notwithstanding

---

[2] More recently, the National Water Policy of 2002 (Government of India, 2002) repeats and updates many of the themes of the 1987 document, but without specifics. Specifics are instead dealt in an amendment to the 1956 Act, recently signed into law.

anything contained in any other law, neither the Supreme Court nor any other court shall have or exercise jurisdiction in respect of any water dispute which may be referred to a Tribunal under this Act' (Ramana, 1992, p. 90). One could interpret this provision as implicitly vesting water tribunals with a status broadly equivalent to the Supreme Court: the decisions of the tribunals have the same force as those of the Supreme Court. Such an interpretation suggests that the Centre can theoretically dismiss a state government, should the latter refuse to accept the tribunal's decision. However, this penalty—the only one seemingly available—is so great that it is hard to imagine it being used solely for a water dispute (although it has been used extensively under other pretexts).

In summary, the resolution of water disputes is complicated by being tangled in the general difficulties of Centre–state federal issues. The wide scope for discretion, the extensive bargaining, and the multiplicity of potential vetoes work in tandem to undermine the clarity and transparency needed for speedy dispute resolution. In May 2002, the ISWD Act was amended to try and place time limits on tribunals: we discuss this development later.

PERSISTENT DISPUTES

We briefly discuss three disputes to illustrate the nature of the costly bargaining process: Krishna-Godavari, Cauvery, and Ravi-Beas. In the first case, relative success was achieved through negotiations and through the working of a tribunal, although the time taken was substantial. In the other two cases, the institutional process was relatively less successful. The Cauvery Tribunal's interim order was implemented after considerable political turmoil and delay, while the judgment of the Ravi-Beas Tribunal was not made official by the Central government—that is, it has yet to be enforced at all. All three cases illustrate delay and ambiguity in procedures, bearing out our earlier general discussion of India's institutions.

Krishna-Godavari

The Krishna-Godavari water dispute among Maharashtra, Karnataka, Andhra Pradesh (AP), Madhya Pradesh (MP), and Orissa could not be resolved through negotiations, which lasted from the mid-1950s till 1969. Here, Karnataka and Andhra Pradesh are the lower riparian states on the river Krishna, and Maharashtra is the upper riparian state. The dispute was mainly about the interstate utilization of untapped surplus water. Separate tribunals were constituted for the Krishna and the Godavari in 1969, but with the same membership.

The Krishna Tribunal reached its decision in 1973, and the award was published in 1976. The Tribunal relied on the principle of 'equitable apportionment' for the actual allocation of the water. It addressed three issues: (1) The extent to which the existing uses should be protected as opposed to future or contemplated uses; (2) Diversion of water to another watershed; (3) Rules governing the preferential uses of water.

The Tribunal's rulings were as follows. On the first issue, it concluded that projects that were in operation or under consideration as in September 1960 should be preferred to contemplated uses and should be protected. It also judged that except by special consent of the parties, a project committed after 1960 should not be entitled to any priority over contemplated uses. On the second issue, the Tribunal concluded that diversion of Krishna waters to another waterline was legal when the water was diverted to areas outside the river basin but within the political boundaries of the riparian states. It was silent regarding the diversion of water to areas of non-riparian states. On the third issue, the Tribunal specified that all existing uses based on diversion of water outside the basin would receive protection.

The Godavari Tribunal commenced hearings in January 1974, after making its award for the Krishna case. It gave its final award in 1979, but meanwhile the states continued negotiations among themselves, and reached agreements on all disputed issues. Hence, the Tribunal was merely required to endorse these agreements in its award. Unlike in the case of other tribunals, there was no quantification of flows, or quantitative division of these flows: the states divided up the area into sub-basins, and allocated flows from these sub-basins to individual states—this was similar in approach to the successful Indus agreement between India and Pakistan. Another difference was that the agreement was not subject to review, becoming, in effect, perpetually valid.

While the Krishna-Godavari dispute was solved relatively successfully, the weakness of institutional arrangements, including the failure to create river-basin authorities, has led to a resurfacing of problems in the case of the Krishna. The states of Andhra Pradesh, Karnataka, and Maharashtra are locked in an increasingly bitter dispute over the use of marginal (i.e. traditionally 'surplus') waters from the Krishna, and spillover effects of various water projects (dams and irrigation) as well as other economic activities (especially logging). Karnataka has petitioned the Supreme Court, which has asked for clarification from the Centre, and the states of Andhra Pradesh and Maharashtra. Newer concerns about ecology and pollution are only complicating matters, and increasing the number of potential actors in the resurfaced dispute.

The Cauvery Dispute

The core of the Cauvery dispute related to the re-sharing of waters that are already being fully utilized. Here, the two parties to the dispute were Karnataka and Tamil Nadu, though the original issues dated back to colonial times. Between 1968 and 1990, twenty-six meetings were held at the ministerial level but no consensus could be reached. Hence, the Cauvery Water Dispute tribunal was constituted on 2 June 1990 under the ISWD Act, 1956.

There was a basic difference between Tamil Nadu on the one hand and the Central government and Karnataka on the other in their approach towards sharing of Cauvery waters. The government of Tamil Nadu argued that since Karnataka was constructing dams on the river and was expanding *ayacuts* (irrigation works), Karnataka was unilaterally diminishing the supply of waters to Tamil Nadu, and adversely affecting the prescriptive rights of the already acquired and existing *ayacuts*. The government of Tamil Nadu also maintained that the Karnataka government had failed to implement the terms of 1892 and 1924 Agreements relating to the use, distribution, and control of the Cauvery waters. It asserted that the entitlements of the 1924 Agreement were permanent, and that clauses dealing only with utilization of surplus water for further extension of irrigation in Karnataka and Tamil Nadu, beyond what was contemplated in the 1924 Agreement, could be changed. In contrast, Karnataka questioned the applicability of the 1924 Agreement, emphasizing equity and regional balance in future sharing arrangements.

There were several reasons why the negotiations held between 1968 and 1990 failed to bring about a consensus. There was a divergence of interest between Karnataka and Tamil Nadu on the question of pursuing negotiations. Karnataka was interested in prolonging the negotiations and thwarting the reference to a tribunal, in order to gain time to complete its new projects. Also, the Cauvery issue became intensely politicized in the 1970s and 1980s. The respective governments in the two states were run by different political parties. Partisan politics in both states made an ultimate solution more difficult. Between 1968 and 1990, there were also frequent changes of government in both states, and at the Centre. Hence, consecutive occasions when the same set of ministers from the same state and the Centre met were rare. The ministerial meetings were held at regular intervals, but no attempt was made to generate technical options to the sharing of Cauvery waters. Expert engineers were not able to work together for a common solution.

While the Cauvery Tribunal passed an interim order in 1991, political tensions heightened, with both state governments pressuring the Centre and the Supreme Court to intervene. The court, in turn, directed the Central government to act. In the end, it was the process of political bargaining that led to the implementation of the interim order, and the formation of a Cauvery River Authority and Monitoring Committee in 1998 (Government of India, 2001). These bodies continue to meet, and the final outcome of the Tribunal remains to be seen. Meanwhile, the dispute continues to simmer. The Cauvery River Authority has been able to adjudicate short-run conflicts over water needs, between Karnataka, the upstream state, and Tamil Nadu, but relations between the chief ministers of the states remain acrimonious. The Central government is in a difficult position, since whatever decision it takes will be seen as politically motivated. Again, the absence of clear and timely mechanisms for dispute resolution makes the conflict prolonged and costly.

The Ravi-Beas Dispute

Punjab and Haryana, the main parties in this dispute at present, are both agricultural surplus states, providing large quantities of grain for the rest of India. Because of the scarcity and uncertainty of rainfall, irrigation is the mainstay of agriculture. An initial agreement on the sharing of the waters of the Ravi and Beas after partition was reached in 1955, through an interstate meeting convened by the Central government.

The present dispute between Punjab and Haryana on the matter started with the reorganization of Punjab in November 1966, when Punjab and Haryana were carved out from the erstwhile state of Punjab. The four perennial rivers, Ravi, Beas, Sutlej, and Yamuna flow through both these states, which are heavily dependent on irrigated agriculture. Irrigation became increasingly important in the late 1960s with the introduction and widespread adoption of high yielding varieties of wheat.

As a result of protests by Punjab against the 1976 agreement allocating water from Ravi-Beas, further discussions were conducted (now including Rajasthan as well), and a new agreement was accepted in 1981. This agreement, reached by a state government allied to the Central government, became a source of continued protest by the political opposition, and lobbies outside the formal political process. Punjab entered a period of great strife, and a complex chain of events led to the constitution of a tribunal to examine the Ravi-Beas issue in 1986. Both states sought clarifications of aspects of the award by this tribunal, but the Centre has not provided these. Hence, the original award has not been notified (listed in the government gazette to give it final force), and does not have the status of a final, binding decision. The proceedings of the Ravi-Beas Tribunal remain in limbo.

ANALYTICAL FOUNDATIONS FOR SUCCESSFUL WATER DISPUTE RESOLUTION

Economic analysis offers helpful guidance to understanding the problems of resolution mechanisms pertaining to interstate water dispute. It is widely recognized that water has a number of features that create potential market failure. These may include non-rivalry, non-excludability, externalities, merit good features, and significant transactions costs (Richards and Singh, 2001). The presence of these factors means that although increased reliance on market forces (e.g. one state selling water to another) can contribute significantly to resolving water issues, there is no escaping the need for parties to agree upon a set of rules, an enforcement mechanism, and a prior distribution of property rights.

Property rights have been claimed on the basis of historical use, as well as on the basis of the 'Harmon Doctrine', that 'what falls on our roof is ours to use, without regard to any potential harm to downstream parties'. Historical use can work against trading water rights, while the Harmon doctrine ignores externalities as well as past investments connected with water use. A third approach, that of the social contract a la Thomas Hobbes, holds more promise. A deal must be struck among the existing decision-making entities, such as Indian states, which (i) decides on an initial allocation of property rights and (ii) creates a mechanism to trade these rights, to regulate uses that generate externalities, etc. Consequently, institutions that support efficient bargaining and can enforce binding agreements are essential.

The obvious starting point for thinking about bargaining over water is the Coasian perspective (Coase, 1960). Coase's ideal bargaining solution provides a benchmark against which one can compare reality. The main lesson of Coase is that one should not presume that Central intervention is desirable or necessary in interstate water disputes. Indeed, when the essential problem faced by states or groups within a state is that the initial allocation of water is suboptimal due to changing circumstances, cooperative bargaining will lead to an optimal allocation.

A bargaining solution will depend on threat points or disagreement payoffs. With multiple layers of decision makers, bargaining may have to occur at different levels: states bargain with each other, and groups within a state also bargain. It is possible in some cases to reach the same outcome regardless of the sequencing of the bargaining (Richards and Singh, 1997).

However, there are (at least) three situations in which bilateral or multilateral bargaining among concerned state governments may not be efficient or equitable on its own:

1. When the Centre can affect starting positions or threat points in the bargaining game between states.

2. When there is incomplete information, even imperfect Central intervention can be better in expected terms than bilateral bargaining. There are potentially two kinds of information: technical and subjective. In principle, technical information may be shared and verified, but in practice this can be very time-consuming, and contribute to lengthy proceedings, as is typical of Indian water tribunals. Further complicating matters is the fact that it is often not possible to objectively verify whether costs and benefits are truly evaluated subjectively. When a rival's objectives are unclear, bargaining becomes far more difficult.

3. When there are multiple issues to be bargained over, there may be spillovers to non-riparian states: the Punjab–Haryana dispute is an example of such a situation.

An additional complication is that the productivity of a given quantity of water depends on the level of complementary investments (Richards and Singh, 1996, 1997). These may be dams, irrigation projects, or even more general investments in agriculture. The first thing to note is that as long as the benefit from a given amount of water is dependent on the amount of investment, the optimal allocation of water will depend on the investments in both states. Hence, even though there are no direct externalities as a result of the investment, the conditional optimum of water allocation involves a linkage of both states. What state A does with its investment will affect the optimal amount of water that state B should receive. This was an important ingredient of the Cauvery dispute.

Even if both investments in dams and the allocation of water are jointly the subject of interstate negotiations, it is unlikely that states are willing or able to negotiate broadly over general investments that affect the utility or productivity of water in the state economy. If investments are chosen non-cooperatively, externalities and strategic considerations both create non-optimalities. The strategic motive for investment to affect subsequent bargaining implies that there is a strong case for avoiding delays in negotiations and agreements, as well as for making agreements permanent, or not subject to review, provided that the information available is relatively complete. This will tend to force efficient investments.

Unforeseen changes in costs and benefits can then be dealt with by trading water, rather than reallocating quantities de novo. This analysis assumes that property rights over water are well specified and clearly understood. But this may not actually be the case. In fact, much of the conflict or disagreement over interstate river waters in India is an attempt to influence or determine the initial allocation of property rights over water, by methods such as political lobbying. The initial quantities of water are not given, but are precisely the main subject of negotiations. In some cases, there is a de facto allocation of rights based on historical usage, but there is a surplus of currently unutilized water that can be used (often only if appropriate investments are made) once it is unambiguously allocated.

It is critical to recognize that in such cases, the situation is one of pure conflict: more for one party means less for another when there is a given total amount of the resource. This situation must be clearly distinguished from the one where initial property rights are well defined, and cooperation is potentially feasible. But in a pure conflict situation, there is no presumption that negotiation among the parties sharing water from a particular river basin will lead to an agreement, and there is a clear role for a higher-level authority. Thus, the suggestion by some analysts of Indian cases that tribunals or courts create an adversarial situation seems to miss the point: tribunals are necessary when the situation is inherently adversarial.

Consider the case of a tribunal allocating initial rights to water. From one perspective, the case of a tribunal is not that different from a political lobbying model. States expend effort to influence the tribunal, which makes its award accordingly. The difference is in the nature of the states' efforts, the public nature of the process, and the objective function of the tribunal. It is the differing nature of accountability and transparency that distinguishes the use of a tribunal.

Clearly, each state will prefer the process—political negotiations or a tribunal—that will favour it. There is no guarantee that the states will have unanimous preferences in this regard. Thus, while each mechanism is designed to overcome the problem of resolving conflict in the absence of property rights, the presence of alternative mechanisms raises the problem of conflict over which mechanism to use. The problem is simply pushed back one step further, and delays occur.

Of course, in India it is specified that if negotiations fail, a tribunal must be appointed. However, this is done at the discretion of the Centre and, in such situations, the Centre would actually prefer a political solution, where it barters an award for political support. Reducing discretion, such as specifying short time limits for negotiation, with a tribunal to take over thereafter, is essential in such cases. Such a recommendation is an old one: our analysis only helps to make a more formal and transparent case for it. The above framework can be used to analyse some additional problems with the political bargaining case, even in the absence of a tribunal as an alternative. These problems arise due to the uncertainty of political regimes (Richards and Singh, 1996). While water agreements are typically very long term, or should be, to permit efficient investments, governments change every few years. The relative value of political support from the two states becomes an important parameter, since one of the states may prefer to postpone the agreement.

POLICY RECOMMENDATIONS

Our analysis implies certain policy recommendations. We offer here specific recommendations for selecting procedures for settlement of disputes, reducing delays, improving enforcement, and reducing the high influence costs that the current federal system fosters. Some of the possibilities have already been mentioned in the introduction.

Constitutionally and legislatively, settlement procedures for interstate river disputes in India involve either of two processes: negotiations or compulsory legal adjudication. There is also room for voluntary processes such as mediation, conciliation, and voluntary arbitration, often by the prime minister or other members of the Central government. Such processes do not foreclose arbitration or adjudication on specific areas of conflicts that remain unresolved after mediation and conciliation.

We emphasized the difference between situations where property rights are well defined (possibly de facto rather than by formal legal mechanisms), and situations where the dispute is over the property rights themselves. In the former case, there is room for a mutually beneficial exchange, and one can think of several different ways of implementing or facilitating a cooperative outcome through bargaining, which also incorporate some elements of fairness, a major component of 'objective settlements'. On the other hand, legal adjudication under the ISWD Act, is a non-voluntary imposed procedure, but it, or some similar externally imposed procedure, may be necessary in situations where the dispute is conflictual in nature, and not over sharing the potential gains of a mutually beneficial exchange. The real issue in such cases is setting up adjudicatory processes or institutions that all parties can agree ex ante to be bound by ex post; in these cases, focusing on voluntary negotiations may be somewhat misguided.

A key insight of our analysis and discussion is that the existing processes and institutions for resolving interstate river disputes are not sufficiently well defined or definite. There are too many options, and there is too much discretion at too many stages of the process. Since water is being more and more fully utilized, the possibility of disputes of conflictual nature arising increases. It is therefore crucial that the dispute resolution mechanism be better defined, in terms of the order of the steps to be taken. Of course, parties to a negotiation can continue to bargain in such cases, and even reach an agreement, as has happened in the case of the Godavari dispute. In fact, the existence of an expected outcome from adjudication may provide a somewhat definite disagreement point, and help to convert a conflictual situation to one of bargaining over (expected) mutual gains. Given this option, a possible recommendation would be the automatic and immediate referral of any dispute to a tribunal if requested by the Centre or any party to the dispute, with the tribunal bound to ratify any agreement reached by negotiation before it had delivered its decision. The 2002 amendment (Interstate Water Disputes [Amendment] Bill, 2002), to the ISWD Act of 1956 goes part way to addressing these concerns.

Extreme delays have been a very costly feature of the process of resolving interstate water disputes in India. There have been three components or dimensions of delay.

Delays in constituting tribunals Under Section 4 of the ISWD Act, the Union government was required to set up a tribunal only when it was satisfied that the dispute could not be settled by negotiations. The Centre could thus indefinitely withhold the decision to set up a tribunal on the ground that it was not yet satisfied that negotiations have failed. The major disputes illustrate this problem. The Godavari and Krishna disputes started around 1956. The states began formal requests for reference in 1962. Ultimately, the disputes were referred to tribunals in 1969. In the Cauvery dispute, two of the basin states, Tamil Nadu and Kerala, asked for reference to a tribunal in the 1970s. The tribunal was constituted only in 1990, after the Supreme Court mediated. The 2002 amendment to the ISWD Act places a limit of one year on the Central government for constituting a tribunal, shortening such delays.

Delays in reaching a decision It took four years in the case of the Krishna Tribunal and ten years in the case of the Godavari Tribunal, while other tribunals have not reached final decisions after longer periods. Such delays may be attributed to the time taken for assembling facts and hearing arguments and abortive attempts to bring about solutions at a political level, which delayed the functioning of constituted tribunals. The new amendment to the ISWD Act does place time limits, but these are still too lengthy (up to six years, with loopholes for extension).

Delays and uncertainties in enforcement This results from delays in notifying the orders of tribunals in the Government of India's official gazette. The process took three years in the case of the Krishna Award and one year in the case of the Godavari Award. These delays naturally tend to complicate the process of dispute settlement. Since this is a general problem of discretion, it cannot be tackled only within the context of water disputes.

Our recommendations with respect to delays (originally made in Richards and Singh, 1996) echo earlier suggestions, such as those of the Administrative Reforms Commission in 1969, and the Sarkaria Commission in 1988. Unlike the Sarkaria Commission, we do not recommend an escape clause, whereby a tribunal can ask for an extension. In this respect we think that the 2002 legislation may still be somewhat weaker than necessary. It is worth reiterating that delays can be extremely costly. Beneficial projects can be delayed (the World Bank, for example, has declined to fund projects related to disputed river basins), and inefficient investments may be undertaken, as we have already discussed. The issue of investment related to water use will become more and more important as the Indian economy continues to grow, and delays will become increasingly damaging.

Finally, we address a set of issues which have not been dealt with in recent legislation. Tribunal decisions are difficult to enforce. State governments have sometimes rejected tribunal awards, as in the case of Ravi-Beas Tribunal and the Punjab government. In this case, the Central government avoided notifying the tribunal's award, to prevent further deterioration of the conflictual political situation in Punjab. In the case of the Cauvery dispute, the Karnataka government sought to nullify the tribunal's interim order through an ordinance. Though the Supreme Court pronounced that the ordinance was unconstitutional, the Karnataka government showed no inclination to implement the tribunal's interim order, until a compromise was reached through political negotiations behind closed doors.

The Sarkaria Commission was of the view that in order to make tribunal awards binding and effectively enforceable, the ISWD Act should be amended to give these awards the same sanction as an order or decree of the Supreme Court. Tribunals seem to have this force in theory, but existing penalties for non-compliance are too low to constrain behaviour. The solution requires separating water disputes from more general problems of Indian federalism and Centre–state relations. This suggests a need to create alternative institutions.

The lack of well-defined procedures, the endemic delays and the weak enforcement of decisions are all at least partially linked to a deficiency in the design of the relevant institutions. A key feature of this deficiency is the subsuming of interstate water disputes into the general political process. In India, federalism, and perhaps the political economy in general, has been characterized by an over-reliance on discretionary allocation; high influence costs have followed. The pattern of interstate water disputes is a prime example of this problem. We have argued that the process of resolving interstate water disputes, and of allocating water more generally, has been made inefficient by getting it entangled in more general political conflicts, conducted within the current structure of Indian federalism.

The solution we propose is the creation of specialized permanent institutions to regulate the allocation of water across states, including the resolution of water disputes. These institutions would themselves respect the federal structure of the country, but will have a greater degree of independence and transparency than the current situation. An analogy may be drawn with public finances: the Finance Commission has done a relatively good job of handling Central–state financial transfers, including making allocations across states according to public and rational criteria. This mechanism is in the process of being extended to the level of state–local transfers (Singh, 1997). Other examples of such sideways delegation are the creation of an independent body to regulate financial markets, and the operation of a relatively independent central bank. In such cases, the government gives up some of its direct powers as a way of pre-committing itself, and insulating certain types of decisions from political pressures. We propose that water rights can also be allocated in a similar manner.

The kind of institutions we propose would incorporate the specific recommendations to clarify and streamline procedures, reduce delays, and improve enforcement that have been made above and by numerous others. However, they would be quite different from the NWRC, which is very much a political creature. A possible guide for specifics of organization is the Murray River Commission (MRC) in Australia, where the states and the Central government have equal representation, and each state typically has drawn its representative from a major rural water management authority, while the Central representative is a senior civil servant.[3] Of course, the MRC is hardly a perfect model. However, a

---

[3] See the articles by David Constable and John Paterson in Eaton (1992).

permanent institution, with rotating membership weighted towards technically knowledgeable administrators, seems a feasible improvement over the current situation.

It is, of course, important to keep in mind that the MRC is a single river basin management authority. We are proposing at the national level an institution that will provide an umbrella for actual river boards or river basin authorities. The legislative framework for such bodies exists, but it has not been effectively used. Even when such entities have been proposed or created, they have not functioned well. State governments fear that they would cede too much decision-making power over their water resources to the Centre. The solution we propose would uniformly remove a set of decisions with respect to water sharing and use from the general political orbit, without tilting power towards the Centre. It should, therefore, be easier for states to accept.

We envisage a hierarchy of water management institutions, with river basin authorities being the next step down from the national commission. One can then think of membership at the national level being drawn from experienced members of individual river board authorities. We can think of institutions at the state and national level as linking up and continuing this kind of hierarchical, federated structure, often found in the context of local water user associations, and federations of such associations. Several different models of such federations exist.[4]

Ultimately, water allocation will be efficient only if decision making is responsive to the end users, and our recommendations seek to ensure that. The role of the institutions at the national and river basin levels is to provide mechanisms for dealing with conflicts associated with externalities, and lack of well-defined property rights, not to allocate water at the micro level. Although the potential to influence activities and associated costs will exist in any kind of hierarchy, we believe that the creation of specialized institutions, with clearly defined limits of authority, can minimize such costs.

We envisage a national-level water institution as incorporating the tasks of dispute resolution, perspective planning, and information gathering and maintenance. These tasks are currently scattered among tribunals, the NWRC, and the NWDA. The last of these organizations seems to be particularly isolated and relatively unsupported. The advantages of integrating information collection and storage with long-range planning and

---

[4] See, in particular, Meinzen–Dick et al. (1994), pp. 25–7. It is interesting to note that a recent study for the United States by Foster and Rogers (1988) makes somewhat similar institutional recommendations to the ones proposed here, including a national and regional councils for water resources policy.

dispute resolution seem manifest. One stumbling block will, of course, be the reluctance of ministries, including politicians and bureaucrats, to give up power over decision making.[5] It is here, perhaps, that ultimately goodwill, emphasized by several analysts of Indian river water disputes, will have to come into play. The possibility of significant, potentially positive institutional change in India is illustrated by recent legislation strengthening local governments. The allocation of water is another aspect of India's federal institutions that can be improved.

MINERALS

Another area of natural resources where federal institutional structures have been important is that of minerals, in particular coal. Coal was historically the major fossil fuel for power generation in India, and its mining has long been the subject of Centre–state disputes. In Chapter 3, we briefly discussed a prominent example of such a dispute. To recapitulate what we presented there, the dispute involved Article 294, which vested control of British Crown property in the pre-independence province of Bengal in the post-independence state of West Bengal. In 1957, the Centre enacted legislation claimed to be derived from an entry in the Union list, empowering Parliament to provide by law for 'the regulation of mines and mineral development to the extent to which such regulation and development under the control of the Union is held to be expedient in the public interest'. The 1957 Act gave the Centre the power to prospect for coal in lands vested in the state of West Bengal. The state government took its case to the Supreme Court, which came down in favour of the Centre's position in the case.

The 1957 legislation was the Mines and Minerals (Development and Regulation) Act. While it was preceded by the 1952 Mines Act, and some rules on mining leases and on worker safety, legislated in 1955 and 1956, the 1957 Act forms the basis for the governance of the mining sector in India. The Act has been amended several times, and supplemented by

---

[5] Currently, the ministry of water resources is responsible for 'overall planning, policy formulation, coordination and guidance in respect of the water resources sector as a whole', according to the National Water Policy of 1987 (quoted in Frederiksen, et al., 1993, p. 39). However, this ministry is essentially the old ministry of irrigation, and it tends to focus on irrigation and flood control only. Other important functions are not directly under its control. An important organization, the Central Water Commission, has a chairman with a rank equivalent to the senior bureaucrat in the ministry, and acts directly as a technical adviser to the planning commission. Other organizations include the Central Groundwater Board, and the National Institute of Hydrology. Overall, there are competing voices and ambiguous lines of authority (Frederiksen, et al., 1993; Chitale, 1992; Rogers, 1992).

additional legislation governing prospecting licences, leasing, and (more recently) environmental concerns. Its key provision with respect to Centre–state relations, titled 'Declaration as to the expediency of Union control', states: 'It is hereby declared that it is expedient in the public interest that the Union should take under its control the regulation of mines and the development of minerals to the extent herein after provided.'

Much of the 1957 Act spells out the various procedures and regulations governing prospecting and mining, both with respect to the states and the Centre. While the states retain significant rights, the Centre is given control over royalty rates, 'dead rents' for leased land that is not being mined, and, by virtue of the key preliminary statement above as well as various specific articles, the ultimate determination of mineral rights. For example, Article 17 gives the Centre broad 'special powers' for reconnaissance, prospecting, and mining. Furthermore, Article 18 gives the Centre broad powers in the form of 'all such steps as may be necessary for the conservation and systematic development of minerals in India ... and for such purposes the Central Government may, by notification in the Official Gazette, make such rules as it thinks fit'.

Note that this language implies that no further legislation is necessary. The language of the Act does enjoin consultation with the relevant state government, but this seems to be in the nature of a perfunctory acknowledgment of concurrent constitutional jurisdiction. On the other hand, for some other categories of state government actions, these are permitted only after the approval of the Centre.

The subordination of the state government with respect to mineral development is also clear from Article 26(3), on the delegation of powers: 'Any rules made by the Central Government under this Act may confer powers and impose duties or authorize the conferring powers and imposition of duties upon any State Government or any officer or authority subordinate thereto.'

As we noted in Chapter 3, the Constitution itself, the Supreme Court's interpretation of it, and the workings of institutions outside the legislative framework, such as intra-party politics, all contributed to a centralizing bias. The Centre's dominance of mineral development has been no different than its dominance of economic decision making in other spheres. Whereas water has had a more ambiguous legislative status, and a closer connection to the state subject of agriculture, minerals as a different kind of natural resource have been firmly under Central control since soon after India's independence. Just as broader economic changes began to take place in the 1990s, mineral policy was also re-examined.

The critical document in setting the stage in the post-reform period was the National Mineral Policy of 1993. The policy reiterates that management of mineral resources is the responsibility of the Centre and the states, in terms of Entry 54 of the Union List and Entry 23 of the State List of the Seventh Schedule. The policy statement still notes the 1957 Act, discussed above, the 1960 Mineral Concession Rules, and the 1988 Mineral Conservation and Development Rules as the key pieces of legislation. Beyond this, however, there appears to be very little, if anything, that is new in the document. While there are plans outlined for improving information about mineral resources and technologies for extraction and use, there appears to be nothing significantly different with respect to policy, with one major exception.

The exception concerns 'Financial Support for Mining' (Section 7.11), which makes the following statement:

Induction of foreign technology and foreign participation in exploration and mining for high value and scarce minerals shall be pursued. Foreign equity investment in joint ventures in mining promoted by Indian Companies would be encouraged. While foreign investment in equity would normally be limited to 50%, this limitation would not apply to captive mines of any mineral processing industry. Enhanced equity holding can also be considered on a case to case basis.

Apart from this, there was nothing in the 1993 policy that appears to change the balance between Centre and states with respect to mineral development.

However, despite no explicit change in relative Centre–state control of mining in the 1993 policy, the 1957 Act was amended in 1999 to delegate more powers to the state governments, as well as to introduce procedural simplifications.[6] Salient features of this delegation included:

- Bestowing full powers of grant of mineral concessions for limestone to the states;
- Allowing the states to have power of renewal of mineral leases and prospecting licences for an important range of minerals;
- Liberalizing area restrictions and making them applicable state-wise;
- Fully authorizing the states to enforce legal provisions and curb illegal mining; and
- Giving the state governments additional powers for granting some kinds of mineral licences and mining plans.

This delegation was not an unmitigated positive from the perspective

[6] The details, summarized in the following discussion, are spelled out in Annexure 1 to the 1999–2000 Annual Report of the Ministry of Mines.

of the mining companies. For example, state government involvement in granting licences was viewed as creating undesirable policy heterogeneity across states, and increasing political pressures for state-level public sector mining companies to be included as partners.

The period 1998–2000 also saw a further liberalization of rules with respect to foreign investment, and partial divestment of the Centre's stake in some public sector mining companies. For example, 51 per cent of Bharat Aluminum Corporation (BALCO) was sold to Sterlite Industries, and the decision was made to sell 26 per cent of Hindustan Zinc Limited (HZL). There were serious questions as to whether the privatization process for the BALCO sale was above board, and whether the Central government received a fair price for the stake it sold. However, the divestment went ahead. The HZL divestment, in contrast, is proposed to be done to small investors and company employees.

Petroleum

Petroleum and natural gas fall into a separate and important category within the broad class of minerals, with their own ministry governing all aspects of the industry. While all other minerals are in the State List of the Constitution, petroleum is separated out in Item 53 of the Union List.

Thus, petroleum and natural gas do not enter into the 1957 Mines and Minerals Act, and are governed by different legislation than other minerals. In particular, the Oil Fields (Regulation and Development) Act, 1948, and the Petroleum and Natural Gas Rules, 1959, deal with the regulation of petroleum operations and the grant of licences and leases for exploration and development of petroleum in India. The 1959 rules provide for the grant of exploration licences and mining leases in respect of land vested in a state government by that state government with the previous approval of the Central government.

Given the existing constitutional constraints, and the strategic role of oil and natural gas, it is unlikely that there will be any significant decentralization of authority to the states, or other changes in the federal arrangements with respect to petroleum and gas. However, the planned privatization in this sector and the entry of private firms, along with the scheduled decontrol of administered prices, will lead to some de facto decentralization by shifting decision making to the market.

ENVIRONMENTAL FEDERALISM

As in other countries, India began to deal with environmental issues over the past few decades, through enactments of various laws, and the creation of regulatory bodies for different aspects of environmental protection. Here, we briefly discuss the federal aspects of India's institutions for forest management, and the control of water and air pollution.

Forests

The Indian Forest Act of 1927 remains in force, and provides the core of regulations and institutions governing forest management and preservation. In essence, control of forests has resided with state governments. This is part of the constitutional assignment of powers. The state governments have appointed forest officers, whose formal position has been that of state bureaucrats, as on-the-ground implementers of forest management. As in the case of irrigation officers (Wade, 1988), these forest officers have often functioned relatively autonomously, and their ability to control the use of the natural resource without adequate monitoring has allowed them to engage in rent seeking. Thus, collusion between state forest officers and logging companies is acknowledged to be widespread, to the detriment of forest preservation.

The Forest Act allows the state to delegate the management of some forests, designated in such cases as village forests, to village community organizations. In practice, the weakness of local government institutions has meant that such assignments were very limited, or useless in effect. While this situation may change in the long run, with the strengthening of local governments, it will require state government decision makers (politicians and bureaucrats) giving up a significant source of rents. As documented by Wade (1988) in the case of irrigation, different levels of the bureaucracy and political structures also collude and share in the rents acquired from those who are given access to the resource (water or trees, as the case may be).

In 1980, the Central government passed the Forest (Conservation) Act, which gave the Centre the power to control state government reclassification of forests for non-forest uses. Thus, the Centre's response to deforestation was to increase monitoring and control, and hence centralization. To the extent that deforestation problems were associated with legal but non-optimal decisions by state governments, this response would seem appropriate, if the Central decision makers were more likely to choose socially optimal decisions than state-level decision makers. As we have discussed in other contexts, this kind of thinking is pervasive in India, where higher levels of government view themselves as benevolent guardians. However, the reality of the situation may be quite different. A pure economic rationale for centralized decision making would emerge from the spillovers that are inherent in decisions with respect to forest cover.

Thus, a state may be willing to incur the costs of some deforestation for a project that provides local benefits, but it might neglect the impacts of such deforestation on areas in neighbouring states. However, it was not clear whether this was the intent or practice of the 1980 Act.

In fact, if one accepts that the true problem lay in monitoring state-level bureaucrats, and quasi-legal or illegal logging activity, increasing Central control would do nothing to tackle the root cause. Instead, more effective local monitoring, through community and local government involvement, would seem to be the appropriate policy response. We discuss the general issues involved with such decentralization in Chapter 13. Those arguments are applicable to the management of local resources including forests.

Pollution

Concerns about pollution began in the 1960s, and the Water (Prevention and Control of Pollution) Act of 1974 was the outcome of over a decade of discussion and study. The Act created pollution control boards at the Central and state government levels. In terms of federal issues, the Central Pollution Control Board has the responsibility of coordinating the activities of the state boards, and resolving disputes among them. In other respects, the Central and state levels have similar responsibilities in terms of information provision, monitoring, investigation, and setting of standards, with the state boards having more direct monitoring responsibilities at the level of industrial plants or factories.

While the central board has an advisory role for the state bodies, it cannot force the adoption of uniform standards. However, it can influence the state boards through the funding it provides. It has been argued that the state boards are at the mercy of their funders (the central board and their respective state governments), and therefore subject to local political whims (Shaman, 1996), but this seems to be no different than any other government agency, where the dividing line between true 'accountability' and mere responsiveness to interest groups is not always clear.

In 1977, a follow-up act was passed, which gave the central and state boards (excepting that of Jammu and Kashmir) with the authority to levy and collect a tax, or cess, on industries using water, to fund pollution control efforts. Since this taxing power was not mentioned in the constitutional assignments, a court opinion was sought at the time of parliamentary debate. The court ruled that the Constitution gave Parliament residual powers in such cases, so the law was implemented.

Air pollution was tackled in the Air (Prevention and Control of Pollution) Act of 1981, which followed a similar model to the Water Act.

It created central and state boards, with almost identical division of responsibilities as in the case of water. One difference, relevant in the case of air, was that the central board has the power to set national ambient air standards. Furthermore, the state boards can petition local magistrates to restrain polluters from exceeding specified standards. In many cases, while the courts have been crucial in trying to enforce standards, the motivation has tended to come from public interest legislation, rather than the vigilance of government agencies.

The Bhopal tragedy of December 1984, which killed and seriously sickened large numbers of people, led to the passage of the Environment (Protection) Act of 1986. As the name suggests, this was broader, umbrella legislation, and it gave the Central government broad authority with respect to a range of environmental issues. We cannot go into the details of the act and its implementation, but simply note that India now has a relatively complete set of laws and institutions with respect to environmental protection.

Despite having the requisite laws on the books, India still faces severe environmental problems. The administrative bodies created for implementation, whether at the Central or state levels, have been only minimally effective. This situation reflects lack of resources, lack of information, and lack of incentives. We would argue that there are two main structural problems. First, since many problems, whether of pollution, forest conservation, or other environmental protection, are local in nature, the lack of institutions at the local level is a major obstacle to implementation. A state-level institution is unlikely to be able to deal effectively with every local problem that arises. Even if problems can be identified at the state level (e.g. widespread groundwater contamination), monitoring and correction will require some decentralized action. Effective incentive mechanisms for decentralized action are lacking in general, and environmental issues are one example. The second structural problem is the overall weakness of the judiciary, due to its inefficient internal processes, lack of resources, and over-centralization. These problems apply strongly to enforcement of environmental regulations.

Our conclusion, with respect to the federal aspects of environmental issues in India, is therefore two-fold. First, decentralization of monitoring and implementation down to the level of local governments may help, if these bodies are given adequate resources. Second, the strengthening of complementary institutions of federal governance (judicial and administrative) is essential to make existing legislation effective. Nothing in this conclusion negates the need for centralized action where there are spillovers, or state or national-level benefits. Our point is that there is less needed to be done in terms of centralized action.

CONCLUSIONS

The main focus of this chapter is India's federal institutions for managing water resources, as these raise interesting issues of federal assignment and dispute resolution between the Centre and states. We described general approaches as well as India's particular institutions for managing water resources and its recent experience with interstate river water allocation. We also discussed three cases in some detail, to give an idea of the issues that have arisen in major interstate water disputes. We discussed analytical issues such as distinguishing between reallocation of water starting from well-defined initial rights—including mechanisms for compensatory transfers—from cases of contests over the allocation of rights themselves, and also the important aspect of potential cooperation over investments that affect the productivity or the availability of water. We examined how some of the issues raised previously in the context of the workings of Indian federalism more generally intersect with thinking about institutions for interstate water disputes. Finally, on the topic of water, we provided an assessment and recommendations drawn from our analysis and case studies. The recommendations included institutions for more rule-bound, transparent procedures to handle dispute resolution. We examined federal issues related to minerals, and noted some of the decentralization that has occurred recently within the existing constitutional framework. Finally, we provided a summary of a set of issues and institutional responses in the area of environmental protection.

PART III

POLITICAL ECONOMY AND INTERGOVERNMENTAL REFORMS

11

⬨

The Political Economy of Centre–state Transfers

INTRODUCTION

One of the main issues debated in the context of Indian federalism is the factors that go into the determination of Centre–state transfers. The salience of this issue is not surprising, given the vertical fiscal imbalance that characterizes the initial structure, evolution, and working of the federal system in India. One aspect of the debates on transfers has been purely normative, namely, what is the optimal design of a transfer system to achieve the economic and political objectives of the federation. We have discussed the Indian system in this light, pointing out some of the problems, and indicating directions for reform. However, there is another aspect of the transfer system that has engendered considerable heat though not light. Many policy makers at the state level, and some academics, have raised concerns about biases in the system of transfers, these being driven by political concerns. However, the political economy aspects of the system have only recently begun to be the subject of rigorous empirical analysis. This chapter reviews our work and that of others on this perspective on India's federal transfer system.

Specifically, we examine various attempts to test the hypothesis that the political and economic influence or importance of the states affect the transfers they receive from the Centre, in ways that are not necessarily captured in transfer formulae. A simple measure of economic importance is the overall economic size of the state, as measured by state domestic product (SDP). Another possible measure of potential for influence is demographic size (population), since the size of a state (viewed in a simplifying assumption as an irreducible unit) will matter for political control at the Centre. More explicit measures of political influence include alignment between ruling political parties at the Centre and state level, political representation of individual states in the ruling party at the Centre (measured by parliamentary strength and/or representation in the Cabinet), whether a state is pivotal in a coalition at the Centre, and so on.

We begin with Riker's view of federalism as 'a constitutional bargain among politicians', which we summarized in Chapter 2. We also summarize some of the literature that complements and extends the Riker perspective. Next, we examine in more detail the political economy factors that affect the institutions governing Centre–state transfers. Subsequently, we provide a summary of some of the recent empirical studies, which, though differing in formulation and implementation, indicate the importance of political economy factors in determining the actual flow of Centre–state transfers in India. In particular, there is evidence to support the hypothesis that states with greater political and economic 'power' receive higher per capita transfers. This is broadly consistent with Riker's view of federalism, even though the Indian system is not the result of an explicit joining of its constituent parts.

POLITICAL ECONOMY MODELS OF FEDERALISM

William Riker, as we discussed in Chapter 2, advances an unequivocally instrumental view of federalism. He focuses on the military and security aspects of the 'constitutional bargain' and on the formation of federations through such bargains. One does not have to accept Riker's dismissal of non-instrumental motives, to acknowledge the importance of instrumental motives. In fact, an instrumental view of federalism realistically should also include broader economic concerns, and continuing bargains that shape the evolution of the federation within the constitutional structure (as well as sometimes leading to amendments in that structure). While India's federal system is not the result of an explicit voluntary combination of its constituent parts, and while it is more centralized than many other federal systems, our broad hypothesis is that its functioning does reflect implicit and explicit bargaining between the Centre and the states which make up the Indian Union. Centre–state fiscal transfers are a particular, quantifiable expression of the complex relationship between the national and sub-national governments in India. As we have discussed in earlier chapters, these transfers are governed by a complicated mix of constitutional assignments, institutional precedents, discretion, and negotiation. The result is therefore often difficult to understand or interpret. Analysts and policy makers in India often focus on minutiae of formulas that govern various components of Centre–state transfers, or bargain behind closed doors over discretionary transfers. While detailed analysis of transfer formulas has normative significance, our approach in this chapter, and our goal, are radically different. We take a positive approach, and we attempt to abstract from institutional details in our empirical exercise.

Modelling in full the idea of federalism as a constitutional bargain is daunting, but one can indicate some of its implications quite simply. Consider a simple Nash bargaining framework, where the constituents of the federation are the bargainers, and joining in the federation represents the cooperative outcome. The threat points are, naturally, the welfare levels achieved in the absence of federation. Suppose for simplicity of exposition that there are only two constituent units, and that utility is transferable, so that total welfare from cooperation is independent of the distribution of the gains from doing so. Let u_i be the utility (welfare) that constituent i gets from joining the federation, and d_i the disagreement payoff, or threat point. Let C be the total welfare of the federation. We may also allow bargaining power to be different across units, and it is denoted by β_i. In this case, it is easy to show that the Generalized Nash Bargaining Solution is given by:

$$u_1 = \beta_1(C - d_2) + \beta_2 d_1 , \tag{11.1}$$

$$u_2 = \beta_1 d_2 + \beta_2(C - d_1) . \tag{11.2}$$

If we normalize so that $\beta_1 + \beta_2 = 1$, the gains from federation for the two units are given by:

$$u_1 - d_1 = \beta_1(C - d_1 - d_2) , \tag{11.3}$$

$$u_2 - d_2 = \beta_2(C - d_1 - d_2) . \tag{11.4}$$

We may view the rules of the federation as the practical means by which the final outcome in (3) and (4) is implemented. Intergovernmental transfers are only one aspect of this allocation of rules. In particular, tax and expenditure assignments, rules governing financial intermediation, location decisions with respect to centrally controlled economic activity, and explicit and implicit subsidies all affect the final distribution of the benefits of the federal bargain. Unfortunately, there is no way that we can imagine implementing a comprehensive empirical model that would test the full impact of this complex of initial conditions and policies. Neither can we estimate the total surplus. Instead, we view the observed pattern of intergovernmental transfers as one channel for distributing the surplus created by federation. We consider the economic and political variables in the regressions we report subsequently as proxies for, or determinants of, the threat points, d_i, and the bargaining powers, β_i. Note that the Nash bargaining model can be viewed as a normative outcome, determined by a set of axioms. However, it may also be thought of as an approximate prediction of the outcome of a strategic bargaining game. The only normative dimension that enters our empirical work is the consideration of equity objectives (though they could also be conceivably driven by instrumental concerns). These have received the most attention in writing on Centre–state fiscal transfers in India, and we allow for them by including per capita income of the sub-national units in the regressions.

The above formalism is, of course, too simple in several respects. It does not explicate the institutional structures and rules that govern the sharing of the surplus created by cooperation. Also, it neglects the fact that the structures laid down at the time of federation cannot specify fully how the surplus will be shared as it is generated over time. Finally, in a point that follows from the second one, federation creates a central authority that has the power to affect the distribution of the surplus across the constituent units of the federation, as well as an interest in preserving its power and the rewards that come with it. The analysis of such behaviour of a central authority is part of a much more general strand of political economy, that examines rent seeking, interest group behaviour, and so on. We briefly describe how some of these issues are tackled in the literature, and the relevance for our empirical approach, which will, in the end, test a combination of hypotheses, not just the pure Rikerian postulate.

One strand of literature examines the economic determinants of nation formation, though not necessarily in the context of explicit ex post federations. An early contribution by Buchanan and Faith (1987) examines secession threats as a limit on taxation of groups within a jurisdiction. This is quite close to the Riker concept. Taxation is used for providing public goods as well as for redistributing surplus from those out of power to those in power. Only those in power receive transfers. The possibility of secession reduces the overall tax rate and the level of redistribution from what they would be in its absence. However, this analysis does not look at disparities within the ruling coalition, and how they affect transfers. Alesina and Spolaore (1997) examine nation formation as determined by a trade-off between scale economies and costs of heterogeneity. They also examine compensation schemes to preserve or alter the boundaries of nations, but find that their assumptions rule out such schemes in equilibrium. Bolton and Roland (1997) also consider the potential break-up of nations, with an explicit focus on conflicts over redistribution. Since they allow for regions with heterogeneous preferences, they find that (unlike in the case of Buchanan and Faith's model) poorer regions that receive transfers might still want to secede. In other words, the overall pattern of benefits and costs of federation matter, not just one component of redistribution. Finally, Warneryd (1998) examines the endogenous formation of jurisdictions in a rent-seeking model, and explicitly compares federalism, with hierarchical rent seeking, to a centralized structure. These papers are only illustrative: Bolton, Roland, and Spolaore (1996) provide a survey of this literature.

An alternative, but related, branch of literature examines distribution and redistribution in the context of existing nations, without the threat of secession or break-up being considered. Again, bargaining perspectives are important in this genre of models. Inman and Rubinfeld (1997) provide a transactions cost analysis of the federal provision of public goods. Their particular focus is on the role of legislative structures in determining this allocation. Given a clear assignment of tasks, a level of representation, and legislative institutions, one can compare the economic efficiency of different combinations of these three institutional variables. Building on the work of Breton and Scott (1978) and Baron and Ferejohn (1989), they make this comparison based on an assessment of different types of transactions costs. They do not explicitly treat intergovernmental transfers in their analysis. Kletzer and Singh (1997, 2000) analyse a median voter model of a federation with taxation, representative government, and intergovernmental transfers. In their model, the constituent units of the federation realize that transfers have to be financed by taxes, and so they care about net transfers. They show in an example how coalitions may form to determine the winners and losers from transfers, based on factors such as income and agenda-setting power.

The analysis of Dixit and Londregan (1998) is the most complete treatment of fiscal federalism in the context of distributive concerns. They also provide an excellent survey of some of the literature in this area. In the Dixit–Londregan model, voters can belong to groups. They care about their private consumption as well as having ideological positions. They allow for political parties, and different political power of groups. The parties determine policies, including ideological positions as well as taxes and transfers. The political power of groups is positively affected by a greater willingness to compromise ideology for private consumption, and greater demographic importance at pivotal points in the preference distribution. Groups with greater power, measured in this way, are therefore predicted to do better in a federal system.

The models of distributive politics in an ongoing federation, whether they consider secession possibilities or not, are mostly positive, in the sense that the Central government—as well as constituent units and individual voters—maximizes its own welfare. This is a feature of Buchanan and Faith's model, as well as Dixit and Londregan's paper. Kletzer and Singh do not explicitly model the Central government's preferences, but assume that its goal is to stay in power, and it therefore responds to the median voter. Inman and Rubinfeld, on the other hand, provide a mix of positive and normative analysis. The important point is that no actor, including the Central government, is assumed to be automatically benevolent in its objectives. This is the perspective in the analyses considered in this chapter, though we do provide critical comments on the efficiency of India's current institutions governing Centre–state transfers.

What is the import of the above models for our empirical analysis? We believe that basic factors such as economic and political size matter for the kinds of distributive issues that are tied to the formation and continued existence of the federation, as we outlined simply in equations (3) and (4). Here, marginal political power, or being pivotal in the ruling coalition, are less significant than basic bargaining power. In our own empirical work, we attempt to capture this power through the impacts of the economic and demographic importance of states on per capita transfers. However, even where secession is not an issue, perhaps being too costly, the framework of federal institutions and rules provides an arena in which bargaining over distribution takes place. In this case, explicitly political variables that we consider, such as the proportion of the ruling party that comes from a state, or whether a state's ruling party matches the party in power at the Centre, come into play. Thus our empirical work gets at both kinds of issues, albeit in an approximate way. The Dixit–Londregan type of analysis suggests that ideally, we would like to have data on the pivotal nature of parliamentary constituencies, aggregated by state. This data is available in raw form, but constructing the appropriate series would require considerable effort.

POLITICAL ELEMENTS IN INDIA'S TRANSFER SYSTEM

In this section we revisit some of the institutional aspects of India's transfer system, detailed in earlier chapters, from a political economy perspective. The Finance Commission was conceived of in the Constitution as a technical body, charged with making transfers, chiefly in the form of tax sharing, but also including grants, to respond to the potential vertical fiscal imbalance created by the constitutional assignment of expenditure and revenue authorities and horizontal imbalances arising from revenue and cost disabilities due to varying income levels, demographic and economic factors. While the Commission has served its role reasonably well within the limits placed on it, it is precisely those limits that seem to reflect political economy considerations on the part of the Central government. The Commission's scope was kept quite narrow from the start, and political considerations tended to intrude into its composition as well as the Central government's response to its recommendations, which formally have only advisory status.

More significant political factors in shaping India's transfer system were the alternative channels that arose along with the narrowing of the practical scope of the finance commissions. The early creation and evolution of the Planning Commission was accompanied by an explicit decision to exclude plan transfers from the scope of the Finance Commission. Initially, plan transfers were discretionary, but in 1969 were made more formulaic. However, over the years, there has been a steady erosion of formula-based plan transfers. Further discretion in Centre–state transfers came to be exercised with the proliferation of project-based transfers governed by various Central government ministries.

While one may critique the efficiency of this complicated system with multiple agencies and methodologies for transfers from a normative perspective, its evolution is quite understandable from a positive political economy perspective. Various Central government decision makers are potentially able to use the discretion and control they have in this system to make transfers that further their political goals, rather than maximizing any measure of aggregate social welfare. Of course, Central decision makers may also represent the interests of sub-national constituents, as in the simple bargaining framework discussed in the previous section.

In the case of all these transfer agencies, several factors can affect the final outcome. The first is the membership of the decision-making bodies. The composition of the Finance Commission and Planning Commission, in terms of the states from which their members originate, can affect transfer patterns wherever there is discretion. Similar considerations would apply to the regional identities of Cabinet members and the senior civil servants in their ministries. Even where transfers are ostensibly rule bound, through formulae or other guidelines, the parameters may themselves be subject to discretion. In the case of centrally sponsored schemes, their proliferation is in part traceable to the perceived political advantage from announcing new schemes. This is to be expected, given their discretionary nature. However, the inefficiency of such schemes can also be traced to political considerations—interest groups such as sub-national politicians, bureaucrats or others may receive the transfers rather than the ostensible recipients.[1] In general, therefore, it is quite plausible to hypothesize that various measures of influence or bargaining strength might be determinants of the actual pattern of transfers in India, with different components of the transfer system being subject to differing degrees of political economy influence.

A final aspect of political influence on the transfer system has been the increasing prevalence of coalitions ruling at the Centre, typically with regional parties having pivotal roles. While single parties may also include implicit regional coalitions within their ranks, explicit coalitions are more likely to require fiscal transfers for stability, since other avenues for rewarding loyalty, such as promotion within the internal hierarchy of the party, are unavailable. This is a further, specific hypothesis that can be tested with Indian data.

EMPIRICAL ANALYSES

Formal theoretical models, as well as casual empiricism, outlined in the previous two sections, have been the basis for several recent attempts to estimate political influences on Centre–state transfers. We summarize the empirical work of Rao and Singh (2000); Singh and Vasishtha (2004), Dasgupta, Dhillon, and Dutta (2001); and Biswas and Marjit (2000). The first two papers are closely related, while each of the others takes a somewhat different approach. We first outline the Rao–Singh work, then the other three papers, and then return to a more detailed look at the results of Rao and Singh.

Overview

Rao and Singh begin with five categories of transfers: shared taxes, non-plan grants, grants for state plan schemes, grants for central plan schemes, grants for centrally sponsored schemes. The first two categories are Finance Commission transfers, the next two are Planning Commission transfers, and the last constitutes transfers directly governed by the Central government's ministries. Rao and Singh aggregate these categories as follows:
1. Statutory Transfers = Shared Taxes + Non-plan Grants
2. Grants for State Plan Schemes
3. Discretionary Transfers = Grants for Central Plan Schemes + Grants for Centrally Sponsored Schemes

---

[1] The wide variety of discretionary transfers from Central ministries also makes it difficult to enforce compliance with conditionalities of the transfers. Incentive provision itself becomes segmented and inefficient.

The argument for the above categorization is that shared taxes and non-plan grants are those determined by the Finance Commission, which is ostensibly free of direct political influence. Grants for Central plan schemes and centrally sponsored schemes, on the other hand, are both directly subject to discretion by the Centre, and this is the obvious place where political influence, if any, should show up. Grants for state plan schemes involve Central approval of state government proposals, so there is scope for discretion, but it is at least potentially different than in the case of transfers based on proposals initiated by the Centre. The Rao–Singh data exclude the loan component of plan transfers, since these are not strictly transfers. They would become so if the loans are forgiven, which is an issue we take up in the conclusion. Furthermore, subsidized loans involve an element of implicit transfer, as we have discussed in Chapter 9; we put aside that issue in the empirical exercise reported here.

Rao and Singh use data on the fourteen large non-special category states in India for ten years, 1983–4 to 1992–3. They estimate a model with state-specific fixed effects. The dependent variables are transfers in the three categories, in per capita terms. The explanatory variables are state domestic product (SDP), SDP per capita, population, and two explicitly political variables, the proportion of the ruling party's members of parliament (lower house only) coming from a particular state, and a dummy variable measuring whether the same party was in power at the Centre and the state level. For brevity, we refer to these variables as roughly measuring 'power' and 'alignment'. Note that the other explanatory variables may also measure political and economic power, while the per capita SDP variable can measure the extent to which transfers meet equity objectives.

Rao and Singh estimated linear, log-linear, and translog functions, to test the robustness of the results. One very robust and plausible result was that the alignment variable always had a positive and statistically significant effect on grants to state plan schemes, albeit with a lag (which may reflect the five-year decision cycle for such transfers). More surprising was the result that in the logarithmic specifications, statutory transfers were positively affected by the 'power' variable. There was also some evidence that political and economic size, as measured by SDP and population had positive impacts on per capita transfers, but these results were not quite as robust across specifications. One consistent result, however, is the differences in explanatory patterns for the three components of transfers that were examined.

One additional institutional feature that was not captured in Rao and Singh's analysis is the five-year cycle of decision making that affects both the Finance Commission and the Planning Commission (though these cycles are no longer contemporaneous). Singh and Vasishtha (2003) have re-estimated the Rao–Singh equations with the following modifications. They estimate separately for the two components of discretionary transfers, they fix the political variables at the levels that are current in the year in which decisions are made, and they include dummy variables for the different planning commissions. The effect of the last factor is very strong: different planning commissions have very different fixed effects on transfers. On the other hand, there is no such effect in the case of Finance Commission transfers, reflecting their overall stability over time as determined by tax revenues and sharing formulae. The political variables are sometimes statistically significant in these additional estimates.

Dasgupta, Dhillon, and Dutta (D3) use data for twenty-nine years, from 1968–9 to 1996–7, and include the smaller state of Goa in their estimations. They begin with a theoretical extension of the Dixit–Londregan model, which was described in the previous section. They use three dependent variables, numbers 3 to 5 of the five basic categories identified by Rao and Singh, in logarithms of per capita transfers. Their 'non-political' control variables are SDP per capita, share of agriculture in SDP, annual rainfall, and voter turnout in the last state legislative assembly election. They use three political explanatory variables: two are somewhat similar to the Rao–Singh measures of 'power' and 'alignment', while the third captures whether a state's legislative assembly election was close or not, reflecting whether the state might 'swing' in a favourable direction as a result of transfers. The alignment variable enters independently as well as determines a switch in the estimated regression for the other political variables. D3 allow for fixed effects as well as various lagged effects in the political variables. D3's results are perhaps the strongest in support of the importance of political effects on discretionary transfers: they find that the 'power', 'alignment', and 'swing' variables all tend to have empirical effects that are consistent with their extension of the Dixit–Londregan model.

Biswas and Marjit use a different specification in their empirical exercise. Their only dependent variable is based on discretionary transfers, but they use the per capita share of such transfers, i.e. transfers to state j in year t are divided by total discretionary transfers in year t, and then by state j's population in year t. This has the advantage of eliminating the effect of aggregate year-to-year fluctuations. There are important differences in their definition of discretionary transfers from that of Rao and Singh and D3, in that they include plan loans, ways and means advances, and special relief for natural disasters. There are some problems with this approach, nevertheless their results are worth discussing. They try various different specifications, including variables similar to Rao and Singh's 'power' variable and their 'alignment' variable, and an alternative 'lobbying power' variable based on representation of different states in the ministerial Cabinet. They also consider voter turnout (as in D3) and an index of opposition unity. They estimate their equations for the same fourteen states as Rao and Singh, but for the period 1974 to 1995 (with several gaps, leaving eighteen years of data). They allow for fixed effects in some of their regressions, and they include dummies for coalition governments and the economic reform period. In each regression, Biswas and Marjit find that the political variables they include are statistically significant, and have the right sign. The results are promising, but are subject to econometric problems: their procedure introduces biases into the estimation by first regressing the dependent variable on SDP per capita, and then regressing the residuals on the political variables. Nevertheless, the results are consistent with those of other authors.[2]

What conclusions can be drawn from these empirical exercises? First, one should not be dismayed by the lack of absolutely clear-cut results. After all, the underlying institutions are often viewed as complex and opaque, perhaps deliberately so. These papers are certainly an excellent start in sorting out the political–economic interactions that determine the actual levels of various kinds of Centre–state transfers in India, and their insights can be combined in future empirical work. Second, the papers taken together do suggest that political factors, whether captured through straight political variables, or through measures of demographic and economic importance, do matter. In particular, Rao and Singh suggest that these effects extend to Finance Commission transfers as well as to more obviously discretionary transfers. We would like to argue, later in this book, that there is a case for institutional reform of the Centre–state transfer system that is supported by the empirical work summarized in this section. Before doing so, we will also first examine the evidence on convergence or divergence across India's states.

It is useful to acknowledge at this stage that the empirical exercises above have all been restricted to explicit transfers. Political considerations can work through a variety of additional channels. The various types of

---

[2] While the data period and specifications used by Biswas and Marjit are different in several respects from those of Rao and Singh, the latter do find that the significance of the political variables is sensitive to the inclusion of fixed effects. In fact, Singh and Vashishta (2002) re-estimate the Rao–Singh fixed-effect specifications with the inclusion of the Biswas–Marjit lobbying power variable, and find that it is statistically insignificant, whether the other political variables are included or not. Hence, there is clearly room for further empirical analysis.

controls, regulations, and the Centre's own investments, have determined resource flows across India's regions. Often these implicit resource transfers were unintended (as in the case of India's freight equalization scheme). Also, financial repression, allocation of loans at below market rates of interest to states, and mandated allocation of loans to priority sectors have all resulted in 'invisible' transfers (Chapter 9) with differential regional impacts. Political economy factors can also manifest themselves in the design of the tax system at the state level, with regional implications. For example, the origin-based sales tax system has caused significant interstate tax exportation (Chapter 7).

EMPIRICAL RESULTS

We use data on fiscal transfers from the Centre to the states that has been compiled and cleaned up at the National Institute for Public Finance and Policy (NIPFP), New Delhi. This institute is primarily responsible for such data compilation and analysis, and we are quite confident about the data quality. There are no missing observations. We use data on fourteen major states: these exclude the so-called special-category states, and the small state of Goa, which was upgraded from union territory status relatively recently. The special-category states are distinguished by being border states, with substantial ethnic and religious differences from the 'mainstream' of India. Their exclusion therefore does not imply unimportance: in fact they are the clearest illustration of a Rikerian view of federalism. However, there are several wrinkles in considering the special-category states (such as differences in cost structures) that suggest a separate analysis with additional data is required. While we have a time series on fiscal transfers that stretches further back, we have, for tractability, restricted our empirical analysis in this paper to the ten-year period from 1983–4 to 1992–3. This NIPFP data set also included figures on state domestic products in current and constant prices, and in total and per capita terms. Thus we recovered state population figures from the ratio of per capita and total values for each year and deflators from the ratio of current to constant price figures. These were used to convert the fiscal data to constant price terms (with 1981 as the base year), and to per capita terms wherever required. We describe the fiscal data in more detail below.

We also use data on political characteristics of the states. In particular, we use data on the share of different states' parliamentary representation in the ruling party or ruling coalition. This data is constructed from Butler, Lahiri, and Roy (1995). The period of estimation included majority Congress governments from 1980 to 1984 and 1985 to 1989, as well as a minority Congress government from 1991 to 1996. From 1989 to 1991 (a period of about a year and a half), there were two Janata Dal minority governments. The existence of 'outside support' for minority governments introduces some noise into using the share variable as a measure of political strength of the state in the central process, but for the present study we work with this variable.[3] We also use data on the control of the various state governments, using this to create a variable that takes the value one if and only if the party at the Centre and the state level are the same in a particular year, and zero otherwise.[4]

We now describe the data on transfers in greater detail. The table below illustrates the tax data we have, using the original (current price) data from Andhra Pradesh for 1983–4. For our present analysis, we consider only the aggregate of shared taxes. Recall that these are centrally collected taxes, which are constitutionally required to be shared with the states. The aggregate share, and the distribution among the states, are both determined by the Finance Commission.

Total Tax Revenue	=	118,440.60
Own Tax Revenue	+	82,352.00
Shared Taxes	=	36,088.60
Shared Income Taxes	+	9069.50
Shared Estate Duty	+	107.50
Share of Union Excise Duties	=	26,911.70
Basic Union Excise Duties	+	23,294.20
Additional Excise Duties		3617.50

The data on non-tax revenue of the states is also available broken down by categories. The table below illustrates the nature of the original data, also using figures from Andhra Pradesh, again at current prices for 1983–4. The four grant categories are further disaggregated in the original data, but we do not present that disaggregated data here.

Total Non-tax Revenue	=	57,966.50
Total Own Non-tax Revenue	+	30,942.44

[3] Ideally, we would like to calculate a power index, such as the Banzhaf Index, to measure the political clout of different states in the ruling party/coalition at the Centre, but such calculations will require implementing a complex computer program, which we have not yet tried.

[4] This data was made available to us by Bhaskar Dutta, who used it in an analysis of the state governments' expenditure patterns (Dutta, 2000). The data is also in Butler, Lahiri, and Roy (1995). Again, the existence of coalition governments in states can make the matching variable we use somewhat less reliable.

Grants from Central Government	=	27,024.06
Non-plan Grants	+	6317.80
Grants for State Plan Schemes	+	7862.07
Grants For Central Plan Schemes	+	3108.55
Grants For Centrally Sponsored Schemes		9735.65

For the empirical analysis, we aggregate transfers into three categories, as indicated earlier in the section. The sum of these three categories constitutes total transfers. We also run regressions using this total variable. The summary statistics suggest that, in general, neither lack of variation nor high correlation between independent variables is likely to be a problem.

Estimation Methodology

We estimated fixed effects models for various specifications. We report selected results in detail in this chapter, and briefly discuss other specifications. All regressions were run alternatively using the three transfer components, and their total, as the dependent variables, in constant price, per capita terms. The independent variables used were state domestic product at 1981 prices (SDP81), per capita constant price SDP (SDPPC81), population (POPN), the proportion of the ruling party's members of Parliament (lower house only) coming from a particular state (PROPN), and the variable measuring whether the same party was in power at the Centre and the state level (ALIGN). Lags of the latter two variables were also tried, with, for example, a three-year lagged variable being denoted PROPNLAG3 and ALIGNLAG3, respectively. We found the results with the lagged variables to be more plausible, as we discuss below, and only those are reported. In addition to these independent variables, state fixed effects were also included. The model without state fixed effects was always rejected in the standard F-tests automatically carried out by LIMDEP and, therefore, those results are not reported. We tried three specifications: linear, log-linear, and translog. In each case the political variables were unchanged. All estimations were carried out using the White heteroscedasticity-corrected variance covariance matrix.

Linear Specification Results

Table 11.1 presents results for the linear specification, for each of the four dependent variables (the three components of transfers, as well as their sum). The first regression, for purposes of illustration, reports the regression without the two explicit 'political' variables. The dependent variable here is statutory transfers. In general, we found that the coefficients of SDP,

TABLE 11. 1
Linear Specification Coefficients

Variable	(1) Statutory transfers per capita	(2) Statutory transfers per capita	(3) Grants for state plan schemes per capita	(4) Discretionary transfers per capita	(5) Total transfers per capita
SDP	–0.162E–04	–0.173E–04	0.328E–06	0.912E–05	–0.261E–04**
	(–1.262)	(–1.328)	(0.036)	(–1.475)	(–2.151)
SDPPC	0.0142**	0.0156**	0.586E–04	0.499E-02	0.0206**
	(2.171)	(2.363)	(0.013)	(1.592)	(2.219)
POPN	1.224***	1.216***	0.295	0.812***	2.323***
	(2.919)	(2.769)	(0.950)	(3.888)	(6.183)
ALIGNLAG3		1.7344	4.784**	0.110	6.628
		(0.636)	(2.481)	(0.085)	(1.631)
PROPNLAG3		52.684	4.687	5.040	62.440
		(1.107)	(0.139)	(0.223)	(1.194)
Adjusted R-squared	0.62681	0.62802	0.21306	0.51408	0.62325

Notes: All financial variables are measured in 1981 Rupees; t-ratios in parentheses
*** significant at 1 per cent level; ** significant at 5 per cent level; * significant at 10 per cent level (all two-sided).

Source: Authors' calculations.

SDPPC, and POPN were not very sensitive to inclusion of the political variables. Therefore, except for the illustrative regression (1), all other regressions reported include the two political variables. As noted, we found that a lag of three years for the political variables gave reasonable results, and we imposed this lag for all the regressions reported. The reasoning behind using lags is that actual transfers would be heavily influenced by factors determined in advance by the Finance Commission, and political impacts would therefore show up with a lag. A rationale for the particular lag can be sought in the five-year cycle of the Finance Commission and Planning Commission awards, with three years representing an approximate 'average' lag, though this is only a rough intuition. The results with the lagged political variables are reported for the linear regressions numbered (2)–(5) of Table 11.1.

Note that, since the three independent variables SDP, SDPPC, and

POPN are multiplicatively related,[5] the coefficients of these variables cannot directly give us marginal impacts of changes in state characteristics. The marginal effects at the unweighted means of the data are therefore also reported in Table 11.2. We use the point estimates to calculate the marginal effects, even though some estimated coefficients are statistically 'insignificant' at conventional levels. In every case, except for regression (3), the 't'-ratios are at least one, and so the point estimates are not only statistically 'best', but are also reasonably precise. For regression (3), with grants for state plan schemes as the dependent variable, none of the three coefficients are even close to statistically significantly different from zero at conventional levels, and we have omitted the calculation of marginal effects for this regression from Table 11.2. For the other regressions, since the marginal effects are linear functions of the coefficients, we are able to calculate the usual t-statistics, and these are reported in Table 11.2 as well.

We discuss the coefficients and marginal effects for each of the regressions

TABLE 11. 2
Linear Specification Marginal Effects

Impact variable (held constant)	(2) Statutory transfers per capita	(4) Discretionary transfers per capita	(5) Total transfers per capita
SDP (SDPPC)	0.43E–04*** (3.14)	0.31E–04*** (4.78)	0.93E–04*** (6.52)
SDP (POPN)	0.12E–04 (1.48)	0.28E–06 (0.07)	0.11E–04 (1.26)
SDPPC (SDP)	–0.014 (–1.41)	–0.015*** (–3.14)	–0.039*** (–3.24)
SDPPC (POPN)	0.006 (1.48)	0.15E–03 (0.07)	0.006 (1.26)
POPN (SDP)	0.66* (1.67)	0.64*** (3.35)	1.74*** (3.76)
POPN (SDPPC)	0.87*** (3.14)	0.63*** (4.78)	1.89*** (6.52)

Notes: t-ratios in parentheses; *** significant at 1% level; ** significant at 5% level; * significant at 10 % level (all two-sided).
Source: Authors' calculations.

[5] Because of the units we have used for the three variables, the relationship is SDP81 = POPN*SDPPC81*10.

(2)–(6) in turn. We have also presented the fixed effects for regressions (2)–(5), in Table 11.3, and we examine them for all four regressions together, once we have presented the discussion of the coefficients and marginal effects.

The regression for statutory transfers per capita, (2), has only the coefficients for SDP per capita and population statistically significantly different from zero. However, the other coefficients are not estimated too imprecisely, and the overall fit is reasonable, though much of the explanatory power comes from the fixed effects. The main story is to be found in the estimated marginal effects in Table 11.2. There we see that the effect of changes in SDP per capita on the per capita statutory transfer, controlling either for economic size (SDP) or demographic size (population), is surprisingly not statistically significant, though in the first case it has the 'right' negative sign. The latter is consistent with equalization objectives and the evidence from simple correlations presented in the last section.

TABLE 11. 3
Linear Specification Fixed Effects

State	(2) Statutory transfers per capita	(3) Grants for state plan schemes per capita	(4) Discretionary transfers per capita	(5) Total transfers per capita
Andhra Pradesh	−32.282	−10.041	−31.045	−73.403
Bihar	−47.652	−18.333	−47.100	−113.122
Gujarat	−31.364	−1.624	−20.254	−53.267
Haryana	15.283	7.830	−1.928	9.403
Karnataka	−21.737	−6.311	−17.990	−46.066
Kerala	5.690	4.207	−11.362	−1.487
Madhya Pradesh	−34.247	−9.233	−32.175	−75.685
Maharashtra	−52.746	−17.923	−35.963	−106.667
Orissa	33.165	6.709	−2.121	37.737
Punjab	−19.024	3.608	−10.104	−25.547
Rajasthan	−9.745	3.626	−9.083	−15.224
Tamil Nadu	−18.331	−5.330	−26.070	−49.759
Uttar Pradesh	−96.628	−27.150	−77.766	−201.597
West Bengal	−19.856	−6.387	−39.529	−65.803

Source: Authors' calculations.

On the other hand, higher SDP is associated with higher per capita statutory transfers. Thus, whether we control for the per capita product of the state, or for its population, a state which is economically more important, as measured by the size of economic activity in the state, receives higher per capita transfers. This result is not an obvious outcome of the complex institutional process of making transfers, and it is our first important observation from our regressions. Finally, population also has a positive effect on per capita transfers: a more populous state receives more per capita, compared either to a state with the same per capita product or to a state with the same total domestic product (i.e. with a higher per capita product).

The political variables in regression (2) are statistically insignificant. We tried several other combinations and lags of the two political variables in the statutory transfers regression. In no case were the coefficients of the two political variables statistically significantly different from zero. As noted, we report only the results for the specification where the variables were lagged by three years. However, we may interpret the population variable as capturing some political effects: in a democracy, the demographic size of a state may be an indicator of its political influence.

Regression (3) in Table 11.1 presents results for the case where the dependent variable is per capita grants for state plan schemes. Only the matching variable is statistically significant, with a lag of three years. The effect is economically important as well. The mean per capita grant for the sample is Rs 13.97, and the average effect of the state being ruled by the same party as the Centre is that the per capita grant in this category is higher by Rs 4.78. The interpretation of this regression is quite plausible: states propose these schemes to the Planning Commission, and states that are ruled by the party in power will tend to receive higher per capita grants. The other political variable is insignificant, as are the measures of state economic activity and demographics (making calculation of those marginal effects moot). Alternative specifications did not change these latter results. The only noteworthy feature was that when the matching variable was included without a lag, it was *negative* and statistically significant at the 10 per cent level. We do not have a plausible explanation for this result: such a switch in sign was not observed when lags were varied in the statutory transfers regression. The results for the grants for state plan schemes regression, when contrasted with those for statutory transfers, show very clearly that different components of transfers are determined by very different factors. This regression's explanatory power is also considerably lower, suggesting that unobserved factors are at work for this component of transfers.

Regression (4) in Table 11.1 presents the results where per capita discretionary (as defined by us) grants are the dependent variable. Neither of the political variables is significant, although when we included only the current ALIGN variable, it was again, surprisingly, negative, and significant at the 10 per cent level. The marginal effects, reported in Table 11.2, are quite similar in size and magnitude to those for statutory transfers, even though the institutional determination of the two different categories is very different. While the coefficients are mostly somewhat smaller in magnitude, it must be noted that transfers in the discretionary category are less than one-third of those in the statutory category. Thus, the marginal impacts are proportionately higher. For example, an increase in SDP by 100,000 units (Rs 1 trillion) is estimated to increase statutory per capita transfers by about Rs 4.40, which is 7.6 per cent of the mean transfer in this category. The estimated effect on discretionary transfers is about Rs 2.80, which is 15 per cent of the mean transfer in this category. Similarly, population has greater proportionate effects for per capita discretionary transfers as compared to statutory transfers. Perhaps discretionary transfers are more politically useful in larger states, irrespective of whether the ruling party currently controls the state or not. Also, the statistical significance levels for the marginal effects are somewhat greater in the case of discretionary transfers, than for statutory transfers. One surprise in the results is the statistically significant negative effect on discretionary transfers per capita of higher per capita SDP, keeping total SDP constant. Our hypothesis would have been that discretionary transfers were less likely to display such equalization effects.

Regression (5) in Table 11.1 presents results for total transfers per capita as the dependent variable. The coefficients of the demographic and income variables, and the resulting marginal effects shown in Table 11.2, are not dissimilar to those for statutory and discretionary transfers. The lagged matching variable appears to reflect the impact on grants for state plan schemes that was discerned in the regression for that component of transfers, and is very close to being significant at the 10 per cent level. The lagged variable measuring the proportionate importance of the different states in the ruling party's parliamentary strength is the closest it comes to statistical significance in any of the linear regressions. In sum, the total transfers regression appears to reflect quite clearly the determinants of the three components of transfers. Of these three components, statutory and discretionary transfers are surprisingly similar in their determinants, while grants for state plan schemes are clearly influenced by a different set of factors, which are not being well captured in this empirical exercise.

Table 11.3 also shows the fixed effects coefficients for the fourteen states, for each of the regressions, (2)–(5). The coefficients for the statutory transfers regression display considerable variation, ranging from –96 to 33. Several of the fixed effect coefficients (particularly those that are larger in magnitude) are statistically significantly different from zero. The variation in the fixed effects suggests, of course, that factors missing from the regressions are important determinants of transfers. One possibility is that the poverty rate is an important missing variable, since Bihar, Madhya Pradesh, and Uttar Pradesh all have negative fixed effects that are large in absolute value. Furthermore, Maharashtra, also with a sizable negative fixed effect, while a high-income state, has a poverty ratio that is relatively high for its SDP per capita, the average being skewed by the large financial centre, Mumbai. However, higher poverty ratios should be reflected in fixed effects that are positive, or less negative, rather than the pattern that is observed. Furthermore, Rajasthan, the fourth 'BIMARU' state[6] does not fit the pattern suggested by the relative poverty explanation (or being part of the Hindi heartland, which also fits the BIMARU states). Neither does the fixed effect for Orissa, another poor state, fit this explanation.

Another possibility is that non-linearities with respect to the impact of the independent variables can account for the variation in the fixed effects. In particular, the fixed effect coefficients are larger in magnitude for states with larger populations (e.g. Bihar, Maharashtra, and Uttar Pradesh). Therefore, we tried to allow for non-linearities by including, alternatively the square and the square root of population, in addition to the other independent variables. However, this resulted in severe multi-collinearity, with unstable and insignificant coefficient estimates, as well as other estimation problems in some cases. Furthermore, the fixed effect coefficients continued to exhibit considerable variation across states. Explaining the fixed effects therefore remains an issue.

The fixed effects for the grants for state plan schemes regressions (column [3] of Table 11.3) are smaller than for the statutory transfers regressions (and now none are statistically significantly different from zero), but almost proportionately so. They display some of the same patterns across states as in the statutory transfers regression. The fixed effects for discretionary transfers also show considerable variation across states. Now their magnitudes are quite large, compared to the fixed effects for the larger category of statutory transfers, and they are mostly statistically significant. The pattern of fixed effects for discretionary transfers does show some differences, compared to the other two categories of

---

[6] The word 'bimar' means 'ill' in Hindi. The term 'BIMARU' comes from the beginning letters of Bihar, MP, Rajasthan, and UP.

transfers. For example, the fixed effects for Tamil Nadu and West Bengal are relatively low than for statutory transfers or grants for state plan schemes. In fact, the differences in the fixed effects mark the greatest difference between the statutory and discretionary transfers regressions, rather than the economic, demographic, and measured political factors.

Log-linear Specification Results

In order to explore the sensitivity of our results to different specifications, we next estimated a log-linear specification. The results for these are reported in Table 11.4, with fixed effects given in Table 11.5. Since the logarithm of SDP is the sum of the logarithms of population and per capita SDP, it is omitted from these regressions. The coefficients of SDP per capita and population are now the elasticities of per capita transfers with respect to these variables, keeping the other variable constant. Since lnSDPPC = lnSDP − lnPOPN, we can substitute this into the equation to derive the other elasticities. The elasticity with respect to SDP, keeping population constant, is the same as the elasticity with respect to per capita SDP (keeping population constant) in this model, while the elasticity with respect to per capita SDP, keeping SDP constant, is the difference in the

TABLE 11. 4
Log-linear Specification Coefficients

State	(6) Statutory transfers per capita	(7) Grants for state plan schemes per capita	(8) Discretionary transfers per capita	(9) Total transfers per capita
LNSDPPC	0.397* (1.868)	1.086 (1.492)	−0.299 (−0.923)	0.380** (1.974)
LNPOPN	0.661** (1.979)	−0.745 (−0.657)	2.704*** (4.868)	0.852*** (2.904)
ALIGNLAG3	0.0093 (0.230)	0.253* (1.950)	−0.012 (−0.196)	0.054 (1.316)
PROPNLAG3	1.397** (2.428)	1.637 (1.222)	1.384 (1.353)	1.300** (2.451)
Adjusted R-squared	0.60946	0.25657	0.49594	0.60212

Notes: All financial variables are measured in 1981 Rupees; t-ratios in parentheses; *** significant at 1 per cent level; ** significant at 5 per cent level; * significant at 10 per cent level (all two-sided).

Source: Authors' calculations.

TABLE 11. 5
Log-linear Specification Fixed Effects

State	(6) Statutory transfers per capita	(7) Grants for state plan schemes per capita	(8) Discretionary transfers per capita	(9) Total transfers per capita
Andhra Pradesh	−1.760	−2.833	−6.129	−2.006
Bihar	−1.747	−2.339	−7.168	−2.118
Gujarat	−1.885	−3.482	−5.021	−1.930
Haryana	−1.236	−4.267	−1.961	−1.040
Karnataka	−1.667	−3.450	−5.052	−1.822
Kerala	−1.121	−3.053	−4.134	−1.230
Madhya Pradesh	−1.765	−2.605	−6.256	−2.001
Maharashtra	−2.218	−3.629	−6.447	−2.497
Orissa	−0.748	−2.700	−3.851	−0.885
Punjab	−1.343	−4.541	−2.804	−1.320
Rajasthan	−1.425	−2.746	−4.667	−1.462
Tamil Nadu	−1.596	−2.947	−5.726	−1.839
Uttar Pradesh	−2.253	−2.009	−8.312	−2.625
West Bengal	−1.597	−2.733	−6.664	−1.954

Source: Authors' calculations.

coefficients (since lnPOPN = lnSDP − lnSDPPC). The two explicit political variables were included in the regression without transformation.

The significance of the variable that measures states' influence in the national parliament (PROPN) changes when we try log-linear regressions. In the logarithmic regressions, the variable PROPNLAG3 now has a positive and significant effect for statutory and for total transfers. This result is again somewhat surprising, since one would have hypothesized that discretionary transfers were more subject to these kinds of influence. The coefficient of this variable is also positive, though statistically insignificant, for the other two components of total transfers. The variable that measures whether there is a match between the national and state government parties is statistically significant only for grants for state plan schemes, as was the case for the linear specifications.

As noted, the coefficients of the population and per capita SDP variables are now elasticities, and the elasticity with respect to the latter, keeping population constant, is positive (i.e. counter to equalizing objectives) in three of the cases, surprisingly excepting discretionary transfers. However, the elasticity with respect to per capita SDP is not statistically significant in the case of grants for state plan schemes. Also, in all four cases, this elasticity is negative when the state fixed effects are omitted (results not reported here). This again points to the role of state fixed effects as capturing some unaccounted-for economic criterion. The state fixed effects in Table 11.5 display patterns similar to those for the linear regressions in Table 11.3.

One noteworthy result is the large positive coefficient of population in the case of discretionary transfers (keeping per capita SDP constant). This is consistent with the point made for the linear regressions, that population may be an indicator of political influence, solely due to the size of the state, and irrespective of its economic base or contribution to the ruling group in parliament. Finally, the elasticity of per capita transfers with respect to economic size, as measured by SDP, is generally positive in the four logarithmic regressions, since it is either the coefficient of SDP per capita (if population is held constant), or the coefficient of population (if per capita SDP is held constant). The impact is largest for the discretionary transfers regression. These results are therefore consistent with the linear regressions.

In broad terms, therefore, the log-linear regressions are consistent with the linear specification results. There is some evidence in the log-linear regressions (perhaps slightly stronger than in the linear case) that political variables matter. This effect arises in the expected way in the regression explaining grants for state plan schemes, but in an unexpected manner in the case of statutory transfers, which one would have hypothesized were less susceptible to political influence than what we have characterized as discretionary transfers. Even in the log-linear case, there are definite patterns in the fixed effects that suggest that unexplained factors might be captured in those variations. It is possible, however, that the variation in fixed effects is a result of misspecification of the regressions. In particular, neither the linear nor the log-linear specification may capture the effect of the complicated formulas that are used for statutory transfers. We therefore also estimated a more flexible functional form, the translog specification described next.

Translog Specification Results

The translog specification is a well-known approximation to a general functional form, based on the idea of a Taylor series expansion of a function. The translog specification results are presented in Table 11.6.

TABLE 11. 6
Translog Specification Coefficients

Variable	(10) Statutory transfers per capita	(11) Grants for state plan schemes per capita	(12) Discretionary transfers per capita	(13) Total transfers per capita
LNSDPPC	9.402*** (3.324)	9.1155 (1.430)	6.472 (1.513)	7.366*** (3.074)
LNSDPPC^2	−0.554** (−2.351)	−0.700 (−1.276)	−0.315 (−0.952)	−0.431** (−2.235)
LNPOPN	1.396 (0.964)	−7.460* (−1.855)	1.976 (0.830)	−0.343 (−0.236)
LNPOPN^2	0.059 (0.178)	0.177 (0.184)	0.570 (1.264)	0.253 (0.960)
LNSDPPC* LNPOPN	−0.149 (−0.369)	0.708 (0.578)	−0.497 (−0.872)	−0.101 (−0.295)
ALIGNLAG3	−0.136E−02 (−0.034)	0.239* (1.959)	−0.363E−02 (−0.060)	0.505E−01 (1.397)
PROPNLAG3	1.373** (2.279)	1.334 (1.002)	0.979 (0.895)	1.095** (2.081)
Adjusted R-squared	0.63575	0.26837	0.50006	0.63185

Notes: All financial variables are measured in 1981 Rupees.
t–ratios in parentheses; *** significant at 1 per cent level; ** significant at 5 per cent level ; * significant at 10 per cent level (all two–sided).
Source: Authors' calculations.

Clearly some of the multi-collinearity that made the linear-quadratic estimates impossible to calculate is present in the translog estimates. For example, population is now no longer statistically significant, when it enters the regression through three different variables. However, the cases of statistical significance of the political variables that were present in the log-linear case survive this generalized specification. There is some evidence of non-linearities in the relationship among the logged variables, indicating that the elasticities of response of transfers to demographic and economic variables are not constant.

It is possible to re-estimate the translog specification in a restricted form, with restrictions varying for each equation, and some preliminary estimates (not reported here) were reasonable, restoring, for example, the statistically significant coefficients on population. However, the main point we wish to emphasize here is that the fixed effects, reported in Table 11.7, are now almost uniform for every one of the regressions in the translog specification. Thus, it is at least possible that non-linearities in the response of per capita transfers to demographic and economic characteristics of the states explain some of the pattern of the fixed effects in the earlier regressions, in addition to the omission of idiosyncratic political and economic factors.

TABLE 11. 7
Translog Specification Fixed Effects

State	*(10)* Statutory transfers per capita	*(11)* Grants for state plan schemes per capita	*(12)* Discretionary transfers per capita	*(13)* Total transfers per capita
Andhra Pradesh	−37.523	−20.831	−30.481	−26.384
Bihar	−37.388	−19.894	−31.614	−26.407
Gujarat	−37.607	−21.503	−29.426	−26.316
Haryana	−36.990	−22.149	−27.383	−25.769
Karnataka	−37.414	−21.515	−29.402	−26.205
Kerala	−36.835	−21.195	−28.624	−25.665
Madhya Pradesh	−37.499	−20.534	−30.598	−26.353
Maharashtra	−37.902	−21.799	−30.736	−26.855
Orissa	−36.408	−20.776	−28.249	−25.256
Punjab	−37.006	−22.249	−27.924	−25.881
Rajasthan	−37.136	−20.765	−28.996	−25.817
Tamil Nadu	−37.372	−21.021	−30.067	−26.231
Uttar Pradesh	−38.124	−19.950	−33.193	−27.216
West Bengal	−37.374	−20.843	−31.030	−26.361

Source: Authors' calculations.

Major Findings

Overall, the regressions suggest that, even with a very simple specification, there is some evidence for the importance of variables that may proxy bargaining power of the components of the Indian federal system. This conclusion is based on the positive estimated effect of economic and demographic size of the states on both statutory and discretionary transfers per capita, and of the lagged effect of a match between the state and Central ruling parties on grants for state plan schemes. In the log-linear case, there is also a positive effect of the proportion of ruling party/coalition MPs on per capita statutory transfers, again with a lag. A cautionary note, besides the general problem of potential fragility of econometric results such as these, is in the limited explanatory power of the independent variables. Most of the explained variance in the regressions reported here is due to the state fixed effects. We have suggested that there may be patterns in these state fixed effects that can be captured by other measurable political and economic characteristics of the states. Examples of such variables include the presence of prominent parliamentary party members with important ministries in their charge, poverty ratios, degree of urbanization, and level of infrastructure. Including such variables may improve the explanatory power of our regressions, and will provide a robustness check on the initial results presented here.

CONCLUSIONS ON THE POLITICAL ECONOMY OF TRANSFER SYSTEM

The motivation for the empirical analysis in this chapter comes from the view of a federal system as a constitutional or political bargain. Even though India was not formed out of an explicit bargaining process (except to some extent with respect to the inclusion of the princely states at the time of independence), the perspective of bargaining is commonly applied informally to resource sharing among the different constituent governments. The states, while not having sovereign status, and, constitutionally speaking, existing at the pleasure of the Central government, represent real and significant political groupings, based on language and culture. We would argue that they are the sub-national political units that matter above all, more so than caste or class. Therefore, Centre–state transfers in India, which are large in relative and absolute terms, provide a natural data set with which to test hypotheses on functioning of a federal system as an ongoing political bargain. We simultaneously tackle the distributive issues that arise due to the possibility of secession, as well as those that are part of the normal politics of ongoing governance.

Given the heterogeneity of methods of transfer, we grouped transfers in the analysis detailed here into two broad categories, which we termed statutory and discretionary transfers, leaving separate a third category, grants for state plan schemes. Surprisingly, results for statutory and discretionary transfers were broadly similar in the linear regressions, despite the very different institutional mechanisms governing them. On the other hand the factors governing grants for state plan schemes seemed to be quite different, and tied to political considerations in a plausible way. The log-linear specifications provide further evidence for the hypothesis that the political and economic importance of the states has a positive influence on per capita transfers.

12

Regional Dimensions of Economic Growth

INTRODUCTION

In the previous chapter, we surveyed some of the emerging literature on the political economy of Centre–state transfers. The evidence suggested that political considerations do affect the actual pattern of such transfers. This result is not surprising, but has only recently emerged from empirical analysis, after being hypothesized for much of India's independent existence. To the extent that political considerations are not aligned with the equity objectives that are part of the normative theory of intergovernmental transfers, the latter objectives may be harder to achieve than otherwise. The importance of intergovernmental transfers in equalization depends in turn on the initial conditions. In this chapter, we examine how India has been doing in terms of economic performance of the different states and regions. Several studies have been done on regional disparities over the last few years, and we review them here, as well as draw out potential implications for India's system of federal transfers.

We begin with an examination of trends in interstate inequalities from different perspectives, including social indicators, state outputs per capita, and measures of infrastructure. Next, we review many of the studies on regional convergence and divergence. On the face of it, some of these studies would suggest that India's states are diverging from each other, or at best converging to very different steady states. Aside from the long-run nature of such arguments, we argue that the evidence is mixed. Nevertheless, the potential negative political implications of perceived increases in regional disparities are quite severe, and we suggest that the topic requires continued attention.

We move on to the potential role of the Centre–state transfer system, in the context of possibly widening interstate economic disparities. We argue that, even aside from any evidence of persistent and widening economic gaps among the states in India, the need for a clear and simple approach to formulating and implementing Centre–state transfers is greater than ever. We also argue that neither the existence of multiple channels for transfers nor the importance of political influence (Chapter 11) vitiates this recommendation.

TRENDS IN INTERSTATE INEQUALITIES

The most obvious measure of the economic performance of the states would be the state-level equivalent of gross national product (GNP), or SDP. Indian data does exist for SDP, though there are some inconsistencies in how these numbers are calculated across states, and they are not consistent with the national accounts statistics themselves. A more serious problem is that SDP does not include net factor incomes from outside the state. To the extent that internal migration is from poorer to richer states, remittances by these migrants would tend to work against, or reduce regional inequalities. The impact of international remittances on regional inequalities is harder to predict, since migrants may be from relatively rich or poor states. To the extent that relatively better-off families are able to support international migration, international remittances might increase household income inequality, but again this does not necessarily imply clear regional impacts. In any case, with these caveats, we either have to use SDP data, or look for alternative measures of economic performance or well-being. We examine both possibilities here.

Table 12.1, taken from Ahluwalia (2002), gives basic data on the growth of the fourteen major states[1] in the 1980s and in the 1990s: the states are ordered from poorest to richest, based on the initial year of 1980–1. As Ahluwalia points out and discusses in greater detail, the picture given by these numbers is mixed. Some of the richer states, such as Maharashtra, have been doing relatively well, while others, such as Punjab, have not. Among the poorer states, Rajasthan and Madhya Pradesh have done well in economic growth, but Uttar Pradesh and Bihar have lagged badly. Ahluwalia goes on to calculate annual Gini coefficients of per capita SDP (weighted by population) for the fourteen major states, finding that interstate inequality by this measure, after being stable for most of the

---

[1] These states account for 93 per cent of population and 91.5 per cent of net domestic product in the country.

TABLE 12.1
Rate of Growth of Gross State Domestic Product

(per cent per year)

State	1980–1 to 1990–1	1991–2 to 1998–9
Bihar	4.66	2.88
Rajasthan	6.60	5.85
Uttar Pradesh	4.95	3.58
Orissa	4.29	3.56
Madhya Pradesh	4.56	5.89
Andhra Pradesh	5.65	5.20
Tamil Nadu	5.38	6.02
Kerala	3.57	5.61
Karnataka	5.29	5.87
West Bengal	4.71	6.97
Gujarat	5.08	8.15
Haryana	6.43	5.13
Maharashtra	6.02	8.01
Punjab	5.32	4.77
Combined GSDP of 14 states	5.24	5.90
GDP (National Accounts)	5.47	6.50

Source: Ahluwalia (2002).

1980s, increased starting from the late 1980s, and even more in the 1990s (Table 12.2).[2]

The picture is quite different when one looks at other indicators of performance. For example, the Centre for Monitoring the Indian Economy (CMIE) constructs a broad-based index of infrastructure, including thirteen different variables that measure diverse aspects of physical and social infrastructure.[3] Ahluwalia (2002) also reports this index over time for the

---

[2] See also Shand and Bhide (2000) for further empirical analysis, including sectoral decompositions. Chaudhuri (2000) also profiles Indian states' growth experience, amplifying the work of Ahluwalia, and highlighting some of the differences between the 1990s and earlier decades. On the other hand, estimated Gini coefficients for personal income distribution do not show any increase from 1990 to 2000.

[3] The thirteen variables in the index are per capita electric power, percentage of villages electrified, railway route length per 1000 sq. km, surfaced road length per 1000 sq. km., unsurfaced road length per 1000 sq. km, handling capacity of major ports, gross irrigated area

TABLE 12.2
Trend in Interstate Inequality

Year	Gini Coefficient
1980–1	0.152
1981–2	0.152
1982–3	0.152
1983–4	0.151
1984–5	0.154
1985–6	0.159
1986–7	0.157
1987–8	0.161
1988–9	0.158
1989–90	0.175
1990–1	0.171
1991–2	0.175
1992–3	0.199
1993–4	0.207
1994–5	0.206
1995–6	0.230
1996–7	0.222
1997–8	0.235
1998–9	0.233

Source: Ahluwalia (2002).

major states. It shows no evidence of increasing inequality across the states. The data show considerable variation across states, but also a remarkable amount of stability over the period, with simple correlations between any two years all being over 0.96, and the coefficient of variation showing a slight decline, from 0.35 in 1980–1 to 0.29 in 1996–7.[4] Of course, the data do not reflect quality variations, and even quantitative

area as a percentage of cropped area, and teledensity plus the following numbers measured per lakh of population: bank branches, post offices, primary schools, hospital beds, and primary health centres. Each indicator is computed for each state relative to an all-India average of 100. The composite index is then constructed as the weighted sum of individual indices. For details see CMIE (1997).

[4] These calculations do not weight the indices by population, but weighting is unlikely to change the conclusion of stability.

statistics may have different degrees of reliability in different states. Nevertheless, the infrastructure index gives an alternative picture of the relative development of the states in the last two decades.

TABLE 12.3

Relative Infrastructure Development Index

(All India = 100)

	1980–1	*1991–2*	*1996–7*
Bihar	83.5	81.7	77.8
Rajasthan	74.4	82.6	83.9
Uttar Pradesh	97.7	102.3	103.8
Orissa	81.5	95.0	98.9
Madhya Pradesh	62.1	71.5	74.1
Andhra Pradesh	98.1	96.8	93.1
Tamil Nadu	158.6	145.9	138.9
Kerala	158.1	158.0	155.4
Karnataka	94.8	96.5	94.3
West Bengal	110.6	92.1	90.8
Gujarat	123.0	122.9	121.8
Haryana	145.0	143.0	137.2
Maharashtra	120.1	109.6	111.3
Punjab	207.3	193.4	185.6

Source: CMIE and Ahluwalia (2002).

A final alternative for measuring state-level economic performance is the Human Development Index (HDI) constructed in the National Human Development Report (Planning Commission, 2002). Table 12.4 shows the HDIs for the fourteen major states, at decade intervals for three years, 1981, 1991, and 2001. The HDI includes measures of literacy, infant mortality, access to safe water and availability of durable constructed housing, as well as formal education, poverty ratios, and per capita expenditure. Not only has the HDI been rising over the two decades, but also the (unweighted) standard deviation of the distribution across states has not risen, resulting in a substantial fall in the coefficient of variation (CV). The CV for the HDI is also lower than the CV for per capita SDP across the states, though this could be an artifact of the scales used for components of the HDI. This data, even more than the infrastructure index, suggests that other factors (e.g. remittances, government expenditures) do mitigate some of the increase in regional inequalities in India that show up when per capita SDP is used as the performance measure.

TABLE 12.4
State Level Human Development Indices

	1981 Value	1981 Rank	1991 Value	1991 Rank	2001 Value	2001 Rank
Andhra Pradesh	0.298	9	0.377	9	0.416	10
Bihar	0.237	14	0.308	14	0.367	14
Gujarat	0.360	4	0.431	6	0.479	6
Haryana	0.360	5	0.443	5	0.509	5
Karnataka	0.346	6	0.412	7	0.478	7
Kerala	0.500	1	0.591	1	0.638	1
Madhya Pradesh	0.245	13	0.328	12	0.394	12
Maharashtra	0.363	3	0.452	4	0.523	4
Orissa	0.267	10	0.345	11	0.404	11
Punjab	0.411	2	0.475	2	0.537	2
Rajasthan	0.256	11	0.347	10	0.424	9
Tamil Nadu	0.343	7	0.466	3	0.531	3
Uttar Pradesh	0.255	12	0.314	13	0.388	13
West Bengal	0.305	8	0.404	8	0.472	8
All India	0.302		0.381		0.472	
Unweighted average	0.325		0.407		0.469	
Standard deviation	0.071		0.075		0.072	
Coefficient of variation	0.219		0.185		0.155	

Source: Planning Commission (2002).

While different measures give different perspectives on what is happening to interstate inequalities, commonly held perceptions of growing inequality or unfairness may be enough to require policy attention. Previous secessionist movements or other, less severe, regional political tensions have been driven by a complex mix of ethnic, linguistic, and economic factors, but economic policies have often been part of the political response.[5] Hence, the role of federal institutions in dealing with

[5] This point also applies if one considers migration. While migration may help to support convergence, in a heterogeneous country such as India, it may bring its own set of problems. If effective equalizing fiscal transfers can reduce inter-regional migration pressures or slow down the process, they may have a positive role in preserving inter-ethnic, or other intergroup, peace. Srivastava (1998), based on micro surveys, suggests that temporary employment opportunities drive a substantial amount of migration in India, beyond what is reflected in national statistics.

such concerns is still worth considering. Before we turn to the policy discussion, however, we consider another, significant set of studies that look at inter-state trends in the context of economic theories of growth.

CONVERGENCE AND DIVERGENCE

While the previous section examined patterns of change in economic performance across the fourteen major states, here we examine approaches to identifying causal factors and hence predictions about future directions. Thus, we examine regression equations that attempt to explain growth differentials across the states in terms of various initial conditions, including, in particular, the starting level of output[6] per capita itself. These regression results can be indicative of whether outputs per capita are getting closer (converging) or not.

The number of papers on convergence or divergence among the Indian states has mushroomed in the past few years. This interest has been driven by the general resurgence of growth theory as much as by the experience of India. Studies of convergence across countries have focused on poorer nations catching up through faster growth. In cases where faster growth is also affected by other variables besides initial income levels, the convergence is termed as 'conditional': in other words, a poorer country (or region) may converge to a steady state that is different from that of the richer country (or region).[7] Variables such as literacy, health, and physical infrastructure may be the conditioning variables, as well as the economic policies followed. Clearly, the conditioning variables themselves may be endogenous in a full structural model. While the evidence for any type of convergence across disparate countries is quite weak, one might expect greater possibilities for convergence across similar sub-national regions or constituent units of a federation such as India, given physical proximity and lower barriers to mobility across units.

[6] As noted earlier, income measures are not available, so the economic performance measure used is SDP per capita. This is not so bad if one is concerned with the relative development of the productive capacity of the different states, rather than economic well-being as measured by income accruing (including interstate remittances).

[7] Thus, one can identify three possible scenarios: absolute convergence, where different entities are moving towards the same steady state; conditional convergence, where they are converging to (possibly very) different steady states; and divergence, where there is no evidence of convergence. The last case is inconsistent with neoclassical growth models, but conceivably fits some endogenous growth models. Note that conditional convergence is quite consistent with increasing disparities across entities. The principal force driving convergence in the neoclassical growth model is diminishing returns to reproducible capital. Thus, economies with lower initial values of capital–labour ratios will have high marginal products of capital and, therefore, tend to grow at higher rates (Evans and Karras, 1996).

In one of the first studies of convergence within India, Cashin and Sahay (1997), examined data for the period 1961–91, thus excluding the reform period of the last decade, but including the Rajiv Gandhi reform period of the 1980s. The analysis is performed on twenty states, thus including some of the special-category states, which receive Central transfers according to different, and typically much more generous formulae than the major states. This is important to note because the authors use state disposable income per capita, adding in all Central transfers, except for shared taxes, to SDP. They find some evidence for unconditional convergence in the period of analysis, with the strongest effect being identified during 1961–71. These results are not changed in essence by controlling for other variables. Furthermore, the results indicate much slower convergence than that found across regions of developed countries such as the US and Japan. This meant that cross-sectional dispersion of per capita incomes across states actually increased over the three decades studied, despite the inclusion of Centre–state transfers (though dispersion was greater when these were excluded). Cashin and Sahay also examine the role of internal migration in convergence, and find it to be weak.

Several analyses followed Cashin and Sahay. Rao and Sen (1997) argue that the inclusion of four special-category states in the Cashin–Sahay sample muddies their analysis. Furthermore, they argue that adding transfers to SDP involves some double counting. Finally, Rao and Sen also take issue with the analysis of the equalizing effect of transfers, arguing that excluding shared taxes gives misleading results. Marjit and Mitra (1996) independently analyse a data set similar to Cashin and Sahay's, but with different empirical methods: they argue that the evidence for convergence is weak.

Nagaraj, Varoudakis and Véganzonès (NVV, 1998) examine data on seventeen states for 1970–94 (including three special-category states). They find no evidence for absolute convergence. Using panel data (rather than a cross-section as in Cashin–Sahay) and per capita SDP (excluding transfers), NVV find that there is evidence for conditional convergence, with the conditioning being done on the share of agriculture and the relative price of agricultural and manufactured goods. Adding infrastructure indicators[8] substantially strengthens the estimated rate of conditional convergence. While NVV do not explicitly consider transfers, they emphasize the importance of infrastructure and non-measured political and institutional factors (captured in state fixed effects) in explaining differences

---

[8] The infrastructure indicators are derived as the first four principal components of a dozen different measures of infrastructure. These individual indicators are very similar to the ones that make up the CMIE index.

in steady state growth rates across states. To the extent that Centre–state transfers have a potential role in affecting these determinants of growth, they are important in this analysis.

Rao, Shand, and Kalirajan (RSK, 1999) examine data for the fourteen major states, for the period 1965–95, using SDP as the output measure. RSK find evidence for absolute as well as conditional divergence, a result that is quite robust across sub-periods as well. They suggest that the speed of divergence increased in the last half-decade of their sample. However, this does not seem to be the decisive factor in explaining the difference from Cashin–Sahay: instead, the exclusion of special-category states, and of Centre–state transfers is of greater importance. The differences in conditioning variables and estimation methodology from NVV (who use a fixed-effects panel model) may explain the difference in conditional convergence results between RSK and NVV. RSK emphasize the role of private investment in explaining growth differences across states. They find that private investment goes disproportionately to higher-income states, as well as to states that have higher per capita public expenditures.[9] RSK also argue that explicit Centre–state transfers have had moderate impacts on interstate inequalities, and that these effects have been outweighed by implicit transfers through subsidized (public and private) lending and through interstate tax exportation.

Two other studies of possible convergence among India's states are those of Bajpai and Sachs (1996) and Aiyar (2001). The former study examines data for a sample of nineteen states for 1961–93. For the sub-period 1961–71, they find some evidence of convergence, but not for later sub-periods or for the period as a whole. Allowing for conditional convergence does not qualitatively alter these results. Aiyar also uses the nineteen-state sample, for 1971–96. He finds weak evidence of absolute convergence for the 1970s, but divergence for later sub-periods (especially the 1990s), as well as for the overall period. He estimates a panel with fixed effects, as do NVV, in which he does find evidence of conditional convergence. His conclusions are similar to those of NVV and RSK, emphasizing the importance of infrastructure, private investment,[10] and non-measured institutional factors.

---

[9] Marjit and Ghosh (2000) obtain results quite consistent to those of RSK, for the period 1970–96, using a slightly different sample of states and somewhat different data. Interestingly, they exclude most of the special-category states 'endogenously', based on an outlier analysis.

[10] Aiyar uses bank credit as a measure of private investment, whereas RSK use lending by all-India financial institutions. Ahluwalia (2002) uses cumulative expenditure in private sector projects as a ratio of GSDP, from the capex database compiled by the CMIE.

Ahluwalia (2002) supplements his calculation of Gini coefficients with regression analysis. He uses the growth of per capita SDP as the dependent variable, and considers various explanatory factors in alternative simple regressions. Since initial year SDP is not included as an explanatory variable, this approach is equivalent to restricting the coefficient to be zero, thus making it impossible to say anything about convergence or divergence. Nevertheless, Ahluwalia's regression results are broadly consistent with the other studies: his measure of private investment (footnote 10) is positive and significant in its impact on growth, and more so when interacted with literacy. On the other hand, neither public investment nor plan expenditure is significant as an explanatory variable. Furthermore, while the broad CMIE index fails to have explanatory power in the growth regressions, three components are individually significant: teledensity, percentage of villages electrified, and per capita energy consumption. Thus, these results are fairly consistent with those of NVV.

Finally, Singh and Srinivasan (2002) examine the most recent data on the performance of India's states, up to 1998–9, as in Ahluwalia, but with explicit convergence regressions. They extend earlier studies by examining if flows of capital to different states affect regional inequalities for the 1990s.[11] They proxy interstate movements of domestic capital, with bank credit–deposit ratios for the fourteen major states. Trends over the last two decades are summarized in Table 12.5. The average credit–deposit ratio shows a slight decline from 1980 to 1995, and is thereafter about the same in 2001. The (unweighted) standard deviation creeps up from the initial year to 1995, and increases further in 2001. While the increase is not great, the sharp decline in the credit–deposit ratio for the states of Bihar and UP is striking. Also, the correlation between the ratio and per capita SDP jumps dramatically from 1995 to 2001, after a much smaller increase in the earlier period (1980 to 1995), even when the coefficient of variation of per capita SDP for these states does not increase.

TABLE 12.5
Credit–Deposit Ratios by State

	1980	1995	2001
Bihar	0.41	0.33	0.24
Rajasthan	0.68	0.46	0.48
Uttar Pradesh	0.42	0.35	0.28
			(contd)

[11] Migration data can allow one to also look at interstate flows of labour. However, such data may underestimate migration (Srivastava, 1998).

(*Table 12.5 contd*)

	1980	1995	2001
Orissa	0.59	0.54	0.41
Madhya Pradesh	0.56	0.53	0.47
Andhra Pradesh	0.74	0.76	0.63
Tamil Nadu	0.94	0.91	0.91
Kerala	0.68	0.45	0.43
Karnataka	0.75	0.68	0.59
West Bengal	0.60	0.54	0.44
Gujarat	0.58	0.47	0.49
Haryana	0.72	0.47	0.42
Maharashtra	0.79	0.70	0.85
Punjab	0.43	0.41	0.41
Average	0.65	0.58	0.57
Std. Deviation.	0.15	0.16	0.18
Coeff. of Var.	0.22	0.27	0.32
Coeff. of Var. (SDP)	0.32	0.40	0.36
Correlation with per capita SDP	0.11	0.18	0.59

Sources: RBI Bulletins, National Accounts Statistics, and Indian Census. Figures for Bihar, Madhya Pradesh and Uttar Pradesh in 2001 include Jharkand, Chhattisgarh, and Uttaranchal, respectively. SDP and population figures used to calculate correlations were for closest available years.

Table 12.6 presents results for some simple convergence regressions, focusing on three different financial variables: FDI approvals per capita over the decade 1991–2001, 1990 per capita bank credit (a proxy for private investment), and 1990 credit–deposit ratios. The results are quite striking. First, the evidence for convergence or divergence is inconclusive, since the coefficient of base-year SDP is never significantly different from one.[12] Second, any one of the financial variables taken individually is estimated to have a significant impact on growth of SDP. When two or more financial variables are included, there is evidence of multi-collinearity, but otherwise the results are robust. They are consistent with a story where domestic and foreign capital are complements, and the evidence is suggestive of mobile domestic and foreign capital driving growth.

---

[12] This is true whether one uses a one-sided or two-sided test.

TABLE 12.6
Growth Regressions

Variable	(1)	(2)	(3)	(4)	(5)	(6)	(7)
Constant	−0.86	−0.02	−0.70	−1.16	0.13	0.84	1.18
	(−0.94)	(−0.02)	(−0.76)	(−1.65)	(0.11)	(0.79)	(1.12)
1990–1 ln SDP	1.14	1.02	1.08	1.14	0.96	0.90	0.85
per capita	(9.75)	(9.79)	(9.71)	(12.71)	(6.41)	(6.21)	(5.95)
FDI approvals		5.4E–05	2.4E–05		6.3E–06	3.3E–05	
p. c 1991–2001		(2.76)	(0.81)		(0.19)	(1.25)	
Credit–deposit			0.35	0.52	0.33		
ratio 1990			(1.34)	(3.10)	(1.26)		
Credit per					8.9E–05	9.7E0–5	16.6E–05
capita 1990					(1.12)	(1.19)	(2.71)

Note: Dependent variable is log of 1998–9 per capita SDP; (t-statistics in parentheses).
Source: Authors' calculations.

REGIONAL AND TRANSFER POLICY IMPLICATIONS

The studies considered in the previous two sections do attempt to draw policy conclusions from their empirical work. For example, Ahluwalia (2002) argues for reform of the Centre–state transfer system, in the direction of imposing more effective conditionalities on transfers, to improve the use of transferred funds by the states. In fact, this would work against any goal of ameliorating the increase in interstate inequalities that he identifies. Furthermore, his recommendation seems to implicitly assume that the Centre (the Planning Commission in particular) is able to impose and monitor such conditionalities in an effective manner, something that has not been true in the past. Our discussion of the political economy evidence in the previous chapter leads us to be more cautious about such an approach. Other suggestions, such as reductions of subsidies at the Central and state level, and privatization of public sector enterprises (PSEs) to release resources for infrastructure are more straightforward, and Ahluwalia gives several examples for the Centre such as highways, railways, and major ports, where benefits could accrue to poor as well as rich states. However, some aspects of Central spending on infrastructure as recommended by Ahluwalia are in the nature of traditional regional policy, and its ability to be successful is not clear, based on previous experience in India and other countries.

NVV provide specific quantitative estimates of the impacts of infrastructure improvements on steady state growth. For example, they estimate that an increase in per capita industrial power consumption by 10 per cent would lead to a 1.3 per cent increase in the steady-state level of per capita income, a 10 per cent increase in the irrigated cropped area would lead to a 2.2 per cent increase in steady-state per capita income, and the density of the road network has a similar effect on irrigation. They also estimate similar or larger impacts for improvements in literacy, primary school enrolment, and infant mortality. NVV's policy conclusions are quite close to those of Ahluwalia, with a focus on the poorer states:

> Our results suggest that targeting public investment in infrastructure for some specific States could improve the overall returns from this investment in terms of better growth performance. On the basis of our results, the States that should be targeted in priority are the nine States [Assam, Orissa, Madhya Pradesh, Rajasthan, Jammu and Kashmir, Himachal Pradesh Andhra Pradesh, Bihar and Uttar Pradesh] whose steady-state SDP gap with respect to the benchmark State is mainly accounted for by inadequate infrastructure.

NVV note that the large infrastructure differences that exist across states are an indication that the planning process for public investment in infrastructure has not come anywhere near achieving goals of balanced growth, but they are silent on how future targeting might avoid repeating this failure. Here, Ahluwalia's discussion of conditionalities for transfers and also of the need for improving governance is helpful. We shall take up the broader themes of institutional reform in Chapter 14, but say more about transfers later in this section.

RSK show explicitly that per capita lending by AIFIs, as a measure of private investment, is positively related to per capita government expenditures incurred by different states. This strengthens the argument that public investment in infrastructure is indirectly important, even though its effects do not show up in direct impacts on growth. They note institutional weaknesses that can hinder growth, covering not just governance but also tenurial relations and the overall environment for doing business. They note that Central investment in PSEs has not contributed to growth, and that poorer states have not been able to reap the full benefits of public investments in industries like steel and coal (predominantly located within their boundaries) due to policies like freight equalization. The transport subsidy given to equalize the prices of these basic inputs throughout the country has not only robbed the forward linkage benefits of locating these industries in poorer regions but has also led to allocative distortions.

Turning from explicit regional policy implemented by the Centre to the issue of intergovernmental transfers and their role in managing regional inequalities, it is important to be clear that reforming the intergovernmental transfer system cannot cancel out increases in interstate income inequalities.

However, they can make the formal transfer system clearer and simpler, which should make it easier to define its proper objective as one of enabling state governments to potentially provide minimal levels of public services. In the Indian case, it is clear that higher per capita expenditures in richer states are caused mainly by their higher revenue capacity. Even when tax rates are identical, the states with higher per capita incomes collect higher per capita taxes and are thus able to provide higher standards of public services. In other words, the states with lower per capita incomes would have to levy taxes at higher rates in order to provide the standards of service available in more affluent states. While intergovernmental transfers in India have had a redistributive impact as measured by a negative elasticity of per capita transfers with respect to per capita SDP, they were nevertheless not adequate to enable the poorer states to provide equal levels of public services at given tax rates.

The data in Table 8.2 gives one an idea of the relative magnitudes of state government revenues and expenditures (and hence Centre–state transfers) compared to SDPs. For the fourteen major states, own revenue ranges from about 5 to 12 per cent of GSDP, and ranges from about 30 to 70 per cent of current expenditure. Thus Centre–state transfers cannot come close to equalizing post-transfer per capita incomes, but they can substantially reduce inequalities in public service provision. The imperative is to do this in a manner that does not adversely affect incentives for raising own revenue. It is also important to note that some of the problems cannot be identified at the state level. States such as Maharashtra and Karnataka have high-income urbanized regions as well as much poorer rural regions within their boundaries. In such cases, the creation of stronger local governments and more formal mechanisms for transfers to them may help, as we discuss further in Chapter 13.

RSK have also documented the impact of implicit or invisible transfers (as we have also discussed in Chapter 9). They show that (i) interstate tax exportation, (ii) subsidized lending to the states from the Central government and the banking system, and (iii) subsidized lending to the private sector by long-term refinancing institutions and assistance from the banking and financial institutions for priority sector activities have all been regressive in their impacts, by favouring the better-off states. While the first two sources of implicit transfers affect the ability of different state governments to undertake expenditures, the third alters the rate of return and, thereby, the regional allocation of private investments.

The conditional regressivity of explicit transfers also emerges from the estimates of Rao and Singh (2000), who look at equalizing effects of different categories of explicit transfers. Their panel regressions tell a somewhat different story than the simple correlation coefficients, which support the view that Finance Commission transfers have favoured states with lower per capita SDP, more so than Planning Commission transfers. Instead, the fixed-effect regressions provide a more ambiguous picture. For example, when state fixed effects are included, per capita Finance Commission transfers do not vary inversely with per capita SDP. While more empirical work needs to be done, the general point is that *conditional* on political and economic factors that may affect bargaining power, the equalizing impact of Centre–state transfers is unclear. Whether this should be of concern when the unconditional impacts—as reflected in the simple correlation coefficients—are in the right direction is a separate matter. We would argue that it is of concern, because economic reform has changed the nature of Central government control of the economy in a way that increases the potential for greater disparities across states, putting more of the burden on an effective system of Centre–state transfers.

CONCLUSIONS

Our conclusion from examining the regional growth experience of India over recent decades, and the 1990s in particular, is that neither the regional policy of the Centre nor Centre–state transfers have been effective in their stated goals. While the evidence on convergence is somewhat mixed, it is unquestionable that disparities among the Indian states are large, even if they have not been growing along the dimensions that ultimately matter. The differences in infrastructure and institutions that seem to explain interstate differences have been persistent, and neither Finance Commission transfers, Planning Commission transfers, nor centrally sponsored schemes have made a substantial dent in regional inequalities in India. One might argue that the Centre–state transfer system is being asked to do too much, both in terms of short-term amelioration of interstate inequalities or in promoting development and poverty alleviation in the long run. If that is the case, however, the present tangle of multiple channels of transfers, with its combination of two extremes of complex formulae on one hand and ad hoc discretion on the other, ought to be simplified dramatically. Alternatively, one may argue that the transfer system has an important role to play in overall national development, and that this role has become more important as the centrifugal force of economic reform will put pressures on the other institutions of India's federal system, and perhaps even on India's political fabric.[13]

[13] This point also applies if one considers migration, a factor that has received relatively little attention after Cashin and Sahay's effort to quantify its impacts. See footnote 5.

We will return to possible reform of the transfer system in greater detail in Chapter 14. Here we emphasize that we are not suggesting that proposed reforms will remove regional inequalities in India. Instead, they will make the formal transfer system clearer and simpler, which should make it easier to understand its objectives and its impacts. This is a first step in actually tackling issues of horizontal equity. We are also not suggesting that this is the only channel for impacts on interstate inequality. RSK have noted the important regressive impacts of implicit transfers and of private sector investment flows. They also point out the unknown regional effects of direct Central government expenditures, which will also incorporate individual MPs' pork barrel efforts. Finally, there will always be some component of explicit transfers that is subject to Central government discretion. However, in our view, removing a significant portion of Centre–state transfers outside the political economy arena, clearly targeting them towards horizontal equity objectives, and doing so in a manner that does not create perverse incentives for recipients, is both feasible and desirable.

13

✧

Issues in Local Government Reform

STRUCTURE OF LOCAL GOVERNMENTS IN INDIA

Local government in India has exhibited several contradictions. Panchayati Raj and local self-government have been cherished concepts, but with little impact in practice. India has over a quarter of a million local governments, but their share of expenditure is only 6 per cent of all government spending. Aside from ideological and political reasons for participatory government (see Chapter 2), there are strong practical or instrumental reasons too: many public goods are local in character, and are best delivered at the local level, both to better respect diversity of preferences across localities, and to better tie benefits to costs. In India, however, casual empiricism suggests that the quality and level of provision of local public goods is very low, even allowing for the nation's low per capita income and low overall government command of resources.

We reviewed the history of local government reform in Chapter 3. To recapitulate, after years of debate on decentralization, a Central government committee recommended that local bodies should be given constitutional status. Two separate amendment bills were introduced, covering panchayats and municipalities, respectively, passed by parliament in 1992, ratified by more than half the state assemblies, and brought into force as the 73rd and 74th amendments to the Constitution of India in 1993. These amendments required individual states to pass appropriate legislation, since local government remained a state subject under the Constitution, and individual states have done so. These legislative changes are the beginning of a process of local government reform in India. Figure 13.1 summarizes the current structure of local governments in India.

This chapter examines ongoing local government reform in India from

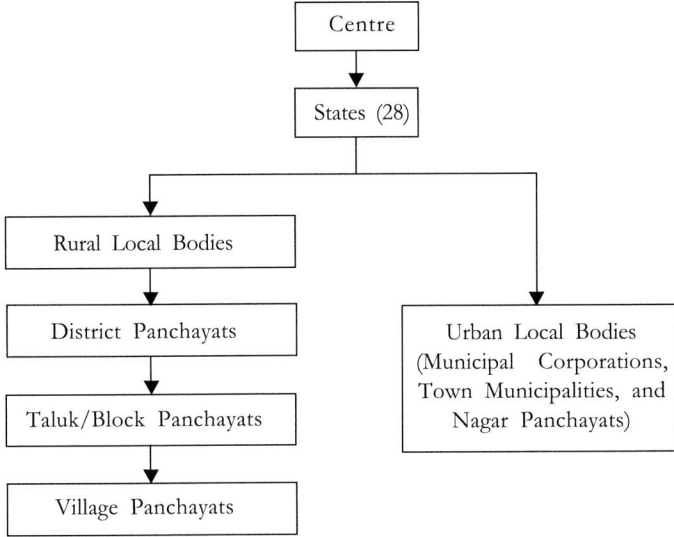

Figure 13. 1: Structure of Multilevel Government in India

the instrumental perspective of improving the provision of local public goods, including things such as sanitation, health services, basic education, roads, and street lights. We categorize reforms under three categories: expenditure responsibilities, revenue authority, and institutions and incentives. The first two categories make up the standard 'assignment problem'. While reform in these areas is important, and has been significant, we argue in this chapter that the most critical aspect of local government reform is in the area of institutions and incentives. Institutional reforms are often viewed from a non-instrumental lens, particularly in terms of how they affect people's participation in government. While that is certainly not to be neglected, we focus solely on the issue of outcomes: how can local government reform lead to a more effective use of scarce resources, and improve standards of living in the crucial dimensions of basic needs such as sanitation, local law and order, and literacy.

The rationale for devolving expenditure authority comes from the principle of fiscal equivalence, which was discussed in Chapters 2 and 6, whereby the jurisdiction responsible for spending should match the locus of beneficiaries as far as possible. In the case of revenue authority, we will focus for now on taxation. We shall discuss borrowing in the specific context of Indian local government reform. The allocational efficiency consequences of different tax assignments may be quite significant, because the incentive effects are quite different across levels of government. In particular, a tax base that is mobile may shrink dramatically in response to a tax. Therefore, it is harder for sub-national jurisdictions to raise revenue from taxes than it is for the Central government.

At any level, if the government is both benevolent and omniscient, government decision makers know the preferences of constituents, in particular their marginal benefits from the provision of any public good, or from an increase in its level. Therefore, it is easy to assign cost shares, in the form of taxes or user charges, to individuals in a manner such that every individual's marginal cost equals her or his marginal benefit. If information and incentives are imperfect, however, the connection between costs and benefits is harder to establish, and voting schemes provide a limited incentive mechanism. The assignment of taxes to a jurisdiction to cover its costs of public goods provision is desirable, but may be counteracted by the dictates of tax base mobility. A further push towards more centralized assignment of taxes may come from redistribution motives.

However, the divergence of revenue and expenditure decisions at the margin can have adverse impacts on incentives, and in the ultimate analysis the assignment of revenue and expenditure authorities must take this into account. In other words, tax and expenditure assignments cannot be entirely independent, particularly at lower levels of government, which predominantly provide public or near-public goods and services. Linking expenditures on public services with prices (user charges or tax payments) in fact supports the provision of appropriate incentives and accountability. The upshot of our discussion is that one cannot consider expenditure and revenue assignments and the structure of incentives and institutions independently. We examine these issues sequentially, however, in the next two sections.

The remaining structure of this chapter is as follows. We start off with an examination of the pre-reform assignments (expenditures and revenues) in Indian local government, the changes introduced by the reforms, and the issues that remain with respect to this aspect of local government reform. We argue that the changes are very much in the right direction, and that effective implementation will really depend on complementary institutional reforms. We move to the issue of institutions and incentives in the context of Indian local government. Again, we summarize the pre-reform situation, the reforms themselves, and the problems that remain. We argue that the crucial problems of reform lie in this area, and we identify these problems from our instrumental analytical perspective, as well as provide suggestions for strengthening the reforms. Finally, we conclude the chapter by putting our analysis in the broader perspective of overall economic reform in India. The novelty of our approach in this chapter is to suggest that the reform of local government in India, while often being pushed by groups opposed to 'liberalization', is in fact complementary, and very close in spirit to the overall reform of the Indian economy.

EXPENDITURE AND REVENUE ASSIGNMENTS

Expenditure Responsibilities

We treat rural local governments first, and then urban local governments. In each case, we discuss the situation prior to the local government reforms enacted in the 1990s, then the changes being effected. We then assess overall the issue of expenditure responsibilities in Indian local government. Two categories of problems are identified with respect to the assignment of responsibilities: (1) excessive narrowness and (2) lack of clarity. The recent reforms provide some improvement with respect to the first, but not with respect to the second.

Rural Local Governments

Pre-reform

Prior to the passage of the 73rd constitutional amendment, the functional responsibilities of rural local governments were in many cases extremely limited. For example, Datta (1992)[1] lists only five areas that were the sole jurisdiction of rural local governments: control of noxious vegetation and animals, sanitation and waste disposal, disposal of the dead, animal pounds and the prevention of cattle trespass, and drinking water supply. Another six areas of rural government responsibility were shared with state government: primary education, roads and bridges, ferries and waterways, agriculture including extension, minor irrigation and water development, and markets and fairs. In most of these latter cases, the local government had a very minor role relative to that of the state.

Since each state had its own Panchayati Raj legislation, there was substantial variation in the assignment of expenditure responsibilities across states. These assignments were often broader on paper than in practice. For example, the Kerala Panchayat Act of 1960, an early example of such legislation, listed thirteen basic responsibilities (the most notable

---

[1] This list, as well as other data on expenditure responsibilities, is in Appendix 4.1 of his chapter.

addition to Datta's list being the maintenance of the village court),[2] and a supplementary list of fifty-nine specific activities, falling in seven areas, including agriculture, animal husbandry, education and culture, social welfare, public health and sanitation, and public works. Despite the impressive list of functional responsibilities in the state's Panchayat Act, there were actually only three main categories of expenditure:[3] public works (maintenance, repairs, and extension of rural roads and bridges, and parks and gardens), water supply and drainage (including installation and maintenance), and street lights (provision, maintenance, and electricity charges). The combined per capita expenditures for 1981–2 in these three areas were only about five rupees. Thus, long legislative assignments did not translate into significant functional responsibilities in practice.

Another dimension of assignment to rural local governments is the division of responsibilities across tiers (these were absent in Kerala): village or group of villages, block, and district. The two higher tiers typically appeared to be implementing agencies of the state government, rather than as local government bodies. A detailed study of the most recent rural fiscal decentralization in Karnataka reveals that at the block and district level, there are no independent revenue sources, and the grants given are tied to a large number of specific schemes. An overwhelming proportion of expenditure on these schemes is for salaries for the employees transferred to these local bodies by the state government. On the whole, the local governments at district and block levels in Karnataka had autonomy to allocate just about three per cent of the funds received by them according to their own preferences (Rao, Amar Nath, and Vani, 2003). In practice, even functions such as education, which might appear only in the list for the lowest tier, were substantially under the control of state government agencies. In many cases, functional responsibilities were notionally assigned to the village level, but village-level decision makers did not have practical control.

---

[2] See Government of Kerala (1986), Appendix IV.

[3] This refers only to expenditure related to service provision: the largest category of expenditure by far was 'establishment charges', representing up to 65 per cent of self-raised income of the panchayats, for the years 1980–1 to 1983–4 (Government of Kerala, 1986, p. 103). Later data for Kerala panchayats (John, 1998) is not dissimilar. Aziz (1993), in a sample of mandal panchayats (groups of villages) in Karnataka, similarly finds that for the years 1987–92 the two main categories of expenditure were civic amenities and public works, with very little spent on health or education. Pande (1994) reports a similar concentration of expenditures for a panchayat in Himachal Pradesh in 1985–90, as do Bhargava and Venkatakrishnan (1998) for two block panchayats in Tamil Nadu. See also Oomen (1995) for further examples.

The assignment of responsibility for the three main categories in Kerala illustrates some further issues. With respect to road maintenance, the expenditure typically went for repeated repairs of earthen roads, which were washed away every monsoon, rather than for conversion to metalled roads as desired by constituents. This illustrates an overly narrow assignment of functional responsibility to the rural governments: metalled roads were beyond their scope. Rural water supply schemes were the responsibility of a state-level special-purpose water authority (or its predecessor, a state government department), with panchayats being charged on a formula basis for a share of the capital costs, as well as for maintenance expenses. Both the capital costs and maintenance charges were not apparently based on any well-articulated economic grounds of benefits provided. The result was disputes with respect to both. The situation with respect to street lighting seemed to parallel that of water, with problems caused by the lack of accurate (or any) metering of electricity usage for this purpose, and disputes between the panchayats and the state electricity board. The problem in all these cases was a combination of narrowness and lack of clarity of the assignment of responsibilities.

Post-reform

The 73rd Amendment created a list of twenty-nine different areas of rural local government functional responsibility. Potentially, therefore, there is a considerable expansion in the expenditure responsibilities of rural local governments. State-level legislation has implemented this expansion on chapter, at least. For example, the Kerala Panchayati Raj Act of 1994 gave 32 obligatory and 124 discretionary (the latter in seventeen areas) expenditure functions to the lowest rural tier.[4]

However, three difficulties loom. The first of these has been illustrated by past examples: most of the items in the new schedule are concurrently state government responsibilities.[5] This new concurrence will require changing the lines of control throughout the layers of government within the states. This includes the division of functional responsibilities among the different rural tiers. State-level legislation based on the amendment does not always clarify this division.[6] Without attention to these issues, situations such as those described for Kerala pre-reform will continue to

---

[4] See John (1998).

[5] Datta (1992), Table 1, identifies only ten relatively minor responsibilities as exclusive to local governments, with the other nineteen involving overlapping responsibility.

[6] See Rajaraman et al. (1996), p. 1074. In the case of Kerala, various departments and staff were transferred from state governments to rural local governments in 1996, but it is not clear if this was more than a chapter transfer (John, 1998).

occur. We discuss this further in the next section, where we examine institutional structures in more detail.

The second issue is in the process of devolving functions. Top–down decentralization has essentially meant that the functions previously undertaken by the state governments are transferred along with employees to local bodies. Safeguarding the interests and powers of the employees in the system has required transferring the functions packaged in terms of detailed schemes and pre-empting their salaries. This has violated the essence of decentralization namely, allocating resources according to the preferences of local citizens. Besides, as pay, transfer, and promotion of employees transferred to local bodies continue to be determined by the state government, the accountability of the employees is to the state government (Rao, Amar Nath, and Vani, 2004).

The third potential difficulty is enforcement, or the assignment of law and order in general. While the 1960 Kerala act did include the maintenance of village courts as a panchayat responsibility, in general, the history of decentralization of such functions to the local level in India has been problematic. Before independence the primary role of traditional panchayats was as petty courts, with limited functions as providers of public goods. The judicial role of panchayats was therefore given some attention after independence. An attempt was made to create separate nyaya panchayats (NPs) to handle judicial matters. Despite the informality and flexibility of procedures in the NPs, there were considerable delays and arrears at that level, attributable to the lack of training of personnel, and ultimately to a lack of adequate funding. Overall, the NP system became effectively moribund.[7]

The idea of devolving law and order to the district level was mooted in discussions of the Karnataka reforms of 1983, but never implemented, and was completely absent from the constitutional amendments: law and order remains a state subject.[8] The lesson from the failure of nyaya panchayats may not be that decentralization of judicial processes will not work, but that the existing structures of the judicial components of government must be decentralized with adequate resources provided for its success.[9] The point is that this is a functional responsibility with important complementarities with other local responsibilities.[10]

[7] Galanter (1989), Chapter 4, examines the judicial role of panchayats and nyaya panchayats in detail.

[8] However, Bihar, Himachal Pradesh, and Punjab have given panchayats some judicial functions in their state-level legislation (Oomen, 1995, p. 14).

[9] In fact, the problems of delay and arrears are pervasive at all levels of the Indian judicial system. See Mookherjee (1993), for example.

[10] The decentralization of law enforcement may be significant for revenue enhancement

Urban Local Governments

Pre-reform

As one would expect, the list of expenditure responsibilities is longer for urban than for rural governments. For the pre-reform phase, Datta (1992) lists fourteen exclusive functions, and sixteen that were concurrent with the state governments. Fire services, health centres, libraries, land use, regulation of industry and commerce, and parks and playgrounds were examples of areas of urban government responsibility not included in the rural government list.

In addition, each state has its own legislation governing urban areas in various classes, typically through general municipal acts, but sometimes, for large metropolitan cities such as Mumbai, through city-specific legislation. As a result, there was great variation in actual functional responsibilities across cities, even those of similar sizes, with cities such as Mumbai and Ahmedabad having broader responsibilities. For example, the Ahmedabad Corporation plays a major role in education, health, water supply, bus transportation, and town planning, while in Chennai, these are provided by state-level institutions (Jetha, 1992). A survey of expenditure patterns of municipalities in six states indicated public health, public works, and general administration as the main categories of spending (Mathur, 1998, Table 9).

Even in the big cities, while functions such as police protection were organized at the local level in terms of jurisdiction, effective control was at the state level, with personnel recruited to state or central police services. Bhagwan (1983) and Jetha (1992) provide detailed information on the functioning of the five biggest Indian cities: Ahmedabad, Kolkata, Chennai, Delhi, and Mumbai, plus Trivandrum. Bhagwan, for example, discusses the expenditures of the Municipal Corporation of Delhi (MCD), focusing on inefficiencies in provision, but also providing examples of lack of clear, permanent assignments of responsibilities.[11]

A striking illustration of the consequences of lack of clear functional responsibility comes from Ludhiana, the largest city and industrial centre of the high-income state of Punjab. The state government has, over the

---

also (tax enforcement for example), once again illustrating our tripartite framework of expenditure, revenue, and incentives. Of course, economies of scale may work in the opposite direction.

[11] On Delhi, see also Jha (1998) and Naresh (1998a,b). Naresh estimates the rate of growth of real expenditure by the MCD, from 1970–1 to 1989–90 at 6.87 per cent, with roads and city 'up-keep' having the highest growth rates. The growth rate of Delhi's population in this period was over 4 per cent.

years, established several special-purpose agencies to perform functions that would normally come under municipal authority. These agencies include the Punjab Housing and Development Board, Punjab Water Supply and Sewerage Board, and various Improvement Trusts. However as Suchdeva (1991) points out:

Labour colony and the adjoining housing areas ... are virtually a hell on earth ... The sewerage has collapsed ... houses built by the Housing Board ... stand in knee deep water. The sewerage had failed *four years ago* and all pleas for repairing it are said to have gone unheeded. The saddest part is that *no department is willing to own responsibility. The Housing Board authorities say they have handed over the colony to the Municipal Corporation while the Corporation dodges the issue by saying it has not taken over the colony. The Public Health Department which laid the sewerage is also not willing to accept responsibility and repair it* (emphases added).

Of course one can also look at this as a failure of accountability, but a major problem is the lack of clear assignment of functional responsibility, due to the existence of multiple government bodies with notional responsibilities for the same function in the same jurisdiction.

Improvement trusts have been set up by the Punjab government for development tasks such as provision of open space, laying out or altering streets, housing the poor, and land management. They are nominated bodies directly under the control of state government, though with some municipal government representatives. The list of tasks of such agencies reflect a common characteristic of local government in India: capital expenditures for a particular function, say, providing roads, are undertaken by a non-local body, while maintenance is left to the local government. The example from Ludhiana is another illustration of this approach. In such cases, there is a clear assignment of tasks, but not one that provides effective incentives for provision of the service.

Post-reform

The 74th Amendment to the Constitution created a list of thirty-seven areas of responsibility for urban local governments. This did not represent as dramatic a potential expansion of responsibility as did the corresponding reform for rural local governments. Examples of additional responsibilities include secondary and adult education, vital statistics, housing and land use, promotion and development of industrial and commercial estates, and electricity distribution. However, some of these were already being carried out by larger urban bodies. Furthermore, there is no change in the state or concurrent lists in the Constitution, and therefore the state governments retain considerable authority over functions now notionally in the urban local government sphere. The issue of law and order has already been discussed in the context of rural local governments. It might be argued that decentralization in this dimension is problematic.[12] However, for cities, the assignment of judicial functions to the local level, with local control, would seem to be feasible. This has not been done in the recent constitutional changes.

Assessment

Local governments, both rural and urban, provide examples of a lack of clarity in the division of functional responsibilities. This occurs in several specific ways. First, the same general expenditure or service category is often the statutory responsibility of the state government as well as its subordinate local governments. Second, even where broad areas are explicitly divided, this is not necessarily done in a manner that promotes incentives for efficiency: the division of capital expenditures by the state and operations and maintenance by the local government for the provision of a given service is the main example of this. Third, there has been a tendency for state governments to encroach on what might otherwise be well-defined municipal responsibilities, through the creation of special-purpose agencies, or through the intervention of state government departments. Fourth, even when local expenditure responsibilities have been clear, they have been too narrowly defined, leading to inefficiencies such as the repeated repair of earthen (rural) roads rather than construction of more durable roads. Finally, the assignment of functional responsibilities has not allowed local control over activities with economies of scope or complementarities: law and order, or judicial services more generally, are the most important case. These five problems clearly overlap. Also, as has been noted, the problem of expenditure assignment is linked very closely to issues of revenue availability and institutional incentives. These issues will be developed further in the rest of the chapter.

We close this section with some positives. Despite the problems highlighted so far, and even though the recent reform legislation does not completely address them, there are several favourable developments in the new assignment of functional responsibilities to local governments. The constitutional amendments take past legislation in various states a step further, providing a ground to local government responsibilities that must, in principle, be respected by the states. This reform also broadens local government responsibilities, reducing to some extent the problem of

---

[12] For example, Bayley (1969, p. 403) notes issues of competence and parochialism.

excessive narrowness. The three-tier system imposed on rural local governments also helps to clarify assignments to the extent that the higher two tiers have specific coordination responsibilities, and are meant to be more like components of local government than agencies of the state government. The recent legislation also has explicit provisions for areas in transition from rural to urban character.

Revenue Authority

Local government responsibilities in India have been broadened and strengthened. How will they be able to carry them out, when even previous narrower responsibilities were often beyond budgetary means of local governments? Obviously, raising additional local government revenue will be a key requirement. We examine past experience with local government revenues, as well as the implications of legislative changes for revenues. We begin with an overview; then turn to individual revenue sources—taxes, user charges, transfers and loans; and finally evaluate prospects in the new framework. In each case, we distinguish between the situations of rural and urban governments

Overview

Datta (1992) provides data on local government revenues, from the last pre-reform comprehensive survey, done in 1975. At that time, grants and shared taxes dominated for rural governments, while taxes were more important for urban governments. Rural local body revenues were heavily skewed towards the upper tier, which was not directly elected, and often nominated by state governments, being just state agencies, with control over their expenditure being effectively determined by state officials. Even so, the per capita revenue of the smallest urban governments, with an average population of 7500, was considerably greater than the per capita revenue of the much larger rural district councils and block councils. Urban local government data for 1979–80 and 1983–4 give a similar picture (Mathur, 1998, Table 1), though by 1992–3, as more states shifted away from octroi, municipalities in non-octroi states were relying more on funding from state governments (Mathur, 1998).

Oomen (1995) provides more recent data on revenue patterns of the lowest and intermediate tiers of rural governments for some states, which indicate that the lowest-level rural governments in some states are much better able to mobilize income from taxes and fees or from land revenue. Some of this difference is a consequence of different legislative assignments, but in other cases the reasons are less obvious. In other states, the panchayats rely much more on grants from higher-level governments.[13] For the intermediate level, there were similar variations across states, with Gujarat standing out with the highest average revenue per block-level government. Table 13.1 provides recent aggregate data that puts local government finances in overall perspective. The quarter million rural local governments still raised negligible revenues, amounting to only 0.04 per cent of GDP, and after transfers they had control over resources of just 1.4 per cent of GDP.

TABLE 13. 1
Fiscal Decentralization in India—1997–8

	Revenue collection	Revenue accrual	Total expenditure
Centre	11.46	6.80	12.00
States	7.80	10.90	13.60
Local Bodies	0.54	2.10	2.20
Urban Local Bodies*	0.50	0.80	0.80
Rural Local Bodies*	0.04	1.40	1.40
District Panchayats*	n	0.60	0.60
Taluk Panchayats*	n	0.30	0.40
Village Panchayats*	0.04	0.40	0.40
Total	19.80	19.80	27.80
Centre	57.88	34.43	43.20
States	39.39	55.03	48.90
Local Bodies	2.73	10.53	7.90
Urban Local Bodies	2.53	4.07	2.90
Rural Local Bodies	0.20	6.46	5.00
District Panchayats	n	3.21	2.20
Taluk Panchayats	n	1.44	1.40
Village panchayats	0.20	1.82	1.40
Total	100.00	100.00	100.00

Note: n-negligible; * Revenue accrual estimates are taken as proxi for expenditures.
Source: Public Finance Statistics 1999–2000, Ministry of Finance, Government of India, 2000. Report of the 11th Finance Commission, Ministry of Finance, Government of India, 2000.

[13] Oomen's data are not completely comparable across states. For example, only the data for Andhra Pradesh and Uttar Pradesh include Central grants under the Jawahar Rozgar Yojana (JRY) scheme of poverty alleviation grants.

Revenue Sources and Structures

We discuss taxes, fees, transfers, and borrowing in turn. Tax sharing is discussed in detail under transfers. Each of these revenue instruments raises different issues: 'The choice of instruments depends on the objectives, and the objectives vary according to the function that is being financed' (Dillinger, 1994, p. 26). In particular, services where benefits are private and the externality (or merit good) aspect is not strong are better candidates for user charges or local taxes. Of course, if revenue sources are not earmarked, there is not necessarily a simple correspondence between functions and instruments in practice.

Taxes

The share of rural government revenue coming from local taxes was quite low in 1989–90. Yet, rural local governments have had twenty-seven different taxes (twenty exclusive, seven concurrent with the state government) available to them.[14] Exclusive taxes included terminal taxes and octroi (a levy on goods entering a local area); property and building taxes; oil engine, food, timber, fishery and produce taxes; and profession and labour taxes. Concurrent taxes included those on commercial crops and on land. For the lowest rural government level in some states, land revenue was a significant proportion of revenue (Oomen, 1995). In other states, the state governments dominated in land taxes: collection would be by the state, with an assigned local share. The figures for tax sharing are also quite small. In sum, the lack of revenue raising through taxes by rural local governments is noteworthy.

Reliable data at the panchayat level are not available. However, primary data on revenues and expenditures of panchayats were collected recently for undertaking a comprehensive study on the finances of rural local governments in Karnataka. This was done for panchayats in four districts, representing different regions and levels of development in the state. The study brought out that, among the three tiers of rural local bodies, the village panchayats are the most meaningful tier as only this tier has independent revenue sources. However, in terms of overall fiscal role, the village panchayats are the least important. The analysis of Karnataka shows that in 2001–02, revenue accruing to village panchayats is just about 5.6 per cent of rural local government revenue, whereas the shares of block and district panchayats repspectively were 54 per cent and 40 per cent. Of the revenues accruing to village panchayats in Karanataka,

[14] See Datta (1992).

revenue from own sources constituted just about 20 per cent in 2001–02. In per capita terms, own revenue of village panchayats was about sixteen rupees in the total revenue of eighty-five rupees.

Almost half of own revenue of village panchayats accrued from one source—property tax, which is essentially a tax on buildings. This is followed by licence fees, rents and water charges, and other miscellaneous revenues. This is broadly the pattern in other states as well, though in Kerala, the local governments have the power to levy profession tax and entertainment tax as well.

Earlier district-level data on Kerala (Government of Kerala, 1986) illustrate three factors in the lack of revenue raising through taxes by rural local governments: (1) rates, (2) assessments, (3) coverage. The data for Kerala also provide further information on the structure of rural government taxes, which complements the more recent Karnataka data. The building tax was the most important rural tax in Kerala, followed by profession and entertainment taxes. The levy of property (building) tax was compulsory, with minimum and maximum rates fixed by the state government. The need for minimum rates is illustrated by the experience in Kerala. Raising the minimum rate from 4 to 6 per cent of annual rental value in 1978 led to a 61 per cent increase in revenue from this source[15] that year. Seventy per cent of panchayats taxed at the lowest possible rate in 1983–4: this reluctance on the part of local governments to tax as much as they are legally allowed to is a general theme in descriptions of Indian local governments. At the same time, it does not seem appropriate to fix maximum rates. In Karnataka, recent data indicate that every panchayat levies the tax at the maximum rate, but that is meaningless in a situation of significant undervaluation.

Thus, a significant dimension in determining the revenue from building taxes is the assessed value. Aside from issues of the details of the system of assessment (often difficult where market transactions are rare or not well recorded), a common problem is simply outdated valuations. This is well illustrated by the Kerala example, where there was a jump of 51 per cent in building tax revenue in 1983–4, when quinquennial assessment revisions were begun. Other states typically still fail to assess values systematically or regularly, making the tax rate itself of limited significance in affecting revenue raised.[16]

Finally, the coverage of a tax such as the building tax is important for

[15] Government of Kerala (1986), p. 16.
[16] In some cases, the building tax is not even ad valorem, but a specific levy: see Rajaraman et al (1996).

revenue. Here, the data are not detailed, but some egregious examples of exemption are provided for Kerala (Government of Kerala, 1986, p. 21): twelve panchayats exempted 50 per cent or more of buildings from the building tax. Another problem is the exemption of certain types of buildings from the tax: for example, in Haryana, all non-residential structures are exempt (Rajaraman et al., 1996).

The most important issue in local taxation is the inability of the local governments to enforce the tax: this goes back to our earlier discussion of enforcement powers. The local governments simply do not have the power and capacity to collect the tax from local elite and the tax is virtually voluntary. The tax rates on the buildings tax, for example are extremely low, both due to low rate of tax and high undervaluation of the buildings and yet, about 30 per cent of the panchayats in Karnataka collected less than 50 per cent of the amounts due.

Other rural property-based local taxes are possible, besides the building tax. Levies on non-agricultural land exist in several states, extending to agricultural land in Bihar, Kerala, and Punjab (Rajaraman et al., 1996). While there is considerable scope for revenue from taxes on land, actual collections in most states are low: in fact, this is true of state-level land taxes as well. Taxes on non-motorized vehicles cannot be a major source of revenue, but there is also scope for sharing motor vehicle tax revenue (collected in urban areas) with rural local governments: currently, Kerala is an exception in doing this. There are also a few instances of other property-based rural taxes. D.S.K. Rao (1995) documents the success of a levy on agricultural pump sets in West Bengal, after the management of tube wells was transferred from the state government to the panchayat level. Betterment levies or developmental charges, which are common for urban local governments, are rare for rural governments (Rajaraman et al., 1996). However, as noted, a critical issue in assigning tax powers is that panchayats should be enabled and empowered to enforce the tax.

Disaggregated data on urban government tax revenues is more plentiful. Urban governments also had many tax instruments available to them. Datta (1992) notes that twenty different taxes were available to urban governments, nine exclusively to them and eleven concurrent with state governments. In contrast to rural governments, several of these were significant taxes, with two of them, octroi and property taxes, accounting for 90 per cent of nationwide municipal tax revenue (70 per cent and 20 per cent, respectively). Other common taxes included vehicle, profession, and terminal taxes. Overall, taxes accounted for a major share of revenue, especially in larger cities or in towns with corporations (Bhagwan, 1983;

Jetha, 1992; Naresh, 1998). Cities such as Chennai and Trivandrum relied on only two taxes (property and entertainment) for the bulk of revenue from this source, even when octroi was not available. The Municipal Corporation of Delhi, had sixteen taxes available to it, but only five of these were significant revenue sources, with property taxes and octroi being dominant.

Problems with rates, assessments, and coverage, noted in the case of rural governments, are pervasive even in larger urban local bodies. In addition, problems with collection compound the problems with rates and bases, restricting tax revenues of local governments. Property tax rates were higher in the big cities than in smaller towns or rural areas, with progressive structures, so that the marginal rate was as high as 30 per cent in Ahmedabad. At the same time, these high rates were undercut by failure to include properties in the base and undervaluation for tax assessment. The problem of valuation in cities and towns is complicated by the existence of rent control laws, combined with the use of annual rental value as the base for taxation. Rates of collection are often below 50 per cent for taxes such as those on property, being as low as 17.8 per cent for Ahmedabad in 1990–1. Furthermore, these collection rates fell through the 1980s.[17] While one can develop sets of normative criteria for reform of urban local tax structure and administration,[18] implementing these requires considering institutional incentives.

Data on tax rates and the composition of tax revenues for smaller urban bodies[19] tell a story consistent with that for the larger cities: the property tax was widely used but inefficiently administered. Sometimes, rates were reduced after revisions in assessment had raised valuations and the number of properties valued, negating some of the impact of reassessment. In many cases, revisions of assessment were conducted after decades.

The focus is on the property tax, because it is the most appropriate local tax in terms of minimizing distortions. On the other hand, octroi, which has been so important for urban local governments, is inefficient, subject to corruption, and excessively distortionary.[20] Some states have abolished it, but others have introduced it in recent years. Madhya Pradesh and Karnataka replaced it with a state entry tax, which has some

---

[17] See Jetha (1992), Table 3.3. Mumbai did relatively well, with a 72 per cent collection rate in the same year. Chennai, Kolkata, and Trivandrum were in between these two extremes.

[18] See Jetha (1992), Datta (1998), Mathur (1998), and Jha (1998).

[19] For example, Dash (1988) examines a sample of thirty-one towns and cities in Orissa.

[20] The inefficiency and distortionary effects of octroi include high collection costs, the high taxation of intermediate and capital goods, and tax exporting. See Jetha (1992, Ch. 6).

of the same effects.[21] Part of the problem is that simple abolition of such a tax does not immediately provide local governments with a replacement source of revenue. Though in the longer run it may give them incentives to improve the collection of property taxes, this will not be an easy administrative task. In some cities and towns, particularly where octroi is not available, entertainment taxes provide significant revenue. While no single tax can replace octroi revenues, better use of taxes on entertainment, motor vehicles, professions, and utilities, which are all reasonable local tax bases, can help collectively. Furthermore, local surcharges on state taxes such as sales taxes are also underutilized. Taxes on utilities such as electricity and water can be quite similar to user fees in practice: this category is discussed below.

Local tax reform has to be part of the national effort at rationalizing the tax system. Some taxes that are properly local are currently pre-empted by state governments. Other taxes (e.g. a surcharge on property transfer duty) are conveniently or effectively collected by the state government on behalf of localities, but the system of transferring or allocating the proceeds to local governments is inefficient. Considerable work has recently been done on reforming central taxes, with attention to how this will impact state-level tax systems. Attention to local governments can and should be a part of such ongoing attempts. The constitutional amendments expand and formalize the assignment of expenditure responsibilities to local governments, but merely instruct the states to provide local governments with adequate revenues or revenue instruments. This requires analysis of rates, bases, and collection, as well as the nature and number of taxes that local governments are permitted to impose.

Users Charges

The boundary between specific or earmarked taxes and fees or user charges is somewhat arbitrary in the case of some goods provided by local governments. The classification partly depends on the closeness of the connection between usage and payment: a pure public good where exclusion is impossible requires taxes. But in the case of goods like water going to individual houses, users can be charged access fees as well as for use—the latter if use can be monitored. In some states, local authorities use these forms of charges as well as taxes for water added on to property tax assessments. This tax revenue may go into a general fund, however. The

---

[21] An entry tax does economize on collection costs, using dealer returns instead of roadside check posts. At the same time, the tax is no longer strictly a local tax. Other alternatives to octroi are discussed by Jha (1998, p. 76).

classification as tax or charge can therefore also depend on the ownership or earmarking of the revenue. With these conceptual complexities acknowledged, we will proceed to follow typical budgetary classifications in our discussion of revenue from fees and user charges. We first treat rural, then urban governments.

State-level data for rural bodies indicate that non-tax revenue is considerably smaller than tax revenue in most states. The most common fees are user charges for water and lighting. These are typically collected at the lowest level and, in the absence of monitoring ability, are flat fees. On the other hand, charges for sanitation, or for public events such as fairs and festivals, are not frequently assigned or employed. Panchayats are also usually not empowered to levy user charges on health and education,[22] even though aspects of these functions are assigned to them. Thus, the general ability of panchayats to charge for services has been quite limited.

A similar situation obtains with respect to local resources. For a sample of panchayats in forested Nainital district (Shah, 1990), tax revenue dwarfed non-tax revenues from the land management committee and the forest panchayat. The latter is particularly interesting because this is a region where deforestation is a serious problem. Forests are a major rural resource, and were traditionally community property. Somanathan (1991) describes these former types of property structures, and their more recent erosion. This process is therefore partly reflected in the lack of income from what might have otherwise been a significant panchayat asset. The lack is particularly significant given the economic structure of the region, with little scope for non-agricultural/forestry activities, and hence of revenue from licence fees for trade or similar charges. The generality of this problem of assignment is noted by Rajaraman et al. (1996). Only Gujarat and Maharashtra share forest revenue with rural governments, in both cases with the highest district-level tier, and at quite low rates. However, Gujarat allows for additional sharing with panchayats in forested areas, as a substitute for land revenue. This is a significant exception, with lessons for other states.[23]

Turning to urban local governments, non-tax revenue varied considerably across states, as a percentage of total state revenue. The categories included in non-tax revenue were income from municipal property, income from municipal enterprises, and interest on investments. In fact, little of the total was derived from enterprises, except for some larger

---

[22] Bihar, Haryana, Rajasthan, and Uttar Pradesh are the exceptions. See Rajaraman et al., 1996.

[23] In Karnataka, also, some panchayats are able to raise revenue from forests, as noted in the section above on taxes.

industrial or commercial cities in Gujarat, Maharashtra, Kerala, and Tamil Nadu (N.R. Rao, 1986, p. 187).

Per capita non-tax revenues for larger cities are small relative to tax revenues, but not as low as in some smaller cities. In Ludhiana, for example, fees provided under 4 per cent of the corporation's revenue in 1982–3. Income from municipal enterprises is also negligible in many smaller urban areas, though not always. For Delhi, income from property and licence fees were the main contributors to non-tax revenue, but the MCD's water and electricity supply enterprises ran deficits in 1977–8 and subsequent years (Bhagwan, 1983, Chapter 7). For Ahmedabad, Chennai, and Trivandrum, user charges and fees provided only small fractions of the costs of providing water, sewerage, bus transportation, and land development (Jetha, 1992, Chapter 4). In some cases, such as water supply, the poor quality of the provision made charging difficult, for technical (e.g. difficulty in metering) or political reasons. In the cases of bus transportation, health, and education, better-off citizens use and pay for private alternatives as distributional considerations are important as the quality of the public service is then further lowered. However, low rates of cost recovery for land development cannot be explained by concern for distribution. Estimates of the subsidies involved in urban land development are as high as 90 per cent (Jetha, 1992, p. 56).

Overall, therefore, fees are used more in urban areas than by rural governments, but are closer to taxes in their application than to service charges. Neither fees nor genuine user charges generate much revenue as a proportion of the cost of service provision, with one or two exceptions in large cities. Non-tax income in urban areas is often generated from the ownership of property and buildings, but again, this is rarely significant. Municipal enterprises are also not a major source of revenue. The problem of low recovery of costs through user charges and fees is not mitigated by provision through special-purpose bodies. Urban water supply, bus transportation, and land development authorities all typically run deficits. There is evidence that private provision can be an effective alternative for urban bus transportation and for solid waste management. In cases of public provision, better regulation and administration are typically required. This problem of raising revenue from user charges and fees is directly traceable to the lack of incentives of government decision makers, as well as indirectly through the low quality of provision. However, the fact that even small urban governments are sometimes able to successfully raise revenue from charges and fees suggests that expanding this method of raising revenues by rural governments, including through ownership of local assets such as forests, is feasible.

Transfers

The two important types of transfers are tax-revenue transfers and grants. There are strong differences between rural and urban local governments with regard to transfers: grants are particularly important for rural governments. The rationale for transferring tax revenues in whole or in part to a lower-level government may lie in lower collection costs at the higher level or in avoiding undue tax competition through better coordination, the higher-level government acting as an agent for the lower level. Formula-based tax-sharing transfers also have the advantage over grants in that they rise with tax revenues, while grants are typically not indexed for inflation. Considerations of fiscal capacity or redistribution do not require that the form of the transfer be through tax sharing: block grants are then appropriate. If the higher-level government wishes to encourage lower-level revenue mobilization, matching grants can be used. And if it wishes to encourage spending in particular categories, specific or categorical grants are appropriate.

A key issue in such transfers is the amount of discretion involved. Dillinger comments, 'Perhaps the most important measure developing countries can take is to reduce the unnecessary side effects of existing transfer programmes—to reduce the uncertainty and bargaining that now accompanies intergovernmental financial flows and remove incentives for strategic behavior'.[24] Until the recent constitutional amendments, transfers from state to local governments have been largely at the discretion of state governments, though mandated in general form by individual state legislative acts.

Transfers from the Central government to rural governments have increased since the 1970s, due to the increase in poverty alleviation schemes (particularly the JRY), as well as developmental projects coordinated with the planning process. These transfers are to the district-level rural governments, and passed down to the lowest level, but are typically controlled by the state governments, since the district level has served as an agency of the state government. The data are also not consistent on these types of transfers: they may or may not show up as rural local government revenue.

The story of transfers in the current set-up in Karnataka is essentially the story of schemes. While the district and block panchayats are essentially the agencies implementing the Central and state schemes devolved

---

[24] Dillinger (1994), p. 30. This point is also made in Rao (1992) and in other studies of transfers to local governments in India, as well as in the context of Central–state transfers in India by Kletzer and Singh (1997).

to them, the village panchyats do have some independent revenue sources assigned to them. However, of the total expenditures incurred by rural local governments, village panchayats spend just about 5 per cent. The remaining 95 per cent is incurred by the district and block panchayats, which, as already mentioned, are merely implementing agencies. They do not have flexibility and autonomy to decide, design, or drop the programmes. Their role is mainly to disburse salaries, distribute transfers to other agencies and, in some cases, spend on specified schemes. Thus, decentralization has not progressed in an essential dimension, that of local fiscal autonomy.

Of shared taxes at the rural level, duty on transfer of property, land revenue, motor vehicle taxes, and entertainment taxes are potentially important. Some of these have been touched on in the discussion of local taxes. There is no reason why entertainment taxes should not be purely local, based on the nature of the service provided (e.g. cinemas). The duty on transfer of property is an important component, on average, of state government revenues, and panchayats typically share a surcharge imposed by the state on this duty,[25] collected by the state along with the basic duty. In Kerala, the duty on transfer of property has been a major contributor to the revenues of its panchayats: this revenue source exceeded the contribution of any other single tax. Of the total revenue (pooled at the *taluk*, or intermediate level), 75 per cent was transferred to panchayats according to population, while the remainder was according to other criteria such as area, resources, and development needs. This kind of well-defined assignment and sharing of a tax is similar in many respects to the approach to Central–state transfers by the Central Finance Commission, but has been rare in state–local transfers. At the same time, it has the problem, present in India's Central–state tax sharing, of weak incentives for collection: distribution by origin would provide local governments with an incentive to aid in collection.

Revenue from agricultural land is, with two or three exceptions, only in the fiscal domain of state governments. State governments give widely varying shares of this levy to rural local governments at one or more of the three tiers. This share is as much as 100 per cent in some states, and is typically divided among local governments by formulae similar to the one described for Kerala's duty on property transfers. Thus, as emphasized by Rajaraman et al. (1996), incentives for collection are almost completely absent. This, together with institutional factors, has reduced the revenue

---

[25] Gujarat and Rajasthan allow panchayats to levy these surcharges, with a state-imposed cap on the rate (Rajaraman et al., 1996, p. 1077).

from this tax to negligible amounts, and there is a strong case for this tax to be made purely local.

Kerala has been the only state that shares the state-level motor vehicles tax with rural as well as urban local governments, though the amounts are relatively small, and payments were made irregularly (Government of Kerala, 1986). There is an economic case for all state governments to do this: maintenance of rural roads is an important panchayat responsibility everywhere, and the current system of funding maintenance, even in Kerala, is inadequate.[26] Similar arguments for sharing with rural governments can also be made for state taxes on liquor and diesel fuel, which are shared with urban local bodies (Rajaraman et al., 1996).

Grants are significant for rural local governments, in relative if not absolute terms. Their importance has been increasing due to poverty alleviation schemes. However, even when spending is nominally at the local level, effective control of the grant moneys has often been at the state government level. Thus, some of the reported differences among states may reflect accounting conventions rather than actual decentralization of funds.

Kerala provides a useful case study on state grants to rural local governments (Government of Kerala, 1986). In addition to statutory tax-sharing transfers, there were twenty-six types of non-statutory grants. Many of these were specific grants, for drainage, water supply, irrigation, road maintenance, and street lighting, for example. Some of these specific grants had matching provisions. Others had distributional motives. At least one had a perverse incentive structure: the establishment grant was paid to meet establishment costs in excess of a fixed percentage of 'normal income'. A large grant category was for of developmental activities, which included communication, irrigation, and construction. Some of these 'development' grants also had matching provisions, others did not: all were part of the Indian five-year planning exercise, and this led to a very lumpy payment of grants, with Rs 100 million being disbursed in 1980–1, and less than Rs 40 million in total over the next four years.

In another example, the panchayats in the Kumaun hills region of Uttar Pradesh (now in Uttaranchal) (Shah, 1990) did not receive any tax-revenue share from the state in 1979–80. On the other hand, as in the case of Kerala (and other states), grants were received for development purposes as part of the planning process. These were matching grants for specific projects proposed by panchayat officials, with funds coming from the intermediate level (block or area councils) or the state government

---

[26] Recall the discussion of this issue under expenditure responsibilities.

development department. The potential grants at the district level were large, exceeding tax revenues. But less than 20 per cent of the allotment had been utilized due to uncertainty about the actual level of funds that would be available to an individual panchayat. Later data from the same state (Saharanpur district, 1992–3, from Oomen, 1995, Appendix B) show panchayats receiving some share of land revenue, but this and all other panchayat revenues are dwarfed by JRY grants.

Various case studies from Himachal Pradesh, Karnataka, and Maharashtra, summarized in Oomen (1995), bear out the large and increasing role played by grants relative to other rural local revenue sources. A variety of grant schemes is noted in these studies, similar to the case of Kerala, and most grants seem to be specific. The case studies also suggest the perverse incentive effects of these grants on revenue effort by local governments. Exceptions are states such as West Bengal, which has a system of incentive grants tied to the collection of state taxes and mobilization of small savings. However, even in West Bengal, JRY grants appeared as the main source of revenue at the highest rural local level, the district (Oomen, 1995, Appendix C), and are perceived as overwhelming state and local incentives (Oomen, p. 11). These studies suggest that improving tax effort, and reforming the system of tax sharing and user charges at the rural local level will require reforming the system of grants to local bodies.

Again, data on transfers to urban governments is more plentiful (Bhagwan, 1983; Jetha, 1992; Naresh, 1998). Assigned or shared taxes were a very small percentage of revenue, with grants providing somewhat more. Shared or assigned taxes for urban governments included duty on transfer of property, motor vehicle taxes, and entertainment taxes. Grants were mostly specific or categorical. Cities such as Trivandrum and Chennai relied more on shared taxes, while Ahmedabad received more grants: these differences were reflections of differing statewide systems for transfers to urban local bodies. In Delhi, after 1970, the only important transfer was statutory educational grants.

Rao (1992) provides a detailed analysis of transfers to urban governments in five states: Gujarat, Kerala, Maharashtra, Tamil Nadu, and West Bengal. Gujarat and Kerala's transfers were relatively systematic, with Gujarat relying more on grants and Kerala on tax sharing. Almost all grants in Gujarat were specific, with nineteen grant categories in the mid-1980s. For corporations—of which Ahmedabad is the largest in the sample—only five categories were used, and the primary education grant constituted almost 74 per cent of transfers. Corporations also received money from an education cess and from entertainment taxes, the latter earmarked for capital expenditures. The main transfers to municipalities were for primary education (40 per cent), capital expenditures from entertainment tax revenue (25 per cent), and dearness allowance[27] (16 per cent), with small percentages from the numerous other specific grants for various health and sanitation expenditures (Jetha, 1992, Table 5.1).

Data for Kerala's transfers to urban local bodies reveal a pattern somewhat similar to that of transfers to its panchayats, but with greater autonomy. The main taxes were on entertainment (cinemas), professions, motor vehicles, and transfers of property. The first two of these were assigned to urban local bodies, while the latter two were shared in different ways. Urban governments were permitted to levy a surcharge on the state duty on property transfers, while the share of vehicle tax revenue was distributed as a specific grant for road maintenance. Tax sharing was also the main transfer vehicle in Tamil Nadu, with entertainment and property transfer taxes being the main sources. Chennai also received a share of receipts from a sales tax surcharge, based on collections within the city limits. Specific grants were relatively minor after the 1990 assumption of primary education financing by the state government. For Maharashtra, 94 per cent of transfers in 1990 were specific grants, including education (29 per cent), dearness allowance (21 per cent), and development grants to backward regions (15 per cent). Several grants, such as those to assist in debt servicing, were highly discretionary in nature. The West Bengal transfer system shared some features with the other states: dearness allowance grants were significant (33 per cent of transfers), followed by education grants (13 per cent). Shared tax revenue was about equal to that of grants, with the entry tax and entertainment tax providing almost all urban revenue from shared taxes.

Other case studies round out the above picture. In Ludhiana and Patiala, in Punjab, general and specific grants from the state government made up about 10 per cent of municipal income (Sachdeva, 1991). Sachdeva notes their inadequate levels, but also points out several cases of lack of full utilization (p. 168) because of two barriers. First, expenditures had to be sanctioned by the state government's local government department. Second, the work, in many cases, had to be carried out by a state government department. In the Orissa sample, grants and shared taxes made up about 30 per cent of revenue in 1975–6 (Dash, 1988, p. 115), most of this being grants. The largest category (51.8 per cent of transfers) was grants given to

---

[27] 'Dearness allowance' is a cost-of-living-based component of income that is adjusted to compensate for inflation, without the necessity of altering the base salary structure.

meet a part of the dearness allowance of local government employees. Still other grants covered part of the base salaries of local government employees. There was an absence of transparency and certainty in such grants, leading Dash to note, 'Thus the system of grants-in-aid is a political weapon in the hands of the State Government to control the working of urban local bodies and to extend patronage ...' (p. 119). Problems of lack of utilization of funds are also described for this sample.[28]

The situation for both rural and urban local governments is one where transfers are often of limited value not just because of their small size, but more significantly because of their discretionary nature, leading to costly uncertainty and bargaining. This effect is compounded by the incomplete nature of the transfers: strings being attached not only to categories of expenditure, but also to specific details of implementation. One can argue such controls were necessary because of the lack of internal controls and expertise, and this argument will be considered later. Furthermore, grants for specific categories such as marginal personnel expenses have obvious perverse incentive effects on expenditure decisions. Distribution formulae used by states, while trying to achieve some equalization of resources for different local bodies, also tend to adversely affect incentives for collection. Finally, many transfers are discretionary, without clear economic rationales.

A simpler, more transparent system of transfers may be desirable and feasible, with more tax sharing, and the use of fewer types of grants, with block grants to achieve equity. These changes may be aided by the new legislation that mandates state finance commissions. While these will still be subject to the discretion of state governments, the experience at the Centre and in states such as Kerala and Karnataka suggests that such commissions do, over time establish rules, conventions, and precedents, and achieve degrees of certainty and transparency that might not obtain otherwise.[29] Mishra (1998) notes some longstanding positive features of grant systems in states such as Gujarat, Kerala, and Madhya Pradesh, in particular the tying of grants to municipal fiscal effort. It is not clear how effective these have been in practice, but they provide examples on which to build the future design of transfers.

---

[28] A similar pattern of inefficiency in state grants to municipalities in Orissa is described by Mishra (1998).

[29] This is no guarantee of optimality: grants with perverse incentives persisted in Kerala despite the existence of its Panchayat Finance Commission. A further complication, which has also existed at the Centre–state level, is that the parallel set of discretionary transfers made for Central sector and Centrally sponsored schemes will continue.

Borrowing

The official literature on Indian government finance often distinguishes between 'developmental' and 'non-developmental' or between 'plan' and 'non-plan' activities or expenditures. The former dichotomy is conceptual, and the latter, in principle, reflects the institutional implementation of the former. However, distinctions made in this way obscure the more fundamental distinction between capital and current expenditures. Investment expenditures whose benefits will accrue in the future are natural candidates for financing through borrowing, and, to the extent that many local services require infrastructure (local roads, street lights, parks), borrowing is potentially important for local governments. The efficiency argument for tax collection to be performed by higher levels of government applies for borrowing as well, but the resulting incentive problems can be severe. We examine these issues in the following discussion. Of course, borrowing is in a different category than the other three revenue sources considered, since it creates future expenditure (repayment) obligations.

Local government borrowing in India has been ad hoc and limited in nature. While rural local governments have not been major borrowers, urban governments have increasingly gone into debt. Statewise data on stocks of municipal debt (N.R. Rao, 1986) indicate differences across states in the growth of such borrowing. Close to 90 per cent of the debt was that of corporations (the urban governments of the larger cities), and of port trusts, the latter having large, specialized infrastructure requirements. Much of the growth in borrowing came via nationalized banks or other government-owned financial institutions. Datta (1992) notes the weak distinction between loans made by state governments as part of the planning process, and institutional financing of local projects, also routed through the states.

Case studies of rural government borrowing come from Kerala and West Bengal, two states that have been most willing to decentralize. The Kerala Panchayat Finance Commission report noted the practice of rural local governments incurring loans from the state's rural development board (RDB) for creating remunerative assets. These projects, however, had to be carried out by the RDB itself. Examples of such projects were rural water supply schemes, for which, until 1984, 50 per cent of the capital cost came from the government-owned Life Insurance Corporation of India as loans to the RDB, and 50 per cent from the state government. Panchayats were charged 25 per cent of the capital cost—that is this was a forced loan. In 1987, ownership of such projects was transferred to a specialized state-level water agency, and the loan liability was also removed. This example indicates the institutional complexities of rural local government 'loans'. However, annual loans directly from the state government to panchayats were a tiny fraction of the aggregate panchayat income in the early 1980s in Kerala.

In West Bengal, we consider implementation of the National Rural Employment Programme (NREP), designed by the Central government to employ the rural poor in creating productive community assets that would further benefit the poor and strengthen rural infrastructure in general.[30] Examples included rural roads, water supply schemes, minor irrigation and flood control, forestry projects, schools, houses, and panchayat offices. Funding for projects was to come from loans from nationalized banks, and from Central government transfers. Implementation in West Bengal was significantly more decentralized than in other states. Plans started with proposals submitted by the gram panchayats to the block-level councils, which in turn made consolidated proposals to the district councils. Execution, monitoring, and maintenance were also largely panchayat responsibilities in West Bengal, much more so than the national average (Lieten, 1992). While the problem of lack of certainty in budgets was also present in this case (leading as usual to sporadic or low utilization of funds), local control was clearer than in previous examples. However, even in West Bengal, rural local governments did not have access to borrowed funds in the same way that large urban governments did. Even district councils, representing populations as large as big cities, did not have the powers or legislative authority available to city corporations.

Rural government borrowing has otherwise been very limited. Oomen (1995, p.6) notes that Uttar Pradesh and Bihar now have panchayat finance corporations that make investment loans to panchayats. Their capital is contributed by rural governments, the state government, and public finance institutions. However, data in Oomen (Tables 1A, 1B) indicate very small percentages (under 1.5 per cent) of revenue from loans for panchayats in Himachal Pradesh, Orissa, and Uttar Pradesh, and 3.5 per cent of revenue for the middle tier in Gujarat, though in some states loans may be hidden in the 'Other' category.

Borrowing is more significant for urban governments. We have noted that city corporations have been the major source of urban local government borrowing (aside from port trusts). For Delhi, in 1978–9, the MCD borrowed almost 20 per cent of its current revenue. A large part of this

---

[30] Subsequently, this was consolidated along with other similar programmes into the Swarnajayanti Grameina Rozgar Yojana (SGRY).

was Central government loans for slum improvement schemes. In the early 1970s borrowing was only 5 to 7 per cent of revenue. However, the MCD began defaulting on loan payments almost every year from 1966–7. This is not surprising, given that in many years the MCD ran deficits on both its current and its capital account. In the 1980s, Ahmedabad, Chennai, and Trivandrum often ran deficits on both current and capital accounts, despite postponing debt service (Jetha, 1992, Table 2.5). Sources of capital finance were varied in these three cities. Grants were a minor source for Ahmedabad, which received substantial loans from the state government, the World Bank, and the Housing and Urban Development Corporation (HUDCO), as well as public borrowing. Chennai and Trivandrum relied more on grants, though the Kerala Urban Development Finance Corporation (KUDFC) was an important borrowing source for Trivandrum. To some extent, these cities were representative of patterns in their respective states, though Tamil Nadu's other municipal bodies relied more on borrowing than did Chennai.[31]

There is similar evidence on borrowing for smaller towns and cities. In Ludhiana (Sachdeva, 1991, Table 8.6) the corporation's repayment of loans were as high as 11.1 per cent of expenditure in 1983–4, but fell to 2.2 per cent or less in the subsequent three years. However, this reflected non-payment: the corporation's finances were in a state of virtual bankruptcy by 1988, with large bills and loans outstanding. At the same time, loans from the state government were made, but not used in a timely manner. Housing, water supply, and sewerage projects for even the bigger cities in Punjab were being handled by bodies such as the housing development board and the water supply and sewerage board created by the state government. These agencies borrowed from the Life Insurance Corporation (LIC), HUDCO, and the World Bank's International Development Authority, and did implement some significant projects. However, while municipal financial contributions were required, the implementation and the recovery of costs from beneficiaries were subject to inefficiencies associated with a lack of clear assignment of responsibilities.

Orissa provides a similar case. Water and housing projects were sometimes funded by state government borrowing from the LIC and HUDCO, respectively. Urban local bodies borrowed for these projects, as well as to finance sanitation projects, commercial infrastructure, street lighting, and even arrears of employee dearness allowance. Their loans came from the state government as well as the LIC. In the mid-1970s, loans to urban local bodies in Orissa were quite small relative to per capita current revenue.

---

[31] These statements are based on various tables in the Appendix to Jetha (1992).

Water supply projects were an important case of loan financing, and the state government required two-thirds of their costs to be met by local loans, arranged by the state, with one-third in grants. However, execution of the projects was the responsibility of the state public health department. Dash (1988) describes problems of implementation in this situation, with overdue and abandoned projects (p. 137) that cost the local government, but generated no benefits or revenue. The state government typically adjusted its grants to localities downward by the amount due on the loans. Local body chairmen in some cases expressed the view that these projects were forced upon them. As in Punjab, borrowed funds were not utilized quickly, even though interest was being charged. Thus, while urban local borrowing was not large, neither was it efficient.

These problems with local borrowing are especially noteworthy given the stringent statutory restrictions on local governments in India. These included restrictions on rates, amounts, aggregate borrowing, and length of terms. Individual loans require approval of the state and or the Central government, as well as consultation with and approval of the Reserve Bank of India (RBI). Open market borrowings are also subject to higher-level government and RBI supervision and approval (Datta, 1984, pp. 77-8). Clearly, no system of monitoring and regulation is perfect, and credit markets are particularly vulnerable, but the evidence suggests a misallocation of effort in some of this regulation in India, resulting in a misallocation (not enough in some cases, in the wrong place in others) of capital for local infrastructure. The situation has already begun to change to some extent, with Ahmedabad leading the way. The city's corporation was able to obtain a respectable credit rating, and issue bonds in the market, instead of relying on the old system (Jha, 1998).

Assessment

Expanded expenditure responsibilities for local government require additional revenue. Rural local governments rely heavily on transfers from state governments for revenue. These transfers are often uncertain and restricted in ways that make their effective use difficult. For the lowest rural tier, taxes are a significant fraction of revenue. While even doubling revenue from this source would still imply low per capita levels, assigning better tax instruments (Rajaraman et al., 1996) can aid in more efficient resource use at the local level (for example, through benefit taxes such as market fees), and establishing a more effective tax administration can aid in building institutional capacity. In some states, there are sufficient tax instruments already assigned by statutes. The problems are in (i) exercising statutory authority,[32] (ii) administering the tax, and (iii) establishing a clear tax assignment. The first problem arises because of inefficiencies in provision, which may need prior improvement by other means. This will also set the stage for more effective use of fees and user charges. These second problem is of administering the tax and this is acute not only because of lack of local capacity but also due to the inability to enforce the tax on powerful groups. The third problem arises because the more significant sources of tax revenue are assigned to state governments. Hence clearer rules for tax-sharing are essential, including options such as complete assignment of taxes like land revenue to the local level.[33]

The new state-level finance commissions, modelled on the Central Finance Commission and previous state-level commissions, will be crucial in achieving clarity, transparency, and certainty with respect to tax-sharing and grants to local governments. This will be beneficial in reducing the costs of bargaining and uncertainty, even if the amount of transfers does not increase. A removal of perverse incentives in such transfers will also help: data on administrative expenditures by local governments suggests that local governments are far from efficient under current incentives. Since the state finance commissions will take time to become operational and effective, the Central Finance Commission, in its last report, had allocated funds for local governments in its recommendations on transfers from the Centre to the states (Finance Commission, 1994).

Borrowing for capital expenditures by rural local governments would be the last piece to fall into place, since it is predicated on a development of institutional capacity, as well as other financial reforms. Borrowing is unlikely to ever be significant at the lowest tier, because of its small size, but there is no reason why the upper two tiers of rural government, now given a more independent status, should not eventually follow in the footsteps of municipalities in borrowing. Organizations such as Kerala's RDB or district rural development agencies in other states are a step in the direction of more transparent channeling of capital for rural infrastructure, but are far from market-driven. The criteria for making loans and for ensuring repayment are not efficient without some market discipline.

---

[32] The following quote from Shah (1990, pp. 137–8), on the nexus of responsibilities, revenues, and institutions, is apt: '... the Gaon Panchayats ... have been vested with considerable powers to raise their revenues. In addition to ... duties like sanitation, road repairing, street lighting, etc. the panchayats have also the responsibility of developing the socio-economic life of the people ... [P]anchayats, though empowered to levy taxes, have been ... slack in collecting them ... [A]rrears could be realized as arrears of land revenues. But no panchayat dares to take such repressive steps ... because it is bound to generate bitterness among the people against the panchayat personnel.'

[33] See also the excellent discussion in Rajaraman (1999).

The issue of the state government's role as a guarantor of such loans, which creates a moral hazard problem for local borrowing, must also be addressed. The issues for urban local government revenue are similar in nature, but urban bodies have greater abilities to tax, and greater scope for charging for services. The importance of taxes for revenue of urban bodies suggests that the pay-off from improving the take from this source will be relatively high. The property tax is less distortionary than octroi, the other main source of urban tax revenue, and improving its enforcement and collection is a priority. As in the case of rural governments, improving efficiency of provision may be a necessary precondition to more effective raising of tax revenue and greater reliance on user charges and fees.

Jetha (1992) and other studies emphasize the critical state of India's urban infrastructure, reflecting both a lack and ineffective use of capital funds. For urban local governments, improving access to capital, through borrowing from the private capital market, can follow more easily if improvements in raising revenue from taxes and fees come first, making repayment more feasible. Reliance on allocation of capital through a political process will then be lessened.

INSTITUTIONS AND INCENTIVES

In this section, we return to the major theme of the chapter that the key issues in local government reform are with respect to the design of appropriate incentives for government decision makers. We begin with some basic description. Table 13.2 gives a state-wise summary of the 'span of control' of rural local governments in India. The population per village government is extremely small, with the median across the state averages being only 2700. There is considerable variation among the states, but the only two obvious outliers are Kerala and West Bengal. These are also the most densely populated states, but the difference is more a reflection of a different institutional arrangement in these states. The small jurisdiction of village governments raises questions of economic efficiency. Populations per block council are considerably larger, with a median of 114,000 across these sixteen states. The block level is important in approximating the constituencies of the lower houses of the state legislatures, known as legislative assemblies. Populations per district council, the highest rural level, are quite large, with a median of close to 1.5 million across the states. The district is approximately the size of the constituency of the member of the Lok Sabha, the lower house of the national parliament.

TABLE 13. 2
Span of Control of Rural Local Governments'

	Population per village government	Population per block council	Population per district council
Andhra Pradesh	2500	45,000	2,210,000
Assam	8000	102,000	463,000
Bihar	6400	127,000	1,443,000
Gujarat	2000	149,000	1,424,000
Haryana	2100	114,000	776,000
Himachal Pradesh	1800	68,000	393,000
Karnataka	5500	NA	1,554,000
Kerala	21,600	141,000	1,530,000
Madhya Pradesh	1600	111,000	1,130,000
Maharashtra	1800	164,000	1,669,000
Orissa	5200	87,000	914,000
Punjab	1200	105,000	1,021,000
Rajasthan	3700	143,000	1,095,000
Tamil Nadu	2900	95,000	1,672,000
Uttar Pradesh	1500	124,000	1,770,000
West Bengal	14,800	145,000	3,086,000
Median population per government	2700	114,000	1,433,500

Notes: Population per village government is rounded to the nearest hundred, for the other two levels to the nearest thousand.
Source: Compiled from Mathew (1994).

The block and district levels—particularly the latter—have been important components of the Central administrative apparatus, even prior to independence. Considerable administrative discretion has rested with appointed officials, usually of the Indian Administrative Service (IAS), at the block and district levels. Although IAS members are assigned to states, they are all part of an all-India bureaucratic structure, and can thus be assumed to be responsive to Central as well as state-level political imperatives. These two levels have also been important in conceptualizing the implementation of India's Central plans, and strengthening block-level implementation has been a significant part of attempts to decentralize the planning process.

Since the lowest level is so small in population size, the intermediate level may be more important for rural local government reform than has been emphasized in previous discussions, both to internalize externalities, and to take advantage of economies of scale and scope. These arguments extend to the highest level, the district, but are counterbalanced by its size, in absolute terms (affecting the span of control), as well as relative to the state level (affecting the ability of state governments to maintain hard budget constraints for the lower level). The highest level of rural local government might not even be characterized as 'local' in this respect: basic public services will typically have smaller constituencies.[34] The issue of the interaction between Central and state bureaucrats and elected local government officials has been, and will continue to be vital.

Until the recent legislative changes, the ability to exercise this suffrage was very limited: at any given time since independence, 40–50 per cent of local government bodies in India had been under state supersession (Dillinger, 1994). Also, there was previously a structural limitation on this exercise, since in most states only the lowest level of rural local government had directly elected local government officials. Only Karnataka and Tamil Nadu had direct local elections above the village level—though in Tamil Nadu, rural local elections were not held for a stretch of fifteen years. States such as Madhya Pradesh and Uttar Pradesh did not even have indirect elections at the higher two levels of rural local government, those bodies being nominated by state governments. Several states had only one or two tiers of rural local government, even though both block and district are part of the nationwide administrative structure.

There is no tier system for urban governments unlike for rural governments. Government types ranged from corporations (which do have smaller units such as wards within them) to municipalities, and then town and notified area committees. Corporations have more autonomy and wider responsibilities than municipalities, with town and notified area committees being most restricted. A major difference between notified or town area committees on the one hand, and municipalities and corporations on the other, is that the former category had not involved any elected governing body: the committees were appointed by state governments. However, to the extent that elected municipalities and corporations have been superseded, the distinction becomes less important. Even in cases where municipalities and corporations had functioning elected governing bodies, state governments typically retained considerable discretion and bureaucratic control over even the largest urban local governments, for example through municipal commissioners (who would typically be IAS members).

---

[34] Here one is implicitly appealing to Olson's principle of fiscal equivalence: see Olson (1986).

Institutional Reform

Key changes brought about by the 73rd and 74th amendments included the reduction of state government discretion concerning elections to rural local government bodies. Under the new laws, direct elections to panchayats must be held every five years. Elections to constitute new bodies must be completed before the term expires. If a panchayat is dissolved prematurely, elections must be compulsorily held within six months, the new body to serve out the remainder of the five-year term. With regard to urban local governments, there is a similar strengthening of the electoral requirements, preventing lengthy supersessions of local powers by the state government, and replacing appointed posts with elected ones.

Various aspects of the elections are also specified. Chairpersons at the intermediate and district levels are to be elected by the panchayat membership, while either direct or indirect elections of chairpersons are permitted at the village level. State-level election commissions are to be created to supervise and manage the electoral processes. At the intermediate and district levels, chairpersons of bodies one level below can be made members, as can MPs (members of parliament), and MLAs (members of legislative assemblies). The act provides for one additional potential avenue of representation and accountability of local government. Each village or group of villages will have a gram sabha, a body comprising all registered voters in the area. The purpose of these gram sabhas is to provide a measure of direct democracy, but their actual role seems likely to remain limited, given their lack of authority or control.

The 74th Amendment provides a parallel set of reforms for urban and transitional areas. For areas in transition from rural to urban, nagar panchayats are to be constituted, and, for most provisions of the Act, be treated equally with municipalities. The composition of municipalities remains under the guidelines of the states, subject to population categories outlined in the amendment. Within larger municipalities, wards and zones become new tiers of urban government with their own committees. As is the case for rural local governments, a key feature is the strengthening of local election procedures, with members at the ward and municipal level being chosen by direct elections. The zonal committees are more of an intermediate level, the chairpersons of the ward committees in the zone.

'Voice' and Accountability

The main thrust of the institutional reforms in Indian local government is the strengthening of 'voice' as a mechanism for promoting accountability. To some extent, this has been done at the expense of 'hierarchy', which had been the main or only mechanism for Indian local government until the recent reforms. If 'voice' provides appropriate incentives to elected officials, and they have the flexibility to act, they will seek to influence non-elected personnel to act in constituents' interests also. Two fundamental departures from this model in the Indian local government context have been the lack of flexibility in designing incentives within local organizations, and the lack of direct electoral incentives for chief decision makers at the local government level. Both these departures reflect the intrusion of higher-level governments into the details of local action. Of course political influence may not be benign. The question is to whom is the elected official responsive. We shall return to this point, which was central to the post-independence constitutional debates that resulted in a weak role for local governments.

In general, the lack of regular, direct local government elections in India, either because of the absence of legislative provisions, or because of the 'overawing' (Riker, 1975) of local elective institutions by state governments, has meant that state or Central non-elected officials have often been key local government decision makers. In such a situation, 'voice' can only work indirectly: rather than being able to vote out a city government with which they are unhappy, constituents have to register their dissatisfaction about a non-elected agent of the state government who is running the city. They complain to the lowest-level elected official available, their MLA, who then pressures the bureaucrat to be responsive to constituents. Such a process loses transparency and certainty, as compared to direct, open elections.

A further problem is that 'voice' is applied at the higher level of government. The state-level politician represents a local constituency, but not just on local matters: he/she will also participate in state-level policy making. This means that voters are not permitted to discriminate as finely as they can when they can separately vote for local and for state-level elected officials, possibly weakening the responsiveness of government overall. This effect is compounded if the local government is smaller than the smallest state government constituency.[35] This is certainly true in India, where legislative constituencies in state government (the constituencies of MLAs) correspond very roughly with the block or other intermediate level of rural local government. But this is much larger than the smallest rural or urban local governments, so constituencies of MLAs do not coincide with single local jurisdictions, and incentives through 'voice' are weakened.

Regular direct elections at the local level, therefore, have the potential to increase the accountability of local government in a fairly obvious and direct way, by providing more direct and refined incentives to please constituents. While state governments may continue to try and postpone local elections when it suits them, they will no longer have the law on their side. The counter argument is that interest groups or powerful individuals will instead have more influence at the local level. However, there is no reason for the presumption that this problem is worse at the local than at the state level. We discuss this below.

'Hierarchy' and Accountability

'Hierarchy', on the other hand, is a less direct mechanism for accountability. In smaller countries, the national government lies directly above local governments. In India, the state governments are the main influence on local governments. However, as already noted, the dual role played by the Central bureaucracy (the IAS, as well as the Indian Police Service), with their state cadres but also a centralized ethos, complicates matters. The Central government's planning process and the vertical fiscal imbalance between the Centre and the states further complicates matters.

Putting aside these institutional complications, we can say that, in practice, the state government in India has been the main body for monitoring local government performance, i.e. 'hierarchy' has been the main mechanism for accountability. This is for two reasons: expertise has been confined to the state government, and it is where true ownership or control of resources has been allocated by law (the assignment of revenue). The second reason in turn is traceable to concerns about elite domination of elected rural local bodies. These concerns have existed since independence, with examples being commonly observed in academic studies (Crook and Manor, 1994, for Karnataka) and journalistic accounts (Naipaul, 1975, for Gujarat).

Yet, examples of misuse of funds through incompetence, malfeasance, or both arc common. It is possible that focusing on selected examples gives a misleading, gloomy picture, but one cannot excuse failures to follow basic accounting procedures, or outright misappropriation. 'Hierarchy' has not been very effective in supporting accountability. Several explanations are possible. Two linked explanations, related to the implementation of administrative and higher-level government control, can be adduced. First, the level of auditing, both quantitatively and qualitatively, has been inadequate. This seems to be borne out by the case studies as well as the

---

[35] A nice formalization of related ideas is in Seabright (1996), which also allows for uncertainty in outcomes that affects the ability of voters to discriminate. In that model, there is a trade-off, since centralization may provide coordination benefits.

surveys by Datta (1984) and Rao (1986), and applies not just to the identification of irregularities, but also to the enforcement of minimum accounting standards.

Second, more effort seems to have been devoted to other kinds of monitoring rather than to auditing or performance monitoring. We can broadly distinguish between input and output monitoring. There is no general case for preferring one type to the other in the provision of incentives, but local government in India has been marked by excessive control of inputs and process, to the detriment of attention to performance and outcomes.[36] Detailed approval is required from higher-level governments for relatively small projects or expenditures, sometimes as part of a top–down national and state planning exercise in which local governments have little input.[37] At the same time, performance could often be neglected, with overdue and abandoned projects being commonly cited. It is useful to characterize this situation as an imbalance in the types of monitoring used. In other words, the implementation of accountability through 'hierarchy' has been flawed.

More broadly, however, both explanations can be traced to the weakness of the accountability of state governments for local government performance, as discussed earlier. 'Hierarchy' as a mechanism for accountability just pushes a greater burden on to 'voice' at a higher government level. This conceptual point does not seem to have been explicitly recognized in the evolving literature on decentralization.[38] Another important conceptual point that emerges is that 'hierarchy' as an accountability mechanism has an inherent tendency to undermine assignments. This is the fundamental problem of the higher-level government in a federal system overawing lower-level governments. Figure 13.2 illustrates how the flow of funds to rural local governments remains largely controlled by agents of higher-level governments, thereby undermining authority of local governments and weakening accountability at both levels. A similar picture can be drawn for urban local governments.

---

[36] The choice between input and output monitoring is a complicated one, since certain means may be undesirable in themselves, if they involve corruption or illegality, even though the ends are thus achieved. Mookherjee (1997) analyses these and other issues in a model of tax administration. See also the references in that piece.

[37] A useful description of monitoring and auditing procedures for panchayats in Tamil Nadu may be found in Bhargava and Venkatakrishnan (1998). They also note some of the problems with implementation of rules, and suggest institutional improvements.

[38] See, for example, World Bank (1997), Litvack et al. (1998), and Litvack and Seddon (1999). Such analyses tend to appeal to lack of institutional 'capacity', rather than the fundamental problems with 'hierarchy' as an accountability mechanism. We return to this issue later in this section.

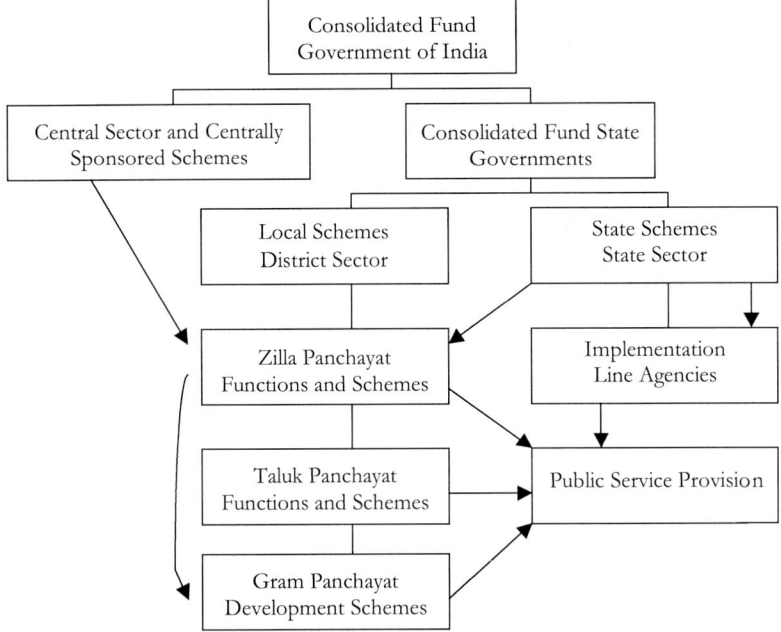

Figure 13.2: Flow of Funds to Rural Local Governments

Information and Transparency

In our framework, we emphasized that accountability is built on transparency, which refers to the public availability of information that allows performance and processes[39] to be measured and evaluated. Information may be self-disclosed, or obtained by monitoring and investigation. Often, though, disclosure of information must be a legal requirement, since the incentive to disclose problems will not exist, and gathering information may be impossible or very costly without legal backing.

Bajaj and Sharma (1995) note the problems that can arise, in terms of the information required to assess elected officials:

When village pradhans were entrusted JRY funds for construction of community assets, the village community at large did not have knowledge about the total funds received and the annual expenditure incurred on various projects. The pradhan and the village panchayat officer, who jointly operated the panchayat account, kept the details a closely guarded secret (p. M-79).

---

[39] Thus transparency helps act as a check on corruption. New technologies permit more transparency at all levels of government. See, for example, Halan (2000).

They go on to describe the resolution of the monitoring problem in their example:

[The higher level] government made it mandatory for information to be posted publicly about the works executed, estimated and actual expenditure and savings if any. The displaying of relevant information on bulletin boards in public places and community halls resulted in community pressure on pradhans to account for public funds, and had the effect of many unfinished projects being rapidly completed.

While all cases may not admit such easy fixes, there is no reason why complete information on a broad range of government activities should not be available to all citizens.

Emphasizing 'voice' as an accountability mechanism highlights the importance of transparency in supporting accountability. On the other hand, the previous emphasis in India on 'hierarchy' as the primary accountability mechanism also led to an inadequate emphasis on transparency.[40] In fact, decision makers at higher levels of government have no general incentive to impose transparency on the lower level when 'hierarchy' is the primary mechanism. On the other hand, a shift to 'voice' at the lower level gives the higher level some incentive to impose transparency at the lower level, or at least not to oppose it, though they may not want it for themselves. The central point to note in this discussion is that a positive feedback exists from accountability mechanisms to transparency, if 'voice' is given an appropriate role to play.

Even with a legal framework that supports transparency, or, more generally, the need to be able to monitor performance, there are issues of implementation. In the case of 'voice', the beneficiaries, the monitors, and the implementers of (electoral) rewards and punishments are all citizens. Having these tasks performed by the same individuals avoids the need to provide incentives to delegated monitors with different preferences. However, there are diseconomies associated with large numbers of principals and with lack of specialization. These factors create a role for more specialized monitoring and regulation, through NGOs acting as watchdog groups, the media, and—where poor performance is connected to illegality—the police and the judiciary.

Exit, and Checks and Balances

Exit and checks and balances are additional accountability mechanisms. 'Exit' in one sense has been of minimal importance in India. Mobility is

---

[40] At a more basic level, the traditional perspective of government shown on the left-hand side of Figure 13.1 gave transparency no conceptual role at all.

low, and is driven by factors that dominate the quality of provision of local public goods. Villagers migrate to cities not because they are following Tiebout-type (1956) logic, seeking the optimal combination of public goods among those offered by competing local governments, but because they are looking for remunerative work. In fact, living in urban slums is a cost that has to be borne by such migrants.

In addition to competition among governments, 'exit' can refer to competition between private and public provision. Some goods are only quasi-public in nature, involving large fixed costs of provision that create a situation close to non-rivalry, but with excludability possible. Other goods are simply provided by the government for distributional reasons, rather than because of any market failure. If private provision is an option, people may exit the public system. Individually, higher-income urban residents in India sink backyard wells and install generators for electricity. Collectively, neighbourhood groups arrange for private garbage disposal services. Unfortunately, such instances do not really represent a major use of 'exit', and they have neither created much competition, nor enhanced accountability.

For 'exit' to work as an accountability mechanism in this way, entire constituencies have to be able to switch to private provision. Waste disposal and transportation are two examples where this is not difficult to achieve, though here again, transparency is important, and private provision is not a panacea. Transparency in bidding and allocation of private contracts is obviously required to prevent corruption. Careful contract design is required to avoid inappropriate incentives, such as occurred with disregard for driving safety among competing private bus operators in Delhi. At the same time, explicit private provision is attractive since inefficient[41] de facto privatization is occurring in any case. Private provision therefore has a role independent of its being an avenue of 'exit'. In this case, 'voice' and 'hierarchy' remain as the primary mechanisms for accountability.

We have discussed the role of the judiciary in the context of assignment of expenditure and revenue authority to local governments. We argued that the power to enforce was an important complement to traditional fiscal assignments, one that had not received enough attention of late. The idea of 'checks and balances' as an accountability mechanism raises a different role for the judiciary. The basic concept of checks and balances,

---

[41] The inefficiencies include both the failure to capture scale economies, and negative externalities. Household-level water and electric power production exhibit both these problems.

or separation of powers, was clearly articulated over two hundred years ago by James Madison (see Persson et al., 1997). In India, the lack of separation of powers between the legislative and executive branches has made the role of the judiciary in providing checks and balances even more important. This role has been exercised differently at different times in independent India, though more prominently only recently.

While there is no easy answer to the question of the optimal structure of checks and balances,[42] federalism raises a further set of issues. Ideally, one would postulate a local judiciary that is both strong enough to enforce the proper authority of the newly strengthened legislative branch of local government, and to place limits on improper exercise of local government powers. Perhaps the state governments are rightly cautious about devolving law and order machinery to the local level, given the well-known vertical and horizontal divisions in India's society. However, there is clearly also a measure of self-interest in the reluctance displayed by state governments: bureaucrats and politicians, for example, seem much less satisfied with judicial activism than are ordinary citizens. A major problem in the past has been lack of resources for the judicial system, not just at the local level. This has been worsened by inefficient procedures for litigation, trial, and judgment (see Mookherjee, 1993). Therefore, an effective local judiciary and legal system may be a long way off. Our framework, however, helps to focus and clarify the conceptual issues with respect to the legal system at the local level.

Responsiveness

A major concern with respect to 'voice' is that the accountability created is not of the appropriate kind. Responsiveness may be still be limited, or may not have positive outcomes. For example, Dash (1988, p. 223) gives examples of the Puri Municipal Council in Orissa providing reductions in, or exemptions from octroi taxes to specific commercial products, benefiting local interest groups. Local governments are reluctant to impose taxes, being responsive to their constituents in this respect. Aziz (1998) expresses similar worries for Karnataka panchayats even after the local government reform (though in some respects, the 1993 Karnataka act represented a retreat from earlier reform). Sachdeva (1991, Chapter 10) provides another argument for limited responsiveness, stating that, counter to our discussion of 'voice' and accountability, local politics can simply reflect state-level rather than local issues, weakening the incentives for local responsiveness.

---

[42] Persson et al. (1997) have recently begun the task of formalizing the analysis of the problem in the context of legislative and executive separation of powers.

In analysing these issues, it is important to separate two distinct problems. First, 'voice' may be an imperfect accountability mechanism at any level of government. One part of this is that interest groups can have a negative influence in any democratic system. The solution is to design institutions that minimize the negative consequences of interest group operations, or to level the playing field. For example, NGOs also are interest groups: they are viewed as positive influences because they typically represent those whose 'voice' is otherwise unheard. Supporting such NGOs can push responsiveness in a positive direction. Another part of this is that voters may rationally choose not to tax themselves. This aspect is actually one that has not been adequately understood by observers of Indian local government. The solution is not to move away from 'voice', but to make it work better. Voters who reject local taxes are being rational, because they either expect the money to flow from higher-level government—the underlying problem in the Karnataka case discussed by Aziz (1998)—or they do not think that the benefits will justify the costs.[43] We return to both these factors later in this section.

A second problem was alluded to earlier: 'voice' might be a weaker mechanism at the local level than at higher levels. This argument must rest on the assumption of lower institutional capacity at the local level, less transparency, greater inequality, or some combination of these factors. The theoretical argument is actually not straightforward, since, even with all these factors operating, direct and refined incentives at the local level might outweigh them. To a large extent, the question is then an empirical one, and positive evidence can be provided as well as the negative instances given. For example, with respect to elite domination, as long ago as 1965, Béteille observed, in his study of a rural area of Tamil Nadu, 'Adult franchise and Panchayati Raj have introduced new processes into village society' (p. 221), and 'political and legislative changes have altered the bargaining positions of the old economic classes' (p. 223). Béteille argues that local elections increased the power of those who were worse off but were in greater numbers, rather than perpetuating or increasing domination by the traditional rural elite. This is not surprising: democracy rewards numerical superiority. Another example is urban. While the Shiv Sena is better known for other aspects of its ideology, its success as a political organization has also been built on its attention to ward and municipal constituencies in Mumbai: it has striven for and achieved electoral rewards by being responsive to those near the bottom of the economic ladder (Naipaul, 1975).

---

[43] A related issue raised by Aziz (1998) and others is tax collection.

Capacity

Much of the argument for hierarchical control of local government, or simply assignment of tasks and authority to the higher level of government, rests on the idea of low local capacity. While this argument may have some force in rural areas, and smaller towns, it can hardly apply to larger urban bodies. To some extent, these have had more autonomy, but hardly commensurate with their situation. Rigid control of municipalities, and even corporations, has often been exercised by state-level functional departments. Bhattacharya (1972), in four case studies,[44] traces the reasons for this control to the role of these functional departments as providers of technical assistance. This, in turn, has been motivated by concerns for efficiency, driven by a perceived lack of expertise at the local government level. In practice, this has translated into direct control of decision making, rather than technical assistance coupled with performance monitoring. The lack of well-designed systems of state–local transfers has reinforced this tendency, since, in the absence of appropriate incentive grants, direct control becomes relatively more appealing.

While Bhattacharya discusses only urban cases, the problems are similar for rural local governments. The solution, to the problem of lack of capacity in both cases is not to centralize or rely on hierarchical control, as has been done in the past. Since local governments will certainly continue to require outside expertise, the answer is to make sure that their new status gives them control in contracting for technical help, including going to the private sector, NGOs, the national government, or even other state and local governments, as alternatives to their own state government. This can be combined with a transfer system that does not provide perverse incentives to the receiving government. It must also be recognized that, to some extent, the lack of capacity in India's local government has been a self-fulfilling expectation, since decision makers at that level have not been given the opportunity to learn by doing.

Monitoring and auditing can be treated in the same way as technical assistance, from the perspective of capacity. Monitoring is often performed by another organization, rather than by constituents: essentially, one agent (for example, the financial auditor) monitors another (the local government).[45] There is no conceptual reason why such auditing or

---

[44] The cases are water supply in Gujarat, primary education in Maharashtra, roads in Tamil Nadu, and health services in West Bengal. Bhattacharya characterizes Tamil Nadu's municipalities as the least autonomous, followed by Maharashtra, West Bengal, and Gujarat.

[45] The case of the media as monitor is somewhat different, in that they are not agents of citizens, but rather independent entrepreneurs in providing monitoring services.

monitoring has to be done by the state government. Some functions of this nature can be and are performed by internal auditors or by private companies. Even if monitoring is to be performed by a higher-level government, it could conceivably be done by the next tier up, for each of the two lower rural tiers. The state government's role can be to set standards, rather than to attempt case-by-case monitoring.

Efficiency

The different aspects of institutions we have discussed—accountability, transparency, and responsiveness—matter to the extent that they improve efficiency in the provision of public services. We can explicitly examine the connection between accountability and efficiency. The issue here is the repeated observation for Indian local governments that their decision makers are reluctant to impose higher taxes, or to collect existing taxes because they fear voters' displeasure. At the same time, the level of local public services is often perceived as too low. A model constructed by Rao and Singh (2000) displays this type of equilibrium. It also shows that increasing efficiency, perhaps even slightly, may lead to a very different equilibrium, with higher levels of provision and higher welfare. The relevance to the above discussion is that if local government reforms provide an environment where the efficiency of provision increases through better regulatory structures,[46] there may be perceptible improvement in the performance of local government in India.

Assignments and Incentives

Finally, we relate our discussion of institutions and incentives back to the issue of assignments. Put simply, expanding assignments at the local level without reducing them at the state level is problematic in terms of incentives. Concurrency in assignments is a pervasive feature of Indian federalism, and has created problems at higher levels as well as the local level. We can think in terms of ownership or property rights, measured by residual control. Local governments in India have had a very restricted locus of control or ownership. While the statutory assignment of responsibilities and authority has been ambitious, it has often overlapped substantially with state government functions and revenue authority. Local decisions have often been made by state or Central bureaucrats. Requirements for approval of specific expenditures have further circumscribed

---

[46] The model does not endogenize this link between regulation and efficiency, but this can be done along the lines of the approach taken in Mookherjee (1997) and the references therein.

the authority of local governments. Personnel practices and assignments have also been heavily state controlled. Control of local land use (such as in the example of forest resources discussed earlier) is also often in the hands of state governments. A key issue in the development of local government will be whether these loci of control change to any substantial degree, despite the absence of these issues from recent legislation.

The provision for regular local elections may still help, if 'voice' develops as an effective mechanism for accountability. For example, an elected city mayor may have stronger incentives to better implement infrastructure projects, to please constituents, than would a state government bureaucrat. To attract capital for such projects,[47] there are incentives to be more efficient in accounting and internal control. At the same time, external agencies may have an easier time dealing with elected governments that will be in office for a predictable amount of time,[48] making specialized state functional departments or specialized state-level agencies (such as housing or water supply boards) relatively less attractive as channels for investment.

On the other hand, there will always be projects where economies of scale or spillover benefits indicate that greater efficiency will be attained by action at a higher government level. For the rural sector, this does not have to be the state: the block and district levels may prove suitable for many larger-scale actions, since they will have an independent existence and electoral support hitherto absent in almost every case. While the block and district levels have been the focus for plan implementation in rural areas, they have typically been (de jure or de facto) state agencies in this role, with effective control remaining at the state government (or even national) level. The key change will be whether local governments at any level can exercise freedom of decision and action. This requires certainty and transparency in transfers, and setting of standards and monitoring of performance by state governments, rather than the old system of case-by-case discretion. New legislative assignments can only be effective in the context of a redesign of institutional structures. In this context, the presence of MLAs and MPs in local government is also a strongly negative feature of the legislative reform.[49]

[47] Of course this was something which the elected panchayat leaders in the example from Bajaj and Sharma (1995) did not have to do, since they chiefly allocated funds received from higher-level governments.

[48] The new legislation will presumably support this by curtailing incentives for state government supersession of elected local bodies. Of course this is not a guarantee that dealing with local government bodies will become easy for outside funding agencies.

[49] The same point is made by Thimmiah (1999), whose general discussion parallels and complements ours.

CONCLUSIONS ON LOCAL FINANCE

This chapter has focused exclusively on local governments, including their interactions with state-level governments and government agencies. The interplay of assignments of functional responsibility, revenue authority, and institutional structures has been stressed in examining ongoing reform of local government. It is useful to conclude by relating these reforms to the country's broader set of changes in the economic policy. This may seem somewhat surprising, since local government reform in India is often associated with ideologies and groups that are critical of economic 'liberalization'. Reform of local government in India certainly had a very different impetus and history than the national economic reforms propelled by the 1991 balance of payments crisis. However, the two reforms are closely connected by the issue of overall fiscal management including tax reform and more efficient delivery of public services. National financial sector reform also has implications for the thorny problems of infrastructure at the local level.

With regard to fiscal deficits, one can make the case that the structure of fiscal federalism in India has contributed to the overall problem of government deficits. The states were used to operating with soft budget constraints, and their finances have deteriorated in the post-reform squeeze, negatively affecting their spending in areas such as education and health. Will local government reform make the fiscal situation worse? For example, the World Bank (1995) country study, in discussing tax reform, tax sharing, and the disincentives for lower-level resource mobilization, offers the following caution:

The 73rd Amendment ... is an important and welcome change, aimed at increasing the autonomy of local governments. However, it may accentuate fiscal indiscipline by establishing between states and local governments a system of transfers similar to the one in place between the central and state governments.

Related concerns, that the Centre will ultimately have to channel resources to local governments, directly and through the states, are expressed in the Tenth Finance Commission report (Finance Commission, 1994, Chapters 10 and 15).

However, state finance commissions have the potential to play an important role in furthering the process of fiscal decentralization and establishing a rule-based equitable transfer system. They can help the state governments identify additional sources of revenue at local levels and ensure a measure of correspondence between the benefits and costs of public service provision. Furthermore, discretion has been the *only* system operating between the state and local levels. State finance commissions can reduce such discretionary transfers from the states to local governments, and increase the transparency, certainty and, ultimately, efficiency of such transfers. The state commissions can also learn from the past, including the experience of the central finance commissions, and avoid grant schemes with perverse incentives, such as those that pay for marginal personnel costs, or 'gap-filling' transfer schemes in general.[50]

While proper design and implementation of the transfer system is necessary, raising local resources more effectively is crucial. Here, broader economic reforms are complementary to the reform of local government. The underlying goal of economic reforms in India is to enhance efficiency in resource allocation (and capital in particular), to support higher growth. Reforms of trade, industry, and financial markets are all, in some way, driven by this basic objective. Relying on smoothly functioning (and well-regulated) financial markets to allocate capital, in this view, is crucial for government as well as for the private sector.

Historically, state and local governments have not been able to engage in market borrowing. Instead, they have relied on top–down funding through the central planning process, which has often not been responsive to the wants of local residents. Since many municipal service projects involve long-lasting capital and equipment, the building up of local capital has been hindered. The creation of urban local governments with independent status, legal authority, and regularly elected officials raises the possibility that these governments may eventually be able to regularly borrow money in the financial markets for local sanitation, roads, and schools. Again, for this to work, hard budget constraints must exist: municipalities should not be allowed to expect a bailout if they overspend. Clearly, the development of market borrowing will take time, but cities such as Ahmedabad have already taken the first steps.

Improving the effectiveness of the tax system is another avenue for revenue enhancement, and is necessary for local government borrowing as well, since borrowing for non-remunerative public projects requires future tax revenues to fund loan repayment. National tax reform predates the 1991 shift in economic policy, and represents an opportunity for local governments as well, for example through local surcharges on redesigned state-level taxes. Effective tax sharing can be an important part of the role of state finance commissions, as it has been at the Centre.

True representative government at the local level is more likely to be able to raise revenue through taxes, if the citizens thereby are able to more

---

[50] For excellent surveys of the current status of fiscal federalism in India, with a focus on the local level and state finance commissions, see Lahiri (1999), Mathur (1999), and Rajaraman (1999).

closely connect benefits received with taxes paid. We have already highlighted several well-known ways in which the assignment and administration of local taxes might be improved. A third route for increasing revenues of local governments to meet their new functional responsibilities is user charges. For many local government goods, user charges and fees can be quite close to taxes in practice, and both these sources of revenue have been constrained partly by the inefficient delivery of public services. Local governments with limited accountability, and typically little freedom of action with respect to expenditures, have tended not to risk upsetting constituents by raising resources through these means, preferring to rely on whatever funding they could obtain from higher-level governments. Constituents have been unwilling to pay more for an inefficient provision of services.

Ultimately, therefore, the central issue is whether decentralization will permit the more efficient use of government funds. Greater responsiveness to constituents due to local democracy and decentralization should certainly help. However, this chapter has stressed that complementary reforms in institutions to improve incentives for government decision makers, are necessary to reap the benefits of greater electoral accountability at the local level. Some possible changes are quite drastic, such as the transfer of existing staff from Central and state government to local government, and the reorganization of administration at all levels. The states such as Kerala, with strong decentralizing traditions, have begun this process. This transfer of human resources can mitigate concerns that increasing local responsibilities will require large increases in 'establishment costs' (Rajaraman et al., 1996). Increasing efficiency of provision can be the basis for more effective use of taxes and fees.

Are increases in efficiency in local government likely? The outcome of even partial economic reforms at the national level has destroyed the idea of a culturally determined 'Hindu rate of growth'. There is a clear conceptual and empirical connection between the nature of past regulation of local governments in India and the overall top-down approach to economic policy, relying on the case-by-case discretion of government decision makers, in areas such as industrial location and expansion, and in the allocation of capital generally. The Central government's shift since 1991 from case-by-case regulation to setting general regulatory standards provides a model for reformulating state regulation of local governments. These issues have not been, and could not be addressed in the general legislation on local government reform.

An important message of our chapter is that the ideas that are guiding changes in how the national government interacts with the private sector are also important for how state governments interact with local governments. The expanded assignments legislated for local governments, and the increased role for local 'voice', together require the state governments to fundamentally change their regulation of local governments underneath them.

14

✡

Policy and Institutional
Dimensions of Reform

THE SETTING

This chapter provides a discussion of various areas of reform in the context of India's federal system. Recent and potential reforms of the Centre–state transfer system are discussed. We argue that, given the evidence of persistent and possibly widening economic gaps among the states in India, the need for a clear and simple approach to formulating and implementing Centre–state transfers is greater than ever. We also argue that this recommendation is not vitiated by the existence of multiple channels for transfers, and the importance of political influence.

We consider broader (actual and possible) reforms in India's fiscal federal institutions, including tax assignments and the system of government finance. We also consider directions of local government reform, extending the discussion in Chapter 13. We suggest that reforms of tax assignments may be tied to other aspects of tax reform in order to achieve joint acceptability to the Centre and the states. We suggest that explicit and implicit intergovernmental transfers for capital projects, as well as lending by public sector institutions, be largely replaced by block grants and by market borrowing.

We examine possible reform of the institutions of federal governance, including political parties and elections, the civil service and other government and public sector unit (PSU) employees, the legal and enforcement system, and tax administration. Finally, we examine the federal dimensions of wider aspects of economic reform, including privatization, infrastructure, and regulation, examining in each case the role of policy at different levels of government, and the interaction between them.

REFORM OF THE TRANSFER SYSTEM

In Chapter 11 we examined the evidence for political effects on the pattern of Centre–state transfers, and found it to be reasonably strong. Chapters 9 and 12 also looked at implicit transfers, and found that these tended to go disproportionately to the richer states, undoing some, if not all, of the equalizing effects of explicit transfers from the Finance Commission. Even explicit transfers from the Planning Commission have not done much to ameliorate regional inequalities in the provision of public services across states with different levels of per capita income. These issues become more salient in the context of concerns that regional inequalities are increasing as a result of economic liberalization and of relaxation of Central government controls in particular.

The overall evidence that we discussed in Chapter 12 was somewhat mixed. Many empirical studies supported a conclusion of absolute divergence among the Indian states in the past three decades (well before liberalization began), with the rate increasing in the 1990s. The evidence on conditional convergence was less decisive, but even if one accepts conditional convergence as descriptive of India's states, they may be converging to very different steady states. The differences in infrastructure and institutions that seem to explain interstate differences in steady states have been persistent, and neither Finance Commission transfers, nor Planning Commission transfers, nor centrally sponsored schemes have made a substantial dent.

One might argue that the Centre–state transfer system is being asked to do too much, both in terms of short-term amelioration of interstate inequalities or in promoting development and poverty alleviation in the long run. If that is the case, however, the present tangle of multiple channels of transfers, with its combination of two extremes of complex formulae on the one hand and ad hoc discretion on the other, ought to be simplified dramatically. Alternatively, one may argue that the transfer system has an important role to play in overall national development, and that this role has become more important as the centrifugal force of economic reform will put pressures on the other institutions of India's federal system, and perhaps even on India's political fabric.[1]

What possible reforms can be made in the transfer system? One example of the process of reform comes from the case of tax sharing arrangements. The Constitution specified certain categories of centrally

---

[1] This point also applies if one considers migration, a factor that has received relatively little attention after Cashin and Sahay's effort to quantify its impacts.

collected taxes that were to be shared with the states, according to criteria to be determined by the Finance Commission. In particular, personal income taxes were a major component of tax transfers from the Centre to the states, which received 87.5 per cent of such tax revenues. On the other hand, income tax surcharges were kept entirely by the Centre. Academic commentators suggested that there were obvious incentive problems with such arrangements, and the Tenth Finance Commission recommended alternative arrangements whereby a proportion of overall central tax revenues would be devolved to the states. This required bargaining and agreement among the Centre and the states, as well as a constitutional amendment, but this has all been accomplished.[2]

Tax sharing between the Centre and the states reflects one dimension of the bargaining that must take place among a federation's constituents. Presumably, the initial effect of the change will be to leave the overall shares of the Centre and the states in aggregate near their previous values, avoiding the problem of creating clear initial losers from the reform. Principles of this sort might be used to tackle a harder problem, that of revising the formulae used to divide the states' share of tax revenue among them. These formulae are quite complex, without embodying any clearly defined objective, either of interstate (horizontal) equity, or of provision of incentives for fiscal prudence. Given that there are other transfer mechanisms as well, and that those will be used with discretion, there is a case for the Finance Commission overhauling its formulae completely, to achieve greater simplicity. Such an overhaul can in theory be designed to respect the present status quo to a great extent, as well as to deal more aggressively with future increases in interstate inequality.

We would argue that an approach that builds equity concerns into a formula is preferable to one in which ad hoc grants are made at the margin. In this respect, one welcome change related to tax sharing is recommended in the Eleventh Finance Commission report. This is the reversal of a practice—introduced by the Eighth Finance Commission—of keeping a portion of shareable tax revenues from Union excise duties exclusively for allocation among states according to the amount of their estimated post-tax-devolution deficits. This amounted to a conversion of a part of the share of taxes into 'gap-filling' grants, lacking both in transparency and efficient incentive provision.

The case for reform of transfer formulae applies equally strongly to the portion of Planning Commission transfers that are calculated on the basis

---

[2] See Rao and Singh (2001) for further detail on the new arrangements, as well as initial implementation by the Eleventh Finance Commission.

of the 1969 'Gadgil formula'. One of the problems in the past has been the overly narrow scope of finance commissions, much narrower than what the Constitution of India implies for their role. Moving away from this restriction, one welcome innovation in the latest Finance Commission's terms of reference was the consideration of the overall fiscal position of India's federal system. The Commission forthrightly recommends a reassessment of plan transfer formulae, with this task to be brought within the scope of the Finance Commission.[3] The latest report also notes the severe muddle with respect to Plan transfers, with meaningless distinction between plan and non-plan expenditures. It recommends reform of the financing of the plans so that plan revenue expenditure is financed from available revenue receipts after meeting non-plan expenditure, with borrowing used only for investments. Finally, a recommendation for multi-year budgeting could presumably be a step away from the artificial cycle of five-year plans, which the evidence in Singh and Vashishta (2001) suggests may introduce temporal distortions in transfers.

We are not suggesting that any of these proposed reforms will solve any problem of increased inequality of per capita SDPs. Instead, they will make the formal transfer system clearer and simpler, which should make it easier to understand its objectives and its impacts. They will also offset the fiscal disabilities of the states better. This is a first step in actually tackling problems of divergence, or of convergence to greatly different steady states. We are also not suggesting that this is the only channel for impacts on interstate inequality. RSK have noted the important regressive impacts of implicit transfers and of private sector investment flows. They also point out the unknown regional effects of direct Central government expenditures, which will also incorporate individual MPs' 'pork barrel' efforts. Finally, there will always be some component of explicit transfers that is subject to Central government discretion. However, in our view, removing a significant portion of Centre–state transfers outside the political economy arena, clearly targeting them towards horizontal equity objectives, and doing so in a manner that does not create perverse incentives for recipients, is both feasible and desirable.

Given an objective of promoting horizontal equity in government expenditures across states, the issue of conditionalities is not directly relevant for such general-purpose transfers. Certainly, perverse incentives that exist in the current system, whereby 'gap-filling' grants are given, should be avoided, but block grants fulfil this criterion well. Also,

---

[3] The much broader issue of what the role of the Planning Commission should be is taken up in the next section.

transparency and accountability can be achieved by a simple transfer system (transparency) and voice as a mechanism at the level of the recipient constituency (accountability). Performance requirements or conditionalities are not necessarily effective, and have their own problems of creating segmented incentives.

Project-based grants and loans are a different matter altogether, and here performance criteria are natural and supported by economic reasoning, since the higher-level government's goal is related to achieving some specific performance through the transfer, and not just one of raising the relative fiscal capacity of the poorer states. Ahluwalia implicitly focuses on these kinds of transfers in his discussion, alluded to in Chapter 12.

We have argued for integrating and simplifying the formulaic components of Centre–state transfers, focusing them more clearly, and expanding their importance relative to discretionary components. We suggested that the success of the recent overhaul of tax sharing arrangements provides evidence that reform in this area is feasible and workable. The recommendation of the Eleventh Finance Commission to bring formulaic plan transfers under the scope of the Finance Commission raises some interesting broader issues. The resources that have been devoted to the operation of the Planning Commission stand in stark contrast to the minimal assistance provided to the Finance Commission. We have already argued that the Finance Commission could be more effective if provided with ongoing resources for conducting its analysis and recommendations.

One might extend the earlier argument to question whether the resources used by the Planning Commission provide any benefit in an economy where liberalization has taken hold. Where there is a justification for national-level coordination because of externalities that cross state borders (as in the case of roads or power, for example), different ministries or even state governments can negotiate and cooperate. Where there is no such justification, unconditional grants, determined by the Finance Commission, that do not distort states' fiscal incentives seem to be the appropriate channel. The Planning Commission may be largely redundant in such an institutional framework. Tackling this issue head-on is likely to be politically infeasible, but gradually shifting responsibility and resources to the Finance Commission may well be a possible approach.

An important component of institutional reform is the resolution of overlapping roles of Finance and Planning Commissions. The issue neeeds to be addressed speedily for, even after market-based reforms were introduced in 1991, the Planning Commission continues its methodology of finalizing the state plans, holding annual plan discussions with the states and giving plan assistance according to the modified Gadgil formula. We have argued in Chapter 9 that the present role assumed by the Planning Commission is not conducive to fiscal discipline. It encourages expenditure profligacy, interferes unduly with states' choice of allocation (through centrally sponsored schemes), promotes a truncated view of state finances, and makes it difficult to fulfil the objectives of the transfer system. It would be better for the Planning Commission to take predominantly an advisory role, plan for physical infrastructure in the country, and provide loan assistance to the states to finance infrastructure facilities. A portion of the loan could be given on concessional terms on the lines of IDA assistance given by the World Bank (Singh and Srinivasan, 2002). All current transfers should be made on the recommendations of the Finance Commission, which is a consitutional body, and which should be made a permanent professional body with a strong research secretariat. Thus, the Planning Commission should be taken out of the business of making grants. The Finance Commission should also have the responsibility of working with Central ministries on specific-purpose transfers, and consolidating them into broad groups. Vesting responsibility of determining both general-purpose and specific-purpose transfers to one agency will help in redesigning the transfer system to be more effective, and vesting the responsibility with a constitutional body with a strong research secretariat may also support the objectives of an equitable and efficient transfer system. The Planning Commission's focus on infrastructure will bring that issue to centre-stage, in line with the goal of greater global competitiveness for India.

REFORM OF FISCAL AND FINANCIAL SYSTEM

In the previous section, we have discussed how to improve the Centre–state transfer system. Three other areas of ongoing reform also bear on the transfer system, either by changing the environment within which it works, or through direct interactions. The assignment of tax authority is obviously important in influencing the starting point from which inter-governmental transfers are made. Second, the explicit strengthening of local governments, with formal transfer systems being introduced for state–local transfers, must impact Centre–state fiscal relations. Finally, financial sector reform interacts with the conditions under which subnational governments or other public entities can obtain funds for capital projects. Since funds are fungible, the institutions for current and capital transfers affect each other. We consider each of these issues in turn.

Tax Reform

Some elements of tax reform in the last decade (some beginning earlier) are well known: a reduction in tariff rates, reductions in direct tax rates coupled with attempts to broaden the tax base, and a gradual movement from excise duties and sales taxes to VAT at both the Central and state levels. If we compare 1990–1 with 1999–2000, the impact of some of these changes has been as follows: an increase in the direct-tax-to-GDP ratio from 2.16 per cent to 3.24 per cent, accompanied by an increase in the number of filers from 6.1 to 17.8 million; more than offset by a decrease in the central indirect-tax-to-GDP ratio from 8.84 per cent to 6.23 per cent, driven by reductions in the percentages of central excise duties as well as customs duties.[4] State sales taxes and excise duties have also shown some proportionate decline, so that the overall tax–GDP ratio has declined by almost two percentage points in the 1990s (Rao, 2000a). While the overall decline merely reverses an increase that took place in the 1980s, the fact that it has occurred at higher income levels, and during a period of economic reform, raises questions about long-term implications. Some of the issues are connected to dimensions of tax reform that have yet to be effectively calibrated.

The Tax Reform Committee of 1991 had also recommended minimizing exemptions and concessions, simplification of laws and procedures, development of modern, computerized information systems, and improvements in administration and enforcement (Rao, 2000a). Work in the mid-1990s by Dasgupta and Mookherjee (1998, Chapter 6) detailed the problems with Indian tax administration, both in terms of the incentives of those paying taxes and those enforcing them. In May 2001, N.K. Singh and Modi (focusing on central tax collection) were led to write, 'The tax enforcement effort has left much to be desired ... from the viewpoint of a decline in total tax collected as a percentage of collectible tax, the pendency of assessment work and the dilatory process of the Appeal redressal mechanism'. Thus it is clear that much remains to be done in this respect. We would like to suggest here that the benefits of improvements in this area are likely to be large, not only because of the direct benefits of improvements in central information systems and institutions of enforcement, but also because these can provide a model for states to improve their tax administration as well.

A reform that more directly affects India's federal system lies in indirect taxes, which, as we have noted, have not increased proportionately

---

[4] These figures are from N. K. Singh and Modi (2001), Tables I, III, and IV.

with GDP in the last decade. As Rao (2000a) puts it, 'The most important challenge in restructuring the tax system in the country is to evolve a coordinated consumption tax system'. We have indicated some of the problems with the current assignments of indirect taxes. Rao provides some detailed recommendations in this regard, with respect to issues such as rates, interstate sales taxes, and tax administration for a dual VAT coordinated between the Centre and the states. Rao also notes the problem created by the failure of the Constitution to explicitly include 'services' within the scope of states' sales tax authority. This problem has been recognized for some time, and is clearly in need of correction, as also recommended by the Eleventh Finance Commission in its report.

Moving taxation of services from the Union List, where it implicitly lies through the Centre's residual powers over taxes not explicitly specified in the Constitution, to the Concurrent List will require a constitutional amendment. Such an amendment must be proposed by the Central government, but will benefit the states. Rao incorporates political economy considerations of the kind that we have discussed, by suggesting that an amendment be tied persuading the states to reduce and eventually eliminate taxation of interstate sales, thus removing some of the internal barriers that have plagued the development of a true national market within India. This will also smoothen the implementation of a destination-based VAT for the states. Note that such reforms can also reduce tax exporting by the richer states, which was discussed in Chapter 7, complementing the role of transfers in keeping interstate divergence from becoming politically unacceptable.

The case of taxation of services illustrates a broader issue that was addressed by the Eleventh Finance Commission. Its report recommended in general terms a reduction in the vertical fiscal imbalance by reassignment of tax authorities, giving the states more power to tax. This approach takes some pressure off the fiscal transfer system, allowing states that can obtain political support to more flexibly tax their own constituents to deliver benefits to them. Another possible example of such a tax reassignment would be to allow states to piggyback on central income taxes. This, too, would require a constitutional amendment. It might seem redundant where tax sharing exists, but with tax sharing no longer applied to specific tax 'handles', but to tax revenues in total, this change would give states more flexibility at the margin, where they properly should have it. Note that states are already assigned the right to tax agricultural income, though their use of this tax is minimal. This separation has no economic justification, and it merely promotes tax evasion. Riding piggyback with a removal of the distinction between non-agricultural and agricultural income would represent a major improvement in tax assignments. The latter would also be an important step forward in broadening the direct tax base. Whether the political economy logic can work for this case of tied reforms, as suggested for the case of services above, is worth considering.

To summarize our discussion, much remains to be done in terms of tax reform. While some measures can be initiated by the Centre acting alone, many others require agreement or coordination between the Centre and the states. These include possible reassignments of tax authority, as well as changes in tax administration. Recognizing the play of differing interests may help in devising reform packages that balance potential losses against gains, and thereby increase the probability of acceptance.

Local Government Reform

In Chapter 13 we characterized local government reform as replacing 'hierarchy' with 'voice' as the primary accountability mechanism, and we have explained this as a positive step based on the ability to provide more refined incentives, subject to the caveat of effective monitoring and transparency being achievable. Local government reform has also changed the nature of tax and expenditure assignments to local governments, and instituted a system of formal state–local transfers modelled on the component of the existing Centre–state system that is governed by the Finance Commission. While there are some serious issues with the new assignments, including problems of local capacity and efficiency, both with respect to revenues and expenditures, we refer readers to our earlier discussions, and focus primarily on the new transfer system.

While one view has been that formal transfers from the Centre and states to local governments have the potential to accentuate fiscal deficit problems, our own perspective is that a formal, rule-governed system will make such problems more transparent. In fact, the evidence suggests that this is the case. Local government finances, particularly for urban bodies, have steadily worsened over the period before local government reform, under a system of hierarchical control and supposedly strict monitoring by state governments. This is not to imply that the new institutions, particularly the state finance commissions (SFCs), represent an immediate improvement. Almost all SFCs have given their initial reports, and the Eleventh Finance Commission sums up its appraisal of them as follows:

Many SFC reports have not addressed the specific terms listed in articles 243I and 243Y, nor have they provided a clear idea of the powers, authority and responsibilities actually entrusted to the local bodies. Many of these reports also do not clearly indicate the principles formulated for sharing or assignment of State taxes, duties, tolls, fees and the grants-in-aid (Paragraph 8.11b).

Again, we would argue that this situation is no worse than the previous one of ad hoc and discretionary transfers and control of local bodies by state governments.

The Central Finance Commission has been reluctant, and rightly so, to provide the states with grants requested by them to supplement the states' own transfers to their local governments, noting that the amendments do not justify this softening of the states' budget constraints. The Commission's main recommendations with respect to local government relate to assignment and incentive issues for various sources of tax revenue. Land and profession taxes are identified as two possible sources of revenue. Perhaps the most promising is the recommendation of surcharges on state taxes earmarked for local government, similar to the piggybacking we proposed for the states on central taxes. These recommendations are straightforward at this general level—the real problems arise in defining details and assuring implementation. This point also applies to the Commission's discussion of property tax, replacements for octroi, and local user charges.

Our analysis in Chapter 13 suggests that incentive efficiency with respect to government expenditure must be the starting point for revenue enhancement efforts. Here, the Commission is right to suggest a quicker transfer of expenditure responsibilities to local governments: they are unlikely to do worse than state governments have so far done, in the provision of basic civic amenities. Grants to the lowest tier of local government recommended by the Commission may help to jumpstart the process of making local governments effective providers, if they can break out of their historical low-level equilibrium of revenue collection and service provision.

The Commission also recommends grants for improved accounting, auditing, and database building for local governments. These measures, if implemented effectively, can have a substantial positive impact on capacity, transparency, and accountability in the delivery of street-level government services. The report also discusses some of the potential conflicts between the existing institutional apparatus of central and centrally sponsored schemes and the role envisaged for local governments, and problems that are arising from states' reluctance to devolve authority to their subordinate governments. One example of the latter problem is the failure of state governments to implement the reports of their own SFCs. In the case of the Central Finance Commission, the bargaining power of the states and the role of precedent have worked to ensure the implementation of most recommendations. In the case of the states, local governments may need outside help, for example from the courts, to pressure reluctant state governments.

The central point here is that the ideas that are guiding changes in how the national government interacts with the private sector are also important for how state governments interact with local governments. The expanded assignments legislated for local governments, and the increased role for local 'voice', together require the state governments to fundamentally change their regulation of local governments underneath them.

Furthermore, expanding and strengthening the scope of the Central Finance Commission in determining Centre–state transfers, while simplifying the formulae that govern them (something we have advocated earlier in this chapter), can have the added benefit of giving states a clearer road in achieving their own devolution to local governments. Currently, central discretionary transfers, which are meant to be implemented at the district or block level, swamp local government capacity for action and for their own revenue raising (Rajaraman, 2001). Replacing these with conditional or unconditional grants from the states (with the ultimate source possibly being unconditional grants from the Centre), will allow more effective functioning of local governments. Thus, our perspective on local government reform ties in with our earlier discussion of reform of the Centre–state transfer system.

Financial Sector Reform

One innovation in the Eleventh Finance Commission's recommendations was its consideration of the overall fiscal position of India's federal system, in particular the Central and state governments. This was, in fact, a significant part of the Commission's terms of reference, and represented a welcome broadening of its scope. It was clearly motivated by the ongoing issue of fiscal deficits that India has struggled with for the past decade. Furthermore, the problem of fiscal deficits has, to a large extent, been pushed down to the level of the state governments, making it very much an issue of federalism.

Fiscal deficits at the state level have increased despite the Central government's apparent formal authority to strictly control state borrowing. There are two causes of this phenomenon. First, the Central government has increasingly used discretionary loans, often with interest subsidies or even ex post conversion of loans to grants, as a component of political influence. This statement is based on casual empiricism, but is consistent with the political effects found in the analyses of explicit transfers. Second, the states have used public sector enterprises and other off-budget devices to run larger deficits in practice.[5] For both the Centre and the states, the ultimate enabler of both these trends has been the nature of India's financial system. Severe financial repression, along with direct ownership and control of much of the financial system, has permitted governments to 'park' deficits in the financial system without having to print money and cause politically dangerous inflation.

The cost of financial repression and deficit parking has been inefficient capital allocation and lower growth. If growth is to be promoted by improvements in the efficiency of capital allocation, and not just increases in savings and investment, reform of the financial sector is required. Such reform has indeed been taking place in areas such as the functioning of Indian stock markets, corporate governance, regulation of banking, and methods of Central government borrowing. Whatever the other specific problems that these reforms have encountered,[6] the constraints imposed by the web of government-controlled financial institutions and their 'bad' loans to the public sector are a severe hurdle to more thorough financial sector reform. Hence, while tax reform and local government reform are directly issues of reform of India's federal structures within the public sector, tackling the ways in which public sector capital finances are handled is a case of interaction of the private and public sectors. Financial sector reform threatens the public sector house of cards, and is therefore held back.

The problem as stated is well recognized. The solution may not be so clear, or easy to implement. The Eleventh Finance Commission recommended a slew of measures to promote fiscal discipline: an overall ceiling of 37.5 per cent of gross receipts of the Centre for all transfers to the states; hard budget constraints for all levels of government with respect to wages and salaries; 'greater autonomy' along with hard budget constraints for public sector enterprises; more explicit controls on debt levels for state governments; and improvements in budgeting, auditing, and control. We would like to suggest that 'greater autonomy along with hard budget constraints for public sector enterprises' might not work. Furthermore, by not working, it will continue to undermine any limits on states' debt levels. The only clear-cut solution is privatization of public sector assets. The political difficulty of this task is highlighted by the absence of any

---

[5] See, for example, Lahiri (1999), Rao (2000b), and Mohan (2001).

[6] Problems have included dealing with moral hazard and corruption, lack of regulatory capacity, political interference, and simple mistakes in institutional design. Nevertheless, the story has often been one of uncovering problems that were earlier hidden, and the overall picture is probably more encouraging than newspaper headlines about financial scandals would suggest.

meaningful privatization in a decade of economic reform. It differs fundamentally from other aspects of reform, involving more than just reform within government or changing the nature and methods of regulating the private sector, instead explicitly shifting the boundary between private and public ownership.

If privatization affects the nature of the demand for credit, the other side of the equation concerns the supply of credit. Deficit parking has been abetted by the existence and operation of public sector financial institutions. The need for privatization applies to these as well. Where does this leave the different levels of government with respect to financing the urgent needs for public infrastructure? One might be tempted to condemn privatization of the financial sector if the past approach of public subsidies and directed lending had been successful in efficiently and effectively building such infrastructure: in fact, it has failed badly.

Note that the issue with respect to the working of the financial sector has not been just one of levels of credit, but also of credit allocation across states. Hence our discussion of fiscal deficits also relates to our analysis of political economy influences and growing interstate disparities. In fact, the problem grew after the nationalization of commercial banks in 1969, which concentrated economic power in the hands of the Centre. With insurance and many other financial institutions already under central control, the Central government became a virtual monopolist in the financial sector. It might even be argued that, in such circumstances, the role of the formal intergovernmental transfer system has been overshadowed by invisible transfers.

Privatization in the financial sector, therefore, can not only have direct impacts on efficiency and growth, but it can also support the objective of allowing explicit Centre–state transfers to meet their own objectives more effectively. With respect to transfers for capital purposes, we suggest that, while Central and state governments will always have the option of making conditional grants and project loans to lower-level governments, the practical limitations on monitoring and incentives of such transfers (including the ultimate fungibility of transferred funds) support the greater use of unconditional block grants, with marginal capital funds coming through market borrowing.[7] Ultimately, since repayment of such borrowing comes from taxes and user charges, this means that each level of government is more responsible at the margin, and responsive to its

[7] Obviously, the smaller the government, the less will be the feasibility of significant reliance on the market. However, as we have emphasized earlier, many of the Indian states are comparable to countries in terms of population size and fiscal domain.

constituents' preferences. This recommendation is perhaps as drastic a reform of 'development finance' in India as that of curtailing the Planning Commission's role, but it seems to be a necessary complement to other aspects of financial sector reform.

We may summarize the main message of this section quite simply. Overall, we are suggesting that a further devolution of expenditure assignments, as is being implemented in the ongoing local government reform, makes sense from an efficiency perspective, because it allows incentives to be more refined and effective. This must be accompanied by devolution of tax assignments, to keep vertical fiscal imbalances from overwhelming such incentives. Since vertical fiscal imbalances will still arise, we argue for a simpler transfer system that does not distort marginal incentives. While there is still room for transfers and loans that are earmarked for capital expenditure, we argue that here, too, marginal incentives are crucial, and that providing these through the market may be the only efficient avenue in practice. This argument is based on the recognition that political influences will distort choices in the absence of such discipline, no matter how legal restraints are structured. Thus, our recommendations here are in keeping with our discussion of the political economy of Centre–state transfers. While decentralization and privatization may seem to exacerbate problems of interstate inequality and divergence, a counter argument is that, instead, they enable higher-level governments to focus more clearly and directly on redistribution objective wherever necessary.

REFORM OF FEDERAL GOVERNANCE

In this section we return to the themes discussed in Chapters 4 and 5, looking at the broader institutions of federal governance. We outlined some of the institutional problems in those chapters, and here we discuss some possible reforms. We will not attempt to suggest unattainable ideals, but propose what we hope are feasible and politically acceptable solutions. Furthermore, we focus on federal dimensions of reform rather than all aspects of how the institutions may be improved in their functioning.

Political Parties

A Central government that involves regional parties in a coalition is inherently more federal, perhaps, since such parties may represent regional interests more strongly. This is especially so since national parties in India tend to be relatively centralized in their working. Regional party leaders may have local power bases through their ability to garner votes, but the tendency for campaign finance to be centralized has weakened them over the years. The two main national parties, the BJP and Congress, are somewhat different in their functioning, with the former having a more formal internal hierarchy. The Congress party's structure was, it seems, irrevocably altered by Indira Gandhi, in the direction of personalized control.

Given the decentralization of economic power that has been an important facet of economic reform, and the contemporaneous rise of regional parties, the lack of well-defined organizational structures in India's political parties is less significant than it was in the 1970s. Furthermore, the retreat from a political system where the party in power at the Centre tried to control all the state governments as well (through devices such as Article 356) has also reduced the impact of internal centralization. There are independent reasons for imposing higher organizational standards on political parties in India, but the impact of centralized parties on the country's federal system does not appear to be critical.

Bureaucracy

In contrast, the bureaucracy's structure appears to be more important in relation to the federal system. To the extent that the national bureaucracy (the IAS) wishes to preserve a centralized system, it can thwart federalist tendencies. For example, national bureaucrats at the state level may be more responsive to their senior colleagues at the central level than elected state government officials. Of course this does not lead to bad outcomes in every case. However, it weakens federalism. The proper response to unsatisfactory political decision making at the state level is the exercise of 'voice' at that level, rather than hierarchical bureaucratic control.

We cannot enter into a full-scale discussion of the merits and problems of the IAS and IPS. We outlined some of the issues in Chapters 4 and 5. Any major change in the structure of the bureaucracy would require a constitutional amendment, and it does not seem that this is a high political priority. Instead, a feasible solution that can reduce the conflict between having a national bureaucracy that operates at the state level and sub-national governments with substantial potential powers is simply to reduce the size of the bureaucracy at the national level. This could lead to IAS members spending more time working within their assigned states, where their expertise could probably be utilized for greater good, given the importance of state-level economic reforms. While the Central government damaged the economy by accepting (and overdoing) the Fifth Pay Commission's pay award without implementing the accompanying recommendation to shrink the size of the government, it is important to keep such a reform on the agenda, and perhaps implement it through attrition.

Law Enforcement and Judiciary

The intrusion of central police forces into law enforcement at the state level is also, to some extent, a problem of bureaucratic organization. Even more than the IAS, the IPS is a vestige of a relatively centralized colonial administration. Its justification, and that of the use of purely central police forces such as the CRPF at the state level, has been specifically to overcome local biases in law enforcement, particularly with respect to groups such as religious minorities or lower castes and untouchables. However, the same point that we made about the IAS applies here: the presumption should be that the constitutionally assigned authority is appropriate, and subject to voice as an accountability mechanism, except when there is a serious and dangerous failure of governance, such as a breakdown of law and order that threatens basic civil rights. It should be noted that public order is the first item in the State List of the Constitution. However, item 2A in the Union List, inserted by the 42nd Amendment in 1976, during the Emergency declared by Indira Gandhi, gives the Centre power to deploy 'any other force subject to the control of the Union'. This sweeping provision is an example of centralization that might be difficult to reverse.

A similar centralization occurred through the same amendment, when the 'Administration of justice; constitution and organization of all courts, except the Supreme Court and the High Courts' was moved from the State List to the Concurrent List. We have noted the centralization of the judiciary in our discussion in Chapter 4. Much of this centralization, however, is a result of the allocation of resources across levels of the judiciary, and of the details of judicial procedures, rather than because of the constitutional assignment. From the perspective of efficiency, resolving such micro issues has the potential to be extremely beneficial, since judicial delays can be extremely costly in property and contractual disputes, and other cases where uncertainty can delay productive investment. These costs are, of course, in addition to the resource costs of lengthy litigation.

Property Rights and Administration

Aside from making the resolution of disputes over property rights more efficient, there are many cases where lower-level governments have a positive role to play in the management of property rights. These include, in particular, urban land. Both state and local governments have failed to create efficient markets in land and housing, and to maintain appropriate records. Not only has investment suffered, but local governments have also failed to collect reasonable amounts of property tax. The issue of state and local tax administration is, in fact, quite general. While considerable attention has been focused on the administration of the central income tax, the improvement of local tax revenues is no less important. Also, one problem throughout the different levels of government is that of incentives of government and PSE employees. In the case of tax administration, some specific organizational improvements have been suggested by Dasgupta and Mookherjee (1998). In many other cases, the more attractive option is simply to privatize, since the government is pervasive in areas where it has no business to be. We will take up privatization in more detail in the next section.

Intergovernmental Institutions

Local government reform has complicated intergovernmental relations in India, by allowing the Centre to bypass state governments to some extent, such as by making direct transfers to local governments. In fact, it has been argued that this was the political motivation for such reform. In general, the economic reform process has changed the nature of Centre–state interactions, and this has been compounded by coalition rule at the Centre. Issues of fiscal deficits, tax reform, policies towards FDI, infrastructure development and regulation all require some coordination between the Centre and the states. In this context, institutions such as the Inter-state Council (ISC) may actually have a greater role to play than earlier.

While states that are pivotal, and hence politically powerful in a coalition government at the Centre may be able to directly extract concessions from the Central government (as the government of Andhra Pradesh appears to have done in some cases), this does not make the ISC redundant. The potential role of the ISC is precisely to provide an alternative to such ad hoc bargaining. Furthermore, bargaining over durable changes in rules governing the federation is quite different from bargaining over specific instances. For example, the ISC was an important forum for gaining acceptance of the change in tax sharing recommended by the Tenth Finance Commission.[8] More recently, it has also been a place where an important change in the rules governing interstate water disputes has been approved by the states (Chapter 10). Clearly, tax reform, changes in the way that states borrow, policies towards FDI, and regulation of sectors such as power are all areas where the ISC can provide a less public, more focused forum for bargaining over issues that jointly affect the Centre and the states than is possible in either house of parliament.

The role of the ISC may also be expanded if the current process of

---

[8] See also Kapur (2001) for additional examples.

planning is reformed, as we have argued earlier in this section. The NDC now serves as the bargaining forum for plan transfers and loans, and we have suggested that these might be replaced by a dual system of block grants and market-based loans. This change would make the NDC redundant. Instead, the ISC may be the place for evolving a new institutional framework. Thus, we envisage the ISC as bargaining over general rules, and not over specific instances. In this respect, our perspective is an extension of Riker's instrumental view of federalism, as 'a constitutional bargain among politicians', with the motives being 'military and diplomatic defense or aggression' (Riker, 1975, pp. 113–14). Our extensions to this concept are to include bargaining not just in constitution making, but also in evolution of subsequent governance, and not just for territorial protection or gain, but also over splitting the economic pie.

CONNECTIONS TO BROADER ECONOMIC REFORM

Government production of private goods, its provision of public infrastructure, and its regulation of industry all have important implications for the performance of the Indian economy. The low productivity and poor return on capital of state-owned enterprises, or PSEs in India have been well documented (e.g. Kapur and Ramamurthi, 2002). With the government owning enterprises in a broad cross-section of industries, the scope of potential privatization is quite sweeping. The political difficulty of this task is highlighted by the absence of any meaningful privatization in the first decade of economic reform, though this situation seems to have improved more recently.

The large implicit subsidies for those employed in public sector enterprises have clearly been an important aspect of the resistance to privatization, and one can guess that patronage and rent-seeking opportunities have contributed to the lack of political enthusiasm from government ministries. Also, in the case of state-level public enterprises such as the state electricity boards (SEBs), there are additional problems of huge deficits and the need for coordinated reform of the power sector (see below). Recently, the Central government created a separate ministry for disinvestment and this has been taking a proactive stand on privatization. However, the resistance from the other ministries has been formidable and although the disinvestment ministry has drawn up a list of twenty-seven central PSEs to be 'disinvested', progress on ground has been chequered and extremely slow.

While the SEBs are directly owned by the state governments, Centre–state relations have also impinged on privatization when central PSEs in particular state jurisdictions have been privatized or proposed for privatization. Since privatization has been so limited, there are few examples, but the initial case served as a test. The first significant privatization that occurred was of the Bharat Aluminium Company (BALCO). As might have been expected, the company's labour unions opposed the privatization and went on strike. Less predictably, perhaps, the government of the new state of Chhattisgarh (carved out of Madhya Pradesh) took an aggressive stance against the disinvestment. While some substantive issues of the fairness of the bidding and the sale of tribal land were involved, the case raised the potential of states obstructing privatization when the Centre had finally got it rolling.

The stance of the chief minister may be understood in terms of responsiveness to a local interest group, and as an attempt to bargain for transfer payments from the Centre. However, the Supreme Court, finally upheld the sale of the company, and dismissed actions by the state government against the new private owners. Kapur and Ramamurthi (2002) have discussed the court judgment in detail, and conclude that it represents a significant precedent for preventing the use of legal manoeuvres such as 'public interest legislation' to obstruct privatization.

Infrastructure includes various physical, social, and economic indicators, but attention is usually focused on public and quasi-public goods such as electric power, irrigation, roads and railways, telecommunications, and ports. In many of these cases, the poor quality of the available infrastructure acts as a constraint on growth (Dollar et al., 2002). Variations in infrastructure also explain a quarter of the difference in high-performing and low-performing states, in the sample analysed by Dollar et al. Various aggregate measures of infrastructure are possible. In Chapter 12 we provided data on the infrastructure development index produced by the CMIE. The fourteen major states listed are ordered according to their per capita gross state domestic product (GSDP) in the initial year, from poorest to richest. The data show considerable variation across states, but also a remarkable amount of stability over the period, with simple correlations between any two years all being over 0.96, and the coefficient of variation showing a slight decline, from 0.35 in 1980–1 to 0.29 in 1996–7.[9] According to this measure, then, up to 1996–7 there was no appreciable divergence in the major Indian states' infrastructure development.

Infrastructure such as telecommunications and power have seen some privatization of PSEs, as well as entry by private firms. These developments

[9] These calculations do not weight the indices by population, but weighting is unlikely to change the conclusion of stability.

require new regulatory structures. In telecommunications, the creation of the Telecoms Regulatory Authority of India (TRAI) has been essentially at the national level, with the Central government shaping its evolution. The TRAI has had problems in creating and implementing a new regulatory framework that does not involve ex ante case-by-case discretion (Dossani, 2002a). However, telecommunications reform has progressed substantially, driven in part by the success of the IT sector.

In the case of electric power, however, the federal issues with respect to regulation are more salient, and have made progress more difficult.[10] Electric power is a concurrent responsibility of the Centre and the states. Each state has had a state electricity board (SEB) that is vertically integrated with respect to generation, transmission, and distribution, and is part of the state government. Various political compulsions and inefficiencies have led to large losses by the SEBs, and they have collectively been the single largest contributor to India's fiscal deficits. Furthermore, power generation has lagged seriously behind targets, and availability of reliable electric power has become a serious bottleneck for growth.

Considering the poor state of the power sector, it is not surprising that it received early attention in the economic reform process. The reform was initiated early with the hope of attracting private investment in the sector. Over the next decade, Rs 373 billion in FDI in the power sector was approved, making up 14 per cent of total approvals, but actual investment has lagged, with several well-publicized disputes and withdrawals by foreign companies, the Enron case being only the most prominent of these (Mukherjee, 2002). The need to dismantle the vertical integration of the power sector, the simultaneous involvement of the Central and state governments, the lack of understanding of the technical details of power contracting by some of those on the Indian side, and the role of various interest groups all had an effect in delaying or even derailing power sector reform.

In 1997, the Central and state governments tried again, with a Common Minimum National Action Plan for Power (CMNAP). The CMNAP recommended corporatization of the SEBs, though within a public ownership framework, and the creation of independent regulatory commissions at the Central and state levels. The CMNAP also recommended some specific regulatory approaches, and private entry in the distribution component of the sector. A number of states and the Centre passed legislation in 1998 to set up its Central Electricity Regulatory Commission,

---

[10] See, in particular, Dossani and Crow (2001) and Dossani (2002b). We draw on these sources for our account of developments in the power sector.

and to enable the states to create their own SERCs. State governments proceeded to do this the following year, and some also moved forward with corporatization and some unbundling of generation, transmission, and distribution. The delay in creating effective independent regulatory bodies, however, has meant that reform has proceeded in a somewhat chaotic manner. The regulatory commissions have not been able to establish the rules of the game, both because they have been pre-empted by earlier ad hoc decisions, and because they have not had much time to establish their own rules of operation. However, independent regulation and private sector participation appear to be the only route out of the political quicksand into which the power sector has fallen.

CONCLUSIONS

In this chapter, we have taken a sweeping look at India's federal institutions in the context of economic reform. Despite its broad scope, there is one basic theme that runs through the chapter, namely the use of the modern approach to institutional design, as a problem of incentive provision. Examining institutional incentives enables one to go beyond relatively mechanistic normative approaches embodied in setting of macroeconomic targets.

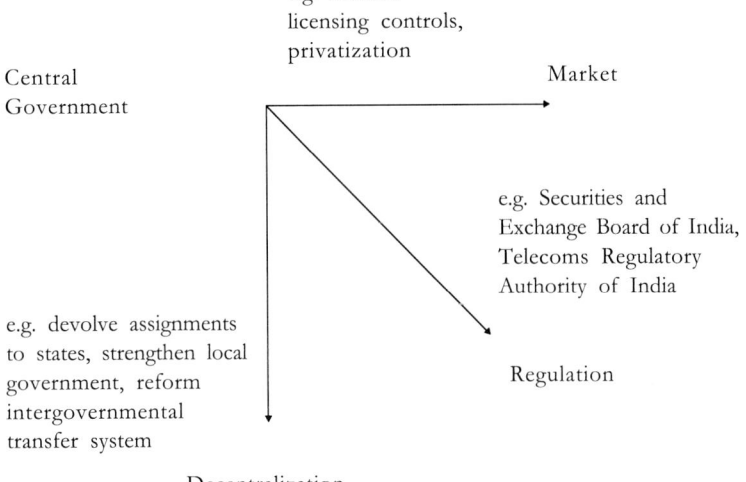

Figure 14.1: Dimensions of Economic Reform

Our central message is that understanding India's federal system is a vital part of conceptualizing economic reform in India. We illustrate this message in Figure 14.1, which is a modified version of a graph we used in Rao and Singh (2001). Shifting the boundary of ownership between state and market (the horizontal arrow in Figure 14.1) is just one aspect of reform. Another dimension involves altering the nature of regulation of the market, moving from case-by-case permission and input control to arm's length regulation and performance-based monitoring (the diagonal arrow).

Various kinds of decentralization, which involve changing the nature of the powers of and interactions among the different levels of government (the vertical arrow), constitute the third, and often most neglected dimension of reform. In this chapter, we have emphasized this dimension, and related it where possible to issues that arise in other dimensions, including privatization and the nature of regulation (whether of private entities or lower-level governments). Ultimately, because India faces bottlenecks in what we might lump together as 'social capital' (using that term somewhat more broadly than is usual), we think that future economic growth will depend on what happens along this third, vertical 'axis', as India attempts to improve its endowments of basic human capital, public physical infrastructure, and public institutions.

15

⟁

Indian Federalism in a Global Environment[1]

REFORM IMPERATIVES IN A GLOBALIZING SCENARIO

In this chapter we examine the interaction between globalization and India's federal system, in the context of the country's past decade of economic reform. Of course, in a formal sense the Constitution allows the interaction of only the Central government with other governments, and with international agencies, and this restriction was the practical norm for much of the past five decades. However, India's sub-national governments have always had a significant economic interest in interactions with the rest of the world and have begun to participate actively in the process of globalization. Therefore, all the layers of government simultaneously interact with foreign governments and corporations in a global economy. These multiple interactions have become more important as reform in India has opened up the economy to foreign trade and investment, and also reduced certain constraints on sub-national governments. Globalization provides challenges as well as opportunities to federal systems such as India's and this chapter seeks to elucidate what these are, while drawing implications for policy and institutional reform.

In economic terms, globalization can be taken as the increased international mobility of goods and services, capital, labour, and knowledge. A cornerstone of Indian economic reform has been opening up to flows of goods and factors, thus integrating more closely with the global economy.[2] This process is continuing with India's involvement in dealing with world trade organization (WTO) initiatives in services and trade-related intellectual property rights, as well as further cuts in overall tariff rates.

---

[1] This chapter draws on the joint work of Singh with T.N. Srinivasan.
[2] See, for example, Srinivasan and Tendulkar (2002).

While all aspects of globalization may not be desirable from a national perspective, the process cannot be avoided, and the focus of national policy must be to make the best of it. This objective is complicated by the existence of multilevel governments in a federal system, with their own objectives and constraints, and potential political strains that might arise. On the other hand, there are distinct potential advantages from globalization, including greater competitiveness, increased productivity, and access to foreign capital and knowledge. If different constituent units of the federation are differentially able to take advantage of these opportunities, however, increased regional inequalities and consequent possible political tensions, which we have discussed in Chapter 12, may be of concern.

We begin the chapter by reviewing the interaction of globalization and the process of economic reform in India, as well as the outcomes in terms of growth and other economic performance indicators. We try to bring out the federal dimensions of the issues that arise. Next, we consider the interplay between globalization, federalism, and economic reform policies that are designed to respond to globalization. We expand on possible policy recommendations that will support the ability to meet the challenges of globalization in India's federal system.

GLOBALIZATION, REFORM, AND ECONOMIC CONSEQUENCES

Although the diversity and size of India required the adoption of a constitution with a federal structure, the public-sector-dominated, heavy-industry-based import substituting development strategy followed since independence gave the Central government a dominant position vis-à-vis the states in economic matters. India's leaders aspired toward an indigenous version of socialism, with government as benevolent guardian, leavened with a smattering of Gandhian influences in favour of smallness, self-sufficiency, and rural traditions. The ruling Congress party adopted a resolution in 1955 that achieving a 'socialistic pattern of society' would be India's objective. This was later incorporated into the Constitution through an amendment in 1976.

Through the 1970s, India's economic growth was reasonable, averaging 3.75 per cent per year, but this was not rapid enough to significantly diminish the number of poor people, nor to deal comfortably with the strains associated with governing a country with substantial ethnic, linguistic, and religious diversity along with economic inequalities. Nevertheless, India was able to preserve its unity, as well as the political system of parliamentary democracy adopted in its early years. However, this political stability was accompanied by the evolution of an economic system riddled with increasing rigidities and inefficiencies, the so-called 'license–quota–permit raj'.

In the 1980s, partly through fresh ideological influences, and partly through the observation of faster growth in many East Asian economies, India's economic policy makers began to seriously attempt some changes in the overall approach to the role of government in the country's economic development. They introduced some liberalization in the trade regime, loosened domestic industrial controls, and promoted investment in modern technologies for areas such as telecommunications. Growth accelerated to 5.8 per cent during 1980–90, but this came at the cost of macroeconomic imbalances (fiscal and current account deficits), which worsened at the beginning of the 1990s as a result of the collapse of the Soviet Union, which had become a major trading partner and ally, and of turmoil in the Middle East.

In 1991, India faced a severe balance of payments crisis, and this circumstance became the occasion for a substantial advance in the pace and nature of economic reforms that were being attempted. In particular, the major steps taken were further trade liberalization, in the form of reductions in tariffs and conversion of quantitative restrictions to tariffs, and a sweeping away of a large segment of restrictions on domestic industrial investment. These two changes in the early 1990s have come to symbolize or encapsulate the term 'economic reform' in India. We may also note that the collapse of the Soviet Union in 1991 and the stellar growth performance of China after its opening to the world economy and initiation of market-oriented reforms in the 1980s were two very significant developments that forced systemic reform in India in the 1990s, as compared to the earlier ad hoc attempts to liberalize the economy.

The move to reduce the role of government in directly controlling the working of markets had additional implications. It was recognized that sectors such as finance and telecommunications required a new set of regulatory structures suitable for an environment in which bureaucrats were no longer making discretionary judgements on a case-by-case basis. This need was strengthened by the direct and indirect impacts of technological change in such sectors. Furthermore, it was recognized that removing controls on industrial investment could not by itself solve India's problem of slow growth. It needed to be complemented by restructuring the working of the labour market, and by improving the economy's physical and institutional infrastructure. Achieving the first of these objectives has been hampered by understandable interest group pressures, while the second goal has been constrained by the continued high level of the government's fiscal deficit.

The high fiscal deficit, in turn, is traceable to subsidies to interest groups, as well as the nature of the interaction between the central and state governments. Table 15.1 summarizes the trends in central and state fiscal deficits over the 1990s.[3] It shows that much of the deterioration in the fiscal deficit has occurred at the state government level. Both the Centre and the states were severely affected by the large pay increases granted to Central government employees in 1997–8, followed by similar increases at the state level the following year.[4]

TABLE 15.1
Central and State Fiscal Deficits

(% of GDP)

	Centre	*States*	*Total*
1990–1	6.6	3.3	9.4
1991–2	4.7	2.7	7.0
1992–3	4.8	2.6	7.0
1993–4	6.4	2.3	8.3
1994–5	4.7	2.8	7.1
1995–6	4.2	2.6	6.5
1996–7	4.1	2.7	6.4
1997–8	4.8	2.9	7.3
1998–9	5.1	4.3	8.9
1999–2000	5.3	4.6	9.4
2000–01	5.1	4.3	9.1

Note: The combined deficit indicators net out the intergovernmental transactions between the Centre and states, and do not equal the sum of the deficits of the Centre and the states.

Sources: Economic Survey of India; RBI Annual Report; Rao (2002); Srinivasan (2002).

Despite the roadblocks to accomplishing comprehensive economic reforms, India was able to achieve a slight acceleration of growth in the

[3] For more detailed discussions of these trends, see Acharya (2002), Rao (2002), and Srinivasan (2002).

[4] This is an example of interest group pressures at work: the pay award was larger than that recommended by the technical advisory body, the Fifth Pay Commission, and was not accompanied by the reduction in staffing that the Commission also recommended. See Acharya (2002) and Srinivasan (2002) for further discussion.

1990s as compared to the previous decade. However, growth statistics indicate that there was a deceleration in the latter half of the 1990s, even before the current global recession took hold. Tables 15.2 and 15.3 provide a summary of the size and structure of India's economy and changes over time (Table 15.2), and economic performance along a wide range of dimensions over the last two decades (Table 15.3). One of the striking features of growth in the last decade has been the anaemic performance of Indian industry, and the associated lack of a shift from agriculture to industry in the share of GDP. On the other hand, services have done well, partly as a result of the boom in software exports and, more recently, in IT-enabled services such as call centres. These aspects of services, and remittances from non-resident Indians have contributed to India's reasonably good export performance, and to its avoidance of further balance of payments difficulties.

TABLE 15.2
Gross Domestic Product and its Sectoral Share

	Gross domestic product (GDP)		Sectoral share in GDP* (per cent)		
	(At factor cost)	(At market prices)	Agriculture & allied	Industry	Services
At 1993–4 prices	Rs Crores				
1950–1	141,557	149,594	55.4	16.1	28.5
1960–1	207,704	222,161	50.9	20.0	29.1
1970–1	298,580	329,227	44.5	23.6	31.9
1980–1	404,246	442,319	38.1	25.9	36.0
1990–1	694,925	773,349	30.9	30.0	39.1
1991–2	705,149	781,575	30.0	29.4	40.6
1992–3	737,018	818,544	30.2	29.1	40.7
1993–4	781,345	859,220	33.6	23.7	42.7
1994–5	835,864	922,289	33.0	24.2	42.8
1995–6	896,990	992,877	30.7	25.3	44.0
1996–7	964,390	1,061,902	31.0	25.2	43.8
1997–8	1,012,816	1,110,384	29.2	25.3	45.5
1998–9	1,081,834	1,185,399	29.2	24.7	46.1

Note: *At factor cost and figures up to 1992–3 relate to prior to revision of GDP.
Source: http://meadev.nic.in/economy/gdp.htm

TABLE 15.3
Major Economic Indicators—Annual Growth Rates (per cent)

Year	Gross national product*	Gross domestic product*	Agricultural production index	Food grains production	Indrustrial production index	Electricity generation	Wholesale price index	Consumer price index	Money supply (M3)	Imports*	Exports*
1981–2	5.8	6.0	5.6	2.9	9.3	9.9	–	12.3	12.0	–4.4	2.6
1982–3	2.7	3.1	–3.8	–2.9	3.2	7.0	4.9	8.8	16.6	–2.6	4.6
1983–4	7.5	7.7	13.7	17.7	6.7	7.6	7.5	12.1	18.2	3.5	3.8
1984–5	4.2	4.3	–1.2	–4.5	8.6	12.1	6.5	6.3	19.0	–5.9	4.5
1985–6	4.5	4.5	2.5	3.4	8.7	8.4	4.4	6.8	16.0	11.5	–9.9
1986–7	4.1	4.3	–3.7	–4.7	9.1	9.8	5.8	8.7	18.6	–2.1	9.4
1987–8	3.6	3.8	–0.8	–2.1	7.3	8.8	8.2	8.8	16.0	9.1	24.1
1988–9	10.1	10.5	21.4	21.0	8.7	10.2	7.5	9.4	17.8	13.6	15.6
1989–90	6.7	6.7	2.1	0.6	8.6	11.2	7.4	6.1	19.4	8.8	18.9
1990–1	5.5	5.6	3.8	3.2	8.2	7.8	10.3	11.6	15.1	13.5	9.2
1991–2	1.1	1.3	–2.0	–4.5	0.6	9.1	13.7	13.5	19.3	–19.4	–1.5
1992–3	5.1	5.1	4.1	6.6	2.3	5	10.1	9.6	15.7	12.7	3.8
1993–4	5.9	5.9	3.8	2.7	6.0	7.3	8.4	7.5	18.4	6.5	20.0
1994–5	7.2	7.3	4.9	3.8	8.4	8.1	12.5	10.1	22.3	22.9	18.4
1995–6	7.5	7.3	–2.7	–5.8	12.8	8.6	8.1	10.2	13.7	28.0	20.9
1996–7	8.2	7.8	9.1	10.5	5.6	4.3	4.6	9.4	15.9	6.5	5.3
1997–8	4.8	4.8	–5.4	–3.5	6.6	6.6	4.4	6.8	17.3	6.1	4.5
1998–9	6.4	6.5	7.5	5.6	4.1	6.5	5.9	13.1	19.4	2.2	–5.1
1999–2000	6.2	6.1	–0.7	1.4	6.7	6.9	3.3	3.4	13.9	17.2	10.8
2000–01	3.9	4.0	1.5	–	5.0	4.5	7.0	3.8	15.0	1.7	21.0

Note: * revised (at 1993–4 prices).

Source: http://meadev.nic.in/economy/mei.htm, http://www.nic.in/stat/stat_act_t1.htm, Reserve Bank of India, http://indiabudget.nic.in/es2001-02/chapt2002/tab12.pdf, http://indiabudget.nic.in/es2001-02/chapt2002/tab16.pdf

Underlying the aggregate performance statistics, we therefore have a story of incomplete economic reforms, with sectors such as agriculture still shackled by an inefficient public procurement and distribution system and severe input market distortions, industry hampered by small-scale reservations and inefficient financing, a financial sector still dominated by direct and indirect public control of investible resources, and labour market rigidities that hamper the entire organized (as opposed to informal) segment of the economy. Liberalization of trade and foreign investment—the 'globalization' aspect of India's reforms—has helped in some areas, but has not been sufficient to promote widespread competitiveness, nor to overcome or rectify the poor state of India's infrastructure. Thus, the economic reform agenda in India remains lengthy as well as complicated.

FEDERALISM, THE REFORM PROCESS, AND GLOBALIZATION

One result of greater openness has been increased competition for Indian manufacturing. Ahluwalia (2002b) notes that Indian firms have upgraded technology and expanded to more efficient scales of production over the last decade. Among larger firms, there have been substantial changes in relative size, indicating a dynamism that was absent before the reforms. Despite these positive signs, India's manufacturing growth has been modest, and manufacturing exports have also not taken off. Many authors have noted that India's rates of protection are still relatively high, contributing to a high cost of production. Continued federal and state-level controls on product markets substantially hinder the growth of this sector. Rigid labour laws and poor infrastructure are other factors contributing to low productivity and high costs, as are rigidities such as small-scale industry reservations.[5]

Manufacturing

While many of the problems of Indian industry can be traced to laws at the national level, it is becoming clear that state-level reforms are also needed. For example, a study by McKinsey & Company (McKinsey Global Institute, 2001) suggests that, starting from a base of 5.5 per cent GDP growth for India, reforms at the state level can add 2 percentage points to growth, almost as much as their estimate of the potential contribution of further reforms by the Central government (2.6 percentage points). The McKinsey report identifies the top three roadblocks to higher growth as product market barriers, land market barriers, and

---

[5] Significant progress on this front has been made very recently. See Mohan (2002).

government ownership. In the case of land markets in particular, state or local-level controls on land use—including protected tenancies, rent controls, and zoning restrictions—are quite significant.[6]

The situation is complicated by the fact that state laws may piggyback, or be enabled by, central-level legislation. Reform therefore requires a coordinated approach, since the Centre is often not in a position to nullify state legislation directly. In the case of labour laws, the main legislation is at the national level, in the form of the Industrial Disputes Act of 1947, the Industrial Employment Act of 1946, and the Contract Labour (Abolition and Regulation) Act of 1970. The national laws require firms with more than 100 workers to get the permission of state governments for closing plants or laying off workers. This permission is rarely given. However, state governments also have the right to restrict contract labour, and variations in their use of this power are significant. Another key source of variation among states is the way that laws relating to worker safety are enforced, with government inspectors in some states using these laws as a significant vehicle of rent extraction.[7]

Dollar, Iarossi, and Mengistae (2002) have examined the quantitative impact of state-level variations in policy on manufacturing productivity. Using a survey of 1000 manufacturing establishments across ten Indian states, they find that states that are poor performers, and identified by survey respondents as having a 'poor investment climate', have total factor productivity (TFP) that is 26 per cent lower than the high-performing states. About a tenth of this gap is found to be due to a higher regulatory burden (specifically, labour market regulations) in the worse states. The advantage of such quantification, of course, is that it enables a basis for policy recommendations with respect to sub-national reforms.

Agriculture

Opening the economy, reducing protection of industry, and exchange rate depreciation have all helped India's agricultural sector by moving relative prices in its favour, and making exports more competitive. The growth performance of agricultural exports, as measured by the increase

[6] For example, Chennai has less restrictive land use controls than Delhi or Mumbai, and has seen a faster growth of more efficient modern food retailing (McKinsey, 2001, p. 8). Note that inefficient and lengthy judicial proceedings compound the problems created by these and other laws. A caveat is that the McKinsey methodology is somewhat vague, and its downgrading of infrastructure as a constraint may not be accurate. Dollar *et al.* (2002, see further in the chapter), emphasize infrastructure.

[7] Forbes (2002, Table 4.2) details eleven kinds of mostly state and local inspection (factory conditions, taxation, etc.), of which eight have not changed in character since 1991.

in share of world exports, has been somewhat better than that of manufacturing (Ahluwalia, 2002b). Nevertheless, there are significant areas where coordinated reforms by the Centre and the states can improve performance. Severe distortions of both input and output prices have distorted cropping patterns and hindered diversification into higher value-added, non-food-grain crops. Some of the price distortions (fertilizers, outputs) are the responsibility of the Centre, whereas others (water, electricity) are due to state governments' subsidies. Restrictions on FDI and domestic distortions have also hindered development of agroprocessing industries.

At the same time that subsidies are removed, farmers need to be freed from a range of outdated laws and institutions. Some of these laws go back in spirit to World War II-era scarcities. The Essential Commodities Act empowers state governments to restrict the movement of agricultural products across state and even district boundaries, and limit the stocks that food traders can hold. Various state-level agricultural produce marketing acts force food traders to buy produce only in regulated markets, making direct contractual relationships difficult, and sometimes reducing the bargaining power of farmers.[8] These restrictions are compounded by an inefficient Central government food procurement and distribution system (Srinivasan, 2002). Ahluwalia (2002b) suggests that, in such cases, the Centre needs to not only repeal its own restrictive laws, but also put limits on the laws that states can pass. From a federalist perspective, however, this may require explicit bargaining between the Centre and the states, since the latter have considerable constitutional authority with respect to agriculture. One can also argue that internal agricultural reform may be important for accelerating growth in the poorer states, which rely more on this sector (Kalirajan, Shand and Bhide, 2000). Thus, agricultural reform may actually play a role in reducing regional disparities.

Finally, the fall in investment in agricultural infrastructure is well known. It appears to have begun in the 1980s, before the current reforms (Gulati and Bathla, 2001). Some kinds of infrastructure relate to production, and require public investment, which has been choked off by the fiscal problems of the state governments. Other infrastructure can support more efficient marketing of agricultural produce. Some of it (airports, roads, etc.) may require public investment, but other investment may simply require removal of a range of outdated and often contradictory

---

[8] Even in the richest, agricultural surplus state of Punjab, intermediaries in both the input and output markets often have monopolistic positions created by government regulations. Nirvikar Singh was told, by a state government official, of at least one case where pesticide distributors successfully lobbied with the state government to prevent direct contracting of farmers with manufacturers, at steep discounts.

legal restrictions on agricultural trade within the country. A symptom of the problems of Indian agriculture is that partial liberalization has, in some cases, made imports of minimally processed foods, such as packaged juices from middle-income Asian countries, cheaper than domestic production. In sum, agriculture may be a major area where the states can take the lead in reform, and push for central reforms as well. To do so, they will have to shift focus from broad subsidies for mostly better-off farmers, to providing infrastructure and basic social services and primary education. As we have argued in Chapter 13, the delivery mechanism for doing this effectively may be the nascent local governments, provided that they are adequately equipped with financial resources, human capital, and incentives to perform.

Services

The rapid growth of India's service sector, reflected in its increasing share of GDP (see Table 15.2) has certainly been supported by the growth of the information technology (IT) sector, particularly in software. The IT sector directly and indirectly demonstrates several possible benefits of reform. While the sector clearly benefited from the availability of the right human capital, and from favourable tax policies, some of the key supporting factors were simply the absence of crippling regulations. Since software did not come under many of the restrictive laws that have strangled Indian manufacturing, new firms were able to operate much more flexibly than they might have otherwise. India's new outward orientation also helped, and software exports grew from $100 million in 1990–1 to $6 billion in 2000–01 (NASSCOM, 2002). This growth was a significant factor in India's avoidance of further balance of payments problems, and by the late 1990s, probably contributed one percentage point to GDP growth. The IT sector also benefited from, as well as spurred, reforms in the telecoms sector that included substantial liberalization and modernization of the regulatory framework.[9]

From a federalist perspective, the IT sector has helped to build a political constituency for reform at the state level. States such as Karnataka and Andhra Pradesh have explicitly competed for investment in IT, through policies to develop physical and educational infrastructure. Other states, such as Punjab, have also tried to catch up in this area, though sometimes with limited success.[10] However, the IT industry remains

---

[9] See Singh (2002) for further discussion of the role of IT in India's economic development.

[10] In the case of Punjab, Singh (2004) argues that broader economic reform is necessary for sectors such as IT to take off in the state.

regionally concentrated. Whether this contributes to regional inequalities depends on the degree of labour mobility, both geographic and occupational, and access to the education system. To the extent that much of the recent growth is coming in IT-enabled services, which require larger numbers of less technically skilled labour, the benefits can accrue to a broader group, and may diffuse some of the regional concentration issues.

Fiscal Federal Issues

Of course India's economic reforms are not taking place in a vacuum. Other countries are also pursuing similar reforms, particularly with respect to integration with the world economy. In many cases, these countries are ahead in the game. Since part of economic reform includes trying to capture the benefits of participating more fully in the global economy, the proper perspective on reform must be one of reform in the context of globalization. Globalization may bring down prices of some goods, lead to more efficient allocations of factors, and allow relatively capital-scarce countries such as India to gain greater access to foreign capital and technology. This is the standard way in which openness supports private (and potentially also public)[11] economic activity. From the perspective of the government, however, there may be new challenges in a world of factor and goods mobility. The ability of the government to tax is affected, since mobile factors can escape the incidence of taxes that are initially placed on them. Furthermore, regulatory policies can be subject to similar problems in the face of factor mobility, as in fears of races to the bottom in standard setting.

An important aspect of openness in a federal system is the extent to which sub-national governments can make policies independently. While only the national government can determine import duties, sub-national governments will typically have some freedom in policies that affect the incentives of foreign capital to enter their jurisdictions. Note that from the perspective of a sub-national government, say an Indian state, capital from another country or from another state can be viewed through the same lens, and must be treated equally in typical policy environments. The final impacts of the entry of capital on a sub-national government will therefore depend also on the internal mobility of capital and labour. Hence, an important point that emerges from considering sub-national jurisdictions in a federal system is that attention must be paid to internal mobility of goods and factors, in addition to external liberalization. Thus sub-national tax and regulatory policies can assume great importance in a

---

[11] This is particularly the case when the government produces private goods.

scenario of economic reform under globalization. A further consideration, which we shall also explore, is that the fiscal health of the states that results from their policies is likely to impinge on the entire nation's credit rating in world capital markets.[12]

In addition to explicit transfers, intergovernmental loans, to the extent that they are subsidized, also constitute transfers to sub-national governments. Ideally, borrowing should be to finance investment, but the state governments have increasingly used borrowing to meet current expenditure needs (approaching 50 per cent in 1998–9). State governments can only borrow from the market with Central government approval if they are indebted to the Centre, and this constraint binds for all the states. Central loans now constitute about 60 per cent of the states' indebtedness, with another 22 per cent being market borrowing, and the remainder made up of pension funds, shares of rural small savings, and required holdings of state government bonds by commercial banks (Rao and Singh, 2002; Srinivasan, 2002). While these captive sources of finance are limited, the states have been able to soften their budget constraints further by off-budget borrowing or non-payment by their PSEs. For example, the SEBs have been tardy in paying the National Thermal Power Corporation, a central PSE (Srinivasan, 2002).

There are other sources of softness in state government budget constraints. The Central government guarantees loans made to state government PSEs by external agencies. The Centre has also in the past forgiven loans made to state governments, presumably to gain political advantage. Even in the case of attempts to impose conditions on state borrowing that would encourage fiscal reforms, the Centre has not been able to harden budget constraints. In particular, in 1999–2000, eleven states signed memoranda of understanding (MOUs) with the Centre, promising fiscal reforms in exchange for ways and means advances (essentially, overdrafts) on tax devolution and grants due to them. In some cases, however, the Centre has had to convert these advances into three-year loans. The Reserve Bank reports stopping payments to three states (Reserve Bank, 2001), but the political difficulty of not bailing out states that are both poor and populous is obvious.[13]

A further complication, which bears on India's federal structure, is that the decade of the 1990s has seen an increase in regional inequality, as

---

[12] The mechanism by which this occurs can be indirect, through contingent liabilities arising from explicit central counter guarantees for state guarantees to foreign corporations, or direct, through the observation of larger deficits for the Centre and states combined.

[13] These kinds of political considerations also constrain the Centre to make plan loans at the same interest rate to all states, removing that marginal incentive device as well.

discussed in Chapter 12. Here we note that while inequalities may have widened within states as well (e.g. the coast and urban areas of Maharashtra and Gujarat versus their interior rural regions), the main focus has been and will be on widening disparities across the states themselves. This is natural, given the size and political importance of the states, and the fact that the states are the direct and indirect channels for numerous kinds of transfers from the Central government.

MEETING THE CHALLENGES OF GLOBALIZATION IN A FEDERAL SYSTEM

Financial Sector

Many of the issues with respect to financial sector reform are at the national level, and so India's federal system is not directly of concern. However, the nature of the financial system overall involves financial repression (essentially, price and quantity controls in the financial sector) which in turn has had implications for Central and state fiscal deficits. In this section, we explore this connection between financial sector reform and federalism. We also address the question of how much India's capital markets should be opened up. While trade barriers have been reduced, and current account convertibility introduced, capital account convertibility remains a topic of policy debate. We examine this debate in the context of India's federal finances.

While securities market reforms have had the highest profile, some steps have also been taken in reforming debt markets and in the banking sector. Most notably, a market for government debt has been established, and the Central government now borrows at rates that are more market-determined. In the banking sector, there has been some reduction in interest rate controls and statutory requirements to invest in government securities, strengthening of prudential norms and regulatory oversight, and policies enabling increased competition from private (domestic and foreign) banks. However, in practice, government control of the banking sector has not changed in some crucial ways.

In the preceding section we observed that the fiscal deficits of the states have increased despite the formal authority of the Centre over the states' borrowing. The effect of this trend of softening the budget constraint has been to weaken the financial system. Direct ownership and control of the financial system along with financial repression policies has helped to accommodate the poor fiscal performance of the States.

Public sector mutual funds such as the Unit Trust of India (UTI), and financial intermediaries such as the Industrial Development Bank of India (IDBI) have suffered from a combination of lack of bottom line objectives and accountability. Though the Central government is rectifying these problems in individual cases,[14] these issues pervade the financial sector. One simple indicator of government financial control is the large percentage of credit allocation by commercial banks that goes to 'priority sectors'. This ratio has not fallen appreciably since reform began, and is much higher than in 1969, when the banks were nationalized.

The large public sector deficits and the policy of financial repression have had adverse growth implication. The lower interest rates on public sector borrowings have led to misallocation of capital. A broad reform in the financial sector is important to enhance capital productivity. The constraints imposed by the web of government-controlled financial institutions and their 'bad' loans to the public sector are a severe hurdle to effective financial sector reform. If thorough financial sector reform is held back because it threatens the public sector house of cards, there may be a case for the government tying its hands through greater external liberalization of capital markets. Even without such liberalization, both the public sector and private financial sector in India are vulnerable to downgrading by international ratings agencies such as Moody's and Standard & Poor's,[15] making India susceptible to the kinds of severe financial crisis that have affected other countries. However, whether capital account liberalization can be a mechanism for financial sector and fiscal discipline probably depends on continued improvements in regulatory oversight.[16]

In suggesting greater exposure to global markets as a disciplining device for the Indian public and private finances, we are not neglecting other

[14] After an earlier bailout, the government has announced that UTI investors must bear all capital risks. It has also announced that the IDBI will be corporatized. In each case, the measures may not go far enough. Bhattacharya and Patel (2002) have made a strong case that incomplete reforms do nothing to deal with the moral hazard problems of India's financial intermediation sector. If anything, the problems may have increased in recent years. However, unlike the case of Argentina, India's state governments cannot directly borrow from banks that they own—nationalized banks are owned by the Central government.

[15] For example Standard & Poor's lowered its long-term local currency rating to 'BBB-' from 'BBB' and revised its outlook on local and foreign currency to negative in August 2001, citing 'the continued deterioration of the government's financial profile, with persistently high fiscal deficits resulting in a rising burden of public debt'. This followed other recent downgrades of other debt categories and outlooks for India. http://www.standardandpoors. com/forums/ratingsanalysis/sovereigns/articles/121201/india.htm. While ratings are imperfect, they do influence foreign investors.

[16] Of course, as significant instances of accounting fraud in the United States remind us, the private sector is also subject to moral hazard in the absence of effective oversight.

policy avenues. As already mentioned, the Eleventh Finance Commission, given a much broader charge than previous commissions, recommended a slew of measures to promote fiscal discipline.[17] It is not at all clear, however, that 'greater autonomy along with hard budget constraints for public sector enterprises' will work in the absence of greater competitive discipline. Furthermore, by not working, it will continue to undermine any limits on states' debt levels. In addition to external competition, internal competition in the financial sector will also be necessary, and here privatization of public sector assets must be considered.

In the financial sector, privatization can affect the nature of the demand for credit by reducing politically motivated subsidies, and by reducing overall interest rates through a reduction in government crowding out of private borrowing. '... As mentioned earlier, accommodating financial system to softening budget constraint has created not just inefficient resource allocation, but has also imported a sense of indiscipline. Subjecting the financial sector to greater market discipline is unavoidable in a more liberalized environment.'

Foreign Direct Investment

Privatization, foreign capital flows, and infrastructure development all intersect in the realm of foreign direct investment (FDI). An important part of the Indian economic reform agenda has been to attract greater levels of FDI, especially those that bring in new technology and improve infrastructure. While there are still restrictions on sectors where FDI is allowed (such as retailing), and the government approval process can still be time-consuming,[18] cumulative FDI approvals have crossed $20 billion for the last decade. A major policy shift allowed state governments to directly seek FDI, rather than having the Central government be the only channel. As a result, state governments have actively competed for FDI,

---

[17] Note that the Centre–state issue with respect to the working of the financial sector has not been just one of levels of credit, but also of credit allocation across states. Hence, our discussion of fiscal deficits also relates to concerns about political economy influences and growing interstate disparities. In fact, the problem grew after the nationalization of commercial banks in 1969, which concentrated economic power in the hands of the Centre. With insurance and many other financial institutions already under central control, the Central government became a virtual monopolist in the financial sector. It might even be argued that, in such circumstances, the role of the formal intergovernmental transfer system has been overshadowed by invisible transfers.

[18] There are two FDI approval routes. Automatic approval through the central bank, for certain categories, is supposed to take only two weeks. The bulk of FDI approvals, however, come through the Foreign Investment Promotion Board (FIPB), which takes several weeks more at a minimum.

though with results that have varied dramatically across states. In that respect, FDI has more transparent regional impacts than foreign portfolio investment, which was allowed from 1993 onward. In terms of magnitude, portfolio investment has been quite significant, in the order of $20 billion since liberalization.

State-wise data for total FDI approvals for the 'reform decade' 1991–2001 are presented in Table 15.4. Using the 1991 population figures from the Census of India, we also calculate per capita approvals. The simple correlation of the per capita FDI approvals with the infrastructure index for any of the three years in Table 15.4 is quite low, ranging from 0.03 to 0.07. To some extent, this reflects the unreliability of FDI approvals as an indicator of actual investment, but more importantly, this is due to the particular infrastructure index used, in which, for example, a state such as

TABLE 15.4
FDI Approvals August 1991– July 2001, 14 Major States

	FDI Approvals (Rs million)	1991 Population (million)	FDI per capita (Rs)
Bihar	8833.43	86.374	102.27
Rajasthan	25,916.69	44.006	588.94
Uttar Pradesh	43,304.25	139.112	311.29
Orissa	82,289.14	31.660	2599.15
Madhya Pradesh	97,709.14	66.181	1476.39
Andhra Pradesh	124,701.31	66.508	1874.98
Tamil Nadu	222,804.00	55.859	3988.69
Kerala	14,360.83	29.098	493.53
Karnataka	208,156.32	44.977	4628.06
West Bengal	84,234.59	68.078	1237.32
Gujarat	168,555.48	41.310	4080.26
Haryana	31,947.46	16.464	1940.44
Maharashtra	456,286.23	78.937	5780.38
Punjab	19,519.22	20.282	962.39
14 States	1,588,618.09	788.846	2013.85

Note: Figures for Bihar, Madhya Pradesh, and Uttar Pradesh include FDI approvals for Jharkhand, Chhattisgarh, and Uttaranchal, respectively.

Sources: FDI – Secretariat for Industrial Assistance Newsletter, August 2001; population – http://www.censusindia.net/data.html

Karnataka is measured as having a lower infrastructure development, despite its high concentration of technical personnel. Most significantly, the coefficient of variation for the per capita FDI approvals (using population-weighted measures of mean and standard deviation) is 0.93, which is much higher than the corresponding measure for the infrastructure index. Thus, it appears that FDI is seeking a few favoured locations, with a concentration even more than would be dictated by broad infrastructure measures. At least one important determinant of the intended destinations of FDI has been the success of India's IT sector.

To the extent that variations in FDI across states are influenced by specific policy initiatives and narrowly focused government investments in infrastructure, such as might be the case in Karnataka, there is scope for state governments to compete more effectively for FDI that might have a longer-term impact on infrastructure. For example, Punjab, with the highest index of infrastructure, lags substantially in FDI, but might conceivably correct this with policy adjustments. In general, the result of economic reform has been to remove Central efforts to direct the location of FDI, as well as to relax restrictions on its nature and amount. The regional concentration of FDI is less of a concern if labour mobility is sufficient to ensure that workers can go where new jobs are created, and if public resources are channelled in ways that allow basic social infrastructure such as urban sanitation to complement private sector investments in aspects of infrastructure such as telecommunications, where the private returns to be captured are potentially higher. In Chapter 12, we presented results that suggested that FDI has a role in growth differential across states. Further results like those would help confirm the importance of FDI, and further focus policies of the Centre and the states on reaping its benefits.

Trade

Trade liberalization can create winners and losers among different groups or factors of production. To the extent that winners or losers are concentrated in particular sub-national jurisdictions, there may be differential pressures on different state governments as a result of greater trade openness. Hence, sub-national governments are also stakeholders in international trade. State governments are also affected more directly, since they may lose tax revenue from expanding exports and diversion from the domestic market. Also, exports of food while gaining the exporters may involve costs to other local constituents. On the other hand, if greater trade openness helps the domestic state economy grow faster, states may ultimately benefit. Central government policies must be designed to correct any externalities that arise, again, perhaps, through regional policies for infrastructure development.

CHALLENGES OF INDIAN FEDERALISM IN A GLOBALIZING ENVIRONMENT

This chapter has attempted to examine the interaction of India's federal system and its ongoing economic reforms in the context of globalization. The analysis explicitly recognizes that the national government has subnational governments below it, and that all these layers of government simultaneously interact with foreign governments and corporations in a global economy. It has analysed real and financial sector reforms and despite its incompleteness, the evidence presented in Chapter 12 suggests that liberalization is making a difference, with foreign and domestic capital together driving growth, and leading to some of the differential growth across states that has been observed in the last decade. It also notes the problems created by government fiscal deficits and government control of the financial sector.

Where does the consideration of globalization leave us in our overall consideration of federalism? We have argued the case in this book for a reform of India's federal institutions, much of that case being independent of the process of globalization. The core of these institutions remains the fiscal transfer system. Making this simpler, more transparent, incentive compatible, and better targeted is a cornerstone of any potential reform. A second key fiscal federal reform lies in the area of taxation, where we have discussed a number of possible reforms that might improve efficiency of collection, reduce allocative distortions, and improve equity. A third important dimension that we have considered is decentralization of spending authority, with control over the resources required to make that effective. In all these cases, we have been cognizant of the political dimensions of reform, that there must be enough winners, or the gains must be demonstrably large enough, for agreement to be possible. Certainly, India has been able to change the status quo in many aspects of the economy, and we have argued in this and the preceding chapter that federal reform necessitates an explicit building of supporting coalitions across levels of government.

Globalization impacts on the reform scenario primarily by exerting pressure for being more competitive, both for governments and the private sector. In fact, the Salmon mechanism of competitive benchmarking (discussed in Chapter 2) impacts across national boundaries as also across the constituent units of a federation. In this chapter, we have suggested that something of that mechanism has been at work in India in driving economic reform.

In this book we have also highlighted some of the political and administrative dimensions of India's federal system, and their interactions with fiscal federal issues. While the political institutions often place constraints on economic reform, they have also proved flexible enough to accommodate a considerable change in perceptions of economic management at different levels of government. Changing the political and administrative institutions themselves will be much more difficult. We have argued that administrative and judicial reform, and reforms in political parties and legislative institutions are all part of improvements that can be made in India's federal system. To some extent, these may be aided by more basic fiscal and financial reforms. Reducing the role of the government in the financial sector, streamlining the system of Central transfers, and reducing the distortions of the tax system while improving equity and administrative efficiency may all help make it easier to see how well government at all levels spends money, and for constituents to more confidently support government's necessary role in the economy. In other words, fiscal federal reforms may ultimately aid the recognition and political acceptability of broader institutional reforms in India's federal system.

Ultimately, politicians who care about long-run economic performance, and the ordinary citizens whom they are supposed to serve, will make the decisions that matter. Our purpose as academics has been to highlight important issues that need to be addressed, and to suggest avenues for going forward in constructive ways. This book has been written to achieve these goals. It will be for readers and practitioners to decide to what extent we have succeeded. Ultimately, only time will tell.

Bibliography

Acharya, S., *India's Macroeconomic Management in the Nineties*, New Delhi: Indian Council of Research in International Economic Relations, 2002.

ACIR, *Studies in Comparative Federalism: Australia, Canada, the United States, and West Germany*, Washington DC: Advisory Commission on Intergovernmental Relations, 1981.

Administrative Reforms Commission of India, *Report of the Study Team on Centre–State Relationships*, Volumes I–III, Delhi: Manager of Publications, Government of India, 1967–8.

—— *Report on Centre–State Relationships*, Delhi: Manager of Publications, Government of India, June 1969.

Ahluwalia, M.S., 'Economic Performance of States in Post-Reforms Period', *Economic and Political Weekly*, May 6, 1637–48, 2000.

—— 'State Level Performance under Economic Reforms in India,' in A. Krueger (ed.), *Economic Policy Reforms and the Indian Economy*, Chicago: University of Chicago Press, 2002.

—— 'Economic Reforms in India Since 1991: Has Gradualism Worked?', forthcoming, (Processed).

Ahmad, E. and R. Thomas, 'Types of Transfers—A General Formulation', in E. Ahmad (ed.), 1997.

Aiyar, S., 'Growth Theory and Convergence across Indian States: A Panel Study', Chapter 8 in Tim Callen, Patricia Reynolds, and Christopher Towe (eds), *India at the Crossroads: Sustaining Growth and Reducing Poverty*, Washington, DC: International Monetary Fund, 2001.

Alesina, A. and E. Spolaore, 'On the Number and Size of Nations', *Quarterly Journal of Economics*, vol. 112, no. 4, pp. 1027–56, 1997.

Arnott, R. and R.E. Grieson, 'Optimal Fiscal Policy for a State or Local Government', *Journal of Urban Economics,* 23–48, 1981.

Arora, B., 'Adapting Federalism to India: Multilevel and Asymmetrical Innovations', in Arora and Verney (eds).

Arora, B. and D. Verney (eds), *Multiple Identities in a Single State: Indian Federalism in Comparative Perspective*, New Delhi: Konark Publishers, 1995.

Aziz, A., *Decentralised Planning: The Karnataka Experience*, New Delhi: Sage Publications, 1993.

—— *Decentralisation: Mandal Panchyat System in Karnataka*, Hyderabad: National Institute of Rural Development, 1994.

—— 'Income Structure of Rural Local Governments: The Karnataka Experience', in Konrad Adenauer Foundation, *Local Government Finances in India*, New Delhi: Manohar, 1998.

Bhattacharya, M., *State Municipal Relations*, New Delhi: Indian Institute of Public Administration, 1972.

Bajaj, J.L. and R. Sharma, 'Improving Government Delivery Systems: Some Issues and Prospects', *Economic and Political Weekly*, May 27, M73–M80, 1995.

Bajpai, N. and J. Sachs, 'Trends in Inter-State Inequalities of Income in India', Development Discussion Paper no. 528, Harvard Institute for International Development, 1996.

Banerjee, A., 'Federalism and Nationalism', Chapter 2 in Nirmal Mukarji and Balveer Arora (eds), *Federalism in India: Origins and Development*, New Delhi: Vikas Publishing, 1992.

Bardhan, P., *The Political Economy of Development in India,* Oxford: Basil Blackwell, 1984.

—— 'Comment on "The Impact of Constitutions on Economic Performance", by Elster', *Proceedings of the World Bank Annual Conference on Development Economics,* 232–5, 1994.

—— 'The Economics of Decentralization in Less Developed Countries', processed, University of California, Berkeley, Department of Economics, 1995.

—— 'Decentralization of Governance and Development', *Journal of Economic Perspectives*, vol. 16, no. 4, Fall 2002, pp. 185–205.

Bardhan, P. and D. Mukherjee, 'Capture and Governance at Local and Governance Levels', *American Economic Review*, vol. 90, no. 2, pp. 135–9, 2000.

Baron, D. and J. Ferejohn, 'Bargaining in Legislatures', *American Political Science Review*, 1181–1206, 1989.

Barthwal, C.P. (ed.), *Public Administration in India,* New Delhi: Ashish Publishing House, 1993.

Baruah, S., 'Cutting States to Size', *Seminar*, 459, pp. 27–30, November 1997.

Basu, K., 'Markets, Laws and Governments', in B. Jalan (ed.), *The Indian Economy: Problems and Prospects*, Delhi: Viking Publishers, 1992.

Bayley, D.H., *The Police and Political Development in India*, Princeton, NJ: Princeton University Press, 1969.

Bergstrom, T.C. and R.P. Goodman, 'Private Demands for Public Goods', *American Economic Review*, vol. 63, no. 3, pp. 280–96, June 1973.

Béteille, A., *Caste, Class, and Power: Changing Patterns of Stratification in a Tanjore Village*, Berkeley: University of California Press, 1965.

Bhadouria, B.P.S. and V.B. Dubey, *Panchayati Raj and Rural Development*, New Delhi: Commonwealth Publishers, 1989.

Bhagwan, J., *Municipal Finance in the Metropolitan Cities of India: A Case Study of Delhi Municipal Corporation*, New Delhi: Concept Publishing, 1983.

Bhargava, B.S. and V. Venkatakrishnan, 'Financial Administration in Panchayati Raj: The Case of Two Panchayat Unions in Tamil Nadu', in Konrad Adenauer Foundation, *Local Government Finances in India*, New Delhi: Manohar, 1998.

Bhattacharya, M., *State Municipal Relations*, New Delhi: Indian Institute of Public Administration, 1972.

—— 'The Mind of the Founding Fathers', Chapter 4 in N. Mukarji and B. Arora (eds), *Federalism in India: Origins and Development*, New Delhi: Vikas Publishing, 1992.

Bhattacharya, S. and U. Patel, 'Financial Intermediation in India: A Case of Aggravated Moral Hazard', chapter presented at the 3rd Annual Stanford Conference on Indian Economic Reform, 2002.

Becker, G.S., 'A Theory of Competition among Pressure Groups for Political Influence', *The Quarterly Journal of Economics*, vol. 98, no. 3, pp. 371–400, 1983.

Besley, T. and C. Anne, 'Incumbent Behaviour: Vote Seeking, Tax-setting, and Yardstick competition', *American Economic Review*, vol. 85, no. 1, pp. 25–45, 1995.

Bird, R.M., *Federal Finance in Comparative Perspective*, Toronto: Canadian Tax Foundation, 1986.

Birch, A.H., 'Approaches to the Study of Federalism', *Political Studies*, vol. XIV, no. 1, pp. 15–33, 1966.

Bird, R.M. and F. Vaillancourt, *Fiscal Decentralization in Developing Countries*, Cambridge: Cambridge University Press, 1999.

Biswas, R. and S. Marjit, 'Political Lobbying and Discretionary Finance in India: An Aspect of Regional Political Influence in a Representative Democracy', processed, Centre for Studies in Social Sciences, Calcutta, 2000.

Boadway, R. and F. Flatters, *Equalization in a Federal State: An Economic Analysis*, Economic Council of Canada, Ottawa: Canadian Government Publishing House, 1982.

Bolton, P., and G. Roland, 'The Break-up of Nations: A Political Economy Analysis', *Quarterly Journal of Economics*, vol. 112, no. 4, pp. 1057–90, 1997.

Bolton, P., G. Roland, and E. Spolaore, 'Economic Theories of the Break-up and Integration of Nations', *European Economic Review*, vol. 40, no. 4, pp. 697–706, 1996.

Bowen, H.R., 'The Interpretation of Voting in the Allocation of Economic Resources', *Quarterly Journal of Economics*, vol. 58, pp. 27–48, November 1943.

Bradbury, K.L., H.F. Ladd, M. Perrault, A. Reschovsky, and J. Yinger, 'State Aid to Offset Fiscal Disparities among Counties', *National Tax Journal*, vol. 37, pp. 151–70, 1984.

Bradford, D. and W. Oates, 'Suburban Exploitation of Central Cities and Government Structure', in H.K. Hochman and C.E. Peterson (eds), *Redistribution through Public Choice*, New York: Columbia University Press, 1974.

Brass, P.R., *The Politics of India since Independence*, 2nd edition, Cambridge: Cambridge University Press, 1994.

Break, G., *Intergovernmental Fiscal Relations in the United States*, Washington DC: Brookings Institution, 1967.

Brennan, G. and J.M. Buchanan, *The Power to Tax: Analytical Foundations of a Fiscal Constitution*, Cambridge: Cambridge University Press, 1980.

Breton, A., 'A Theory of Government Grants', *Canadian Journal of Economics and Political Science*, vol. 31, no. 2, pp. 175–87, 1965.

—— 'Towards the Theory of Competitive Federalism', *European Journal of Political Economy*, Special Issue, vol. 3, no. 1+2, pp. 263–328, 1987.

—— *Competitive Governments: An Economic Theory of Politics and Public Finance*, New York: Cambridge University Press, 1995.

—— 'Federalism and Decentralization: Ownership Rights and Superiority of Federalism', *Publius: The Journal of Federalism*, vol. 30, 2, pp 1–16, 2000.

—— 'An Introduction to Decentralization Failure in Ahmad, Ehtisam, and Vito Tanzi, *Managing Fiscal Decentralization*, London and New York: Routledge, pp. 31–45, 2002.

Breton, A. and A. Scott, *The Economic Constitution of Federal States*, Toronto: Toronto University Press, 1978.

Buchanan, J.M., 'Federalism and Fiscal Equity', *American Economic Review*, vol. 40, no. 4, September 1950, pp. 583–99.

—— *Fiscal Theory and Political Economy*, University of North Carolina Press, North Carolina, 1960.

Buchanan, J.M. and R.L. Faith, 'Secession and the Limits of Taxation: Toward a Theory of Internal Exit', *American Economic Review*, vol. 77, no. 5, pp. 1023–31, 1987.

Burgess, R., S. Howes, and N. Stern, 'Tax Reform in India', Working Paper no. 45, The Development Economics Research Programme, London School of Economics, 1993.

Butler, D., A. Lahiri, and P. Roy, *India Decides: Elections 1952–1995*, 3rd edn, New Delhi: Books & Things, 1995.

Cashin, P. and R. Sahay, 'Internal Migration, Center-State Grants, and Economic Growth in the States of India: A Reply to Rao and Sen', *International Monetary Fund Staff Papers*, vol. 44, no. 2, pp. 289–91, 1997.

Chaturvedi, S. K., *Metropolitan Police Administration in India,* Delhi: B.R. Publishing Corporation, 1985.

Chanda, A., *Federalism in India*, George Allen and Unwin Ltd, 1965.

Chelliah, R.J., *Towards a Decentralized Polity*, L.K. Jha Memorial Lecture, New Delhi: The Fiscal Foundation, 1991.

Chitale, M.A., 'Water Resources Management in India: Achievements and Perspectives', in Guy Le Moigne et al. (eds), *Country Experiences with Water Resources Management: Economic, Institutional, Technological, and Environmental Issues*, World Bank Technical Paper Number 175, Washington DC: The World Bank, 1992.

Chaudhuri, S., 'Economic Growth in the States—Four Decades-1', *Money and Finance*, pp. 45–69, October–December, 2000.

CMIE, *Infrastructure*, Centre for Monitoring Indian Economy, Mumbai, 1997.

Coase, R., 'The Problem of Social Cost', *Journal of Law and Economics*, vol. 1, pp. 1–44, 1960.

Coleman, J.S., 'Norms as Social Capital', in Gerard Radnitzky and Peter Bernholz (eds), *Economic Imperialism: The Economic Approach Applied Outside the Field of Economics*, New York: Paragon House, 1987.

Cornes, R. and T. Sandler, *The Theory of Externalities, Public Goods, and Club Goods*, 2nd edn, New York: Cambridge University Press, 1996.

Courchene, T., *Equalization Payments: Past, Present and Future*, Toronto: Ontario Economic Council, 1984.

Cremer, J., A. Estache, and P. Seabright, 'The Decentralization of Public Services: Lessons From the Theory of the Firm', in Antonio Estache (ed.), *Decentralizing Infrastructure: Advantages and Limitations*, World Bank Discussion Paper 290.

Crook, R. and J. Manor, *Enhancing Participation and Institutional Performance: Democratic Decentralization in South Asia and West Africa*, Report to Overseas Development Administration, UK, 1994.

Dasgupta, A. and D. Mookherjee, *Incentives and Institutional Reforms in Tax Enforcement: An Analysis of Developing Country Experience*, Delhi: Oxford University Press, 1998.

Dasgupta, S., A. Dhillon, and B. Dutta, 'Electoral Goals and Centre–State Transfers in India', processed, Indian Statistical Institute, New Delhi, 2001.

Dash, G., *Municipal Finance in India: Based on Orissa*, New Delhi: Concept Publishing, 1988.

Datta, A., *Municipal Finances in India*, New Delhi: Indian Institute of Public Administration, 1984.

—— 'Local Government Finances: Trends, Issues and Reforms', in Amaresh Bagchi, J.L. Bajaj, and William A. Byrd (eds), *State Finances in India*, New Delhi: Vikas Publishing House, 1992.

—— 'Rent Control and Municipal Property Tax Base: Reform Attempts in India', in Konrad Adenauer Foundation, *Local Government Finances in India*, New Delhi: Manohar, 1998.

Datta Chaudhuri, M., 'Labour Markets as Social Institutions in India', paper presented at IRIS Conference on Institutions, Incentives and Economic Reforms in India, New Delhi, 4–5 March 1994.

Davis, L.E. and D.C. North, *Institutional Change and American Economic Growth*, Cambridge: Cambridge University Press, 1971.

Davoodi, H. and Heng-fu Zou, 'The Effects of Fiscal Decentralization on Economic Growth: A Cross-Country Study', Policy Research Department, The World Bank, March 1996.

Desai, V., *Panchayati Raj: Power to the People*, Mumbai: Himalaya Publishing House, 1990.

Diaz-Cayeros, A., 'Do Federal Institutions Matter? Rules and Political Practices in Mexico', W.P., Centro de Investigacion para el Dessarrollo, A.C. Mexico, 1999.

Dillinger, W., *Decentralization and Its Implications for Urban Service Delivery*, UNDP/UNCHS/World Bank Urban Management Programme Discussion Chapter, UMP 16, 1994.

Dixit, A. and J. Londregan, 'Fiscal Federalism and Redistributive Politics', *Journal of Public Economics*, vol. 68, pp. 153–80, 1998.

Dollar, D., G. Iarossi, and T. Mengistae, 'Investment Climate and Economic Performance: Some Firm Level Evidence from India', chapter presented at 3rd Annual Stanford Conference on Indian Economic Reform, 2002.

Dossani, R., *Telecommunications Reform in India*, Asia/Pacific Research Centre, Stanford University, June 2002a.

—— *India's Power Sector Reforms*, Asia/Pacific Research Centre, Stanford University, June, 2002b.

Dossani, R. and R.T. Crow, 'Restructuring the Electric Power Sector in India: Alternative Institutional Structures and Mechanisms', Working Paper, Asia/ Pacific Research Centre, Stanford University, 2001.

Downs, *An Economic Theory of Democracy*, New York: Harper and Row, 1957.

Dréze, J. and A. Sen, *India: Economic Development and Social Opportunity*, Delhi: Oxford University Press, 1995.

Dwivedy, S. and G.S. Bhargava, *Political Corruption in India,* New Delhi: Popular Book Services, 1967.

Dua, B.D., India: Federal Leadership and Secessionist Movements on the Periphery, in Ramashray Roy and Richard Sission (eds), *Diversity and Dominance in Indian Politics*, vol. 2, New Delhi: Sage, 1990.

Dutta, B., 'Fragmented Legislatures and Electoral Systems: The Indian Experience,' in Anthony Lanyi (ed.), *Institutions, Incentives, and Economic Reforms in India*, New Delhi: Sage Publications (forthcoming), 2000.

Eaton, D.J. (ed.), *The Ganges–Brahmaputra Basin: Water Resource Cooperation between Nepal, India, and Bangladesh*, Austin: Lyndon B. Johnson School of Public Affairs, 1992.

Elster, J., 'The Impact of Constitutions on Economic Performance', Proceedings of the World Bank Annual Conference on Development Economics, 209–26, 1994.

Estache, A. and S. Sinha, 'Does Decentralization Increase Public Infrastructure

Expenditure?', in Antonio Estache (ed.), *Decentralizing Infrastructure: Advantages and Limitations*, World Bank Discussion Paper 290.

Evans, P. and G. Karras, 'Convergence Revisited', *Journal of Monetary Economics*, vol. 37, no. 2, 249–65, April 1996.

Farrell, J., 'Information and the Coase Theorem', *Journal of Economic Perspectives*, vol. 1, no. 2, pp. 113–29, 1987.

Feldstein, M.S., 'Wealth Neutrality and Local Choice in Public Education', *American Economic Review*, vol. 65, pp. 75–89, 1975.

Finance Commission, *Report for 1995–2000*, New Delhi: Government of India, 1994.

—— *Report for 2000–2005*, New Delhi: Government of India, 2000.

Forbes, N., 'Doing Business in India: What Has Liberalization Changed?', in A. Krueger (ed.), *Economic Policy Reforms and the Indian Economy*, Chicago: University of Chicago Press, 2002.

Foster, C.H.W. and P.P. Rogers, 'Federal Water Policy: Toward an Agenda for Action', Report of the Harvard Water Policy Project, Energy and Environmental Policy Center, JFK School of Government, Harvard University, 1988.

Frederiksen, H.D., J. Berkoff, and W. Barber, *Water Resources Management in Asia: Volume 1, Main Report*, World Bank Technical Paper Number 212, Washington DC: The World Bank, 1993.

Galanter, M., *Law and Society in Modern India*, Delhi: Oxford University Press, 1989.

Gordon, R.H., 'An Optimal Taxation Approach to Fiscal Federalism', *Quarterly Journal of Economics*, pp. 567–86, 1983.

Gould, H.H., *Grass-Roots Politics in India: A Century of Political Evolution in Faizabad District*, New Delhi: Oxford and IBH, Chapter 2, p. 33, 1994.

Government of India, *Report of the Finance Commission*, Rajamannar (Chairman), New Delhi: Ministry of Finance, 1965.

—— *National Perspectives for Water Resources Development*, New Delhi: Ministry of Irrigation, 1980.

—— *Report of the Expert Committee on Replacement of Sales Tax on Vanaspati, Drugs and Medicines, Cement, Paper and Paperboard, and Petroleum Products by Additional Excise Duty*, Kamalapati Tripathy (Chairman), New Delhi: Ministry of Finance, 1983.

—— *Report of the Commission on Centre–State Relations* (Sarkaria Commission), Nasik: Government of India Press, 1988.

—— *Final Report of the Tax Reforms Committee*, Pt. I, R.J. Chelliah (Chairman), New Delhi: Ministry of Finance, 1992.

—— *Report of the Eleventh Finance Commission*, New Delhi: Ministry of Finance, 2000.

—— *Annual Report, 2000–2001*, Chapter 8, Ministry of Water Resources, New Delhi, http://wrmin.nic.in/publication/ar2001/default13.htm., 2001.

—— *National Water Policy*, Ministry of Water Resources, New Delhi: Government of India Press, April, http://wrmin.nic.in/policy/nwp2002.pdf., 2002.

—— The Inter-State Water Disputes (Amendment) Bill, 2002, http://indiacode.nic. in/incodis/whatsnew/Interstatewater.htm.

Government of Karnataka, *Report of the Finance Commission for Zilla Parishads and Mandal Panchayats*, Bangalore: Govt. of Karnataka, 1989.

Government of Kerala, *Report of the Panchayat Finance Commission*, Trivandrum: Govt. of Kerala, 1986.

Gramlich, E., 'Intergovernmental Grants: A Review of Empirical Literature', in W.E. Oates (ed.), *The Political Economy of Fiscal Federalism*, Lexington, Mass.: Lexington Books, pp. 219–40, 1977.

—— 'A Policymaker's Guide to Fiscal Decentralization', *National Tax Journal*, vol. XLVI, no. 2, pp. 229–35, 1993.

Groves, T. and J.O. Ledyard, 'Optimal Allocation of Public Goods: A Solution to the "Free Rider" Problem', *Econometrica*, vol. 45, no. 4, May 1977.

Grossman, S.J. and O.D. Hart, 'The Costs and Benefits of Ownership: A Theory of Vertical and Lateral Integration', *Journal of Political Economy,* vol. 94, pp. 691–719, 1986.

Guhan, S., 'Centre and States in the Reform Process', in Robert Cassen and Vijay Joshi (eds), *India: The Future of Economic Reform*, New Delhi, Oxford University Press, pp. 71–112, 1993.

Gulati, A. and S. Bathla, 'Capital Formation in Indian Agriculture: Revisiting the Debate, *Economic and Political Weekly*, vol. 36, 20, May 2001.

Gurumurthi, S., *Fiscal Federalism in India: Some Issues,* New Delhi: Vikas Publishing House, 1995.

Halan, M., 'Ungreasing Palms in India: An anticorruption crusader discovers the Internet cuts bureaucracy and bribes', www.thestandard.com/article/display/ 0,1151,15851,00.html, June 12, 2000.

Hall, R.L. and B. Grofman, 'The Committee Assignment Process and the Conditional Nature of Committee Bias', *American Political Science Review*, vol. 84, no. 4, pp. 1149–66, December 1990.

Hamid, N., *Process of Agricultural Development—A Case Study of the Punjab,* Ph.D. Dissertation, Stanford University, Ann Arbor: University Microfilms International, 1981.

Hausman, J., 'Specification Tests in Econometrics', *Econometrica*, vol. 46, no. 6, pp. 1251–72, 1978.

Hirschman, A.O., *Exit, Voice, and Loyalty; Responses to Decline in Firms, Organizations, and States,* Cambridge, Mass.: Harvard University Press, 1970.

Hommes, R., 'Conflicts and Dilemmas of Decentralization', Annual World Bank Conference on Development Economics 1995, pp. 331–50, 1995.

Humes, S. and E. Martin, *The Structure of Local Government*, The Hague: International Union of Local Authorities, 1969.

Hunter, J.S.H., *Federalism and Fiscal Balance*, Canberra: Australian National University, 1977.

Iaryczower, M., S. Saiegh, and M. Tommasi, 'Coming Together: The Industrial Organization of Federalism', WP, Universidad de San Andres, Argentina, 2000.

Inman, R.P., 'The "New" Political Economy', in Alan Auerbach and Martin Feldstein (eds), *Handbook of Public Economics,* vol. 2, Amsterdam: North Holland, 1985.

—— 'Federal Assistance and Local Services in the United States: The Evolution of a New Fiscal Order', in H. Rosen (ed.), *Fiscal Federalism: Quantitative Studies,* Chicago: University of Chicago Press, 1988.

Inman, R.P. and D.L. Rubinfield, 'Can We Decentralize Our Unemployment Policies? Evidence from the United States', Paper presented at the International Seminar on Public Economics, Hitotsubhashi University, Tokyo, 31 August–1 September 1992.

—— 'The Political Economy of Federalism', processed, University of California at Berkeley and University of Pennsylvania, June, 1994.

—— 'The Political Economy of Federalism', in Dennis C. Mueller (ed.), *Perspectives on Public Choice: a Handbook,* Cambridge, UK; New York: Cambridge University Press, 1997.

Iyer, R.R., 'Federalism and Water Resources', *Economic and Political Weekly,* March 26, 733–38, 1994a.

—— 'Indian Federalism and Water Resources', *Water Resources Development,* vol. 10, no. 2, pp. 191–202, 1994b.

Jetha, N., 'Financing of Municipal Services in India: Selected Issues', World Bank Report no. 10452–IN, 1992a.

—— 'Gujarat State Finances', in Amaresh Bagchi, J.L. Bajaj, and William A. Byrd (eds), *State Finances in India,* New Delhi: Vikas Publishing House, 1992b.

Jha, G., 'Enhancing Municipal Fiscal Capability: Issues in Local Resource Mobilization', in Konrad Adenauer Foundation, *Local Government Finances in India,* New Delhi: Manohar, 1998.

John, O., 'Panchayati Raj Finances in Kerala: Tasks Ahead', in Konrad Adenauer Foundation, *Local Government Finances in India,* New Delhi: Manohar, 1998.

Joshi, V. and I.M.D. Little, *India's Economic Reforms: 1991–2002,* New Delhi: Oxford University Press, 1996.

Kalirajan, K.P., R.T. Shand, and S. Bhide, 'Economic Reforms and Convergence of Incomes Across Indian States: Benefits for the Poor', in S. Gangopadhyay and W. Wadhwa (ed.), *Economic Reforms for the Poor,* Chapter 2, Delhi: Konark, 2000.

Kapur, D., 'India's Institutions and Economic Performance', chapter presented at the Conference on Public Institutions in India: Performance and Design, Harvard University, February, 2001.

Kapur, D. and R. Ramamurthi, 'Privatization in India: The Imperatives and Consequences of Gradualism', chapter presented at the 3rd Annual Stanford Conference on Indian Economic Reform, 2002.

King, D.N., *Fiscal Tiers: The Economics of Multi-Level Government*, London: George Allen & Unwin, 1984.

Kletzer, K. and N. Singh, 'The Political Economy of Indian Fiscal Federalism', in Sudipto Mundle (ed.), *Fiscal Policy in India*, New Delhi: Oxford University Press, 1997.

—— 'Indian Fiscal Federalism: Political Economy and Issues for Reform', in Anthony Lanyi (ed.), *Institutions, Incentives, and Economic Reforms in India*, New Delhi: Sage Publications, 2000.

Kornai, J., 'The Hungarian Reform Process: Visions, Hopes and Reality', *Journal of Economic Literature*, vol. 24, no. 4, December, 1986.

Kraemer, M., 'Intergovernmental Transfers and Political Representation: Empirical Evidence from Argentina, Brazil, and Mexico', Inter-American Development ment Bank, Working Paper 345, January 1997.

Krueger, A.O., 'The Political Economy of the Rent Seeking Society', *American Economic Review*, vol. 64, pp. 291–303, 1974.

Kumar, D. (ed.) with M. Desai, *The Cambridge Economic History of India*, vol. II, c.1757–c.1970 Cambridge: U.K. and New York, U.S.A., 1982.

Kumar, S. and K. Venkataraman, *State-Panchayati Raj Relations: A Study of Supervision and Control in Tamil Nadu*, New York: Asia Publishing House, 1974.

Kydland, F. and E. Prescott, 'Rules Rather than Discretion: The Inconsistency of Optimal Plans', *Journal of Political Economy*, 85, pp. 473–91, 1977.

Lahiri, A.K., 'Practising Sub-National Public Finance in India', NIPFP, New Delhi, chapter presented at The First Meeting of the Global Network Conference, Session on Decentralization, Governance, and Public Goods in Large Economies, Bonn, Germany, December, 1999.

Lazear, E.P. and Sherwin Rosen, 'Rank-Order Tournaments as Optimum Labor Contracts', *Journal of Political Economy*, vol. 89, no. 5, pp. 841–64, 1981.

Leaf, M., *Song of Hope: The Green Revolution in a Panjab Village*, New Brunswick, N.J.: Rutgers University Press, 1984.

Lewis, J.P., *India's Political Economy: Governance and Reform*, Delhi: Oxford University Press, 1995.

Lieten, G.K., *Continuity and Change in Rural West Bengal*, New Delhi: Sage Publications, 1992.

Litvack, J., J. Ahmed, and R. Bird, 'Rethinking Decentralization at the World Bank', PRMPS Discussion Chapter, World Bank, 1998.

Litvack, J. and J. Siddon (eds), 'Decentralization Briefing Notes', World Bank Institute Working Chapter, World Bank, 1999.

Majeed, A., untitled paper presented at Roundtable on Mechanisms of Intergovernmental Relations in India, New Delhi: Institute of Social Sciences, 22 April, 2002.

Malimath, V.R., Report of the Arrears Committee 1989–90, headed by Justice V.R. Malimath, Supreme Court, Government of India, 1990.

Manor, J., 'Regional Parties in Federal Systems', in Arora and Verney (eds), pp. 105–35, 1995.

Marjit, S. and B. Ghosh, 'Economic Growth and Regional Divergence in India, 1970-1996', processed, Centre for Studies in Social Sciences, Kolkata, 2000.

Marjit, S. and S. Mitra, 'Convergence in Regional Growth Rates: Indian Research Agenda', *Economic and Political Weekly*, vol. 31, no. 1, 1966.

Marshall, A., *Principles of Economics*, 8th edn, London: Macmillan, 1920.

Mathew, G. (ed.), *Status of Panchayati Raj in the States of India, 1994*, Institute of Social Sciences, New Delhi: Concept Publishing Company, 1994.

Mathur, M.P., 'Municipal Finances in India: Present Status and Future Prospects', in Konrad Adenauer Foundation, *Local Government Finances in India*, New Delhi: Manohar, 1998.

Mathur, O.P., 'Decentralization in India: A Report Card', Working Chapter, New Delhi: National Institute of Public Finance and Policy, March 1999.

Mehra, A.K., *Police in Changing India*, New Delhi: Usha Publications, 1985.

Meinzen-Dick, R., M. Mendoza, L. Sadoulet, G. Abiad-Shields, and A. Subramanian, 'Sustainable Water User Associations: Lessons from a Literature Review', paper presented at World Bank Water Resources Seminar, Lansdowne, Virginia, 13–15 December, 1994.

Menon, N.R. Madhava, and B. Debroy (eds), *Legal Dimensions of Economic Reforms*, New Delhi: Allied Publishers, 1995.

Milgrom, P. and J. Roberts, 'An Economic Approach to Influence Activities in Organizations', *American Journal of Sociology*, Supplement, S154–S179, 1988.

—— 'Bargaining Costs, Influence Costs, and the Organization of Economic Activity', in J. Alt and K. Shepsle (eds), *Perspectives on Positive Political Economy*, Cambridge: Cambridge University Press, 1990.

—— 'The Efficiency of Equity in Organizational Decision Processes', *American Economic Review*, Papers and Proceedings, pp. 154–9, 1990.

—— *Economics, Organization, and Management*, New Jersey: Pearson Education, 1992.

Mishra, R., 'State–Municipal Financial Relations: Grants-in-Aid', in Konrad Adenauer Foundation, *Local Government Finances in India*, New Delhi: Manohar, 1998.

Mishra, R. and S. Mohanty, *Police and Social Change in India*, New Delhi: Ashish Publishing House, 1992.

Mohan, R., 'Achieving Higher Economic Growth: The Fiscal Deterrent', chapter presented at Stanford Conference on Indian Economic Reform, June, 2001.

—— 'Small Scale Industry Reservations' in A. Krueger (ed.), *Economic Policy Reforms and the Indian Economy*, Chicago: University of Chicago Press, 2002.

Mookherjee, D., 'Incentive Reforms in Developing Country Bureaucracies: Lessons from Tax Administration', chapter presented at Annual World Bank Conference on Development Economics, Washington, D.C., 30 April–1 May, 1997.

—— 'Redefining the Economic Role of the State: The Role of 'Positive' and

'Negative' Institutional Reforms in India', chapter presented at conference on Economic Liberalization in South Asia, University of California, Berkeley, April 1993.

Mukherjee, A., 'Foreign Firms Pulling Out of Power Projects', *The Hindu*, 8 July, 2002. *www.hinduonnet.com/stories/2002070802271300.htm*

Mukherjee, B.C., *Administration in Changing India*, New Delhi: Blaze Publishers, 1994.

Musgrave, R.A., *The Theory of Public Finance*, New York: McGraw Hill, 1959.

—— 'Approaches to Fiscal Theory of Political Federalism', in *Public Finances: Needs Sources and Utilization*, National Bureau of Economic Research, Princeton, NJ: Princeton University Press, 1962.

Musgrave, R.A., 'Who Should Tax, Where and What?', in C. McLure (ed.), *Tax Assignment in Federal Countries*, Canberra: Australian National University Press, pp. 2–19, 1983.

Nagaraj, R., A. Varoudakis, and M.A. Veganzones, 'Long-Run Growth Trends and Convergence across Indian States', OECD Technical Paper no. 131, 1998.

Naipaul, V.S., *India: A Wounded Civilization*, New York: Alfred Knopf, 1975.

Naresh, G., *Financing of Local Governments in India*, Delhi: Gayatri Publications, 1998a.

—— 'Municipal Expenditure in India: A Cross-Sectional and Time-Consistent Analysis', in Konrad Adenauer Foundation, *Local Government Finances in India*, New Delhi: Manohar, 1998b.

NASSCOM (National Association of Software and Service Companies), 'Software Export', 2002, *http://www.nasscom.org/it_industry/sw_export.asp*

National Water Development Agency, *National Perspectives for Water Resources Development*, July, New Delhi: NWDA, 1992.

NIPFP, *The Ninth Finance Commission: Issues and Recommendations*, New Delhi: National Institute of Public Finance and Policy, 1993.

—— 'Reform of Domestic Trade Taxes in India: A Report of the Study Team on Value Added Taxation', Ministry of Finance, Government of India, 1994.

Niskanen, W., Jr., *Bureaucracy and Representative Government*, New York: Aldine-Atherton, 1971.

North, D.C., *Structure and Change in Economic History*, New York: Norton Publishing Co., 1981.

North, D.C. and B. Weingast, 'Constitutions and Commitment: The Evolution of Institutions Governing Public Choice in Seventeenth-Century England', *Journal of Economic History*, vol. 49, pp. 803–32, 1989.

Oates, W.E., *Fiscal Federalism*, New York: Harcourt, Brace and Jovanovich, 1972.

—— 'An Economist's Perspective of Fiscal Federalism', in W.E. Oates (ed.), *Political Economy of Fiscal Federalism*, Lexington Books, pp. 3–20, 1977.

—— 'Principles of Fiscal Federalism: A Survey of Recent Theoretical and Empirical Research', IRIS Working Paper no. 21, University of Maryland, College Park, 1991.

Oates, W.E., 'An Essay on Fiscal Federalism', *Journal of Economic Literature*, vol. 37, pp. 1120–49, 1999.

Oates, W.E. and R.M. Schwab, 'Economic Competition among Jurisdictions: Efficiency Enhancing or Distortion Inducing?' *Journal of Public Economics*, vol. 35, pp. 333–54, 1988.

Olson, M., *The Logic of Collective Action* Cambridge: Harvard University Press, 1965.

—— 'The Principle of Fiscal Equivalence', *American Economic Review*, vol. 59, no. 2, pp. 479–87, 1969.

—— *The Rise and Decline of Nations*, New Haven and London: Yale University Press, 1982.

—— 'Toward a More General Theory of Governmental Structure', *American Economic Review*, May 1986.

Oomen, M.A., 'Panchayats and their Finances', Institute of Social Sciences Chapter, New Delhi, 1995.

Ostrom, E., *Crafting Institutions for Self-Governing Irrigation Systems,* San Francisco: Institute for Contemporary Studies Press, 1992.

Pande, A.K., 'Flow of Funds in Panchayat Benkala During the Seventh Five Year Plan', *Journal of Rural Development*, vol. 13, no. 2, 1994.

Persson, T., G. Roland, and G. Tabellini, 'Separation of Powers and Political Accountability', *Quarterly Journal of Economics*, vol. 102, no. 4, pp. 1163–202, 1997.

Picciotto, R., 'Putting Institutional Economics to Work', World Bank Discussion Paper 304, 1995.

Pigou, A.C., *The Economics of Welfare,* 4th ed, 1932.

Pauly, M., 'Income Redistribution as a Local Public Good', *Journal of Public Economics*, vol. 2, no. 1, pp. 35–58, February 1973.

Prud'homme, R., 'The Dangers of Decentralization', *The World Bank Research Observer*, vol. 10, no. 2, pp. 201–20, 1995.

Putnam, R.D., 'Comment on "The Institutions and Governance of Economic Development and Reform" by Williamson', Proceedings of the World Bank Annual Conference on Development Economics, pp. 198–200, 1994.

Rajaraman, I., 'Fiscal Features of Rural Local Government in India', in J.J. Dethier (ed.), *Governance in India, China and Russia,* Berlin: Springer-Verlag, 1999.

—— 'Growth-Accelerating Fiscal Devolution to the Third Tier', paper presented at NIPFP-DFID-World Bank Conference on India: Fiscal Policies To Accelerate Economic Growth, New Delhi, May 2001.

Rajaraman, Indira, O.P. Bohra, and V.S. Renganathan, 'Augmentation of Panchayat Resources', *Economic and Political Weekly*, May 4, pp. 1071–83, 1996.

Ramasubramaniam, K.A., 'Historical Development and Essential Features of the Federal System', in Nirmal Mukarji and Balveer Arora (eds), *Federalism in India: Origins and Development*, New Delhi: Vikas Publishing, pp. 105–24, 1992.

Ramana, M.V.V., *Inter-State River Water Disputes in India,* Madras: Orient Longman, 1992.

Raychaudhuri, T., and I. Habib (eds), *The Cambridge Economic History of India,* volume 1, ca.1100–ca.1750, Cambridge, 1982.

Rao, D.S.K. 1995, 'Farmer Management of Public Tubewells in West Bengal', *Economic and Political Weekly,* September 30, pp. A117–A122, 1995.

Rao, M.G., 'State Government Transfers to Urban Local Bodies', processed, New Delhi: National Institute of Public Finance and Policy, 1992.

—— 'Intergovernment Transfers in India', processed, paper presented at Conference on Fiscal Transfer Systems, Qingdao, China, 25–29 July, 1994

—— 'Fiscal Federalism in India: Problems and Prospects', forthcoming, Sudipto Mundle (ed.), *Fiscal Policy in India,* New Delhi: Oxford University Press, 1995.

—— 'Tax Reform in India: Achievements and Challenges', *Asia-Pacific Development Journal,* vol. 7, no. 2, pp. 59–74, 2000a.

—— 'Invisible Transfers in Indian Federalism', *Public Finance/ Finances Publiques,* 2000c.

—— 'State Level Fiscal Reforms in India', paper presented at Cornell University, Conference on Indian Economic Reform, 19-20, April, 2002.

—— 'Fiscal Decentralization in Indian Federalism', in Ehtisham Ahmad and Vito Tanzi, *Managing Fiscal Decentralization,* Routledge, pp. 286–306, 2002.

—— 'Reform of Central Sales Tax in the Control of Vat', *Economic and Political Weekly,* vol. XXXVIII, no. 7, 15–21 February, pp. 627–36, 2003.

—— 'Fiscal Federalism in India: Problems and Prospects', processed, Australian National University, Canberra, 1995.

—— 'Indian Fiscal Federalism from a Comparative Perspective', processed, National Institute of Public Finance and Policy, New Delhi, 1993.

Rao, M.G. and A. Dasgupta, 'Intergovernmental Transfers as an Instrument to Alleviate Poverty', *Environment and Planning C: Government and Policy,* vol. 13, pp. 1–23, 1995.

Rao, M.G. and F. Vaillancourt, 'Subnational Tax Disharmony in India: A Comparative Perspective', *Publius, The Journal of Federalism,* vol. 24 (Fall), pp. 99–114, 1994.

Rao, M.G., G. Pradhan, and O.P. Bohra, *Alternatives to Octroi in Rajasthan,* New Delhi: National Institute of Public Finance and Policy, 1985.

Rao, M.G. M.H.K. Amar Nath, and B.P. Vani, 'Rural Fiscal Decentralization in Karnataka', in G Sethi (ed.), *Fiscal Decentralization to Rural Local Governments,* Oxford University Press, pp. 43–106, 2004.

Rao, M.G. and K. Sen, 'Internal Migration, Center–State Grants, and Economic Growth in the States of India: A Comment on Cashin and Ratna Sahay', *International Monetary Fund Staff Papers,* vol. 44, no. 2, pp. 283–8, 1997.

Rao, M.G. and N. Singh, 'Local Government Reform in India: Assignments, Institutions and Incentives', Working Chapter, Centre for Economic Development and Policy Reform, Stanford University, 1999.

Rao, M.G. and N. Singh, 'The Political Economy of Center–State Fiscal Transfers in India', in John McLaren (ed.), *Institutional Elements of Tax Design and Reform*, World Bank, Washington D.C., 18–19 February, 2000.

—— 'India's Federal Institutions and Economic Reform', paper presented at the conference on India's Public Institutions at Harvard University, 9–10 February, 2001.

Rao, M.G., R. Shand, and K.P. Kalirajan, 'Convergence of Incomes across Indian States: A Divergent View', *Economic and Political Weekly*, 27 March–2 April, 1999.

Rao, N.R., *Municipal Finances in India (Theory and Practice)*, New Delhi: Inter-India Publications, 1986.

Richards, A. and N. Singh, 'Inter State Water Disputes in India: Institutions and Policies,' UC Santa Cruz Working Paper, 2002.

Richards, Alan R., and Nirvikar Singh, 'Two Level Negotiations in Bargaining Over Water', in T. Parthasarathy, B. Dutta, J.A.M. Potters, T.E.S. Raghavan, D. Ray and A. Sen, (ed.), *Game Theoretical Applications to Economics and Operations Research*, Boston: Kluwer Academic Publishers, 1997.

—— 'No Easy Exit: Property Rights, Markets, and Negotiations over Water', (with A. Richards), *International Journal of Water Resources Development*, vol. 17, no. 3, pp. 409–25, 2001.

—— 'Water and Federalism: India's Institutions Governing Inter-State River Waters', report prepared for the Center on Institutional Reform and the Informal Sector (IRIS), at the University of Maryland, under Cooperative Agreement No. DHR-0015-A-00-0031-00 with US Agency for International Development, 1996.

Riker, W., *Federalism: Origins, Operation, Significance*, Boston: Little, Brown, 1964.

—— 'Federalism,' in *Handbook of Political Science*, vol. 5, Fred I. Greenstein and Nelson W. Polsby (eds), Reading, MA: Addison-Wesley, 1975.

Riker, W. and R. Schaps, 'Disharmony in Federal Government', *Behavioural Science*, vol. 2, pp. 276–90, 1957.

Rivlin, A.M., *Reviving the American Dream: The Economy, the State and the Federal Government*, Washington DC: Brookings Institution, 1992.

Rogers, Peter, 'Comprehensive Water Resource Management: A Concept Paper', World Bank Policy Research Paper, WPS 879, March, Washington DC: The World Bank, 1992.

Rondinelli, D., 'Government Decentralization in Comparative Perspective: Theory and Practice of Developing Countries', *International Review of Administrative Sciences*, vol. 47, no. 2, pp. 133–45, 1981.

—— 'What is Decentralization?', in Jennie Litvack and Jessica Seddon (eds), *Decentralization Briefing Notes*, Washington, DC: World Bank Institute, pp. 2–5, 1999.

Rubinstein, A. and A. Wolinsky, 'Renegotiation-Proof Implementation and Time Preferences', *American Economic Review*, vol. 82, pp. 600–14, 1992.

Sachdeva, Pardeep, *Dynamics of Municipal Government and Politics in India*, Allahabad: Kitab Mahal, 1991.

—— *Urban Local Government and Administration in India*, Allahabad: Kitab Mahal, 1993.

Saleth, R.M., 'Towards a New Water Institution: Economics, Law and Policy', *Economic and Political Weekly*, 24 September 1994.

Salmon, P., 'Decentralization as an Incentive Scheme', *Oxford Review of Economic Policy*, vol. 3, no. 2, pp. 24–43, 1987.

—— 'Decentralization and Supranationality: The Case of the European Union', in Ehtisham A. and V. Tanzi (eds), *Managing Fiscal Decentralization*, London and New York: Routledge, pp. 99–121, 2002.

Samuelson, P.A., 'The Pure Theory of Public Expenditure', *Review of Economics and Statistics*, vol. 36, pp. 387–9, 1954.

Scott, A.D., 'The Economic Goals of Federal Finance', *Public Finance/Finances Publiques*, vol. 13, no. 3, pp. 241–88, 1964.

Seabright, P., 'Accountability and Decentralization in Government: An Incomplete Contracts Model', *European Economic Review*, vol. 40, pp. 61–89, 1996.

Seth, V., *A Suitable Boy: A Novel*, New York: Harper Collins, 1993.

Shah, B.L., *The Role of Panchayats in Integrated Rural Development*, New Delhi: Cosmo Publications, 1990.

Shah, R.B., 'Inter-state River Water Disputes: A Historical Review', *Water Resources Development*, vol. 10, no. 2, pp. 175–89, 1994.

Shand, R. and S. Bhide, 'Sources of Economic Growth: Regional Dimensions of Reforms', *Economic and Political Weekly*, 14 October, pp. 3747–57, 2000.

Shapley, L.S. and M. Shubik. 'A Method of Evaluating the Distribution of Power in a Committee System', *American Political Science Review*, vol. 48, no. 3, pp. 787–92, 1954.

Sharma, R.N. and D. Kumar, *Municipal Government in India: An Annotated Bibliography*, New Delhi: Indian Institute of Public Administration, 1981.

Sharman, D., 'India's Pollution Regulatory Structure and Background' (5 January 1996), retrieved from http://www.worldbank.org/nipr/india/india-back.htm

Shiviah, M. and K.B. Srivastava, *Factors Affecting Development of the Panchayati Raj System*, Hyderabad: National Institute of Rural Development, 1990.

Shleifer, A., 'Establishing Property Rights', Proceedings of the World Bank Annual Conference on Development Economics, pp. 93–117, 1994.

Shleifer, A. and R. Vishny, 'Corruption', *Quarterly Journal of Economics*, vol. 108, pp. 599–617, 1993.

Singh, H., 'Constitutional Base for Panchayati Raj in India: The 73rd Amendment Act', *Asian Survey*, vol. 34, no. 7, July, pp. 818–27, 1994.

Singh, L.P., *Role of the Council of States in our Federal System*, New Delhi: Centre for Policy Research, 1991.

Singh, N.K. and A. Modi, 'Direct Tax Reform in India', chapter presented at Stanford Conference on Indian Economic Reform, June, 2001.

Singh, N., 'Conflict in India: Panjab and Kashmir', Institute of International Studies Working Paper, UC Berkeley, 1995.

—— 'The Economic Consequences of India's Institutions of Governance', paper presented at International Conference on Law and Economics, New Delhi, India, 11–13 January, 1996.

—— 'Governance and Reform in India', forthcoming, *Journal of International Trade and Economic Development,* 1997.

—— 'Information Technology and India's Economic Development', in K. Basu (ed.), in *India's Emerging Economy: Performance and Prospects in the 1990s and Beyond,* MIT Press, pp. 223–61, 2002.

Singh, N. and G. Vashista, 'The Political Economy of Centre–State Transfers in India: Further Analysis' in progress, 2004.

Singh, N. and T.N. Srinivasan, 'Indian Federalism, Globalization and Economic Reform', UC Santa Cruz Working Paper, 2002.

Singh, S.S. and S. Misra, *Legislative Framework of Panchayati Raj in India,* New Delhi: Intellectual Publishing House, 1993.

Sivaraman, B., *Bitter Sweet: Governance of India in Transition,* New Delhi: Ashish Publishing House, 1991.

Sitaramayya, B.P., *History of the Indian National Congress,* Delhi: S. Chand and Co., 1969.

Siwach, J.R., *Dynamics of Indian Government and Politics,* New Delhi: Sterling Publishers, 1985.

Somanathan, E., 'Deforestation, Property Rights and Incentives in Central Himalaya', *Economic and Political Weekly,* 26 January, pp. PE37–PE46, 1991.

Srinivasan, T.N., 'India's Fiscal Situation: Is a Crisis Ahead?' in A. Krueger (ed.), *Economic Policy Reforms and the Indian Economy,* Chicago: University of Chicago Press, 2002.

Srinivasan, T.N. and Suresh D. Tendulkar, *Reintegrating India with the World Economy,* Washington, DC: Institute for International Economics, 2002.

Srivastava, R., 'Migration and the Labour Market in India', *The Indian Journal of Labour Economics,* vol. 41, pp. 583–616.

Tang, S.Y., *Institutions and Collective Action: Self-Governance in Irrigation,* San Francisco: Institute for Contemporary Studies Press, 1992.

Tanzi, V., 'Fiscal Federalism and Decentralization: A Review of Some Efficiency and Macroeconomic Aspects', Annual World Bank Conference on Development Economics 1995, pp. 295–316, 1995.

Thimmiah, G., 'Making PRIs and ULBs More Autonomous and Effective', chapter presented at Chennai Conference on Second Generation Reforms, 1999.

Tiebout, C., 'A Pure Theory of Local Government Expenditures', *Journal of Political Economy,* vol. 64, 1956.

Tresch, R.W., *Public Finance: A Normative Theory,* Plano, Taxes: Business Publications, 1981.

Tulasidhar, V.B. and M.G. Rao, 'Cost and Efficiency of Fiscal Incentives—The

Case of Sales Tax Subsidy', *Economic and Political Weekly*, vol. XXI, no. 41, 11 October, pp. 1799–806, 1986.

Tullock, G., 'The Welfare Cost of Tariffs, Monopolies, and Theft', *Western Economic Journal*, vol. 5, pp. 224–32, 1967.

Tummala, K.K., *Public Administration in India,* Singapore: Times Academic Press, 1994.

Venkatarangaiya, M. and M. Pattabhiram, *Local Government in India: Select Readings, Calcutta: Allied Publishers*, 1969.

Verney, D.V., 'Federalism, Federative Systems, and Federations: The United States, Canada, and India', *Publius*, Spring, pp. 81–97, 1995.

Wade, R., *Village Republics: Economic Conditions for Collective Action in South India*, Cambridge: Cambridge University Press, 1988.

—— 'Politics and Graft: Recruitment, Appointment, and Promotions to Public Office in India,' in P.M. Ward (ed.), *Corruption, Development and Inequality,* London: Routledge, pp. 73–109, 1989.

—— *Governing the Market: Economic Theory and the Role of Government in East Asian Industrialization,* Princeton, N.J.: Princeton University Press, 1990.

Waldman, P., 'India's States Poised to Grab More Power: Wobbly New Ruling Coalition Needs Regional Support', *The Wall Street Journal*, 30 May, 1996.

Warneryd, K., 'Distributional Conflict and Jurisdictional Organization', *Journal of Public Economics*, vol. 69, pp. 435–50, 1998.

Weingast, B., 'Constitutions as Governance Structures', *Journal of Institutional and Theoretical Economics*, vol. 149, pp. 233–61, 1993.

—— The Economic Role of Political Institutions: Market Preserving Federalism and Economic Development', *Journal of Law, Economics and Organization*, vol. 11, no. 1, pp. 1–18, 1995.

Weingast, B.R. and W.J. Marshall, 'The Industrial Organization of Congress (Or Why Legislatures, Like Firms, Are Not Organized as Markets)', *Journal of Political Economy*, vol. 96, February, 1988.

Weldon, J., 'Public Goods (and Federalism)', *Canadian Journal of Economics and Political Science*, vol. 32, no. 2, pp. 230–8, 1966.

Wheare, K.C., *Federal Government*, 3rd edn, London: Oxford University Press, 1953.

Wildasin, D.E., *Urban Public Finance*, New York: Harwood Academic Publishers, 1986.

Wilde, J.E., 'Grants-in-aid: Analytics of Design and Response', *National Tax Journal*, vol. 24, no. 2, pp. 143–55, 1971.

Williamson, O., 'The Institutions and Governance of Economic Development and Reform', *Proceedings of the World Bank Annual Conference on Development Economics,* pp. 171–97, 1994.

Wiseman, J., 'The Political Economy of Federalism: A Critical Appraisal', *Environmental and Planning C: Government and Policy*, vol. 5, pp. 383–410, 1987.

Wittman, D., *The Myth of Democratic Failure: Why Political Institutions Are Efficient*, Chicago: University of Chicago Press, 1995.

World Bank, *Water Resources Management: A World Bank Policy Paper*, Washington DC: The World Bank, 1993.

—— *India: Recent Economic Developments and Prospects*, Washington DC: The World Bank, 1995.

—— *World Development Report: The State in a Changing World*, Washington DC: Oxford University Press for World Bank, 1997.

Zink, H., A. Whlstrand, F. Benvenuti, and R. Bhaskaran, *Rural Local Government in Sweden, Italy and India: A Comparative Study*, London: Stevens & Sons, 1957.

Index